Film Noir **Reader**

Also by Alain Silver

David Lean and His Films
The Vampire Film
The Samurai Film
*Film Noir: An Encyclopedic Reference to the
American Style,* Editor
Robert Aldrich: a guide to references and resources
The Film Director's Team
Raymond Chandler's Los Angeles
More Things Than Are Dreamt Of
What Ever Happened to Robert Aldrich?

Also by James Ursini

David Lean and His Films
The Life and Times of Preston Sturges, An American Dreamer
The Vampire Film
*Film Noir: An Encyclopedic Reference to the
American Style,* Editor, 3rd Edition
More Things Than Are Dreamt Of
What Ever Happened to Robert Aldrich?

Film Noir

R E A D E R

EDITED BY
ALAIN SILVER AND JAMES URSINI

LIMELIGHT EDITIONS
NEW YORK

Limelight Editions
512 Newark Pompton Turnpike
Pompton Plains, New Jersey 07444

First published in 1996 by Limelight Editions
Eighth printing, 2006

Printed in the United States of America

Library of Congress Cataloging-in-Publication Data

Film noir reader / edited by Alain Silver and James Ursini
     p.   cm.
  ISBN 0-87910-197-0
  1. Film noir—United States—History and criticism. I. Silver, Alain, 1947-
II. Ursini, James.
PN1995.9.F54F57 1996
741.93'655—dc20

                                      96-11102
                                           CIP

The editors are grateful for permission to reprint copyrighted material as detailed in the Acknowledgments.

www.limelighteditions.com

Contents

Part Three: *Noir* Then and Now

Acknowledgments

Our idea to publish a series of essays on *film noir* goes back to fall of 1974. At that time we talked to several prospective collaborators—Janey Place, Lowell Peterson, Richard Thompson, and Tim Hunter—some of whom helped to formulate our original outline. That book concept was dropped when Peter Mayer asked Alain Silver and Elizabeth Ward to produce *Film Noir: An Encyclopedic Reference to the American Style*. The extensive research done by Elizabeth Ward on that book included acquiring copies of many of the seminal pieces which are reproduced in this volume.

We refined the idea for an anthology of old and new writings while researching and revising the third edition of *Film Noir: An Encyclopedic Reference*, which includes a 15,000 word essay on "Other Studies of Film Noir" (and an even longer piece on neo-*noir*). During that time we also had discussions about neo-*noir* with Todd Erickson and Bob Porfirio, who had discussed an anthology project with Edward Dimendberg at the University of California Press. Out of all that came the outline of the "classic" essays on *film noir* which became the basis for this book.

We were most fortunate to be able to acquire the rights to reprint all but one of the essays on our original "wish list." We would have liked to use an excerpt from Barbara Deming's *Running Away from Myself*, but we were unable to locate the rights holder for that long out-of-print book. We also considered Amir Karimi's *Towards a Definition of Film Noir*, which we ultimately decided was too derivative of Borde and Chaumeton's book from which its title is taken, and David Bordwell's essay "The case of *film noir*" from *The Classical Hollywood Cinema*, which is in print and readily available.

In the actual permissions process, in addition to the authors themselves, we are grateful for the assistance of Robin Wood at *CineAction!*, James Schwoch at Northwestern University/*Film Reader*, Gary Morris at *Bright Lights Film Journal*, Sayre Maxfield at *Film Comment*, Caroline Beven at *Screen*, Roma Gibson at the B.F.I., Tomm Carroll at the *DGA Magazine*, and Jerôme Lindon at Les Éditions de Minuit. Although this is not a DGA Publication, Selise Eiseman, the DGA Special Projects Officer, suggested several potential contributors; and Adele Field, who is in charge of DGA publications, made suggestions about software and design.

Many of the prints for the essay of TV *Noir* were screened at the UCLA Television Archives. Others were from the Mark Haggard Archives. Bruce Kimmel also loaned us prints. While many of the films from the classic period are available on videotape, reviewing the John Farrow pictures was made easier by the existence of the American Movie Channel and our VCRs.

Other research was done at the Academy of Motion Picture Arts and Sciences Library in Beverly Hills and at the UCLA University Research Library. Janey Place not only loaned us the illustrations for "Some Visual Motifs of *Film Noir*" but also several other scene stills and frame enlargements which she assembled with Lowell Peterson. Other stills/frame enlargements are from the Robert Porfirio Collection at Brigham Young University administered by James D'Arc; Jeremy Butler; David Chierichetti; Robert E. Smith; and Adell Aldrich. All of other photographs are from the editors' personal collections. These stills are reproduced courtesy of Allied Artists, Cineville, Columbia, Live, MGM, Miramax, Paramount, Quinn Martin, RKO, Shapiro-Glickenhaus, 20th Century-Fox, United Artists, Universal, and Warner Bros. .

Bob Hoover typed portions of the manuscript; and, as they have so often done before, Glenn Erickson and Linda Brookover proofread drafts of the book. And, of course, Mel Zerman at Limelight Editions made the entire endeavor possible.

While we have attempted to reproduce the original pieces as closely as possible, some formal or practical considerations resulted in a few changes. While film titles may have been all caps or underlined in the original, for the sake of stylistic consistency we have chosen to italicize them as well as the term *film noir*. Except for this, any other underlining or italics in the text is that of the original authors. Most of the authors used end notes, so we have adopted that format throughout. We also changed the punctuation of the titles of some of the pieces previously published elsewhere when it differed from the style used here. The original format is reproduced below.

With regard to the illustrations, we have, where available or as far as possible, reproduced those used with the original article. The authors of "Some Visual Motifs of *Film Noir*" and "No Way Out: Existential Motifs in the *Film Noir*" could not locate one or two of the original frame enlargements and opted either to substitute another image ("No Way Out") or delete the original text reference ("Visual motifs"). In selecting and organizing new stills we have attempted to key photographs to the text, whether reprinted or new, but we have occasionally taken the liberty of injecting our own viewpoint in the captions.

"Towards a Definition of Film Noir" from *Panorama du Film Noir Américain* by Raymond Borde and Étienne Chaumeton. Copyright © 1955 by Les Éditions de Minuit. Reprinted by permission of Les Éditions de Minuit.

"Noir Cinema" from *Hollywood in the Forties* by Charles Higham and Joel Greenberg. Copyright © 1968 by Charles Higham and Joel Greenberg. Reprinted by permission of the authors.

"PAINT IT BLACK: the Family Tree of Film Noir" by Raymond Durgnat. Copyright © 1970 by *Cinema* (U.K.)/Raymond Durgnat. Reprinted by permission of the author.

"notes on film noir" by Paul Schrader, *Film Comment*, Spring, 1972. Copyright © 1972 by Film Comment Publishing Corporation. Reprinted by permission of the Film Society of Lincoln Center.

"SOME VISUAL MOTIFS OF FILM NOIR" by J.A. Place and L.S. Peterson, *Film Comment*, January-February, 1974. Copyright © 1974 by Film Comment Publishing Corporation. Reprinted by permission of the Film Society of Lincoln Center.

"NO WAY OUT: Existential Motifs in the film noir" by Robert Porfirio, *Sight and Sound*, Autumn, 1976 [vol. 45, no. 4]. Copyright © 1976 by the British Film Institute. Reprinted by permission of the British Film Institute/Robert Porfirio.

"FILM NOIR: A MODEST PROPOSAL" by James Damico, *Film Reader*, No. 3. Copyright © 1978 by The Silver Screen. Reprinted by permission of the Film Division, School of Speech, Northwestern University.

"Out of what past? Notes on the B *film noir*" by Paul Kerr, *Screen Education*, Nos. 32/33, Autumn/Winter, 1979-80. Copyright © 1979 by SEFT [Society for Education in Film and Television]. Reprinted by permission of *Screen*/Paul Kerr.

"*Phantom Lady*, Cornell Woolrich, and the Masochistic Aesthetic" by Tony Williams, *CineAction!*, Nos. 13-14, Summer, 1988. Copyright © 1988 by *CineAction!* Reprinted by permission of *CineAction!*/Tony Williams.

"JOHN FARROW, UNSUNG AUTEUR" by James Ursini and Alain Silver, *Film Screening Co-op Journal*, Winter, 1970. Copyright © 1970 by James Ursini and Alain Silver. Reprinted by permission of the authors.

"At the Margins of Film Noir: PREMINGER'S *ANGEL FACE*" by Richard Lippe, *CineAction!*, Nos. 13-14, Summer, 1988. Copyright © 1988 by *CineAction!* Reprinted by permission of *CineAction!*/Richard Lippe.

"*The Killers*: Expressiveness of Sound and Image in *Film Noir*" adapted from *The Dark Age of American Film: A Study of American* Film Noir *(1940-1960)* [doctoral dissertation, Yale University] by Robert Porfirio. Copyright © 1979 and 1995 by Robert Porfirio. Printed by permission of the author.

"Mann in the Dark: THE FILMS NOIR OF ANTHONY MANN" by Robert K. Smith, *Bright Lights*, No. 5 [vol. 2, no. 1]. Copyright © 1977 by Gary Morris. Reprinted by permission of Gary Morris.

"Expressionist Doom in *Night and the City*" by Glenn Erickson. Copyright © 1995 by Glenn Erickson. Printed by permission of the author.

"*KISS ME DEADLY*: Evidence of a Style" by Alain Silver, *Film Comment*, March-April, 1975. Copyright © 1975 by Film Comment Publishing Corporation. Reprinted by permission of the Film Society of Lincoln Center. Revisions Copyright © 1994 by

Film Noir **Reader**

Above, Robert Mitchum and Jane Greer in *Out of the Past* and, below, Dick Powell with Jane Wyatt and Jimmy Hunt in *The Pitfall*. "Different directors, cinematographers, and screenwriters adapting different original stories for different stars at eight different studios...created eight otherwise unrelated motion pictures with one cohesive style."

Introduction

Alain Silver

> The existence over the last few years of a "série noir" in Hollywood is obvious. Defining its essential traits is another matter.
>
> *Panorama du Film Noir Américain*

I.

Forty years after Raymond Borde and Étienne Chaumeton defined the challenge, critical commentators on *film noir* continue to grapple with it. Ironically, American writers did not immediately take up consideration of this indigenous phenomenon and the question of its "essential traits." Only gradually in a frequently cross-referenced series of essays in the 1970s did they begin to express themselves. There are now a dozen full-length books in English concerning *film noir* and undoubtedly more to follow. As noted in the Acknowledgments, the sometimes difficult process of tracking down significant earlier writings for an essay in *Film Noir: An Encyclopedic Reference to the American Style* (Overlook/Viking, 1992) gave us the idea for this book. As it happens the two most recent volumes on *noir, Shades of Noir* (Verso, 1993) and *The Book of Film Noir* (Continuum, 1993) are anthologies of new essays by mostly non-American writers.

Past and present commentators have brought and continue to bring to bear on the *noir* phenomenon a variety of critical approaches, and that is the foundation of *Film Noir Reader*. Of course, we are bypassing the point of view of someone like Barry Gifford, author of the informal survey *The Devil Thumbs A Ride*, who deems all such endeavors to be "academic flapdoodle." In 1979, the introduction, other essays, and individual entries in *Film Noir: An Encyclopedic Reference* were the first published attempt in English to search the entire body of films for "essential traits." I remarked there that the full range of the *noir* vision depends on its narratives, its characterizations, and its visual style. In fact, that style is a translation of both character emotions and narrative concepts into a pattern of visual usage. No doubt a pop critic such as Gifford could assert that it is formalist mumbo-jumbo to "detect" alienation lurking beyond the frame line in a vista of the dark, wet asphalt of a city street or obsession in a point-of-view shot that picks a woman's face out of crowd. I would argue that to resist such readings is to deny the full potential of figurative

3

meaning not merely in *film noir* but in all motion pictures. Obviously none of the various elements of visual style—angle, composition, lighting, montage, depth, movement, etc.—which inform any given shot or sequence are unique of *film noir*. What sets the *noir* cycle apart is the unity of its formal vision. There is nothing in the films themselves which precludes or invalidates any established critical method as the various essays reprinted in this volume will confirm.

Michael Walker's opening comments in *The Book of Film Noir* reveal a fairly straightforward auteurist bias. But what can one say about a viewpoint such as French critic Marc Vernet's in his introductory essay, "Film Noir at the Edge of Doom" in *Shades of Noir*? Certainly it epitomizes the sort of criticism which Gifford scorns; but Gifford's opprobrium is not the issue. In the third edition of *Film Noir: An Encyclopedic Reference* our review of the literature on *film noir* included Vernet's previously published conclusion that "a hero cannot be both strong and vulnerable, the woman good and evil." The assertion made there—that his observations were part of a simplistic, structuro-semiological rush to judgment clearly at odds with the narrative position of *film noir* as a whole—still pertain. Where once Vernet merely puzzled over contradictory icons, in "Edge of Doom" he indulges in pointless deconstruction. On the one hand Vernet now bemoans "complacent repetition" about *film noir*. On the other hand he presents the ultimate obfuscation by calling it "impossible to criticize." What then is he writing about?

One can tolerate being abstractly dismissed by Vernet and even overlook having one's actual name misspelled, as when he changes "Alain" to "Alan." Vernet's is certainly not the first bibliographic reference with that particular misspelling. Nor am I suggesting that critical writing should be about crossing every "t" or including every "i." This is particularly true with writers on motion pictures, who are addressing an expressive medium that is the most complex in the history of art. But Vernet's assumption about how a particular name should be spelled is telling in that it reveals his tendency towards pre-judgment and succinctly exposes the problem with his critical outlook. Vernet sees a simple contradiction: a French first name like those in the credits of *L'Année Dernière à Marienbad* and an English last name right out of *Treasure Island*. "Of course," he deduces, "this must be an error." Some unnamed researcher has made a mistake, which he is correcting by Anglicizing the spelling. It seems quite clear from this where Vernet's outlook is rooted. It derives from a solipsistic arrogance that can presume to "correct" anomalies which it does not understand and can generate the offhanded observation that *film noir* is "the triumph of European artists even as it presents American actors."

Aside from its remarkably unembarrassed Eurocentric bias, such a statement completely ignores Paul Schrader's decades-old warning that "there is a danger of over-emphasizing the German influence in Hollywood"; and it typifies many recent attempts both to break down the "myth" of *film noir* and to relocate its origins. As Borde and Chaumeton realized from the first, there is no easy answer. The *noir* cycle is an event garmented in the uneasy synthesis of social upheaval and Hollywood.

Given its brief history *film noir* has inspired more than its share of discussion. Part of what has always troubled some critics of *film noir* are its character themes, its protagonists who often perish because of an obsessive and/or alienated state of mind. Must it be really so remarkable, when methodologies from Marxism to Freudianism to Existentialism assailed the moral and political status quo, that a movement such a *film noir* should develop characters with a sense of alienation and despair? It may be unduly simplified to erect such a causality or to cite a fortuitous confluence of factors as responsible for the appearance of the *noir* movement, but that does not make it incorrect.

Much has been made of the crisis of masculinity in *film noir*. Much could be made of the crisis in Judeo-Christian patriarchal structures since the mid-point of the 20th Century. The dramatic crisis of *film noir* is the same as that which drives any convergent group of characterizations. The unprecedented social upheaval of two world wars compounded by economic turmoil and genocides on every continent was globally promulgated by broadcasts and newsreels and all condensed into a thirty year span from 1915 to 1945. Just as the technique and technology of filmmaking has progressed in its hundred year history, the ideological outlook of its artists cannot have been unaffected by the other events in the world during that span of time.

Whatever one may believe about the delimiting factors of *film noir*, then or now, its first expression in what is generally accepted as "the classic period" was solely in American movies made in America by American filmmakers. Vernet seems to imply that Fritz Lang, Robert Siodmak, Anthony Mann, Otto Preminger, and Billy Wilder were European or, more specifically, German artists. The issue of European expatriates is a significant one, not just for *film noir* but for American filmmaking in general. But how can it be glibly summarized as a "triumph of European artists presenting American actors"? Putting aside for a moment questions of auteurism or whether these filmmakers were more significant to the cycle of *noir* films than American-born directors from Robert Aldrich to Robert Wise, does the national origin of the directors change the nationality of a film? Did Joseph Losey continue to make American movies in England? Do John Farrow's origins make his films for Paramount and RKO "early Australian" *film noir*?

When Borde and Chaumeton wrote the first book-length study of the phenomenon in 1955 they called it, naturally enough, *Panorama du Film Noir <u>Américain</u>*. The title itself expresses the second truism of *film noir*. Vernet and others may have some reason other than Eurocentric bias for stressing the non-American aspects of *film noir*. The three British and French publishers of *Film Noir: An Encyclopedic Reference* probably did not delete "to the American Style" from the title just because they thought it was too long. Still, while many subsequent writers have questioned both specifics and generalities of Borde and Chaumeton's seminal work, none have questioned the very existence of the phenomenon which they tried to define.

In 1979 I wrote that, with the Western, *film noir* shares the distinction of being an indigenous American form. But unlike Westerns which derive in great part from a preexisting literary genre and a period of American history, the antecedents of *film noir* are less precise. As a consequence, the *noir* cycle has a singular position in the brief history of American motion pictures: a body of films that not only presents a relatively cohesive vision of America but that does so in a manner transcending the influences of auteurism or genre. *Film noir* is not firmly rooted in either personal creation or in the translation of another tradition into movie terms. Rather *film noir* is a self-contained reflection of American culture and its preoccupations at a point in time. As such it is the unique example of a wholly American film style.

Vernet makes some assertions about *film noir*'s origins, about censorship and prejudices in both America and France from which he concludes that post-World War II French critics "created" *film noir*. Can anyone seriously contend that critics created anything but the term? As Edgardo Cozarinsky notes "*film noir* defies transla-tion into English, though its object of study is mainly (and, one may argue, its only le-gitimate examples are) English-speaking."[1] The suggestion of Vernet and others arrogates the very concept of creation. At the risk of belaboring the obvious, films are made by filmmakers not by critics, whose understanding of the process is neces-sarily limited. To paraphrase Vernet, the primary consideration is not the technical process nor the financial process, but the expressive process, which relies on the audience—the perceivers of the expression—for completion. This is the fundamen-tal transaction on which Vernet or any critic should concentrate.

> They are, therefore, not revolutionary but conservative. Actually,
> they are reactionary, for they try to roll back the wheel of history.
>
> *The Communist Manifesto*

In order to see the subject of *film noir* as it is, one need look no farther than the films. Vernet's revisionism is like any of the neo-Freudian, semiological, historical, structural, socio-cultural, and/or auteurist assaults of the past. *Film noir* has resisted them all. Why then are critics like Vernet interested in the phenomenon of *film noir*? Are they at heart all neo-Platonists and *Il Conformista* the film that they watch over and over late at night? Perhaps many of the new European essayists need to tear apart the foundation laid by Borde and Chaumeton in order to build something new. Certainly there is justification in James Damico's lament in "*Film Noir*: A Modest Proposal" that an "order of breezy assumption seems to have afflicted *film noir* criticism from its beginnings." Unfortunately, in this latter context, a reactionary commentator like Vernet offers nothing new but just another brand of breezy assumptions. Actually, he offers a void, a *noir* hole where there once was a body of films.

Much of *Shades of Noir* progresses from the suggestion made by David Bordwell in *The Classical American Cinema* that *film noir* is merely an invention of critical com-mentators. In discussing this concept in *Film Noir: An Encyclopedic Reference*, Bord-well's assertion was cited to the effect that "critics have not succeeded in defining specifically noir visual techniques... or narrative structure. The problem resembles one in art history, that of defining 'non-classical' styles." At first glance there is nothing to dispute in Bordwell's remark. The tautological nature of his position is clearer in a more recent expression by a reviewer: "Genres are invented by critics. When the first *film noir*—whatever you might consider that to be— was released, nobody yelled, 'Hey, let's go on down to the Bijou! The first *film noir* is out!' What is at first innovation or anomaly only becomes a genre through repetition and eventual critical classification."[2] If nothing else, this is certainly a more cogent expression of the obvious that either Vernet or Bordwell make. So they didn't go down to the Bijou to see *Stranger on the Third Floor* or *Two Seconds* (Vernet's candidate from 1932) because it was the "first *film noir*." To answer in kind, "So what?" Did the first audiences for *The Great Train Robbery* or *Nosferatu* congratulate themselves on attending the first Western or the earliest adaptation of Bram Stoker's *Dracula*? The best answer to anyone's assertion that filmmakers of the classic period never specifically decided to make "a *film noir*" is still cinematographer John Alton's evocation of the *noir* milieu in his book *Painting with Light*: "The room is dark. A strong streak of light sneaks in from the hall under the door. The sound of steps is heard. The shadows of two feet divide the light streak. A brief silence follows. There is suspense in the air."

If Bordwell was not aware of Alton's book when he wrote "critics have not succeeded in defining specifically *noir* visual techniques," he certainly must have known Janey Place and Lowell Peterson's essay on visual motifs in *noir*. Place and Peterson themselves quoted Higham and Greenberg's 1968 book *Hollywood in the Forties* on the subject of visual style. The visual analysis of *film noir* was further developed by Janey Place in *Women and Film Noir* and by Robert Porfirio's extensive work in his dissertation *The Dark Age of American Film: A Study of American Film Noir*.

In fact, the evocation of a "*noir* look" goes all the way back to Borde and Chaumeton. In 1979 I cited the years of production immediately after World War II as the most visually homogeneous of the entire *noir* cycle. One might still consider a random selection of motion pictures released over an eighteen month period such as *The Big Clock* (Paramount, 1948), *Brute Force* (Universal, 1947), *Cry of the City* (20th Century-Fox, 1948), *Force of Evil* (MGM, 1948), *Framed* (Columbia, 1947), *Out of the Past* (RKO, 1947), *The Pitfall* (United Artists, 1948), and *The Unsuspected* (Warner Bros., 1947) and discover that eight different directors, cinematographers, and screenwriters adapted different original stories for different stars at eight different studios. These people of great and small technical reputations created eight otherwise unrelated motion pictures with one cohesive style.[3]

I have previously contended that the *noir* cycle's consistent visual style is keyed specifically to recurrent narrative patterns and character emotions. Because these patterns and emotions are repeatedly suggestive of certain abstractions, such as alienation and obsession, it may seem that *film noir* is overly dependent on external constructions, such as Existentialism or Freudianism, for its dramatic meanings. Irrefutably *film noir* does recruit the ethical and philosophical values of the culture as freely as it recruits visual conventions, iconic notations, and character types. This

process both enriches and dislocates the *noir* cycle as a phenomenon so that it resists facile explanation.

Criticism is often less a search for meaning than for sub-text. In film the dilemma
is that narrative is usually explicit and style is usually not. Charts of narrative patterns,
icons, and the like are easy to make. For example, one could assign critical allegiances to *noir* figures:

Alienated characters < = > Existentialism

Obsessed characters < = > Freudianism

Proletarian characters < = > Marxism

Femme fatales < = > Feminism

All of the above < = > Structuralism

A writer like Gifford might well accuse chart makers of chasing their own tall
tales. For him, *film noir* is more about Lawrence Tierney's sneer than statistics or
structures. The real question, as suggested by Bordwell, is neo-formalist: if *film
noir* is heavily reliant on visual style, how does that affect meaning?

What I answered in *Film Noir: An Encyclopedic Reference* was that there is no
grammar attached to this visual substance because its conventions of expression are
not analogous to those of language. Or, as Pasolini put it, "The cinema author has no
dictionary."[4] Divergent concepts of "signs and meaning" notwithstanding, the side-lit
close-up, the long take, or the foreground object bisecting the frame may imply respectively a character's indecision, a building tension, a figurative separation of the
other persons and things in the frame; or they may not. The potential is always
there. The specific image may or may not participate in that potential. Without denotation, it is the connotations which *film noir* repeatedly creates that are telling. The
dark streets become emblems of alienation; a figure's unrelenting gaze becomes obsessive; the entire environment becomes hostile, chaotic, deterministic. Some critics
have found a conflict between the documentary import of certain police dramas,
which are ostensibly realistic, and the low-key style of detective films, which are ostensibly expressionistic. In fact, the issue is really one of convention. Which is more
lifelike, a man in a dark alley, his face illuminated by a match as he lights a cigarette
or a woman on a veranda built on a sound stage cottage, her body casting three
shadows as she shoots her victim? Hollywood reality is by convention. The visual
conventions of *film noir* are, as often as not, actually more naturalistic.

What *Film Noir Reader* will quickly reveal is the breadth of theories which critics
have brought to the *noir* phenomenon. Whatever one calls it—series, style, genre,
movement, school, cycle—none of the seminal essayists on *film noir* represented in
this book have contradicted Borde and Chaumeton's remark that the existence of a
noir series is "obvious." Certainly they did not all agree (when have critics ever done
that?), but they did address the visual techniques and narrative structures of *film noir*
in dozens of articles.

History is to take an arbitrarily selected series of continuous events and examine it apart from others, although there is and can be no beginning to any event, for one event always flows uninterruptedly from another.

War and Peace

It should go without saying that any investigator must first look at the heart of the matter, to the films themselves. How then could Marc Vernet look at those films and conclude that "*film noir* is a collector's idea that for the moment can only be found in books"? Actually, this may be the most accurate statement that Vernet makes; although, borrowing a touch of his condescension, he probably doesn't even know why. Obviously there is nowhere in the literal history of cinema, that is, in the films themselves, a "*film noir*," any more than there is a Western, a war film, or a screwball comedy. Even straining credibility and accepting Bordwell's assertion that the makers of *noir* films did not in any way realize what they were doing, is conscious intentionality a prerequisite for creative expression? It can only be assumed that it is Vernet's lack of knowledge about the real process by which films are made which leads to his confusion. Of course, it does not take a rocket scientist to realize that one is hard pressed to make a samurai film without swords or a Western without horses.

Fresh from the translation of Borde and Chaumeton, I am moved to slip for a moment into a free-form, anecdotal, somewhat French style. In 1975, I sit in an almost empty theater in Santa Monica watching Walter Hill's Hard Times, *the directorial debut of the screenwriter of the remarkable neo-noir* Hickey and Boggs; *and I am somehow reminded of Kihachi Okamoto's* Samurai Assassin. *Two years later, I sit in a living room in the Hollywood hills, interviewing Walter Hill for* Movie *magazine. In the preliminary banter, I remark that the Charles Bronson character in* Hard Times *is like a Japanese* ronin, *a masterless* samurai. *Hill goes to a shelf and brings over two scripts. One is a Western, still unproduced, entitled* The Last Gun. *While I flip through, noting that the main character is named Ronin and that the act breaks are marked by quotes from* bushido, *the code of the warrior, Hill finds a particular page in the* Hard Times *script. As he hands it to me, his thumb indicates a line of stage direction in which the street fighter "crouches in the corner like a samurai."*

Is *Hard Times* a samurai film? Of course not. No more than the elements borrowed even more extensively in Hill's *The Warriors* can make it a samurai film. Neither Hill nor Clint Eastwood nor John Milius nor George Miller, as much as they might admire the genre, have made anything more than allusions to samurai films; just as reciprocally Akira Kurosawa could never make a John Ford Western. Styles of films have more than requisite icons to identify them. Filmmakers know this when the films are made. Contemporary filmmakers understand, as actor Nick Nolte asserts, that "film noir is putting a style over the story."[5] "Collectors," as Vernet brands them, only realize it after the fact. In the end, does it matter what the filmmakers of the classic period of *film noir* thought about the films they were making? *Film noir* is a closed system. To some extent, it is defined after the fact. How could it be otherwise? Was the Hundred Years War, something else after only fifty years of fighting? So when did *film noir* become what it is? For those more interested in the phenomenon than the phenomenology, the answer must be from the first, when that first *noir* film opened at the Bijou. But perhaps a more eloquent answer is a question. Consider the photograph reproduced below. Why did Robert Aldrich, producer/director of *Kiss Me Deadly*, pose with a copy of the first edition Borde and Chaumeton's book (in which he is not even mentioned) as he stood on the set of *Attack!* in 1956?

2.

A fact thus set down in substantial history cannot easily be gainsaid.
Nor is there any reason it should be.

Moby Dick

Questions of phenomenology aside, film history is as clear now about *film noir* as ever: it finds its existence as obvious as Borde and Chaumeton did forty years ago. If observers of *film noir* agree on anything, it is on the boundaries of the classic period, which begins in 1941 with *The Maltese Falcon* and ends less than a score of years later with *Touch of Evil*. Issues of pre-*noir* or neo-*noir* aside, the editors of this book and many other commentators have long considered *film noir* to be more than either a genre or a movement. Exactly what Borde and Chaumeton claim to mean by their term "series," which they define as a group of "motion pictures from one country sharing certain traits (style, atmosphere, subject matter...) strongly enough to mark them unequivocally and to give them, over time, an unmistakable character," is not clarified by their lists of analogies to *film noir*, which include both genres and movements. Because so many of the essayists on the *noir* phenomenon in the 70s were still deliberating the question of "essential traits" posed by Borde and Chaumeton in 1955, there is no consensus on *film noir* to be found in this book.

Beginning with Borde and Chaumeton's first chapter, "Towards a Definition of *Film Noir*," Part One of *Film Noir Reader* contains eight Seminal Essays. Taken together they represent the proliferation and divergence of significant published opinions on *film noir* through 1979. It was in 1979 that the first edition of *Film Noir: An Encyclopedic Reference* appeared; and since then, as already noted, eleven other book-length compendiums and anthologies in English have followed.

It was in the 1983 Afterword to the reprint of *Panorama du Film Noir Américain*, which was based on an article about *film noir* in the 70s, that Borde and Chaumeton asserted that "*film noir* had fulfilled its role, which was to create a specific malaise and to drive home a social criticism of the United States." Whether the authors were injecting the issue of "social criticism" in hindsight is unknown; but it underlines the second main theme which many of the seminal essayists also consider: the relationship of the *noir* cycle to the socio-cultural history of the United States.

As Borde and Chaumeton wrestle through lists of films, considering plot points and character types, they also make a telling observation about the style of *film noir*. In their subsequent chapter on the "sources" of *film noir*, they introduce not only the obvious influence of hard-boiled fiction but also the prevalence of psychoanalysis in the 1940s as a popular treatment of nervous disorders. The original edition of *Panorama du Film Noir Américain* had a unique perspective being not merely the first but also the only study of *film noir* written contemporaneously with the classic period. From this position, Borde and Chaumeton's initial attempt at definition of *film noir* cannot be superseded as the benchmark for all subsequent work making the same attempt.

By 1962, French film historian George Sadoul was offhandedly remarking in his *Histoire du Cinéma* that *film noir* "was a school,... where psychoanalysis was applied [so that] a childhood trauma became the cause of criminal behavior just as unemployment explained social unrest." Both the term and the concept took longer to gain acceptance with English-language critics. The first extensive discussion of film noir in English appeared in the chapter, "Black Cinema," of Charles Higham and Joel Greenberg's *Hollywood in the Forties*. Beginning with an evocative and oft-cited paragraph about the dark wet streets and flashing neon signs that create the "ambience of *film noir*," what follows is an overview of what Higham and Greenberg consider "a genre," but no usable definition of *film noir* emerges from this impressionistic piece.

In 1970, an article by Raymond Durgnat appeared in the British magazine *Cinema*. "Paint It Black: the Family Tree of the *Film Noir*" is the first structural approach to *film noir* which asserts that "it is not a genre as the Western or gangster film is, and takes us into the realms of classification by motif and tone." As Durgnat rambles through scores of titles in less than a dozen pages the branches of his family tree twist around and entangle themselves with each other. In the end Durgnat has no time, and perhaps no inclination, to plot these intertwinings. Ironically, Durgnat's "family tree" is better known in a truncated version stripped down to a two-page chart of just categories printed by *Film Comment* in 1974. Curiously, Vernet claims that Durgnat's self-professed "imperfect schematizations" helped "to paralyse reflection on *film noir*."

Paul Schrader's "notes on *film noir*" originally appeared in a program accompanying a retrospective of *noir* films at the first Los Angeles Film Exposition. When it was published in *Film Comment* in 1972, it was the first analysis of *film noir* for many American readers. If any single essay had the possibility of "paralyzing reflection on *film noir*," it was this one. Schrader cited and embraced Durgnat's assertion that *film noir* is not a genre. Rather than charting his own types, Schrader summarizes the mediating influences on the *noir* phenomenon and then discusses its style and themes. Schrader steps over the question of definition with a disclaimer about subjectivity: "Almost every critic has his own definition of *film noir*, and a personal list of film titles.... How many *noir* elements does it take to make a *film noir noir*?" While he is the first to summarize succinctly four "causes"—(1) World War II and post-War disillusionment; (2) post-War realism; (3) the German influence; and (4) the hard-boiled tradition—Schrader considers the "uneasy, exhilarating combination of realism and expressionism" to be contradictory; and, surprisingly, he never considers how oneirism or nightmarish images can reflect a psychological truth as mentioned by Borde and Chaumeton.

The ground-breaking aspect of Schrader's article is the outline of *film noir* style and characterization. For Schrader the classic period ends early but still produces a plethora of chiaroscuro and an multitude of haunted protagonists. The stylistic discussion carries over as the piece ends tellingly on the question of *film noir* and auteurism: "Auteur criticism is interested in how directors are different; *film noir* criticism is interested in what they have in common."

In early 1974 *Film Comment* published another article as influential as and perhaps even more widely cited than the Durgnat and Schrader pieces: Janey Place and Lowell Peterson's "Some Visual Motifs of *Film Noir.*" "Visual Motifs" is actually two separate pieces. In the first part, Place and Peterson introduce the concept of what they call "anti-traditional elements," that is, a mise-en-scene by directors and a lighting scheme by cinematographers that radically diverges from the studio "norm." In doing so, they are the first to attempt a systematic if abbreviated assessment of *film noir* style. The second part of the article is meant to illustrate the first; but the stills and frame enlargements which appear there have detailed annotations which permit them to stand alone as an analysis of the *noir* form.

Published in *Sight and Sound* in 1976, Robert Porfirio's "No Way Out: Existential Motifs in the *Film Noir*" was extracted from a larger work in progress and partially assimilated into *Film Noir: An Encyclopedic Reference.* Before beginning an analysis of the motifs of alienation and despair, as promised in the piece's title, Porfirio notes that "visual style rescued many an otherwise pedestrian film from oblivion." Porfirio's analytical style is more closely aligned to that of Place and Peterson than to Durgnat or Schrader, as he makes extensive use of frame enlargements to illustrate such prototypical moments of existential *angst* in *film noir* as the narrator's lament in *Detour* that "fate or some mysterious force can put the finger on you or me for no reason at all."

James Damico's 1978 *"Film Noir:* A Modest Proposal" from *Film Reader* makes a case for *noir* as a genre but also focuses on the limitations of a genre model that is based on "plot structure and character type." Damico's principal alternative concept—his modest proposal—is an archetype based on Northrup Frye's model, largely dependent on the *femme fatale,* and in many respects reminiscent of Borde and Chaumeton, to whom he frequently refers. Damico's piece has itself often been cited as a first major article to express a viewpoint opposed to Paul Schrader's because of his search for a narrative model. Actually Damico seems to admire Schrader's genealogy of *noir* even as he decries Durgnat's unfocused and/or too broad categories. Perhaps Damico's most radical assertion is consigned to a note at the very end of the piece. Damico briefly surveys all the preceding essays on *noir* except Place and Peterson's, yet in his note he casually dismisses the concept of visual style because he can "see no conclusive evidence [of] anything cohesive."

The last of the seminal pieces is Paul Kerr's "Out of What Past? Notes on the B *Film Noir.*" As the title suggests, its aim is "to refocus...on one important, industrially-defined, fraction of the genre—the B *film noir.*" Kerr regards *film noir* as a genre but also accepts that "the curious cross-generic quality of *film noir* is perhaps a vestige of its origins as a kind of 'oppositional' cinematic mode." He begins a search for a new definition by reviewing past assessments from Borde and Chaumeton to Damico then presents his own digest of observations keyed to economic issues. His most original points, such as low-key lighting being used to mask low-budget sets or night shooting as a strategy to get more set-ups into each production day, are part of a "technological determinism" for *film noir*. While his use of statistical data is extensive, a few of Kerr's conclusions are marginally backed by the facts. For instance, he asserts that the studios with larger financial reserves, Pararmount, Fox, and MGM, made "not only fewer...but also more lavish" *noir* films. While RKO and United Artists clearly had the highest tally of titles in the classic period, Paramount made almost as many; and Fox's total was equal to Warners. Despite his basically "non-aesthetic" discussion, Kerr's influence on later writers seeking alternatives to the auteurist or structural models still continues.

The second section of *Film Noir Reader* contains "case studies" of individual films and directors. While most of the writers follow a convention that goes back to Borde and Chaumeton's assertion that they would "deem films to be created by their directors," not all of these case studies are auteurist. In fact, the critical biases and methodologies from Porfirio's visual analysis of *The Killers* to Tony Williams on *Phantom Lady* cover as broad a range as the seminal articles reproduced in Part One. While the distinction may not be as simple as Paul Schrader suggested, *film noir* has never been "about" auteurism or particular directors, any more than silent Soviet dramas were about Eisenstein or Neo-realism about Rossellini. But as it is with all of film history, auteurism is part of *film noir*. For many directors *noir* provided a "B" context to display his or her talent and make the transition to "A" pictures. This is a key point which Robert Smith makes in his essay about Anthony Mann's early work.

Part Three of *Film Noir Reader* goes farther afield into the question: "What is this Thing called *Noir*?" (which is, not coincidentally, the title of one of the new essays). It and another new piece also consider issues from the "classic period": fugitive couples and, as Karen Hollinger extracts from her dissertation, narrative structure and the *femme fatale*. Another original article considers the influence of classic *noir* on the television productions of the period and a reprint from 1985 ponders the "legacy" of *noir* on more recent TV as evidenced by the visual style of *Miami Vice*. Of course, no anthology would be complete without considering neo-*noir*, its popularity with contemporary producers and influence on the independent and "neo-B" filmmakers. Todd Erickson's revision of his thesis topic explores the parallels in technological developments which underlie both the classic period and neo-*noir* and traces how a new generation of filmmakers have transformed a movement into a genre.

Anyone who has searched in vain for an article or used a dog-eared photocopy of any of the pieces in Part One already understands the researcher's frustration which motivated the creation of a compendium of classic texts in *Film Noir Reader*. Not only are all the key essays in one volume but, thanks to the originals provided by the authors and twenty years of technological improvements, there are also better quality reproductions of frame enlargements in the "Motif" articles. But having now read and reread all these essays, old and new, the most important reason for *Film Noir*

Reader is clearer than ever: the historical and ongoing importance of *film noir* itself to American motion pictures. Without going as far as Schrader's assertion that "picked at random, a *film noir* is likely to be a better made film than a randomly selected silent comedy, musical, western, and so on," it is fair to ask how many fifty-year-old movies can still hold the attention of a contemporary average filmgoer? Scores of classic period *noir* films are as fascinating for current audiences as they were for the French filmgoers who suddenly discovered them en masse after World War II. If there were a critical consensus of the best films from the 40s and 50s, many if not most of them would be *noir* films. In fact, in the years since Borde and Chaumeton, "noir" itself has so become a part of the American idiom that journalists can now write about a dark aspect of society without fear of misunderstanding that "this is America *noir*, a moral nether world plumbed by tabloid television and pulp fiction."[6]

Notes

1. "American Film Noir" in *Cinema: A Critical Dictionary* (New York: Viking, 1980), edited by Richard Roud, p. 57.

2. Andy Klein, "Shady Characters, A Fortnight of *Noir* Nihilism," *Los Angeles Reader*, V. 17, n. 16 (January 27, 1995), p. 15.

3. The particulars: *The Big Clock* directed by John Farrow, photographed by John Seitz, from a script by Jonathan Latimer based on a novel by Kenneth Fearing, and starring Ray Milland and Charles Laughton; *Brute Force* directed by Jules Dassin, photographed by William Daniels, from a script by Richard Brooks based on a story by Robert Patterson, and starring Burt Lancaster and Yvonne DeCarlo; *Cry of the City* directed by Robert Siodmak, photographed by Lloyd Ahern, from a script by Richard Murphy based on a novel by Henry Edward Helseth, and starring Victor Mature and Richard Conte; *Force of Evil* directed and co-scripted by Abraham Polonsky, photographed by George Barnes, co-script by Ira Wolfert based on his novel, and starring John Garfield; *Framed* directed by Richard Wallace, photographed by Burnett Guffey, from a script by Ben Maddow based on a story by Jack Patrick, and starring Glenn Ford and Barry Sullivan; *Out of the Past* directed by Jacques Tourneur, photographed by Nicholas Musuraca, from a script by Daniel Mainwaring [using the pseudonym Geoffrey Homes] and Frank Fenton [uncredited] based on Mainwaring's novel, and starring Robert Mitchum, Kirk Douglas, and Jane Greer; *The Pitfall* directed by André de Toth, photographed by Harry Wild, from a script by Karl Kamb basd on a novel by Jay Dratler, and starring Dick Powell and Lizabeth Scott; and *The Unsuspected* directed by Michael Curtiz, photographed by Woody Bredell, from a script by Ranald MacDougall based on a novel by Charlotte Armstrong, and starring Claude Rains.

4. *Cahiers du Cinéma* (English), No. 7, p. 36. Pasolini's presentation at the First New Cinema Festival at Pesaro in June, 1965 introduced the concept of a "styleme" or a unit of "stylistic grammar." That essay and Umberto Eco's "Articulations of Cinematic Code" delivered the following year at Pesaro are the foundation texts on "Style and Meaning."

5. Nick Nolte interviewed by Jim Brown, NBC *Today Show*, August 31, 1995.

6. Stephen Braun, "Contract Killings in Suburbia," *Los Angeles Times* (February 10, 1995), p. A1.

Above, Barry Fitzgerald (center) as a traditional "brave and incorruptible" hero, Lt. Muldoon, "the diminutive Irish detective of *The Naked City*, who believes in God and works on his own time to see justice done." His short stature is emphasized when flanked by his much taller partner, Halloran (Don Taylor, left) and an ambulance doctor (Russ Conway); but in his dark suit he nonetheless dominates the scene.

Towards a Definition of *Film Noir*

Raymond Borde and Étienne Chaumeton (1955)

[The following is excerpted from the book *Panorama du Film Noir Américain*[1]]

It was during the summer of 1946 that French moviegoers discovered a new type of American film. In the course of a few weeks, from mid-July to the end of August, five movies flashed one after the other across Parisian screens, movies which shared a strange and violent tone, tinged with a unique kind of eroticism: John Huston's *The Maltese Falcon*, Otto Preminger's *Laura*, Edward Dmytryk's *Murder, My Sweet*, Billy Wilder's *Double Indemnity*, and Fritz Lang's *The Woman in the Window*.

Long cut off from the United States, with little news of Hollywood production during the war, living on the memory of Wyler, of Ford and Capra, ignorant even of the newest luminaries in the directorial ranks, French critics could not fully absorb this sudden revelation. Nino Frank, who was among the first to speak of "dark film" and who seemed to discern from the first the basic traits of the *noir* style, nonetheless wrote of *The Maltese Falcon* and *Double Indemnity* that "[these films] belong to what we used to call the police genre but that we should more appropriately describe from now on by the term 're criminal adventure' or, better still, 're criminal psychology'."[2] This was also the reaction of genre critics who, it must be said, failed to grasp the full impact of these releases.

But a few months later Frank Tuttle's *This Gun for Hire*, Robert Siodmak's *The Killers*, Robert Montgomery's *The Lady in the Lake*, Charles Vidor's *Gilda*, and Howard Hawks' *The Big Sleep* imposed the concept of *film noir* on moviegoers. A new "series" had emerged in the history of film.

A series can be defined as a group of motion pictures from one country sharing certain traits (style, atmosphere, subject matter...) strongly enough to mark them unequivocally and to give them, over time, an unmistakable character. Series persist for differing amounts of time: sometimes two years, sometimes ten. To some extent, the viewer decides on this. From the point of view of "filmic evolution," series spring from certain older features, from long-ago titles. Moreover they all reach a peak, that is, a moment of purest expression. Afterwards they slowly fade and disappear leaving traces and informal sequels in other genres.

17

The history of film is, in large part, a history of film cycles. There are, of course, certain titles that resist classification: Welles' *Citizen Kane* or Clifford Odets' *None but the Lonely Heart* are among these. Often a remarkable film cannot be classified because it is the first in a new movement and the observer lacks the necessary perspective. *Caligari* was unclassifiable before it engendered "Caligarism."

Since the start of talkies, one could cite many examples: in the United States, social realism, gangster films; in Germany, the farces from 1930 to 1933 which inspired a like movement in American comedy; in the USSR, films dedicated to the October Revolution; in France, the realism of Carné, Renoir, and Duvivier.

More recently, we have seen British comedies, a French series dealing with mythic evasions (from *L'éternal Retour* to *Singoalle* and *Juliette*), the social documentaries of Daquin, Rouquier and Nicole Védrès. From the USSR come paeans to the glory of collective labor and the Kolkhoz cycle. In the United States: the crime documentary (Hathaway, Kazan, Dassin), the psychological melodrama, and the new school of the Western—so many types of films, each having its particular locales, traditions, and even fans.

The existence over the last few years of a "*série noir*" in Hollywood is obvious. Defining its essential traits is another matter.

One could simplify the problem by assigning to *film noir* qualities such as nightmarish, weird, erotic, ambivalent, and cruel. All these exist in the series; but at one moment, reverie may dominate and the result is *Shanghai Gesture*, at another, eroticism comes to the fore in *Gilda*. In still other titles, the cruelty of some bizarre behavior is preeminent. Often the *noir* aspect of a film is linked to a character, a scene, a setting. *The Set-up* is a good documentary on boxing: it becomes a *film noir* in the sequence when scores are settled by a savage beating in a blind alley. *Rope* is a psychological melodrama which attaches itself to *film noir* through its intriguing sadism. Alternately, *The Big Sleep, This Gun for Hire*, and *The Lady in the Lake* seem to be typical "thrillers." We will begin by addressing the problem of definition by discussing the pictures which critics have most often dubbed "*films noirs*."

One last note: by convention we will deem films to be created by their directors. This is a convention because one can never know with regard to American productions whether the director is really the ultimate creator of a work. Sternberg himself said "I work on assignment, that is to say by the job. And each job order, just like those given to a cabinet maker, bookbinder, or cobbler, is for a specific piece of work."[3] What is the contribution of the producer, the screenwriter, the editor? Is it coincidental that the late Mark Hellinger produced three such distinctive pictures as *The Killers, Brute Force*, and *The Naked City*? Who can say, other than those who were there, whether Hellinger put his own mark on these films or gave Dassin and Siodmak free rein?

In reality, while there may be few instances of a director who has the final word in Hollywood, his role is certainly a significant one; and his degree of independence will logically enough increase with his commercial success. This could explain the persistence of vision in a given director's work: the theme of failure and adventure in John Huston, the theme of violence with Raoul Walsh, the theme of urban realism with Dassin, and even Sternberg, who has never strayed far from exotic sensuality. By all accounts, this convention of authorship is entirely apt.

The bloody paths down which we drive logic into dread.[4]

The noir film is black *for us*, that is, specifically for the Western and American moviegoers of the 1950s. It exists in response to a certain mood at large in this particular time and place. Accordingly one who seeks the root of this "style" must think in terms of an affected and possibly ephemeral reaction to a moment in history. This is what links productions as diverse as *The Shanghai Gesture* and *The Asphalt Jungle*.

From this vantage, the method is obvious: while remaining as scientifically and objectively grounded as possible, one must examine the most prominent characteristics of the films which critics have classed as *noir*. From these characteristics one may then derive the common denominator and define that unique expressive attitude which all these works put into play.

It is the presence of crime which gives *film noir* its most constant characteristic. "The dynamism of violent death," is how Nino Frank evoked it, and the point is well taken. Blackmail, accusation, theft, or drug trafficking set the stage for a narrative where life and death are at stake. Few cycles in the entire history of film have put together in seven or eight years such a mix of foul play and murder. Sordidly or bizarrely, death always comes at the end of a tortured journey. In every sense of the word a *noir* film is a film of death.

But *film noir* has no monopoly on death, and an essential distinction must be overlaid. In principle, *film noir* is not a "crime documentary." We know that since 1946 Hollywood has exported a score of films to France which have as their main themes criminal inquiries supposedly based on actual cases. In fact, a title card or a narrator often alert the viewer at the start of the film that this is a true story which took place in such and such a time at such and such a place. The shots on the screen faithfully reconstruct the start of the process: a call to the homicide bureau, the discovery of a body. Sometimes it may be a seemingly inconsequential incident or some report from a neighborhood police station that sets events in motion. Then comes the tedious "leg" work by the cops: the careful but fruitless searches, ineffective surveillance, and futile decoys. Finally there is a glimmer, some object found, a witness, which leads to a climactic chase and uncovering a den of cutthroats. This series, which has produced interesting pictures (Henry Hathaway's *Call Northside 777* and *The House on 92nd Street*, Elia Kazan's *Boomer-*

Above, the realistic detail of the precinct station in the "police documentary," *House on 92nd Street*.

ang and *Panic in the Streets*, Laslo Benedek's *Port of New York*, Jules Dassin's *Naked City*, and, testing the limits of the genre, Bretaigne Windust's *The Enforcer*), shares several characteristics with *film noir*: realistic settings, well developed supporting roles, scenes of violence, and exciting pursuits. In fact, these documentary-style films often have typically *noir* elements: we won't soon forget the repellent aspect of the head of Murder Inc. in *The Enforcer* or the laconic gangster in *Panic in the Streets*. It sometimes happens that a given director will alternate between the genres. Jules Dassin is credited with *Naked City* and also with *Night and the City*. Joseph H. Lewis produced a classic *noir* work in 1950 with *Gun Crazy*, while a year earlier he had detailed the work of treasury agents in *The Undercover Man*.

Still there are differences between the two series. To begin with there is a difference in focus. The documentary-style picture examines a murder from without, from the point of view of the police official; the *film noir* is from within, from the point of view of the criminals. In features such as *The Naked City*, the action begins after the criminal act, and the murderers, their minions, and other accomplices move across the screen only to be followed, marked, interrogated, chased, and killed. If some flashback depicts a scene between gangsters it is to illustrate a disclosure or some testimony, a transcript of which is already in the police file. The police are always present, to act or to overhear. Nothing of this sort occurs in *film noir*, which situates itself within the very criminal milieu and describes it, sometimes in broad strokes (*The Big Sleep* or *Dark Passage*), sometimes in depth with correlative subtlety (*The Asphalt Jungle*). In any case, *film noir* posits a criminal psychology which recalls, from another discipline, the popular psychology in vogue at the end of the last century; both delve into forbidden milieus.

The second difference between the series is one of moral determinism, and this may be even more essential. In the police documentary investigators are traditionally portrayed as righteous men, brave and incorruptible. The naval medical officer in *Panic in the Streets* is a hero. So is, if less obviously so, the diminutive Irish detective of *The Naked City*, who believes in God and works on his own time to see justice done. As message film, the American "police documentary" is more accurately a glorification of the police, much as is the French production *Identité Judiciare* or the British *The Blue Lamp*.

This is not the case for the *noir* series. If police are featured, they are rotten— like the inspector in *The Asphalt Jungle* or the corrupt hard case portrayed by Lloyd Nolan in *The Lady in the Lake*—sometimes even murderers themselves (as in Otto Preminger's *Fallen Angel* or *Where the Sidewalk Ends*). At minimum, they let themselves get sucked into the criminal mechanism, like the attorney in *The File on Thelma Jordon*. As a result of this, it is not haphazardly that screenwriters have frequently fallen back on the private detective. It would have been too controversial always to impugn American police officials. The private detective is midway between lawful society and the underworld, walking on the brink, sometimes unscrupulous but putting only himself at risk, fulfilling the requirements of his own code and of the genre as well. As if to counterbalance all this, the actual law breakers are more or less sympathetic figures. Of course, the old motto of the pre-War shorts from MGM, "Crime does not pay," is still the order of the day, and there must be moral retribution. But the narrative is manipulated so that at times the moviegoer sympathizes, identifies with the criminals. Remember the suspenseful scene of the jewel theft in *The Asphalt Jungle*. What viewer failed to identify with the thieves? And *Gun Crazy*, we dare say, brought an exceptionally attractive but murderous couple to the screen.

As to the unstable alliances between individuals in the heart of the underworld, few films have described them as well as *The Big Sleep* and, in its *noir* sequence (Rico's testimony), *The Enforcer*. We perceive in this rogue's gallery of suspects and convicts, a complex and shifting pecking order based on bribery, blackmail, organized crime and the code of silence. Who will kill and who will be killed? The criminal milieu is an ambiguous one, where a position of strength can be quickly eroded.

This uncertainty is also manifest in the ambivalence of the characters themselves. The integral protagonist, the elemental figure of the *Scarface* type, has disappeared from *film noir* and given way to a crowd of sanctified killers, neurotic gangsters, megalomaniac crime bosses, and their perplexing or tainted cronies. Notable examples are the solitary and scientific serial killer in *He Walked by Night*, the self-destructive loser in *Night and the City*, or the hyperactive gang boss so attached to his mother in *White Heat*. Just as twisted are the vicious, drunken, grub-like henchmen in *The Enforcer*.

There is ambiguity, too, with regard to the victims, who usually are under some suspicion as well. Their ties to the unsavory milieu are what attract the attention of their executioners. Often, they are victims precisely because they cannot be executioners. The decadent partner in *The Lady from Shanghai* is such a type, a man who finds death when he tries to simulate his own murder and who will long remain a prototype of the sham victim. One could also cite the terrorized woman, who seems destined to be killed before the end of Jacques Tourneur's *Out of the Past* but who had already set up her would-be assassin for a fall. This tough guy had no more chance than a steer consigned to the slaughter-house.

As for the ambiguous protagonist, he is often more mature, almost old, and not too handsome. Humphrey Bogart typifies him. He is also an inglorious victim who may suffer, before the happy ending, appalling abuse. He is often enough masochistic, even self-immolating, one who makes his own trouble, who may throw himself into peril neither for the sake of justice nor from avarice but simply out of morbid curiosity. At times, he is a passive hero who allows himself to dragged across the line into the gray area between legal and criminal behavior, such as Orson Welles in *The Lady from Shanghai*. As such, he is far from the "superman" of adventure films.

Finally, there is ambiguity surrounding the woman: the *femme fatale* who is fatal for herself. Frustrated and deviant, half predator, half prey, detached yet ensnared, she falls victim to her own traps. While the inconstancy of Lauren Bacall in *The Big Sleep* may not cost her her life, Barbara Stanwyck cannot escape the consequences of her murderous intrigues in *The File on Thelma Jordon*. This new type of woman, manipulative and evasive, as hard bitten as her environment, ready to shake down or to trade shots with anyone—and probably frigid—has put her mark on "*noir*" eroticism, which may be at times nothing more that violence eroticized. We are a long way from the chaste heroines of the traditional Western or historical drama.

Film noir has renovated the theme of violence. To begin with, it abandoned the adventure film convention of the fair fight. A sporting chance has given way to settling scores, beatings, and cold-blooded murders. Bodyguards kick a powerless victim back and forth like football then toss his bloody body on a common thoroughfare (*Ride the Pink Horse*), in a back alley (*The Set-up*), or with the garbage (*I Walk Alone*). Crime itself is performed by the numbers, professionally, by a contract killer who does his job "without anger or hate." The opening of Robert Siodmak's *The Killers*, the celebrated scene in a roadhouse, where two men searching for their victim terrify the other patrons with their callous confidence, will remain one of the most gripping moments in American film, an unforgettable slice of life. Twitching and stigmatized, an unknown breed of men rose up before us. Their lot includes mild-mannered hit men (Alan Ladd in *This Gun for Hire*), indiscriminate brutes (William Bendix), and the clear-eyed menacing organizers (Everett Sloane in *The Enforcer*). It also includes the twisted, corpulent killers, sweating in fear, humiliated by their cronies, who suddenly boil over (Laird Cregar and Raymond Burr).

As for the ceremony of execution itself, *film noir* has the widest array of examples. Random samplings are the offhanded gesture of a wealthy publisher who sends a bothersome witness who was washing windows down an elevator shaft; all that was needed was to tip over the stool with the handle of his cane while idly chatting (*The High Wall*)—or the atrocious death by razor in *The Enforcer*—or a kick to a car jack (*Red Light*). In other films, a paralyzed woman is tied to her wheelchair and hurled down a stairway (*Kiss of Death*); an informer is locked inside a Turkish bath and the steam valve is opened [(*T-Men*)]; a convict is impelled under a pile driver by the threat of red-hot irons (*Brute Force*); one man is crushed by a tractor, another drowned in slime (*Border Incident*)... An unparalleled range of cruelties and torments are paraded before the viewer in *film noir*.

The anxiety in *film noir* possibly derives more from its strange plot twists than from its violence. A private detective takes on a dubious assignment: find a

Below, "the ambiguous protagonist... Humphrey Bogart typifies him" and "ambiguity surrounding the woman: the *femme fatale* [typified by] the inconstancy of Lauren Bacall in *The Big Sleep*."

woman, eliminate a blackmail threat, throw someone off track, and suddenly corpses are scattered across his path. He is followed, beaten, arrested. He asks for some information and finds himself trussed up and bloodied on the floor of a cellar. Men glimpsed in the night shoot at him and run off. There is something of the dream in this incoherent and brutal atmosphere, the atmosphere common to most *noir* films: *The Big Sleep, Ride the Pink Horse, The Lady in the Lake, Chicago Deadline.* Georges Sadoul remarked in this regard that "The plot is murky, like a nightmare or the ramblings of a drunkard."[5] In fact, one of the rare parodies of the genre, Elliott Nugent's *My Favorite Brunette,* begins exactly this way. Bob Hope wants to play detective and Dorothy Lamour gives him a retainer to tackle one of these vague assignments that only Americans understand, such as "Find my brother" or "Find my sister." Immediately a hail of daggers menaces him, bodies pile up by the roadside, and inexorable gears of mischance drag him towards the electric chair by way of a hospital that doubles as a gangland hide-out.

Usually the mystery is a bit more realistic: an amnesiac tries to discover his past and flushes a crime out of its den. This theme was explored by Robert Florey in *The Crooked Way* and by Joseph Mankiewicz in *Somewhere in the Night.* But in these instances, the context of the narrative dilemma is such that the viewer expects confusion. In a true *film noir,* the bizarre is inseparable from what might be called the *uncertainty of motivations.* For instance, what are Bannister and his partner hoping to accomplish with their shadowy intrigues in *The Lady from Shanghai?* All the weirdness of the movie is focused on this: in these mysterious and metamorphosing creatures who tip their hands only in death. Elsewhere does a fleeting figure in a nightclub indicate a possible ally or an enemy? The enigmatic killer, will he be an executioner or a victim? Honor among thieves, an extortion network, unexplained motives, all this verges on madness.

In our opinion, this resounding confusion is at the core of *film noir*'s peculiar oneirism. It is simple to find several titles the action of which is deliberately associated with dreams, such as Fritz Lang's *The Woman in the Window.* The same is true of pictures where the artifice focuses on the symbolic and the imaginary, as with Sternberg's *Shanghai.* But, as a general rule, the perspective of *film noir* is realistic and each scene in isolation could pass for an excerpt from a documentary. It is the sum total of these realistic snapshots of a weird theme which creates the atmosphere of the nightmare.

As we might have guessed, all the components of *film noir* yield the same result: disorienting the spectator, who can no longer find the familiar reference points. The moviegoer is accustomed to certain conventions: a logical development of the action, a clear distinction between good and evil, well-defined characters, sharp motives, scenes more showy then authentically violent, a beautiful heroine and an honest hero. At least, these were the conventions of American adventure films before the War.

Now the moviegoer is being presented a less severe version of the under-world, with likable killers and corrupt cops. Good and evil go hand in hand to the point of being indistinguishable. Robbers become ordinary guys: they have kids, love young women, and just want to go home again (*The Asphalt Jungle*). The victim seems as guilty as the hit man, who is just doing his job. The primary reference point of earlier days, the moral center, is completely skewed.

The heroine is depraved, murderous, doped-up or drunk. The hero is under the gun or, as they say in boxing, he absorbs a lot of punishment when accounts are settled up. So the secondary reference point, the myth of Superman and his chaste fiancée, also fades.

The action is confused, the motives are unclear. There is nothing resembling classic dramas or the moral tales from a realistic era: criminals vie against each other (*The Big Sleep*), a policeman arrives on the scene, reveals his criminal intent, and does nothing but enhance the viewer's apprehension (*The Lady in the Lake*); the sober process by which a man's fate is determined concludes in a fun house (*The Lady from Shanghai*). A film takes on the characteristics of a dream and the viewer searches in vain for some old-fashioned logic.

In the end, the chaos goes "beyond all limits." Gratuitous violence, the over-weening rewards for murder, all this adds to the feeling of alienation. A sense of dread persists until the final images.

The conclusion is simple: the moral ambivalence, the criminality, the complex contradictions in motives and events, all conspire to make the viewer co-experi-ence the anguish and insecurity which are the true emotions of contemporary *film noir*. All the films of this cycle create a similar emotional effect: *that state of tension instilled in the spectator when the psychological reference points are removed.* The aim of *film noir* was to create *a specific alienation*.

Translated from the French by Alain Silver

Notes

1. The Authors wish to thank Mr. Freddy Buache, secretary-general of the Cinématheque of Lausanne, who agreed to publish this Introduction in the review *Carreau*.

2. *Écran Français*. No. 61, August 28, 1946.

3. *Le Figaro*, May 8, 1951.

4. Editors' Note: the quote is from Isidore Ducasse, Count Lautréamont, 19th Century pre-surrealistic writer. The French reads: "Les filières sanglantes par où l'on fait passer la logique aux abois."

5. Review of *The Big Sleep* in *Les Lettres Françaises*.

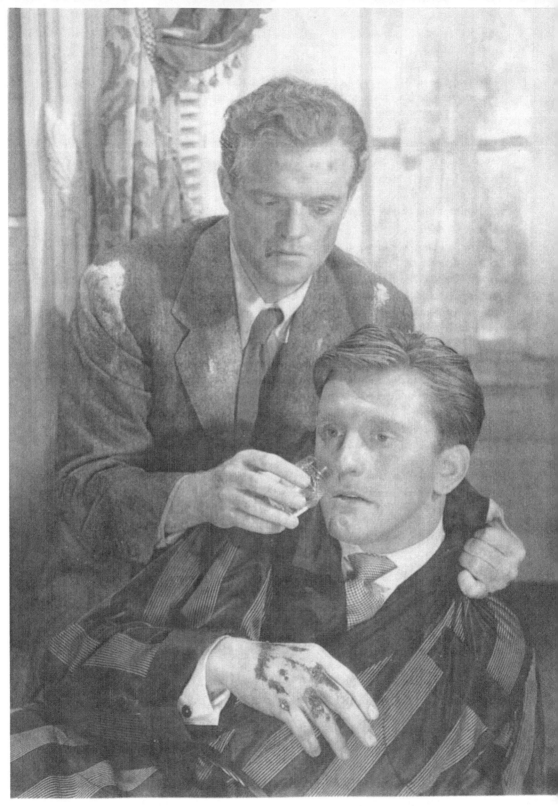

Above, Van Helfin (left) and Kirk Douglas in *The Strange Love of Martha Ivers* (1946).

Noir Cinema

Charles Higham and Joel Greenberg (1968)

[The following is excerpted from the book *Hollywood in the Forties*[1]]

A dark street in the early morning hours, splashed with a sudden downpour. Lamps form haloes in the murk. In a walk-up room, filled with the intermittent flashing of a neon sign from across the street, a man is waiting to murder or be murdered...the specific ambience of *film noir*, a world of darkness and violence, with a central figure whose motives are usually greed, lust and ambition, whose world is filled with fear, reached its fullest realisation in the Forties. A genre deeply rooted in the nineteenth century's vein of grim romanticism, developed through U.F.A. and the murky, fog-filled atmosphere of pre-war French movies, flowered in Hollywood as the great German or Austrian expatriates—Lang, Siodmak, Preminger, Wilder—arrived there and were allowed more and more freedom to unleash their fantasies on the captive audience.

To that scene of night streets, recurring again and again in the films of the period, most notably in Michael Curtiz's *The Unsuspected*, can be added images of trains: clanking and swaying through storm-swept darkness, their arrival at remote stations signalled by the presence of mysterious raincoated figures, while in the narrow corridors, the antiseptic cramped compartments, assignations are made and, more often than not, a murder is planned. Elevators often figure as well, most notably in *Dark Passage*, where the lift gives an entrance, for the fugitive central figure, to an enclosed world of luxury and safety, where the gates clanging shut on the tear-stained face of the defeated villainess forebode her own incarceration in Tehachapi. Cocktail bars, too, exercise a special fascination: mirrors, stretching to the ceiling, reflect the stew of faces, each one predatory, doomed or afraid, and the glasses are piled in pyramids, often—this was an especial passion of Curtiz's—to be smashed by one of the principals in an outburst of rage. Standard lamps fallen on pile carpets, spilling a fan of light about the face of a corpse; interrogation rooms filled with nervous police, the witness framed at their centre under a spotlight; heels clicking along subway or elevated platforms at midnight; cars spanking along canyon roads, with anguished faces beyond the rain-splashed windscreen...here is a world where it is always night, always foggy or wet, filled with

27

gunshots and sobs, where men wear turned-down brims on their hats and women loom in fur coats, guns thrust deep into pockets.

The soundtracks, laced by the minatory scores of Franz Waxman, Max Steiner, Miklós Rózsa or Erich Wolfgang Korngold, also create the flavour: one remembers the whine of Dan Duryea in Fritz Lang's *Woman in the Window* and *Scarlet Street*, the breathlessness and the faked sob in the voice of Mary Astor in *The Maltese Falcon*, the scream of the elevated across the luxurious self-contained world of the threatened woman in *Sorry, Wrong Number* and the cold hard voices on the telephone switchboard; the cry of the train in *The Strange Love of Martha Ivers*, carrying away, in the rain of course, the escaping adolescents to a lifetime of suffering; the rapping of Ella Raines's heels on the platform and the hysterical jangle of the jazz-band in *Phantom Lady*, the shuffle of the husband's feet on the ceiling in *Gaslight* and the dissonant woodwind of Bronislau Kaper's score as the gaslights dim; the sound of "Tangerine" floating from a radio down the street as the lovers enter their death-clinch in the shuttered room in *Double Indemnity*.

And above all, shadow upon shadow upon shadow...Lee Garmes, Tony Gaudio, Lucien Ballard, Sol Polito, Ernest Haller, James Wong Howe, John F. Seitz and the other great cameramen of the era pitched every shot in glistening low-key, so that rain always glittered across windows or windscreens like quicksilver, furs shone with a faint halo, faces were barred deeply with those shadows that usually symbolised some imprisonment of body or soul. The visual mode was intensely romantic, and its precise matching to the stories of fatal women and desperate men—straight out The Romantic Agony—gave Forties *film noir* its completeness as a genre. A world was created, as sealed off from reality as the world of musicals and of Paramount sophisticated comedies, yet in its way more delectable than either.

Hitchcock's notable *film noir* of the period, *Shadow of a Doubt* (1943), was pitched in a calm world, its darkness suggested rather than stated. The opening takes place on a sunny, dusty day, Charlie, the widow-murderer, dodging the police, lying wearily back in his walk-up room or standing looking at his pursuers, puffing proudly at a cigar. Later as he enters the chintzy little world of his small-town Californian relatives, he shows himself a genuine occupant of *film noir*: in a cafe, he tells his niece that the universe is a "foul sty," and over dinner he discloses something of his neurotic, perhaps basically homosexual loathing of women. Joseph Cotten's performance cleverly suggests the psychotic tension under the bland generous front; here is a creature of the darkness blinking against the light of a very American innocence.

Rope (1948) and *The Paradine Case* (1948) are more firmly centered on a world of evil. In *Rope* two homosexuals murder a "straight" youth, serving his father, aunt and fiancée dinner from the chest he is entombed in; while in *The Paradine Case* "une belle dame sans merci," the heartless Maddelena Paradine, murders her blind husband and shows complete contempt for the defence counsel engaged to save her. Hitchcock and his writers here delineate lives lived without conscience and without love. In *Rope*, the homosexual ambience is ably suggested: the slightly over-decorated apartment, the "understanding" housekeeper, the elliptical, wounding and sharp-witted exchanges between the killers, played by Farley Granger and John Dall, and their mutually suspicious and resentful relationship with the dead boy's girl-friend. The gradual breakdown from smooth party badinage to nerves and finally dissolution of the psyche, arrest and ruin, is charted with precision, and the endlessly gliding takes, moving from death-chest to window spangled with New York lights to shifting trays of food, create an atmosphere as stifling as the interior of a coffin.

The Paradine Case has as its centre a fatal woman of whom Wedekind would have been proud: as played by Alida Valli, she is a leprous madonna, her lips permanently twisted into a smile of contempt, her hair tightly drawn back, her skin stretched on the delicate skull. The prison scenes are pure *film noir*: echoing corridors, barred with Lee Garmes's famous shadows, enclose her in a world of stone; the shadows deepen in her face as her foolish, infatuated counsel drones on and on. No less sinister, in Hitchcock's black vision, the judge Lord Horfield (Charles Laughton) smacks his lips over Mrs. Paradine's forthcoming hanging while gobbling a meal, dwelling on the convolutions of a walnut ("they resemble the human brain") while framed through a silver candelabra in his mansion, the reward of a lifetime of judicial murder.

Closely allied to Hitchcock, Robert Siodmak—a colleague of Billy Wilder and Fred Zinnemann at U.F.A. in the early 1930s—expresses a more detached, urbane and less cynical observation of the dark side of human nature. Nevertheless, his Germanic pessimism and fascination with cruelty and violence are not in doubt.

Phantom Lady (1944), produced by Joan Harrison (who also worked with Hitchcock), created, with aid of John Goodman's art direction and Woody Bredell's nocturnal camerawork, a powerful mise-en-scene of squalor and violence. The story—from a pulp novelette about a search for an accused murderer's alibis, most notably a mysterious woman in a bizarre hat met in a bar to the strains of "I Remember April"—becomes an excuse for the exploration of the underworld, for a series of descending spirals into hell.

New York is evoked during the toxic heat of midsummer: menace and poetry come together in images of pursuit, as the accused's girl (Ella Raines) tries to break down the bribed witnesses to her lover's innocence. A bartender is tracked across an elevated platform: heels tap on stone, a turnstile groans, a train shrieks to a stop. A tap-drummer sweats through a fog of cigarettes and alcohol in a dive rocking to the sounds of a jazz-band. Behind the suave apartment blocks, Siodmak is telling us, there is a world waiting to pounce in: at the gates of the respectable, the jungle is already thrusting upwards.

Christmas Holiday (1944) is no less black: after an opening of gaiety—Robert and Abigail are idyllic newlyweds—Robert is gradually exposed as a crook, squandering the family fortune in gambling. One morning he burns a pair of blood-stained trousers: Abigail finds that he has murdered a bookmaker, hiding the body with his mother's help. Moreover, his relationship with his mother is depicted as incestuous, and his manner suggests homosexual tendencies. Siodmak's elliptical direction and cleverly off-beat casting of Deanna Durbin and Gene Kelly help to create an atmosphere of lightly suggested menace, of wickedness just an inch below the suburban surface.

The Suspect (1945), based on the Crippen case and set in late Victorian London, is equally merciless about human nature: a tobacconist (Charles Laughton), flabby and dominated by a vicious wife (Rosalind Ivan), murders her, but he is made to seem less evil than the inquisitive neighbour (brilliantly played by Henry Daniell) and the cruelly observant detective (Stanley Ridges) who brings about his downfall. In thickly cluttered, stifling sets, full of aspidistras, wax fruit and gewgaws, Siodmak discloses the horror of breakdown, a lifetime of genteelly endured misery collapsing into moral disintegration, ruin and death.

Again, in *Conflict* (1945), from a Siodmak story but not directed by him, a husband is dominated by a vicious wife whom he murders, and is destroyed by a detective—here once more the genteel suburban world is shown to contain cracks which at any moment can bring about its destruction. *The Strange Affair of Uncle Harry* (1945) shows a "nice" New England family: celibate, careful Harry (George Sanders) and his two sisters (Geraldine Fitzgerald and Moyna MacGill). When Harry falls in love, his younger sister Lettie, insane with incestuous jealousy, tries to destroy the relationship and finally goes to the gallows for her pains. The bickering, despair and repressed sexual longing of this tight little clan are exposed in shadows as black as those which blanket the characters' psyches. And in *The Spiral Staircase* (1946), the story of a mute terrified girl in a town haunted by a killer of maimed women, the darkness closes in. A murder in a room above a flickering bioscope display; an eye lurking deep in a cupboard; a face that swims out of focus as the dumb mouth blurs into a hole, watched by the killer: here is direction of the boldest Gothic flair.

The Dark Mirror (1946), about twins, one evil, one good, *The Killers* (1946) and *Criss Cross* (1949) were less successful, although patches of technique—the grim first sequence of *The Killers*, based on Hemingway's story, a robbery sequence in *Criss Cross*—are justly remembered. But in *Cry of the City* (1948), Siodmak returned strongly to form. In this story about a conflict between a sanctimonious policeman (Victor Mature) and an accused killer (Richard Conte), the director evokes a fine range of low-life locales: the sense of a lived-in night city is admirably managed. The gross, six-foot masseuse (Hope Emerson) is a memorable monster, gobbling her breakfast or striding through her house to receive a nocturnal guest, observed by the camera through a glass-topped doorway as she switches on the lights in successive rooms. And so is the furtive shyster of Barry Kroeger, white and plump as a slug. Little scenes like a police interview with abortionists—mostly European refugees—show Siodmak's talent for observing squalor in full display. A tense prison hospital escape matched to an almost imperceptibly swelling drum-beat; a murder in a swinging, creaking office chair—the film is crammed with sequences like these, powerfully realised and charged with an oppressive coldness.

Fritz Lang's *Woman in the Window* (1944) and *Scarlet Street* (1945) were equally rancid portraits of darkness and the city. In both, a weakling played by Edward G. Robinson, sexually unfulfilled, lonely and depressed, becomes the victim of a pretty and ruthless seductress played by Joan Bennett. Lang and his writers disclose without mercy how the beautiful can feed on the ugly, and the films—set in classic surroundings of wet, dark streets, rooms full of hideous knick-knacks, shimmering street lamps—remain memorable for the viciousness of the characterisations, notably Dan Duryea's stripe-suited pimps, and the unblinking look at middle-class life: a retirement party with bawdy jokes accompanying the presentation of a watch, a quarrel across a cluttered flat, a close-up of a clerk's embarrassed face as his fly-by-night asks him for money in a public place.

In *Laura* (1944) and *Fallen Angel* (1945) Otto Preminger made two remarkable contributions to the genre. On the surface, *Laura* looks atypical: from the first shot, a slow left to right pan across a series of shelves filled with *objets d'art*, the world we are shown is cool, sunlit or filled with the soft light of standard lamps: a world of apartments in the highest brackets of New York. But the characters cast their own shadows: Waldo Lydecker, played expertly by Clifton Webb, is a brittle jealous killer behind the front of a Woollcott-like columnist; Shelby Carpenter (Vincent Price) is a parasite feeding on rich women; his mistress (Judith Anderson) is a purchaser of male flesh. Only Laura herself, played as the Eternal Woman by Gene Tierney, remains beyond reach of the mire. Preminger's direction, calm and detached, and Jay Dratler's and Samuel Hoffenstein's sophisticated dialogue, turn the women's magazine conventions of the story inside out, so that at the end we are given a portrait of the utmost corrosiveness. Elegance and taste are balanced by greed and cruelty, and these endlessly bright rooms, these soft carpets and clocks and screens and china figures express a menace not reduced by the high-key handling.

Conversely, *Fallen Angel* (1945) is set in the lower rungs of the American milieu: this story of a man who marries for money in a small town so he can afford a floozie has an admirable mise-en-scene, evoking the contrast between suburban house and end-of-the-road hotel, a fine Forties range of seedy rooms, neons flashing in the dark, doors opening from dark streets into the cosy vibrant warmth of a cafe or bar.

Much the same atmosphere pervades Michael Curtiz's *Mildred Pierce* (1945) and *The Unsuspected* (1947). Mildred Pierce, wittily adapted by Ranald MacDougall from the novel by James M. Cain, charts the rise of a housewife (Joan Crawford) from waitress to owner of a chain of restaurants on the Californian coast, with mayhem along the way. No film has caught so completely the feel of Southern California, and it is not surprising that a restaurant commemorates it in Hollywood, with dishes named after Cain's characters. The coast roads, the plush taut atmosphere of restaurants, and the endless jostling greed of the environment are conveyed with an aficionado's knowledge. The opening is typical Curtiz: a series of shots fired into a mirror, following distant views of a beach-house at night, the murdered lover (Zachary Scott) lurching past his reflected face, gasping a last word "Mildred." The film conveys Curtiz's love of the American night world, of piers shining under rain, dark beaches, the Pacific moonlight seen through a bar's windows, and the tough direction of the players at all times pays dividends. In their respective portrayals of ambition, sisterly humour and brainless lust, Joan Crawford, Eve Arden and Zachary Scott are in splendid form.

The Unsuspected is even more beguiling: here Curtiz surpassed himself with U.F.A.-esque camera effects. As Victor Grandison, superbly hammed by Claude Rains, moves from harmless Waldo Lydecker-like crime story-telling on radio to committing murder himself, Curtiz charts a vivid course of greed and heartlessness. In order to satisfy his desire for possessions, for control of a fortune and his niece's mansion, Grandison murders and risks his life: he is finally arrested while broadcasting to America on a particularly violent murder case.

The images have an unusually massive opulence: the huge house, with its tables covered in black mirrors, pyramids of glasses in the cocktail bar, and a record library which plays a complex role in the action, is a triumph of the Warners art department. A girl's poisoning is seen through the bubbles of a glass of champagne, as though she were drowning in alcohol. A chest containing a body that has to be got rid of in a hurry is lifted high on a crane above a disposal-ground, watched desperately by the murderer's accomplice. And one sequence remains the quintessence of Forties *film noir*. The camera moves out of a train window, across a narrow street filled with neon signs, and up to a room where a killer lies smoking, terrified in the dark, listening to the story of his crimes related by Victor Grandison on the radio.

Lewis Milestone, in *The Strange Love of Martha Ivers* (1946), also created a striking addition to the lists. An aunt murdered and a getaway on a freight-car at night; the rise of an ambitious woman, definitively played by Barbara Stanwyck, and her no less ruthless mate, the attorney O'Neill; with the aid of her childhood companion Martha plans her husband's murder. Replete with impressive images of cruelty and destructiveness, this *chef d'oeuvre* could not have been more persuasively directed. Nor could the similar Joan Crawford vehicle *The Damned Don't Cry* (1949-50) of Vincent Sherman's, made at the very end of the period. Here, the sense of an enclosed world of criminals is masterfully suggested, as the pushing girl played by Crawford moves from a ravishingly photographed Tobacco Road setting to furs, luxury, guns and the company of murderers and thieves.

Still more black a portrait of the underworld—but this time of a different kind—is Edmund Goulding's Nightmare Alley (1947), based by Jules Furthman on the novel by William Lindsay Gresham. This is the story of a small-town carnival operator, Stanton Carlisle (Tyrone Power) who obtains the secrets of a fake mind-reader and climbs to the big time in Chicago by setting himself up as a spiritualist. On the way, he acquires a partner in crime, Zeena, a sideshow fortune teller, and a remarkably clever accomplice, the psychologist Dr. Lilith Ritter, played brilliantly, with icy, calculating intelligence by Helen Walker. Huge-eyed, sly as a cat, Dr. Ritter's gestures suggest a soulless ambition; the web of hair, the smoothly disciplined face are unforgettable.

Nightmare Alley is a work of great daring, even risking a few shots at human belief in immortality. People are shown as venal, gullible, and hell-bent on success at any cost. Memorable are the portraits of Ezra Grindle (Taylor Holmes), the millionaire determined to materialise his dead mistress Addie so that he can again make love to her; of the alcoholic ex-mind reader (Ian Keith); and of the shrewd and wealthy Mrs. Peabody bamboozled by spiritualism. Joan Blondell is perfect as Zeena, the warm, fleshy, blowsy carny queen out of the sticks; Lee Garmes's photography effectively evokes the circus settings; but the film's greatest triumph lies in its uncompromising portrait of American corruption. As Carlisle rises from hick to ace charlatan and crashes to become a "geek"—a creature tearing the heads off live chickens in a bran-pit—we see a frightening glimpse of life without money or hope in a society that lives by both. Scenes like the one in the cheap hotel when a waiter asks the now stricken Carlisle if he would "like anything else" convey, with the aid of sleazy sets, an ambience of almost unbearable squalor, achieved through the bitter, heartless writing, and through direction of an unusually cutting edge.

Only one director could exceed Goulding in sophisticated observation of greed: Billy Wilder. But whereas Goulding's was an honest understanding, Wilder's was a cynical and corrosive criticism. Double Indemnity (1944), one of the highest summits of film noir, is a film without a single trace of pity or love.

A blonde, Phyllis Dietrichson (Barbara Stanwyck), sets out to seduce an insurance man, Walter Neff (Fred MacMurray), so she can dispose of her unwanted husband for the death money. Infatuated, he succumbs, and helps her work out a complicated scheme; this misfires, the couple meet desperately after the killing in supermarkets or risk telephone calls; finally, they shoot each other in a shuttered room, with "Tangerine," most haunting of numbers, floating through the windows. As in Mildred Pierce, the Californian ambience is all important: winding roads through the hills leading to tall stuccoed villas in a Spanish style 30 years out of date, cold tea drunk out of tall glasses on hot afternoons, dusty downtown streets, a huge and echoing insurance office, Chinese checkers played on long pre-television evenings by people who hate each other's guts. The film reverberates with the forlorn poetry of late sunny afternoons; the script is as tart as a

Above, the blonde, Phyllis Dietrichson (Barbara Stanwyck) and Walter Neff
(Fred MacMurray), "meet desperately after the killing in supermarkets."

lemon; and Stanwyck's white rat-like smoothness, MacMurray's bluff duplicity, are
beautifully contrasted. A notable scene is when the car stalls after the husband's
murder, the killing conveyed in a single close-up of the wife's face, underlined by
the menacing strings of Miklós Rózsa's score.

Lana Turner impersonated a *femme fatale* not unlike Stanwyck's in a similar
story, *The Postman Always Rings Twice* (1946), directed by Tay Garnett, based by
Harry Ruskin and Niven Busch on the novel by James M. Cain, already adapted for
the screen twice before: as *Le Dernier Tournant* (Pierre Chenal, 1939), and *Ossessione* (Visconti, 1942). Cold and hard in brilliant high-key lighting, Garnett's film
captured Cain's atmosphere as perfectly as Curtiz's *Mildred Pierce*: in this story of
a girl in a roadside cafe (Lana Turner) who seduced a ne'er do well (John Garfield)
and induces him to murder her husband (the estimable Cecil Kellaway) the tension is drawn very tight. Lana Turner, almost always dressed in ironical white, introduced when she drops her lipstick case to the floor in a memorable sequence,
is cleverly directed to suggest a soulless American ambition; and Garfield, tense,
nervous, unwillingly drawn into a web of crime, makes an excellent foil. This is the
perfect *film noir*, harsh and heartless in its delineation of character, disclosing a
rancid evil beyond the antiseptic atmosphere of the roadside diner.

But one should accord an even greater accolade to Welles's *The Lady from
Shanghai* (1948); here is a film Shakespearean in the complexity of its response to
an evil society. Rita Hayworth, sex symbol of the Forties, is made to play a deadly
preying mantis, Elsa Bannister; her husband, Arthur Bannister, the great criminal
lawyer, is, as interpreted by Everett Sloane, an impotent and crippled monster
whose eyelids are like the freckled hoods of a snake's.

The Fatal Woman theme is reworked in brilliant detail; the fake sex symbol
that beamed down from the hoardings along the American highways and glittered

from the period's front-of-house is stripped bare, while the husband becomes a
no less striking symbol of the emasculated American male. Only Michael, played
by Welles himself, the sailor trapped into a charge of murder by his love of Elsa, is
made to seem decent and free. At the end of the film, when Elsa and her husband
shoot each other to death in a hall of mirrors, Michael walks across a wharf sparkling with early morning sunlight, released from an evil civilisation to the clean life
of the sea.

Physically, the film is Welles' most mesmerizing achievement. It conjures up the
"feel" of the tropics, of the lazy movement of a yacht at sea, of the beauty of
marshes and palms, and the misty calm of remote ports-of-call. In the film's most
beautiful sequence, when Elsa Bannister lies on her back on deck singing, and
Bannister and his partner Grisby exchange wisecracks ("That's *good*, Arthur!"—
"That's good, George!") Welles's love of luxury, of relaxation and pleasure, flash
through the bitter social comment and show him to be essentially a poet of the
flesh.

The soundtrack is no less exhilarating than the images of Charles Lawton, Jr.,
Heinz Roemheld's menacing arrangements of Latin American themes match the
tensions of the yachting holiday, the journey through Mexican backwaters. Wood-
winds and castanets echo throughout the preparations for a mammoth party near
Acapulco, a commercial jingle on the yacht's radio mockingly underlines the
sailor's seduction; and while the wife in a white dress runs through the pillars of
an Acapulco street a male chorus sings a primitive song, followed by two startlingly harsh chords from the brass section. Throughout the film, the feral shrieks
and neurotic whispers or giggles of the cast, the sneezes, coughs and chatter of
the trial scene extras, give the listener the impression of being trapped in a cage
full of animals and birds.

From a film loaded with detail, baroque and sumptuous, one can pick out a
handful of memorable scenes. The picnic party, lights strung out across an inlet,
men wading through water, and the sailor emerging from the darkness to tell his
sweating, hammocked employers a symbolic tale about a pack of sharks which
tore each other to pieces off the Brazilian coast. A talk about murder high on a
parapet above the fjords of Acapulco harbour, interrupted by a gigolo's shrill
"Darling, of course you pay me!" A conversation in the San Francisco Aquarium,
the wife's fake passion breathed in silhouette against the mindless pouting of a
grouper fish. The trial, and the final shoot-out in the mirror hall, the lawyer firing
at his wife through layers and layers of deceiving glass panes.

Note

1. In 1968, this chapter was called "Black Cinema," in an attempt to render into English
   the sense of the French term *"film noir."* To avoid misunderstanding about the subject,
   the authors have asked that it be retitled.

Above, Dana Andrews as the cop who commits murder in *Where the Sidewalk Ends*.

Paint It Black: The Family Tree of the *Film Noir*

Raymond Durgnat (1970)

In 1946 French critics having missed Hollywood films for five years saw suddenly, sharply, a darkening tone, darkest around the crime film. The English spoke only of the "tough, cynical Hammett-Chandler thriller," although a bleak, cynical tone was invading all genres, from *The Long Voyage Home* to *Duel in the Sun*.

The tone was often castigated as Hollywood decadence, although black classics are as numerous as rosy (Euripides, Calvin, Ford, Tourneur, Goya, Lautréamont, Dostoievsky, Grosz, Faulkner, Francis Bacon). Black is as ubiquitous as shadow, and if the term *film noir* has a slightly exotic ring it's no doubt because it appears as figure against the rosy ground of Anglo-Saxon middle-class, and especially Hollywoodian, optimism and puritanism. If the term is French it's no doubt because, helped by their more lucid (and/or mellow, or cynical, or decadent) culture, the French first understood the full import of the American development.

Greek tragedy, Jacobean drama and the Romantic Agony (to name three black cycles) are earlier responses to epochs of disillusionment and alienation. But the socio-cultural parallels can't be made mechanically. Late '40s Hollywood is blacker than '30s precisely because its audience, being more secure, no longer needed cheering up. On the other hand, it was arguably insufficiently mature to enjoy the open, realistic discontent of, say, *Hotel du Nord, Look Back In Anger*, or Norman Mailer. The American *film noir*, in the narrower sense, paraphrases its social undertones by the melodramatics of crime and the underworld; *Scarface* and *On the Waterfront* mark its limits, both also "realistic" films. It's almost true to say that the French crime thriller evolves out of black realism, whereas American black realism evolves out of the crime thriller. Evolution apart, the black thriller is hardly perennial, drawing on the unconscious superego's sense of crime and punishment. The first detective thriller is *Oedipus Rex*, and it has the profoundest twist of all; detective, murderer, and executioner are one man. The Clytemnestra plot underlies innumerable *films noirs*, from *The Postman Always Rings Twice* to *Cronaca di Un Amore*.

The nineteenth century splits the classic tragic spirit into three genres: bourgeois realism (Ibsen), the ghost story, and the detective story. The avenger ceases to be a ghost (representative of a magic order) and becomes a detective, private or public. The butler did it. *Uncle Silas, Fantomas,* and *The Cat and the Canary* illustrate the transitional stage between detective and ghost story. For ghosts the *film noir* substitutes, if only by implication, a nightmare society, or condition of man. In *Psycho,* Mummy's transvestite mummy is a secular ghost, just as abnormal Norman is, at the end, Lord of the Flies, a Satanic, megalomaniac, hollow in creation. The *film noir* is often nihilistic, cynical or stoic as reformatory; there are Fascist and apathetic denunciations of the bourgeois order, as well as Marxist ones.

There is obviously no clear line between the threat on a grey drama, the sombre drama, and the *film noir,* just as it's impossible to say exactly when a crime becomes the focus of a film rather merely a realistic incident. Some films seem black to cognoscenti, while the public of their time take the happy end in a complacent sense; this is true of, for example, *The Big Sleep. On the Waterfront* is a *film noir,* given Brando's negativism and anguished playing, whereas *A Man Is Ten Feet Tall* is not, for reasons of tone suggested by the title. *Mourning Becomes Electra* is too self-consciously classic, although its adaptation in '40s Americana with Joan Crawford might not be. *Intruder in the Dust* is neither Faulkner nor *noir,* despite the fact that only a boy and an old lady defy the lynch-mob; its tone intimates that they tend to suffice. The happy end in a true *film noir* is that the worst of danger is averted, with little amelioration or congratulation. The *film noir* is not a genre, as the Western and gangster film, and takes us into the realm of classification by motif and tone. Only some crime films are *noir,* and *films noirs* in other genres include *The Blue Angel, King Kong, High Noon, Stalag 17, The Sweet Smell of Success, The Loves of Jeanne Eagels, Attack, Shadows, Lolita, Lonely Are The Brave* and *2001.*

The French *film noir* precedes the American genre. French specialists include Feuillade, Duvivier, Carné, Clouzot, Yves Allegret and even, almost without noticing, Renoir (of *La Chienne, La Nuit du Carrefour, La Bête Humaine, Woman on the Beach*) and Godard. Two major cycles of the '30s and '40s are followed by a gangster cycle in the '50s, including *Touchez Pas Au Grisbi* (Becker, 1953), *Du Rififi Chez Les Hommes* (Dassin, 1955), *Razzia Sur La Chnouf* (Decein, 1957), *Mefiez-vous Fillettes* (Allegret, 1957), and the long Eddie Constantine series to which Godard pays homage in *Alphaville. Fantomas,* made for Gaumont, inspired their rival Pathé to the Pearl White series, inaugurated by the New York office of this then French firm. *La Chienne* becomes *Scarlet Street, La Bête Humaine* becomes *Human Desire, Le Jour se Leve* becomes *The Long Night,* while *Pepe-le-Moko* becomes *Algiers* ("Come with me to the Casbah") and also Pepe-le-Pew. The American version of *The Postman Always Rings Twice* (1945) is preceded by the French (*Le Dernier Tournant,* 1939) and an Italian (*Ossessione,* 1942). The '50s gangster series precedes the American revival of interest in gangsters and the group-job themes. Godard was offered Bonnie and Clyde, before Penn, presumably on the strength of *Breathless* rather than *Pierrot Le Fou.*

The Italian *film noir,* more closely linked with realism, may be represented by *Ossessione,* by *Senza Pieta, Caccia Tragica, Bitter Rice* (neo-realist melodramas which pulverize Hollywood action equivalents by Walsh, et al.), and *Cronaca di Un Amore*, Antonioni's mesmerically beautiful first feature. The American black Western, which falters in the early '60s, is developed by the Italians. Kracauer's *From Caligari to Hitler* details the profusion of *films noirs* in Germany in the '20s, although the crime theme is sometimes overlaid by the tyrant theme. *The Living Dead*, a compendium of Poe stories, anticipates the Cormans. The Germans also pioneered the horror film (*Nosferatu* precedes *Dracula*, *Homunculus* precedes *Frankenstein*). German expressionism heavily influences American *films noirs*, in which German directors (Stroheim, Leni, Lang, Siodmak, Preminger, Wilder) loom conspicuously (not to mention culturally Germanic Americans like Schoedsack and Sternberg).

The English cinema has its own, far from inconsiderable, line in *films noirs*, notably, the best pre-war Hitchcocks (*Rich and Strange*, *Sabotage*). An effective series of costume bullying dramas (*Gaslight*, 1940), through *Fanny by Gaslight* and *The Man in Grey* to *Daybreak* (1947), is followed by man-on-the-run films of which the best are probably *Odd Man Out*, *They Made Me a Fugitive* and *Secret People*. The also-rans include many which are arguably more convincing and adventurous than many formula-bound Hollywood cult favorites. The following subheadings offer, inevitably imperfect schematizations for some main lines of force in the American *film noir*. They describe not genres but dominant cycles or motifs, and many, if not most, films would come under at least two headings, since interbreeding is intrinsic to motif processes. In all these films, crime or criminals provide the real or apparent centre of focus, as distinct from films in the first category from non-criminal "populist" films such as *The Crowd*, *Street Scene*, *The Grapes of Wrath*, *Bachelor Party*, *Too Late Blues* and *Echoes of Silence*.

1. CRIME AS SOCIAL CRITICISM

A first cycle might be labelled: "Pre-Depression: The Spontaneous Witnesses." Examples include *Easy Street* (1917), *Broken Blossoms* (1919), *Greed* (1924), *The Salvation Hunters* (1925). Two years later the director of *The Salvation Hunters* preludes with *Underworld*, the gangster cycle which is given its own category below. The financial and industry-labour battles of the '30s are poorly represented in Hollywood, for the obvious reason that the heads of studios tend to be Republican, and anyway depend on the banks. But as the rearmament restored prosperity, the association of industry and conflict was paraphrased in politically innocent melodrama, giving *Road to Frisco* (1939) and *Manpower* (1940). (Realistic variants like *The Grapes of Wrath* are not *noir*). *Wild Harvest* (1947) and *Give Us This Day* (1949) relate to this genre. The former has many lines openly critical of big capitalists, but its standpoint is ruralist-individualist and, probably, Goldwaterian. The second was directed by Dmytryk in English exile, but setting and spirit are entirely American.

Another cycle might be labelled: "The Sombre Cross-Section." A crime takes us through a variety of settings and types and implies an anguished view of society as a whole. Roughly coincident with the rise of neo-realism in Europe this cycle includes *Phantom Lady, The Naked City, Nightmare Alley, Panic in the Streets, Glory Alley, Fourteen Hours, The Well, The Big Night, Rear Window* and *Let No Man Write My Epitaph*. The genre shades into Chayefsky-type Populism and studies of social problems later predominate. European equivalents of the genre include *Hotel du Nord, It Always Rains on Sunday, Sapphire* and even *Bicycle Thieves*, if we include the theft of bicycles as a crime, which of course it is, albeit of a non-melodramatic nature. The American weakness in social realism stems from post-puritan optimistic individualism, and may be summarised in political terms. The Republican line is that social problems arise from widespread wrong attitudes and are really individual moral problems. Remedial action must attack wrong ideas rather than the social set-up. The Democratic line is a kind of liberal environmentalism; social action is required to "prime the pump," to even things up sufficiently for the poor or handicapped to have a fairer deal, and be given a real, rather than a merely theoretical equality in which to prove themselves. Either way the neo-realist stress on economic environment as virtual determinant is conspicuous by its absence, although the phrase "wrong side of the tracks" expresses it fatalistically. It's a minor curiosity that English liberal critics invariably pour scorn on the phrases through which Hollywood expresses an English liberal awareness of class and underprivilege.

Two remarkable movies, *He Ran All the Way* and *The Sound of Fury*, both directed by victims of McCarthy (John Berry, Cy Enfield) illustrate the slick, elliptic terms through which serious social criticisms may be expressed. In the first film, the criminal hero (John Garfield) holds his girl (Shelley Winters) hostage in her father's tenement. The father asks a mate at work whether a hypothetical man in this position should call in the police. His mate replies: "Have you seen firemen go at a fire? Chop, chop, chop!" A multitude of such details assert a continuity between the hero's paranoid streak ("Nobody loves anybody!") and society as a paranoid (competitive) network. Similarly, in *The Sound of Fury*, the psycho killer (Lloyd Bridges) incarnates the real energies behind a thousand permitted prejudices: "Beer drinkers are jerks!" and "Rich boy, huh?" His reluctant accomplice is an unemployed man goaded by a thousand details. His son's greeting is: "Hullo father, mother won't give me 90 cents to go to the movies with the other kids," while the camera notes, in passing, the criminal violence blazoned forth in comic strips. When sick with remorse he confesses to a genteel manicurist, she denounces him. An idealistic journalist whips up hate; the two men are torn to death by an animal mob, who storming the jail, also batter their own cops mercilessly.

Socially critical *films noirs* are mainly Democratic (reformist) or cynical-nihilistic, Republican moralists tend to avoid the genre, although certain movies by Wellman, King Vidor, and Hawks appear to be Republican attempts to grasp the nettle, and tackle problems of self-help in desperate circumstances (e.g. *Public Enemy, Duel in the Sun, Only Angels Have Wings*).

However, certain conspicuous social malfunctions impose a black social realism. These are mostly connected with crime, precisely because this topic reintroduces the question of personal responsibility, such that right-wing spectators can congenially misunderstand hopefully liberal movies. These malfunctions give rise to various subgenres of the crime film:

(a) **Prohibition-type Gangsterism**. It's worth mentioning here a quiet but astonishing movie, *Kiss Tomorrow Good-bye* (1949), in which Cagney, as an old-time gangster making a comeback, corrupts and exploits the corruption of a whole town, including the chief of police. His plan, to murder his old friend's hell-cat daughter (Barbara Payton) so as to marry the tycoon's daughter (Helena Carter) and cement the dynasty, is foiled only by a personal quirk (his mistress's jealousy). The plot is an exact parallel to *A Place in the Sun* except that Dreiser's realistically weak characters are replaced by thrillingly tough ones. (Its scriptwriter worked on Stevens' film also.) Post-war gangster films are curiously devoid of all social criticism, except the post-war appeal of conscience, apart from its devious but effective reintroduction in *Bonnie and Clyde*.

(b) **A Corrupt Penology** (miscarriages of justice, prison exposes, lynchlaw). Corrupt, or worse, merely lazy, justice is indicted in *I Want To Live, Anatomy of a Murder*, and *In the Heat of the Night*. Prison exposés range from *I Am a Fugitive from a Chain Gang* to Dassin's brilliant *Brute Force* and Don Siegel's forceful *Riot in Cell Block 11*. Lynching films range from *Fury* (1936) through *Storm Warning* (1951) to *The Chase*, and, of course, *In the Heat of the Night*.

(c) **The fight game** is another permitted topic, the late '40s springing a sizzling liberal combination (*Body and Soul, The Set-Up, Champion, Night and the City*).

(d) **Juvenile delinquency** appears first in a highly personalized, family motif concerning the youngster brother or friend whom the gangster is leading astray. The juvenile gang (*Dead End*, 1937) introduces a more "social" motif. *Angels with Dirty Faces* combines the two themes, with sufficient success to prompt a rosy sequel called *Angels Wash Their Faces*, which flopped. The late '40s seem awkwardly caught between the obvious inadequacy of the old personal-moral theme, and a new, sociology-based sophistication which doesn't filter down to the screen until *Rebel without a Cause* and *The Young Savages*. Meanwhile there is much to be said for the verve and accuracy of *So Young So Bad* and *The Wild One*.

Rackets other than prohibition are the subject of *Road to Frisco* (1939), *Force of Evil* (1947), *Thieves' Highway* (1949) and, from *The Man with the Golden Arm* (1955), drugs.

The first conspicuous post-war innovation is the neo-documentary thriller, much praised by critics who thought at that time that a documentary tone and location photography guaranteed neo-realism (when, tardily, disillusionment set in it

Above, Glenn Ford, "the cop hero," and Gloria Grahame in Lang's *The Big Heat*

was, of course, with a British variant—*The Blue Lamp*). In 1945 a spy film (*The House on 92nd Street*) had borrowed the formula from the *March of Time* news-series, to give a newspaper-headline impact. The most open-air movies of the series (*The Naked City, Union Station*) now seem the weakest, whereas a certain thoughtfulness distinguishes *Boomerang, Call Northside 777* and *Panic in the Streets.* The cycle later transforms itself into the *Dragnet*-style TV thriller. Several of the above films are *noir*, in that, though the police (or their system) constitute an affirmative hero, a realistic despair or cynicism pervade them. A black cop cycle is opened by Wyler's *Detective Story* (1951), an important second impetus coming from Lang's *The Big Heat*. The cop hero, or villain, is corrupt, victimized or berserk in, notably, *The Naked Alibi, Rogue Cop*, and *Touch of Evil*. These tensions remain in a fourth cycle, which examine the cop as organization man, grappling with corruption and violence (*In the Heat of the Night, The Detective, Lady in Cement, Bullitt, Madigan* and *Coogan's Bluff*). Clearly the theme can be developed with either a right or left-wing inflection. Thus the post-*Big Heat* cycle of the lone-wolf fanatic cop suggest either "Pay the police more, don't skimp on social services" or "Give cops more power, permit more phone tapping" (as in *Dragnet* and *The Big Combo*). The theme of a Mr. Big running the city machine may be democratic (especially if he's an extremely WASP Mr. Big), or Republican ("those corrupt Democratic city machines!") or anarchist, of the right or the left. If a favourite setting for civil rights themes is the Southern small town it's partly because civil rights liberalism is there balanced by the choice of ultra-violent, exotically backward, and Democratic, backwoods with which relatively few American filmgoers will identify. *Coogan's Bluff* depends on the contrast of Republican-fundamentalist-small town with Democratic-corrupt-but-human-big-city. The neo-documentary thrillers created a sense of social networks, that is, of society as organizable. Thus they helped to pave the way for a more sophisticated tone and social awareness which appears in the late '40s.

A cycle of films use a crime to inculpate, not only the underworld, the dead-ends and the underprivileged, but the respectable, middle-class, WASP ethos as well. *Fury* had adumbrated this, melodramatically, in the '30s; the new cycle is more analytical and formidable. The trend has two origins, one in public opinion, the second in Hollywood. An affluent post-war America had more comfort and leisure in which to evolve, and endure, a more sophisticated type of self-criticism. Challengingly, poverty no longer explained everything. Second, the war helped Hollywood's young Democratic minority to assert itself, which it did in the late '40s, until checked by the McCarthyite counter-attack (which of course depended for its success on Hollywood Republicans). These films include *The Sound of Fury*, the early Loseys, *Ace in the Hole, All My Sons* (if it isn't too articulate for a *film noir*), and, once the McCarthyite heat was off, *The Wild One, On The Waterfront* and *The Young Savages*. But McCarthy's impact forced *film noir* themes to retreat to the Western. Such films as *High Noon, Run of the Arrow* and *Ride Lonesome* make the '50's the Western's richest epoch. Subsequently, Hollywood fear of controversy mutes criticism of the middle-class from black to grey (e.g. *The Graduate*). *The Chase, The Detective*, even *Bonnie and Clyde* offer some hope that current tensions may force open the relentless social criticism onto the screen.

2. GANGSTERS

Underworld differs from subsequent gangster films in admiring its gangster hero (George Bancroft) as Nietzschean inspiration in a humiliating world. If *Scarface* borrows several of its settings and motifs it's partly because it's a riposte to it. In fact public opinion turned against the gangster before Hollywood denounced him with the famous trans-auteur triptych, *Little Caesar, Scarface* and *Public Enemy*. To Hawk's simple-minded propaganda piece, one may well prefer the daring pro- and contra-alternations of *Public Enemy*. The mixture of social fact and moralizing myth in pre-war gangster movies is intriguing. Bancroft, like Cagney, represents the Irish gangster, Muni and Raft the Italian type, Bogart's deadpan grotesque is transracial, fitting equally well the strayed WASP (Marlowe) and the East European Jews, who were a forceful gangster element. It's not at all absurd, as NFT audiences boisterously assume, that *Little Caesar* and *Scarface* should love their Italian mommas, nor that in *Angels With Dirty Faces* priest Pat O'Brien and gangster Cagney should be on speaking terms. 1920s gangsters were just as closely linked with race loyalties as today's Black Muslim leaders—the latter have typical gangster childhoods, and without the least facetiousness can be said to have shifted gangster energies into Civil Rights terms. It helps explain the ambivalence of violence and idealism in Black Muslim declarations; dialogues between "priest"

(Martin Luther King) and advocates of violence are by no means ridiculous. Disappointed Prohibitionist moralists found easier prey in Hollywood, and the Hays Office, and cut off the gangster cycle in its prime. A year or two passes before Hollywood evolves its "anti-gangster"—the G-Man or FBI agent who either infiltrates the gang or in one way or another beats the gangster at his own game. *Angels With Dirty Faces* (1938) combines the Dead End kids (from Wyler's film of the previous year) with gangster Cagney. When he's cornered, priest Pat O'Brien persuades him to go to the chair like a coward so that his fans will be disillusioned with him. By so doing, Cagney concedes that crime doesn't pay, but he also debunks movies like *Scarface*. In 1940 *The Roaring Twenties* attempts a naive little thesis about the relationship between gangsterism and unemployment.

Between 1939 and 1953 Nazi and then Russian spies push the gangster into the hero position. A small cycle of semi-nostalgic gangster movies appears. A unique, Hays Code-defying B feature *Dillinger* (1945), is less typical than *I Walk Alone* (1947). This opposes the old-fashioned Prohibition-era thug (Burt Lancaster) who, returning after a long spell in jail, finds himself outmoded and outwitted by the newer, nastier, richer operators who move in swell society and crudely prefigure the "organization men" who reach their climax in the Marvin-Galager-Reagan set-up of Siegel's *The Killers*. *Murder Inc.* (*The Enforcer*) is another hinge movie. putting D.A. Bogart against a gang which while actually Neanderthal in its techniques is felt to be a terrifyingly slick and ubiquitous contra-police network. *Kiss Tomorrow Good-bye* and *White Heat* are contemporary in setting but have an archaic feel. *The Asphalt Jungle* is a moralistic variant within this cycle rather than a precursor of *Rififi* and its gang-job imitations (which include *The Killing* and *Cairo*, a wet transposition of Huston's film).

The next major cycle is keyed by various Congressional investigations, which spotlight gangsterism run big business style. "Brooklyn, I'm very worried about Brooklyn," frowns the gang boss in *New York Confidential* (1954); "It's bringing down our average—collections are down 2%." An equally bad sequel, *The Naked Street* handles a collateral issue, gangster (or ex-gangster?) control of legitimate business (a tardy theme: during the war Western Union was bought by a gangster syndicate to ensure troublefree transmission of illegal betting results). Executive-style gangsterism has to await *Underworld U.S.A.* and *The Killers* for interesting treatment. For obvious reasons, the American equivalent of *La Mani Sulla Citta* has still to be made. *Johnny Cool* is a feeble "sequel" to *Salvatore Giuliano*.

Instead, the mid-'50's see a new cycle, the urban Western, which take a hint from the success of *The Big Heat*. A clump of movies from 1955-1960 includes *The Big Combo, Al Capone, The Rise and Fall of Legs Diamond, Babyface Nelson, The Phenix City Story* and *Pay Or Die*. Something of a lull follows until the latter-day Technicolour series (*The Killers, Bonnie and Clyde, Point Blank*). With or without pop nostalgia for the past, these movies exist, like the Western, for their action (though the killings relate more to atrocity than heroism). The first phase of the cycle is ultra-cautious, and falters through sheer repetition of the one or two safe moral clichés, while the second phase renews itself by dropping the old underworld mystique and shading Illegal America into virtuous (rural or grey flannel suit) America. The first phase carries on from the blackest period of the Western. The second coincides with the Kennedy assassinations and Watts riots.

3. ON THE RUN

Here the criminals or the framed innocents are essentially passive and fugitive, and, even if tragically or despicably guilty, sufficiently sympathetic for the audience to be caught between, on the one hand, pity, identification and regret, and, on the other, moral condemnation and conformist fatalism. Notable films include *The Informer, You Only Live Once, High Sierra, The Killers, He Ran All The Way, They Live By Night, Cry of the City. Dark Passage* and a variant, *The Third Man. Gun Crazy* (*Deadlier Than The Male*), an earlier version of the Bonnie and Clyde story, with Peggy Cummins as Bonnie, fascinatingly compromises between a Langian style and a Penn spirit, and, in double harness with the later film, might assert itself, as a parallel classic.

4. PRIVATE EYES AND ADVENTURERS

This theme is closely interwoven with three literary figures, Dashiell Hammett, Raymond Chandler and Hemingway. It constitutes for some English critics the poetic core of the *film noir*, endearing itself no doubt by the romanticism underlying Chandler's formula: "Down these mean streets must go a man who is not himself mean..." This knight errant relationship has severe limitations. The insistence on city corruption is countered by the trust in private enterprise; and one may well rate the genre below the complementary approach exemplified by *Double Indemnity* and *The Postman Always Rings Twice*, in which we identify with the criminals. The genre originates in a complacent, pre-war cycle, the *Thin Man* series (after Hammett) with William Powell, Myrna Loy and Asta the dog, being both sophisticated and happily married (then a rarity) as they solve crimes together. The motif is transformed by Bogart's incarnation of Sam Spade in the misogynistic *Maltese Falcon*, and the bleaker, lonelier, more anxious Hemingway adventurer in *To Have and Have Not*. In the late '40s Chandler's Marlowe wears five faces—Dick Powell's, Bogart's, Ladd's, Robert Montgomery's and George Montgomery's, in *Farewell My Lovely* (*Murder, My Sweet*), *The Big Sleep, The Blue Dahlia, Lady In The Lake* and *The High Window* (*The Brasher Doubloon*). An RKO series with Mitchum (sometimes Mature) as a vague, aimless wanderer, hounded and hounding, begins well with *Build My Gallows High* (*Out Of the Past*) but rapidly degenerates. The series seeks renewal in more exotic settings with *Key Largo, Ride the Pink Horse, The Breaking Point*, and *Beat The Devil*, but concludes in disillusionment. In *Kiss Me Deadly, Confidential Agent* and a late straggler, *Vertigo*, the private eye solves the mystery but undergoes extensive demoralization. In retrospect, films by well respected auteurs like Hawks, Ray, Siegel and Huston seem to me to have worn less well than the most disillusioned of the series, Dmytryk's visionary *Farewell My Lovely* prefiguring the Aldrich-Welles-Hitchcock pessimism. *The Maltese Falcon*, notably, is deep camp. Huston's laughter deflates villainy into the perverted pretension of Greenstreet and Lorre who are to real villains as Al Jolson to Carmen Jones. In the scenes between Bogart and Mary Astor (a sad hard not-so-young vamp with more middle class perm than "it") it reaches an intensity like greatness. Huston's great *film noir* is a Western (*Treasure of Sierra Madre*).

5. MIDDLE CLASS MURDER

Crime has its harassed amateurs, and the theme of the respectable middle-class figure beguiled into, or secretly plotting, murder facilitates the sensitive study in black. The '30s see a series centering on Edward G. Robinson, who alternates between uncouth underworld leaders (*Little Caesar, Black Tuesday*) and a guilt-haunted or fear-bourgeoisie (in *The Amazing Dr. Clitterhouse, The Woman In The Window, Scarlet Street, The Red House*, and *All My Sons*). Robinson, like Laughton, Cagney and Bogart, belongs to that select group of stars, who, even in Hollywood's simpler-minded years, could give meanness and cowardice a riveting monstrosity, even force. His role as pitiable scapegoat requires a little excursion into psychoanalytical sociology. Slightly exotic, that is, un-American, he symbolized the loved, but repudiated, father/elder sibling, apparently benevolent, ultimately sinister, never unlovable—either an immigrant father (Little Rico in *Little Caesar*) or that complementary bogey, the ultra-WASP intellectual, whose cold superior snobbery infiltrates so many late '40s movies (Clifton Webb in *Laura*). The evolution of these figures belongs to the process of assimilation in America. Robinson's '50s and '60s equivalents include Broderick Crawford, Anthony Quinn, Rod Steiger and Vincent Price. The theme of respectable eccentricity taking murder lightly is treated in *Arsenic and Old Lace, Monsieur Verdoux, Rope*, and *Strangers On A Train*. The theme of the tramp corrupting the not-always-so-innocent bourgeois is artistically fruitful, with *Double Indemnity, The Postman Always Rings Twice, The Woman in the Window, The Woman On the Beach* and, a straggler *The Pushover*. *The Prowler* reverses the formula: the lower-class cop victimizes the DJ's lonely wife. The theme can be considered an American adaptation of a pre-war European favourite (cf. *Pandora's Box, La Bête Humaine*), and the European versions of *The Postman Always Rings Twice*. The cycle synchronizes with a climax in the perennial theme of Woman: Executioner/Victim, involving such figures as Bette Davis. Barbara Stanwyck, Gene Tierney, Joan Crawford and Lana Turner. Jacques Siclier dates the misogynistic cycle from Wyler's *Jezebel* (1938), and it can be traced through *Double Indemnity, Gilda, Dragonwyck, The Strange Love of Martha Ivers, Ivy, Sunset Boulevard, Leave Her To Heaven, Beyond The Forest, Flamingo Road, The File on Thelma Jordan, Clash By Night, Angel Face, Portrait in Black* and *Whatever Happened To Baby Jane?*. A collateral cycle sees woman as grim heroic victim, struggling against despair where her men all but succumb or betray her (*Rebecca, Phantom Lady*). Many films have it both ways, perhaps by contrasting strong feminine figures, the heroine lower-class and embittered, the other respectable but callous (like Joan Crawford and her daughter in *Mildred Pierce*), or by plot twists proving that the apparent vamp was misjudged by an embittered hero (as Rita Hayworth beautifully taunts Glenn Ford in *Gilda* "Put the blame on mame, boys..."). The whole subgenre can be seen as a development out of the "confession" stories of the Depression years, when Helen Twelvetrees and others became prostitutes, golddiggers and kept women for various tear-jerking reasons. Replace the tears by a glum, baffled deadpan, modulate self pity into suspicion, and the later cycle appears. Maybe the misogyny is only an aspect of the claustrophobic paranoia so marked in late '40s movies.

Double Indemnity is perhaps the central *film noir*, not only for its atmospheric power, but as a junction of major themes, combining the vamp (Barbara Stanwyck), the morally weak murderer (Fred MacMurray) and the investigator (Edward G. Robinson). The murderer sells insurance. The investigator checks on claims. If the latter is incorruptible, he is unromantically so; only his cruel Calvinist energy distinguishes his "justice" from meanness. The film's stress on money and false friendliness as a means of making it justifies an alternative title: *Death of A Salesman*. This, and Miller's play all but parallel the relationship between *A Place In The Sun* and *Kiss Tomorrow Good-bye* (realistic weakness becomes wish fulfillment violence).

6. PORTRAITS AND DOUBLES

The characteristic tone of the '40s is sombre, claustrophobic, deadpan and paranoid. In the shaded lights and raining night it is often just a little difficult to tell one character from another. A strange, diffuse play on facial and bodily resemblances reaches a climax in Vidor's *Beyond The Forest* (where sullen Bette Davis is the spitting image, in long-shot, of her Indian maid) and, in exile, in Losey's *The Sleeping Tiger*, where dominant Alexis Smith is the spitting image of her frightened maid. A cycle of grim romantic thrillers focused on women who, dominant even in their absence, stare haughty enigmas at us from their portraits over the fireplace. Sometimes the portrait is the mirror of split personality. The series included *Rebecca, Experiment Perilous, Laura, The Woman in the Window, Scarlet Street* and *The Dark Mirror*. Variants include the all-male, but sexually inverted, *Picture of Dorian Gray, Portrait of Jennie* (rosy and tardy, but reputedly one of Buñuel's favourite films), *Under Capricorn* (the shrunken head), and a beautiful straggler, *Vertigo*.

7. SEXUAL PATHOLOGY

In *The Big Sleep* Bogart and Bacall, pretending to discuss horse-racing, discuss the tactics of copulation, exemplifying the clandestine cynicism and romanticism which the *film noir* apposes to the Hays Office. Similarly, "love at first sight" between Ladd and Lake in *The Blue Dahlia* looks suspiciously like a casual, heavy pick-up. *In A Lonely Place*, *The Big Heat* (and, just outside the *film noir*, *Bus Stop*) make another basic equation: the hero whose tragic flaw is psychopathic violence meets his match in the loving whore.

The yin and yang of puritanism and cynicism, of egoism and paranoia, of greed and idealism, deeply perturbs sexual relationships, and *films noirs* abound in love-hate relationships ranging through all degrees of intensity. Before untying Bogart, Bacall kisses his bruised lips. Heston rapes Jennifer Jones in *Ruby Gentry*, and next morning she shoots her puritanical brother for shooting him. Lover and beloved exterminate each other in *Double Indemnity* and *Build My Gallows High*. He has to kill her in *Gun Crazy* and lets her die of a stomach wound in *The Lady From Shanghai*.

Intimations of non-effeminate homosexuality are laid on thick in, notably, *Gilda*, where loyal Glenn Ford gets compared to both his boss's kept woman and swordstick. A certain flabbiness paraphrases effeminacy in *The Maltese Falcon* (the Lorre-Greenstreet duo repeated in the Morley-Lorre pair in *Beat The Devil*), and in *Rope* and *Strangers On A Train* (where Farley Granger and Robert Walker respectively evoke a youthful Vincent Price). Lesbianism rears a sado-masochistic head in *Rebecca* (between Judith Anderson and her dead mistress) and *In A Lonely Place* (between Gloria Grahame and a brawny masseuse who is also perhaps a symbol for a coarse vulgarity she cannot escape). Homosexual and heterosexual sadism are everyday conditions. In *Clash By Night* Robert Ryan wants to stick pins all over Paul Douglas's floosie wife (Barbara Stanwyck) and watch the blood run down; we're not so far from the needle stuck through a goose's head to tenderize its flesh in *Diary of A Chambermaid* ("Sounds like they're murdering somebody," says Paulette Goddard).

Below, Robert Walker (left) and Farley Granger in *Strangers on a Train*.

Slim knives horrify but fascinate the paranoid '40s as shotguns delight the cool '60s. Notable sadists include Richard Widmark (chuckling as he pushes the old lady down stairs in her wheelchair in *Kiss of Death*), Paul Henreid in *Rope of Sand* (experimenting with a variety of whips on Burt Lancaster's behind), Hume Cronyn in *Brute Force* (truncheoning the intellectual prisoner to the strains of the *Liebestod*), Lee Marvin flinging boiling coffee in his mistress's face in *The Big Heat*; and so on to Clu Gulager's showmanlike eccentricities in *The Killers* and, of course, Tony Curtis in *The Boston Strangler*.

8. PSYCHOPATHS

Film noir psychopaths, who are legion, are divisible into three main groups: the heroes with a tragic flaw, the unassuming monsters, and the obvious monsters, in particular, the Prohibition-type gangster. Cagney's *Public Enemy* criss-crosses the boundaries between them, thus providing the moral challenge and suspense which is the film's mainspring. Cagney later contributes a rousing portrait of a gangster with a raging Oedipus complex in *White Heat*, from Hollywood's misogynistic period. Trapped on an oil storage tank, he cries exultantly: "On top of the world, ma!" before joining his dead mother via the auto-destructive orgasm of his own personal mushroom cloud. The unassuming monster may be exemplified by *The Blue Dahlia*, whose paranoid structure is almost as interesting as that of *Phantom Lady*. Returned war hero Alan Ladd nearly puts a bullet in his unfaithful wife. As so often in late '40's films, the police believe him guilty of the crime of which he is nearly guilty. The real murderer is not the hero with the motive, not the wartime buddy whom shellshock drives into paroxysms of rage followed by amnesia, not the smooth gangster with whom the trollop was two-timing her husband. It was the friendly hotel house-detective.

On our right, we find the simple and satisfying view of the psychopath as a morally responsible mad dog deserving to be put down (thus simple, satisfying films like *Scarface* and *Panic In Year Zero*). On the left, he is an ordinary, or understandably weak, or unusually energetic character whose inner defects are worsened by factors outside his control (*Public Enemy, The Young Savages*). These factors may be summarised as (1) slum environments, (2) psychological traits subtly extrinsic to character (neurosis) and (3) a subtly corrupting social morality. In Depression America, the first explanation seems plausible enough (*Public Enemy*, with exceptional thoughtfulness, goes for all three explanations while insisting that he's become a mad dog who must die). In 1939, *Of Mice and Men* prefigures a change of emphasis, and in postwar America, with its supposedly universal affluence, other terms seem necessary to account for the still festering propensity to violence. Given the individualism even of Democratic thought, recourse is had to trauma, either wartime (*The Blue Dahlia, Act of Violence*) or Freudian (*The Dark Corner, The Dark Past*). A second group of films, without exonerating society, key psychopathy to a tone of tragic confusion (*Of Mice and Men, Kiss The Blood Off My Hands*). A third group relates violence to the spirit of society (*Force of Evil, The Sound of Fury*). A cooler more domestic tone prevails with *Don't Bother To Knock*, with its switch-casting (ex-psychopath Richard Widmark becomes the embittered, kindly hero, against Marilyn Monroe as a homicidal baby-sitter). This last shift might be described as anti-expressionism, or coolism, with psychopathy accepted as a normal condition of life. Critics of the period scoff at the psychopathic theme, although in retrospect Hollywood seems to have shown more awareness of American undertones than its supercilious critics. *The Killers, Point Blank* and *Bonnie and Clyde* resume the "Democratic" social criticism of *Force of Evil* and *The Sound of Fury*. A highly plausible interpretation of *Point Blank* sees its hero as a ghost; the victims of his revenge quest destroy one another, or themselves. The psychopathy theme is anticipated in pre-war French movies (e.g. *Le Jour Se Leve*) with a social crisis of confidence, a generalised, hot, violent mode of alienation (as distinct from the glacial variety, a la Antonioni). With a few extra-lucid exceptions, neither the French nor the American films seem to realize the breakdown of confidence as a social matter.

9. HOSTAGES TO FORTUNE

The imprisonment of a family, an individual, or a group of citizens, by desperate or callous criminals is a hardy perennial. But a cycle climaxes soon after the Korean War with the shock, to Americans, of peacetime conscripts in action. A parallel inspiration in domestic violence is indicated by *The Petrified Forest* (1938), *He Ran All The Way* and *The Dark Past*. But the early '50s see a sudden cluster including *The Desperate Hours, Suddenly, Cry Terror* and *Violent Saturday*. The confrontation between middle-class father and family, and killer, acts out, in fuller social metaphor, although, often, with a more facile Manicheanism, the normal and abnormal sides of the psychopathic hero.

10. BLACKS AND REDS

A cycle substituting Nazi agents and the Gestapo for gangsters gets under way with *Confessions Of A Nazi Spy* (1939). The cold war anti-Communist cycle begins with *The Iron Curtain* (1948), and most of its products were box-office as well as artistic flops, probably because the Communists and fellow-travellers were so evil as to be dramatically boring. The principal exceptions are by Samuel Fuller (*Pick Up On South Street*) and Aldrich (*Kiss Me Deadly*). Some films contrast the good American gangster with the nasty foreign agents (*Pick Up On South Street*); *Woman On Pier 13* links Russian agents with culture-loving waterfront union leaders and can be regarded as ultra-right, like *One Minute To Zero* and *Suddenly*, whose timid liberal modification (rather than reply) is *The Manchurian Candidate*. *Advise and Consent* is closely related to the political *film noir*.

11. GUIGNOL, HORROR, FANTASY

The three genres are clearly first cousins to the *film noir*. Hardy perennials, they seem to have enjoyed periods of special popularity. Siegfried Kracauer has sufficiently related German expressionist movies with the angst of pre-Nazi Germany. Collaterally, a diluted expressionism was a minor American genre, indeterminate as between *film noir* and horror fantasy. Lon Chaney's Gothic grotesques (*The Unknown, The Phantom of the Opera*) parallel stories of haunted houses (*The Cat and the Canary*) which conclude with rational explanations. Sternberg's *The Last Command* can be considered a variant of the Chaney genre, with Jannings as Chaney, and neo-realistic in that its hero's plight symbolizes the agonies of the uprooted immigrants who adapted with difficulty to the tenement jungles. The Depression sparked off the full-blown, visionary guignol of *Dracula, Frankenstein* (with Karloff as Chaney), *King Kong* (with Kong as Chaney!), *The Hounds of Zaroff, Island of Lost Souls*, etc. (the Kracauer-type tyrant looms, but is defeated, often with pathos). Together with gangster and sex films, the genre suffers from the Hays Office. After the shock of the Great Crash, the demoralizing stagnation of the depressed '30's leads to a minor cycle of black brooding fantasies of death and time (*Death Takes A Holiday, Peter Ibbetson*). The war continues the social unsettledness which films balance by cosy, enclosed, claustrophobic settings (*Dr. Jekyll and Mr. Hyde, Flesh and Fantasy, Cat People*). A post-war subgenre is the thriller, developed into plain clothes Gothic (*The Spiral Staircase, The Red House, Sorry Wrong Number*). *Phantom Lady* (in its very title) indicates their interechoing. A second Monster cycle coincides with the Korean War. A connection with scientists, radioactivity and outer space suggests fear of atomic apocalypse (overt in *This Island Earth, It Came From Outer Space* and *Them*, covert in *Tarantula* and *The Thing From Another World*). *The Red Planet Mars* speaks for the hawks, *The Day The Earth Stood Still* for the doves. *Invasion of the Bodysnatchers* is a classic paranoid fantasy (arguably justified). As the glaciers of callous alienation advance, the Corman Poes create their nightmare compensation: the aesthetic hothouse of Victorian incest. *Psycho* crossbreeds the genre with a collateral revival of plainclothes guignol, often revolving round a feminine, rather than a masculine, figure (Joan Crawford and Bette Davis substitute for Chaney in *Whatever Happened To Baby Jane?*). The English anticipate of the Corman Poes are the Fisher *Frankenstein* and *Dracula*. With *Dutchman*, the genre matures into an expressionistic social realism.

The '60s obsession with violent death in all forms and genres may be seen as marking the admission of the *film noir* into the mainstream of Western pop art, encouraged by (a) the comforts of relative affluence, (b) moral disillusionment, in outcome variously radical, liberal, reactionary or nihilist, (c) a post-Hiroshima sense of man as his own executioner, rather than nature, God or fate, and (d) an enhanced awareness of social conflict. The cinema is in its Jacobean period, and the stress on gratuitous tormenting, evilly jocular in *The Good, the Bad and the Ugly,* less jocular in *Laughter In the Dark,* parallel that in Webster's plays. Such films as *Paths of Glory, Eva,* and *The Loved One* emphasize their crimes less than the rottenness of a society or, perhaps, man himself.

The beginning and end of the *noir* cycle as recapped by Paul Schrader: above, Bogart, Lorre, Astor, and Greenstreet in the 1941 *Maltese Falcon*. Below, Orson Welles in the 1958 *Touch of Evil*.

Notes on *Film Noir*

Paul Schrader (1972)

In 1946 French critics, seeing the American films they had missed during the war, noticed the new mood of cynicism, pessimism and darkness which had crept into the American cinema. The darkening stain was most evident in routine crime thrillers, but was also apparent in prestigious melodramas.

The French cineastes soon realized they had seen only the tip of the iceberg: as the years went by, Hollywood lighting grew darker, characters more corrupt, themes more fatalistic and the tone more hopeless. By 1949 American movies were in the throes of their deepest and most creative funk. Never before had films dared to take such a harsh uncomplimentary look at American life, and they would not dare to do so again for twenty years.

Hollywood's *film noir* has recently become the subject of renewed interest among moviegoers and critics. The fascination *film noir* holds for today's young filmgoers and film students reflects recent trends in American cinema: American movies are again taking a look at the underside of the American character, but compared to such relentlessly cynical *films noir* as *Kiss Me Deadly* or *Kiss Tomorrow Goodbye*, the new self-hate cinema of *Easy Rider* and *Medium Cool* seems naive and romantic. As the current political mood hardens, filmgoers and filmmakers will find the *film noir* of the late Forties increasingly attractive. The Forties may be to the Seventies what the Thirties were to the Sixties.

Film noir is equally interesting to critics. It offers writers a cache of excellent, little-known films (*film noir* is oddly both one of Hollywood's best periods and least known), and gives auteur-weary critics an opportunity to apply themselves to the newer questions of classification and transdirectorial style. After all, what is *film noir*?

Film noir is not a genre (as Raymond Durgnat has helpfully pointed out over the objections of Higham and Greenberg's *Hollywood in the Forties*). It is not defined, as are the western and gangster genres, by conventions of setting and conflict, but rather by the more subtle qualities of tone and mood. It is a film *"noir,"* as opposed to the possible variants of film gray or film off-white.

Film noir is also a specific period of film history, like German Expressionism or the French New Wave. In general, *film noir* refers to those Hollywood films of the

Forties and early Fifties which portrayed the world of dark, slick city streets, crime and corruption.

Film noir is an extremely unwieldy period. It harks back to many previous periods: Warner's Thirties gangster films, the French "poetic realism" of Carné and Duvivier, Sternbergian melodrama, and, farthest back, German Expressionist crime films (Lang's *Mabuse* cycle). *Film noir* can stretch at its outer limits from *The Maltese Falcon* (1941) to *Touch of Evil* (1958), and most every dramatic Hollywood film from 1941 to 1953 contains some *noir* elements. There are also foreign offshoots of *film noir*, such as *The Third Man, Breathless* and *Le Doulos*.

Almost every critic has his own definition of *film noir*, and personal list of film titles and dates to back it up. Personal and descriptive definitions, however, can get a bit sticky. A film of urban night life is not necessarily a *film noir*, and a *film noir* need not necessarily concern crime and corruption. Since *film noir* is defined by tone rather than genre, it is almost impossible to argue one critic's descriptive definition against another's. How many *noir* elements does it take to make *film noir noir*?

Rather than haggle definitions, I would rather attempt to reduce *film noir* to its primary colors (all shades of black), those cultural and stylistic elements to which any definition must return.

At the risk of sounding like Arthur Knight, I would suggest that there were four conditions in Hollywood in the Forties which brought about *film noir*. (The danger of Knight's *Liveliest Art* method is that it makes film history less a matter of structural analysis, and more a case of artistic and social forces magically interacting and coalescing.) Each of the following four catalytic elements, however, can define the *film noir*; the distinctly *noir* tonality draws from each of these elements.

War and post-war disillusionment. The acute downer which hit the U.S. after the Second World War was, in fact, a delayed reaction to the Thirties. All through the Depression, movies were needed to keep people's spirits up, and, for the most part, they did. The crime films of this period were Horatio Algerish and socially conscious. Toward the end of the Thirties a darker crime film began to appear (*You Only Live Once, The Roaring Twenties*) and, were it not for the War, *film noir* would have been at full steam by the early Forties.

The need to produce Allied propaganda abroad and promote patriotism at home blunted the fledgling moves toward a dark cinema, and the *film noir* thrashed about in the studio system, not quite able to come into full prominence. During the War the first uniquely *film noir* appeared: *The Maltese Falcon, The Glass Key, This Gun for Hire, Laura*, but these films lacked the distinctly *noir* bite the end of the war would bring.

As soon as the War was over, however, American films became markedly more sardonic—and there was a boom in the crime film. For fifteen years the pressures against America's amelioristic cinema had been building up and, given the freedom, audiences and artists were now eager to take a less optimistic view of things. The disillusionment many soldiers, small businessmen and house-wife/factory employees felt in returning to a peacetime economy was directly mirrored in the sordidness of the urban crime film.

This immediate post-war disillusionment was directly demonstrated in films like *Cornered, The Blue Dahlia, Dead Reckoning,* and *Ride the Pink Horse,* in which a serviceman returns from the war to find his sweetheart unfaithful or dead, or his business partner cheating him, or the whole society something less than worth fighting for. The war continues, but now the antagonism turns with a new vicious-ness toward the American society itself.

Post-war realism. Shortly after the War every film-producing country had a re-surgence of realism. In America it first took the form of films by such producers as Louis de Rochemont (*House on 92nd Street, Call Northside 777*) and Mark Hellin-ger (*The Killers, Brute Force*), and directors like Henry Hathaway and Jules Dassin. "Every scene was filmed on the actual location depicted," the 1947 de Rochemont-Hathaway *Kiss of Death* proudly proclaimed. Even after de Rochemont's particular "March of Time" authenticity fell from vogue, realistic ex-teriors remained a permanent fixture of *film noir.*

The realistic movement also suited America's post-war mood; the public's de-sire for a more honest and harsh view of America would not be satisfied by the same studio streets they had been watching for a dozen years. The post-war real-istic trend succeeded in breaking *film noir* away from the domain of the high-class melodrama, placing it where it more properly belonged, in the streets with every-day people. In retrospect, the pre-de Rochemont *film noir* looks definitely tamer than the post-war realistic films. The studio look of films like *The Big Sleep* and *The Mask of Dimitrios* blunts their sting, making them seem more polite and conven-tional in contrast to their later, more realistic counterparts.

The German Influence. Hollywood played host to an influx of German expatri-ates in the Twenties and Thirties, and these filmmakers and technicians had, for the most part, integrated themselves into the American film establishment. Holly-wood never experienced the "Germanization" some civic-minded natives feared, and there is a danger of over-emphasizing the German influence in Hollywood.

But when, in the late Forties, Hollywood decided to paint it black, there were no greater masters of chiaroscuro than the Germans. The influence of expression-ist lighting has always been just beneath the surface of Hollywood films, and it is not surprising, in *film noir,* to find it bursting to find a larger number of German and East Europeans working in *film noir*: Fritz Lang, Robert Siodmak, Billy Wilder, Franz Waxman, Otto Preminger, John Brahm, Anatole Litvak, Karl Freund, Max Ophuls, John Alton, Douglas Sirk, Fred Zinnemann, William Dieterle, Max Steiner, Edgar G. Ulmer, Curtis Bernhardt, Rudolph Maté.

On the surface the German expressionist influence, with its reliance on artificial studio lighting, seems incompatible with post-war realism, with its harsh unadorned exteriors; but it is the unique quality of *film noir* that it was able to weld seemingly contradictory elements into a uniform style. The best *noir* technicians simply made all the world a sound stage, directing unnatural and expressionistic lighting onto realistic settings. In films like *Union Station, They Live by Night, The Killers* there is an uneasy, exhilarating combination of realism and expressionism.

Perhaps the greatest master of *noir* was Hungarian-born John Alton, an expressionist cinematographer who could relight Times Square at noon if necessary. No cinematographer better adapted the old expressionist techniques to the new desire for realism, and his black-and-white photography in such gritty *film noir* as *T-Men, Raw Deal, I the Jury, The Big Combo* equals that of such German expressionist masters as Fritz Wagner and Karl Freund.

The hard-boiled tradition. Another stylistic influence waiting in the wings was the "hard-boiled" school of writers. In the Thirties, authors such as Ernest Hemingway, Dashiell Hammett, Raymond Chandler, James M. Cain, Horace McCoy and John O'Hara created the "tough," cynical way of acting and thinking which separated one from the world of everyday emotions—romanticism with a protective shell. The hard-boiled writers had their roots in pulp fiction or journalism, and their protagonists lived out a narcissistic, defeatist code. The hard-boiled hero was, in reality, a soft egg compared to his existential counterpart (Camus is said to have based *The Stranger* on McCoy), but he was a good deal tougher than anything American fiction had seen.

When the movies of the Forties turned to the American "tough" moral understrata, the hard-boiled school was waiting with preset conventions of heroes, minor characters, plots, dialogue and themes. Like the German expatriates, the hard-boiled writers had a style made to order for *film noir*; and, in turn, they influenced *noir* screenwriting as much as the German influenced *noir* cinematography.

The most hard-boiled of Hollywood's writers was Raymond Chandler himself, whose script of *Double Indemnity* (from a James M. Cain story) was the best written and most characteristically *noir* of the period. *Double Indemnity* was the first film which played *film noir* for what it essentially was: small-time, unredeemed, unheroic; it made a break from the romantic *noir* cinema of [the later] *Mildred Pierce* and *The Big Sleep*.

(In its final stages, however, *film noir* adapted and then bypassed the hard-boiled school. Manic, neurotic post-1948 films such as *Kiss Tomorrow Goodbye, D.O.A., Where the Sidewalk Ends, White Heat,* and *The Big Heat* are all post-hard-boiled: the air in these regions was even too thin for old-time cynics like Chandler.)

STYLISTICS. There is not yet a study of the stylistics of *film noir*, and the task is certainly too large to be attempted here. Like all film movements *film noir* drew upon a reservoir of film techniques, and given the time one could correlate its techniques, themes and causal elements into a stylistic schema. For the present, however, I'd like to point out some of *film noir*'s recurring techniques.

■ The majority of scenes are lit for night. Gangsters sit in the offices at midday with shades pulled and the lights off. Ceiling lights are hung low and floor lamps are seldom more than five feet high. One always has the suspicion that if the lights were all suddenly flipped on the characters would shriek and shrink from the scene like Count Dracula at sunrise.

■ As in German expressionism, oblique and vertical lines are preferred to horizontal. Obliquity adheres to the choreography of the city, and is in direct opposition to the horizontal American tradition of Griffith and Ford. Oblique lines tend to splinter a screen, making it restless and unstable. Light enters the dingy rooms of *film noir* in such odd shapes—jagged trapezoids, obtuse triangles, vertical slits— that one suspects the windows were cut out with a pen knife. No character can speak authoritatively from a space which is being continually cut into ribbons of light. The Anthony Mann/John Alton *T-Men* is the most dramatic but far from the only example of oblique *noir* choreography.

■ The actors and setting are often given equal lighting emphasis. An actor is often hidden in the realistic tableau of the city at night, and, more obviously, his face is often blacked out by shadow as he speaks. These shadow effects are unlike the famous Warner Brothers lighting of the Thirties in which the central character was accentuated by a heavy shadow; in *film noir*, the central character is likely to be standing in the shadow. When the environment is given an equal or greater weight than the actor, it, of course, creates a fatalistic, hopeless mood. There is nothing the protagonist can do; the city will outlast and negate even his best efforts.

■ Compositional tension is preferred to physical action. A typical *film noir* would rather move the scene cinematographically around the actor than have the actor control the scene by physical action. The beating of Robert Ryan in *The Set-Up*, the gunning down of Farley Granger in *They Live by Night*, the execution of the taxi driver in *The Enforcer* and of Brian Donlevy in *The Big Combo* are all marked by measured pacing, restrained anger and oppressive compositions, and seem much closer to the *film noir* spirit than the rat-tat-tat and screeching tires of *Scarface* twenty years before or the violent, expressive actions of *Underworld U.S.A.* ten years later.

■ There seems to be an almost Freudian attachment to water. The empty *noir* streets are almost always glistening with fresh evening rain (even in Los Angeles), and the rainfall tends to increase in direct proportion to the drama. Docks and piers are second only to alleyways as the most popular rendezvous points.

■ There is a love of romantic narration. In such films as *The Postman Always Rings Twice, Laura, Double Indemnity, The Lady from Shanghai, Out of the Past* and *Sunset*

Boulevard the narration creates a mood of *temps perdu:* an irretrievable past, a predetermined fate and an all-enveloping hopelessness. In *Out of the Past* Robert Mitchum relates his history with such pathetic relish that it is obvious there is no hope for any future: one can only take pleasure in reliving a doomed past.

■ A complex chronological order is frequently used to reinforce the feelings of hopelessness and lost time. Such films as *The Enforcer, The Killers, Mildred Pierce, The Dark Past, Chicago Deadline, Out of the Past* and *The Killing* use a convoluted time sequence to immerse the viewer in a time-disoriented but highly stylized world. The manipulation of time, whether slight or complex, is often used to reinforce a *noir* principle: the how is always more important than the what.

THEMES. Raymond Durgnat has delineated the themes of *film noir* in an excellent article in the British *Cinema* magazine ("The Family Tree of *Film noir*," August, 1970), and it would be foolish for me to attempt to redo his thorough work in this short space. Durgnat divides *film noir* into eleven thematic categories, and although one might criticize some of his specific groupings, he does cover the whole gamut of *noir* production (thematically categorizing over 300 films).

In each of Durgnat's *noir* themes (whether Black Widow, killers-on-the-run, *dopplegangers)* one finds that the upwardly mobile forces of the Thirties have halted; frontierism has turned to paranoia and claustrophobia. The small-time gangster has now made it big and sits in the mayor's chair, the private eye has quit the police force in disgust, and the young heroine, sick of going along for the ride, is taking others for a ride.

Durgnat, however, does not touch upon what is perhaps the over-riding *noir* theme: a passion for the past and present, but also a fear of the future. The *noir* hero dreads to look ahead, but instead tries to survive by the day, and if unsuccessful at that, he retreats to the past. Thus *film noir's* techniques emphasize loss, nostalgia, lack of clear priorities, insecurity; then submerge these self-doubts in mannerism and style. In such a world style becomes paramount; it is all that separates one from meaninglessness. Chandler described this fundamental *noir* theme when he described his own fictional world: "It is not a very fragrant world, but it is the world you live in, and certain writers with tough minds and a cool spirit of detachment can make very interesting patterns out of it."

Film noir can be subdivided into three broad phases. The first, the wartime period, 1941-'46 approximately, was the phase of the private eye and the lone wolf, of Chandler, Hammett and Greene, of Bogart and Bacall, Ladd and Lake, classy directors like Curtiz and Garnett, studio sets, and, in general, more talk than action. The studio look of this period was reflected in such pictures as *The Maltese Falcon, Casablanca, Gaslight, This Gun for Hire, The Lodger, The Woman in the Window, Mildred Pierce, Spellbound, The Big Sleep, Laura, The Lost Weekend, The Strange Love of Martha Ivers, To Have and Have Not, Fallen Angel, Gilda, Murder My Sweet,*

The Postman Always Rings Twice, Dark Waters, Scarlet Street, So Dark the Night, The Glass Key, The Mask of Dimitrios, and *The Dark Mirror.*

The Wilder/Chandler *Double Indemnity* provided a bridge to the post-war phase of *film noir.* The unflinching *noir* vision of *Double Indemnity* came as a shock in 1944, and the film was almost blocked by the combined efforts of Paramount, the Hays Office and star Fred MacMurray. Three years later, however, *Double Indemnitys* were dropping off the studio assembly line.

The second phase was the post-war realistic period from 1945-'49 (the dates overlap and so do the films; these are all approximate phases for which there are many exceptions). These films tended more toward the problems of crime in the streets, political corruption and police routine. Less romantic heroes like Richard Conte, Burt Lancaster and Charles McGraw were more suited to this period, as were proletarian directors like Hathaway, Dassin and Kazan. The realistic urban look of this phase is seen in such films as *The House on 92nd Street, The Killers, Raw Deal, Act of Violence, Union Station, Kiss of Death, Johnny O'Clock, Force of Evil, Dead Reckoning, Ride the Pink Horse, Dark Passage, Cry of the City, The Set-Up, T-Men, Call Northside 777, Brute Force, The Big Clock, Thieves' Highway, Ruthless, Pitfall, Boomerang!,* and *The Naked City.*

The third and final phase of *film noir,* from 1949-'53, was the period of psychotic action and suicidal impulse. The *noir* hero, seemingly under the weight of ten years of despair, started to go bananas. The psychotic killer, who in the first period been a subject worthy of study (Olivia de Havilland in *The Dark Mirror*), in the second a fringe threat (Richard Widmark in *Kiss of Death*), now became the active protagonist (James Cagney in *Kiss Tomorrow Goodbye*). There were no excuses given for the psychopathy in *Gun Crazy*—it was just "crazy." James Cagney made a neurotic comeback and his instability was matched by that of younger actors like Robert Ryan and Lee Marvin. This was the phase of the "B" *noir* film, and of psychoanalytically-inclined directors like Ray and Walsh. The forces of personal disintegration are reflected in such films as *White Heat, Gun Crazy, D.O.A., Caught, They Live by Night, Where the Sidewalk Ends, Kiss Tomorrow Goodbye, Detective Story, In a Lonely Place, I the Jury, Ace in the Hole, Panic in the Streets, The Big Heat, On Dangerous Ground,* and *Sunset Boulevard.*

This third phase is the cream of the *film noir* period. Some critics may prefer the early "gray" melodramas, other the post-war "street" films, but *film noir*'s final phase was the most aesthetically and sociologically piercing. After ten years of steadily shedding romantic conventions, the later *noir* films finally got down to the root causes of the period: the loss of public honor, heroic conventions, personal integrity, and, finally, psychic stability. The third-phase films were painfully self-aware; they seemed to know they stood at the end of a long tradition based on despair and disintegration and did not shy away from the fact. The best and characteristically *noir* films—*Gun Crazy, White Heat, Out of the Past, Kiss Tomorrow Goodbye, D.O.A., They Live by Night,* and *The Big Heat*—stand at the end of the pe-

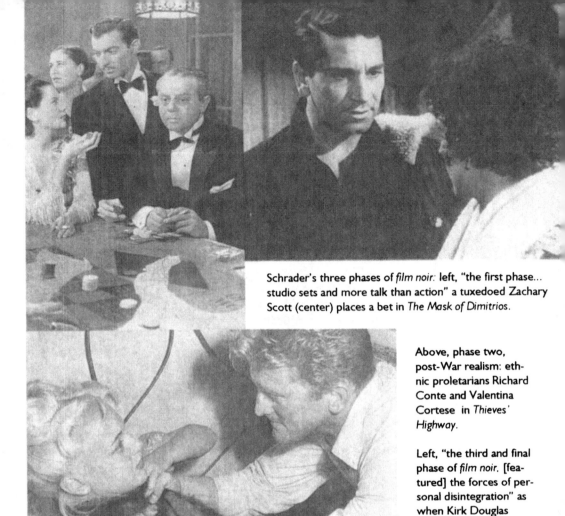

Schrader's three phases of *film noir:* left, "the first phase...
studio sets and more talk than action" a tuxedoed Zachary
Scott (center) places a bet in *The Mask of Dimitrios.*

Above, phase two,
post-War realism: eth-
nic proletarians Richard
Conte and Valentina
Cortese in *Thieves'
Highway.*

Left, "the third and final
phase of *film noir.* [fea-
tured] the forces of per-
sonal disintegration" as
when Kirk Douglas
menaces Jan Sterling in
Ace in the Hole..

Right, "there were a
few notable stragglers"
such as the John Alton
photographed *The Big
Combo*

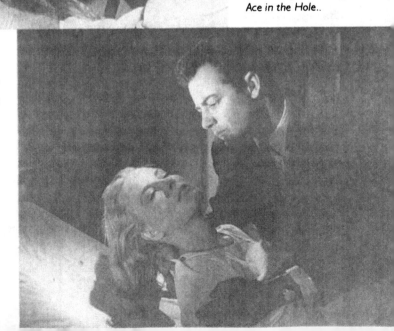

riod and are the results of self-awareness. The third phase is rife with end-of-the-line *noir* heroes: *The Big Heat* and *Where the Sidewalk Ends* are the last stops for the urban cop, *Ace in the Hole* for the newspaper man, the Victor Saville-produced Spillane series (*I, the Jury, The Long Wait, Kiss Me Deadly*) for the private eye, *Sunset Boulevard* for the Black Widow, *White Heat* and *Kiss Tomorrow Goodbye* for the gangster, *D.O.A.* for the John Doe American.

Appropriately, the masterpiece of *film noir* was a straggler, *Kiss Me Deadly*, produced in 1955. Its time delay gives it a sense of detachment and thoroughgoing seediness—it stands at the end of a long sleazy tradition. The private eye hero, Mike Hammer, undergoes the final stages of degradation. He is a small-time "bedroom dick," and makes no qualms about it because the world around him isn't much better. Ralph Meeker, in his best performance, plays Hammer, a midget among dwarfs. Robert Aldrich's teasing direction carries *noir* to its sleaziest and most perversely erotic. Hammer overturns the underworld in search of the "great whatsit," and when he finally finds it, it turns out to be—joke of jokes—an exploding atomic bomb. The inhumanity and meaningless of the hero are small matters in a world in which The Bomb has the final say.

By the middle Fifties *film noir* had ground to a halt. There were a few notable stragglers, *Kiss Me Deadly*, the Lewis/Alton *The Big Combo*, and *film noir*'s epitaph, *Touch of Evil*, but for the most part a new style of crime film had become popular.

At the rise of McCarthy and Eisenhower demonstrated, Americans were eager to see a more bourgeois view of themselves. Crime had to move to the suburbs. The criminal put on a gray flannel suit and the footsore cop was replaced by the "mobile unit" careening down the expressway. Any attempt at social criticism had to be cloaked in ludicrous affirmations of the American way of life. Technically, television, with its demand for full lighting and close-ups, gradually undercut the German influence, and color cinematography was, of course, the final blow to the "*noir*" look.

New directors like Siegel, Fleischer, Karlson and Fuller, and TV shows like *Dragnet, M-Squad, Lineup* and *Highway Patrol* stepped in to create the new crime drama. This transition can be seen in Samuel Fuller's 1953 *Pickup on South Street*, a film which blends the black look with the red scare. The waterfront scenes with Richard Widmark and Jean Peters are in the best *noir* tradition, but a later, dynamic fight in the subway marks Fuller as a director who would be better suited to the crime school of the middle and late Fifties.

Film noir was an immensely creative period—probably the most creative in Hollywood's history—at least, if this creativity is measured not by its peaks but by its median level of artistry. Picked at random, a *film noir* is likely to be a better made film than a randomly selected silent comedy, musical, western and so on. (A Joseph H. Lewis "B" *film noir* is better than a Lewis "B" western, for example.) Taken as a whole period, *film noir* achieved an unusually high level of artistry.

Film noir seemed to bring out the best in everyone: directors, cameramen, screenwriters, actors. Again and again, a film noir will make the high point on an artist's career graph. Some directors, for example, did their best work in film noir (Stuart Heisler, Robert Siodmak, Gordon Douglas, Edward Dmytryk, John Brahm, John Cromwell, Raoul Walsh, Henry Hathaway); other directors began in film noir and, it seems to me, never regained their original heights (Otto Preminger, Rudolph Maté, Nicholas Ray, Robert Wise, Jules Dassin, Richard Fleischer, John Huston, Andre de Toth, and Robert Aldrich); and other directors who made great films in other molds also made great film noir (Orson Welles, Max Ophuls, Fritz Lang, Elia Kazan, Howard Hawks, Robert Rossen, Anthony Mann, Joseph Losey, Alfred Hitchcock, and Stanley Kubrick). Whether or not one agrees with this particular schema, its message is irrefutable: film noir was good for practically every director's career. (Two interesting exceptions to prove the case are King Vidor and Jean Renoir.)

Film noir seems to have been a creative release for everyone involved. It gave artists a chance to work with previously forbidden themes, yet had conventions strong enough to protect the mediocre. Cinematographers were allowed to become highly mannered, and actors were sheltered by the cinematographers. It was not until years later that critics were able to distinguish between great directors and great noir directors.

Film noir's remarkable creativity makes its longtime neglect the more baffling. The French, of course, have been students of the period for some time (Borde and Chaumeton's Panorama du Film Noir was published in 1955), but American critics until recently have preferred the western, the musical or the gangster film to the film noir.

Some of the reasons for this neglect are superficial; others strike to the heart of the noir style. For a long time film noir, with its emphasis on corruption and despair, was considered an aberration of the American character. The western, with its moral primitivism, and the gangster film, with its Horatio Alger values, were considered more American than the film noir.

This prejudice was reinforced by the fact that film noir was ideally suited to the low budget "B" film, and many of the best noir films were "B" films. This odd sort of economic snobbery still lingers on in some critical circles: high-budget trash is considered more worthy of attention than low-budget trash, and to praise a "B" film is somehow to slight (often intentionally) an "A" film.

There has been a critical revival in the U.S. over the last ten years, but film noir lost out on that too. The revival was auteur (director) oriented, and film noir wasn't. Auteur criticism is interested in how directors are different; film noir criticism is concerned with what they have in common.

The fundamental reason for film noir's neglect, however, is the fact that it depends more on choreography than sociology, and American critics have always been slow on the uptake when it comes to visual style. Like its protagonists, *film noir* is more interested in style than theme, whereas American critics have been traditionally more interested in theme than style.

American film critics have always been sociologists first and scientists second: film is important as it relates to large masses, and if a film goes awry it is often because the theme has been somehow "violated" by the style. *Film noir* operates on opposite principles: the theme is hidden in the style, and bogus themes are often flaunted ("middle-class values are best") which contradict the style. Although, I believe, style determines the theme in *every* film, it was easier for sociological critics to discuss the themes of the western and gangster film apart from stylistic analysis than it was to do for *film noir*.

Not surprisingly it was the gangster film, not the *film noir*, which was canonized in *The Partisan Review* in 1948 by Robert Warshow's famous essay, "The Gangster as Tragic Hero." Although Warshow could be an aesthetic as well as a sociological critic, in this case he was interested in the western and gangster film as "popular" art rather than as style. This sociological orientation blinded Warshow, as it has many subsequent critics, to an aesthetically more important development in the gangster film—*film noir*.

The irony of this neglect is that in retrospect the gangster films Warshow wrote about are inferior to *film noir*. The Thirties gangster was primarily a reflection of what was happening in the country, and Warshow analyzed this. The *film noir*, although it was also a sociological reflection, went further than the gangster film. Toward the end *film noir* was engaged in a life-and-death struggle with the materials it reflected; it tried to make America accept a moral vision of life based on style. That very contradiction—promoting style in a culture which valued themes—forced *film noir* into artistically invigorating twists and turns. *Film noir* attacked and interpreted its sociological conditions, and, by the close of the *noir* period, created a new artistic world which went beyond a simple sociological reflection, a nightmarish world of American mannerism which was by far more a creation than a reflection.

Because *film noir* was first of all a style, because it worked out its conflicts visually rather than thematically, because it was aware of its own identity, it was able to create artistic solutions to sociological problems. And for these reason films like *Kiss Me Deadly, Kiss Tomorrow Goodbye* and *Gun Crazy* can be works of art in a way that gangster films like *Scarface, Public Enemy* and *Little Caesar* can never be.

5410-69

Above, silhouetted figures standing in rigid position become abstracted Modern Man and Woman in the final sequence of *The Big Combo*. The back-lighting of heavy smoke and an ominously circling light visible in the background further abstracts the environment into a modern nether world. Below, direct, undiffused lighting of Barbara Stanwyck in *Double Indemnity* creates a hard-edged, mask-like surface beauty. By comparison, "hard-boiled" Fred MacMurray seems soft and vulnerable.

Some Visual Motifs of *Film Noir*

Janey Place & Lowell Peterson (1974)

> A dark street in the early morning hours, splashed with a sudden downpour. Lamps form haloes in the murk. In a walk-up room, filled with the intermittent flashing of a neon sign from across the street, a man is waiting to murder or be murdered... shadow upon shadow upon shadow... every shot in glistening low-key, so that rain always glittered across windows or windscreens like quicksilver, furs shone with a faint halo, faces were barred deeply with those shadows that usually symbolized some imprisonment of body or soul.
>
> Joel Greenberg and Charles Higham.
> *Hollywood in the Forties*

Nearly every attempt to define *film noir* has agreed that visual style is the consistent thread that unites the very diverse films that together comprise this phenomenon. Indeed, no pat political or sociological explanations—"postwar disillusionment," "fear of the bomb," "modern alienation"—can coalesce in a satisfactory way such disparate yet essential *film noir* as *Double Indemnity, Laura, In a Lonely Place, The Big Combo* and *Kiss Me Deadly*. The characteristic *film noir* moods of claustrophobia, paranoia, despair, and nihilism constitute a world view that is expressed not through the films' terse, elliptical dialogue, nor through their confusing, often insoluble plots, but ultimately through their remarkable style.

But how can we discuss style? Without the films before us it is difficult to isolate the elements of the *noir* visual style and examine how they operate. Furthermore, while film critics and students would like to speak of the shots and the images, we often lack a language for communicating these visual ideas. This article is an attempt to employ in a critical context the technical terminology commonly used for fifty years by Hollywood directors and cameramen, in the hope that it might be a good step toward the implementation of such a critical language. The article is not meant to be either exhaustive or exacting. It is merely a discussion— with actual frame enlargements from the films—of some of the visual motifs of the *film noir* style: why they are used, how they work, and what we can call them.

The "Noir" Photographic Style: Antitraditional Lighting and Camera

In order to photograph a character in a simple, basic lighting set-up, three different kinds of light, called by some cinematographers the "key light," "fill light," and "back light," are required. The key light is the primary source of illumination, directed on the character usually from high and to one side of the camera. The key is generally a hard direct light that produces sharply defined shadows. The fill light, placed near the camera, is a soft, diffused or indirect light that "fills in" the shadows created by the key. Finally, the back light is a direct light shining on the actor from behind, which adds interesting highlights and which has the effect of giving him form by differentiating him from the background.

The dominant lighting technique which had evolved by the early Forties is "high-key lighting," in which the ratio of key light to fill light is small. Thus the intensity of the fill is great enough to soften the harsh shadows created by the key. This gives what was considered to be an impression of reality, in which the character's face is attractively modeled, but without exaggerated or unnatural areas of darkness. Noir lighting is "low-key." The ratio of key to fill light is great, creating areas of high contrast and rich, black shadows. Unlike the even illumination of high-key lighting which seeks to display attractively all areas of the frame, the low-key noir style opposes light and dark, hiding faces, rooms, urban landscapes—and, by extension, motivations and true character—in shadow and darkness which carry connotations of the mysterious and the unknown.

The harsh lighting of the low-key noir style was even employed in the photography of the lead actresses, whose close-ups are traditionally diffused (by placing either spun glass or other diffusion over the key light, or glass diffusion or gauze over the camera lens itself) in order to show the actress to her best advantage. Far removed from the feeling of softness and vulnerability created by these diffusion techniques, the noir heroines were shot in tough, unromantic close-ups of direct, undiffused light, which create a hard, statuesque surface beauty that seems more seductive but less attainable, at once alluring and impenetrable.

The common and most traditional placement of lights, then and now, is known as the "three-quarter lighting" set-up, in which the key light is positioned high and about forty-five degrees to one side in front of the actor, and the fill is low and close to the camera. Because the attractive, balanced, harmonious face thus produced would have been antithetical to the depiction of the typical noir moods of paranoia, delirium, and menace, the noir cinematographers placed their key, fill and back light in every conceivable variation to produce the most striking and offbeat schemes of light and dark. The elimination of the fill produces areas of total black. Strange highlights are introduced, often on the faces of the sinister or demented. The key light may be moved behind and to one side of the actor and is then called the "kick light" Or it can be moved below or high above the characters to create unnatural shadows and strange facial expressions. The actors may play a scene totally in shadow, or they may be silhouetted against an illuminated background.

Above all, it is the constant opposition of areas of light and dark that characterizes *film noir* cinematography. Small areas of light seem on the verge of being completely overwhelmed by the darkness that now threatens them from all sides. Thus faces are shot low-key, interior sets are always dark, with foreboding shadow patterns facing the walls, and exteriors are shot "night-for-night." Night scenes previous to *film noir* were most often shot "day-for-night"; that is, the scene is photographed in bright daylight, but filters placed over the camera lens, combined with a restriction of the amount of light entering the camera, create the illusion of night. Night-for-night—night scenes actually shot at night—required that artificial light sources be brought in to illuminate each area of light seen in the frame. The effect produced is one of the highest contrast, the sky rendered jet black, as opposed to the gray sky of day-for-night. Although night-for-night becomes quite a bit more costly and time-consuming to shoot than day-for-night, nearly every *film noir*, even of the cheapest "B" variety, used night-for-night extensively as an integral component of the *noir* look.

Another requirement of *noir* photography was greater "depth of field." It was essential in many close or medium shots that focus be carried into the background so that all objects and characters in the frame be in sharp focus, giving equal weight to each. The world of the film is thus made a closed universe, with each character seen as just another facet of an unheeding environment that will exist unchanged long after his death; and the interaction between man and the forces represented by that *noir* environment is always clearly visible. Because of the characteristics of the camera lens, there are two methods for increasing depth of field: increasing the amount of light entering the lens, or using a lens of wider focal length. Obviously, because of the low light levels involved in the shooting of low-key and night-for-night photography, wide-angle lenses were used in order to obtain the additional depth of field required.

Beside their effect on depth of field, wide-angle lenses have certain distorting characteristics which, as *noir* photography developed, began to be used expressively. As faces or objects come closer to the wide lens they tend to bulge outward. (The first shot of Quinlan in *Touch of Evil* is an extreme example.) This effect is often used in *noir* films on close-ups of porcine gangsters or politicians, or to intensify the look of terror on the hero's face as the forces of fate close in upon him. These lenses also create the converse of the well-known "endistancing effects" of the long, telephoto lenses: wide-angle has the effect of drawing the viewer into the picture, of including him in the world of the film and thus rendering emotional or dramatic events more immediate.

The "Noir" Directorial Style: Antitraditional Mise-en-scène

Complementary to the *noir* photographic style among the better-directed films is a *mise-en-scène* designed to unsettle, jar, and disorient the viewer in correlation with the disorientation felt by the *noir* heroes. In particular, compositional balance within the frame is often disruptive and unnerving. Those traditionally harmonious triangular three-shots and balanced two-shots, which are borrowed from the compositional principles of Renaissance painting, are seldom seen in the better *film noir*. More common are bizarre, off-angle compositions of figures placed irregularly in the frame, which create a world that is never stable or safe, that is always threatening to change drastically and unexpectedly. Claustrophobic framing devices such as doors, windows, stairways, metal bed frames, or simply shadows separate the character from other characters, from his world, or from his own emotions. And objects seem to push their way into the foreground of the frame to assume more power than the people.

Often, objects in the frame take on an assumed importance simply because they act to determine a stable composition. Framed portraits and mirror reflections, beyond their symbolic representations of fragmented ego or idealized image, sometimes assume ominous and foreboding qualities solely because they are so compositionally prominent. It is common for a character to form constant balanced two-shots of himself and his own mirror reflection or shadow. Such compositions, though superficially balanced, begin to lose their stability in the course of the film as the symbolic Doppelgänger either is shown to lack its apparent substantiality or else proves to be a dominant and destructive alter ego. Similarly, those omnipresent framed portraits of women seem to confine the safe, powerless aspects of feminine sexuality with which the *noir* heroes invariably fall in love. But in the course of the film, as the forces mirrored in the painting come closer to more sinister flesh and blood, the compositions that have depended on the rectangular portrait for balance topple into chaos, the silently omniscient framed face becoming a mocking reminder of the threat of the real women.

In the use of "screen size," too, the *noir* directors use unsettling variations on the traditional close-up, medium and long shots. Establishing long shots of a new locale are often withheld, providing the viewer with no means of spatial orientation. Choker close-ups, framing the head or chin, are obtrusive and disturbing. These are sometimes used on the menacing heavy, other times reserved to show the couple-on-the-run whose intimacy is threatened or invaded. The archetypal *noir* shot is probably the extreme high-angle long shot, an oppressive and fatalistic angle that looks down on its helpless victim to make it look like a rat in a maze. *Noir* cutting often opposes such extreme changes in angle and screen size to create jarring juxtapositions, as with the oft-used cut from huge close-up to high-angle long shot of a man being pursued through the dark city streets.

Camera movements are used sparingly in most *noir* films, perhaps because of the great expense necessary to mount an elaborate tracking or boom shot, or perhaps simply because the *noir* directors would rather cut for effect from a close-up to a long shot than bridge that distance smoothly and less immediately by booming. What moving shots that were made seem to have been carefully considered and often tied very directly to the emotions of the characters. Typical is the shot in which the camera tracks backward before a running man, at once involving the audience in the movement and excitement of the chase, recording the terror on the character's face, and looking over his shoulder at the forces, visible or not, which are pursuing him. The cameras of Lang, Ray, and Preminger often make short tracking movements which are hardly perceptible, yet which subtly undermine a stable composition, or which slightly emphasize a character to whom we then give greater notice.

The "dark mirror" of *film noir* creates a visually unstable environment in which no character has a firm moral base from which he can confidently operate. All attempts to find safety or security are undercut by the antitraditional cinematography and *mise-en-scène*. Right and wrong become relative, subject to the same distortions and disruptions created in the lighting and camera work. Moral values, like identities that pass in and out of shadow, are constantly shifting and must be redefined at every turn. And in the most notable examples of *film noir*, as the narratives drift headlong into confusion and irrelevance, each character's precarious relationship to the world, the people who inhabit it, and to himself and his own emotions, becomes a function of visual style.

Below, the "normalcy" of this typical couple in love in *Beyond a Reasonable Doubt* is undercut by their unsettling positions in an unbalanced frame.

The Big Heat: Above left, high-key lighting to convey normalcy, the everyday, Glenn Ford's bourgeois wife. Above right, low-key lighting of a dame who inhabits the "other world." Shadow areas hint at the hidden, the unknown, the sinister.

Below, Bogart finally realizes it is Lupino he loves in *High Sierra*. The low-placed key light creates a stark lighting in which interior feelings of the characters are finally exposed and laid bare.

Below left, hard direct lighting on an unmade-up face creates an unpretty close-up of a bitter and cynical Cathy O'Donnell at the beginning of *They Live by Night*. Below right, the same actress in softer light shot through a heavy diffusion filter over the camera lens. The sense of intimacy is further conveyed through use of choker close-up.

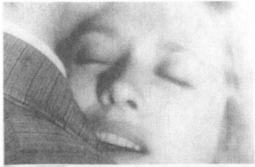

Left, a strange high-light under Bogart's eyes injects a sinister, demented quality into his mock description of his part in the murder in *In a Lonely Place*.

Right, Barbara Stanwyck under the rich, black sky of a night-for-night shot in *Double Indemnity*. Each illuminated area in the shot required that an artificial light source be brought in.

Below, one of the very few traditionally balanced two-shots of these two characters in all of *In a Lonely Place*. Bogart and Grahame experience a rare moment of safety and security. This shot cuts to this upsetting two-shot at right as the policeman who has been trailing the couple walks into the bar. Two characters each in tight close-up convey intimacy being invaded.

Above, *Night and the City:* left, bold, architectural lines carried in sharp focus over the large depth of field of a wide-angle lens minimize Richard Widmark's compositional importance. Right, as the night-club owner makes the decision to "get Harry," this low, wide-angle close-up distorts his already grotesquely fat face. Strong cross-light from the right throws unusual shadows on the left side of his face, carrying connotations of the sinister and evil.

Left, Dana Andrews framed behind a cabinet in *Laura.* The powerful foreground objects seem at once constricting and symbolic of a precarious situation which threatens at any moment to shatter to the floor.

Below, extreme framing devices: left, differences in lighting and screen size, and action played on different planes in depth separate a man and woman in *Night and the City.* Right: lonely characters isolated by framing devices in a composition of constricting vertical and horizontal lines manage to bridge the distance between them with a dramatic diagonal of exchanged glances from *In a Lonely Place.*

Above, a low-angle shot expresses the menace of Grahame's Lesbian masseuse in *In a Lonely Place*.

Top right and right, a short track-in to close two-shot expresses the fear and claustrophobia felt by Grahame in *In a Lonely Place*.

The Big Heat: right, Ford and Gloria Grahame are linked in space by the shadow area on the wall, which creates a bridge between their looks. Below, kick-lighting of the first shot of Lee Marvin immediately establishes him as a heavy threatening to erupt into violence. The restriction of depth of field and the turning of his head towards the camera give his figure power and control of the frame

Above left, a choker (extreme) close-up emphasizes the grotesque face of Howard da Silva in his last scene in *They Live by Night*. Right, an extreme close-up of Bogart's eyes, framed by the isolating darkness of night and the city in the credits of *In a Lonely Place*.

Below, Edmond O'Brien's shadow in *The Killers* suggests an alter ego, a darker self who cohabits that frame's space. This and the frame enlargement at bottom page left are actually "two-shots" of only one character.

Below left, the many mirror reflections of Gloria Grahame in *The Big Heat* suggest her "other side" which during the course of the film is revealed. Right, isolated by labyrinth staircases in an extreme high-angle long shot from *Kiss Me Deadly*.

Above, an ominous portrait, emphasized by its dominant compositional function in making a balanced two-shot, stares out over the proceedings of *Woman in the Window*. The constant mirror reflections of Joan Bennett and the other characters subtly hint at their alter egos, revealed at the end of the film when the protagonist wakes up to discover it was all a dream. Below, two policemen form a dark, vertical mass not counterbalanced by the smaller, lighter horizontal figure of the punk hoodlum upon whom they are about to administer the third degree in *On Dangerous Ground*. The cops' downward looks, the position of their bodies, and the line of the bed frame create a heavy top-left to bottom-right diagonal in a precarious and unbalanced composition.

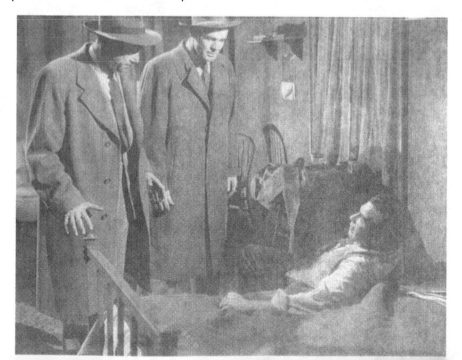

Above: "I'm nobody's friend." Robert Montgomery as Gagin, "the man with no place," speaks with government agent Retz (Art Smith) in *Ride the Pink Horse*.

No Way Out: Existential Motifs in the *Film Noir*

Robert G. Porfirio (1976)

The *film noir*, a Hollywood staple of the 1940s and 1950s, has come into its own as a topic of critical investigation. By now both its foreign and domestic roots (German expressionism, French poetic realism; the gangster film and the hard-boiled novel) have been clearly established. The mordant sensibilities of the "Germanic" emigrés and their penchant for a visual style which emphasised mannered lighting and startling camera angles provided a rich resource for a film industry newly attuned to the commercial possibilities of that hard-boiled fiction so popular in the 1930s. It was a style and sensibility quite compatible with a literature dealing with private eyes and middle-class crime, one bent on taking a tough approach towards American life. Following the success of *Double Indemnity* and *Murder, My Sweet*, both made in 1944, this "Germanic" tradition was quickly assimilated by others and the era of *film noir* was in full bloom. The one major domestic contribution to the style, the post-war semi-documentary, moved the *film noir* out of the "studio" period into new directions. The police documentaries (*T-Men, Street with No Name*), the exposés (*Captive City, The Enforcer*) and the socially oriented thrillers (*Crossfire, The Sound of Fury*) in turn gave way to films which could no longer be placed within the *noir* tradition (*The Line-Up, Murder, Incorporated, On the Waterfront*). It is as if the *film noir* tradition fragmented as its initial energies dissipated along new lines, and all but disappeared in the 1950s when audiences dwindled and Hollywood resorted to new styles, subjects and techniques.

I have refrained for a number of reasons from referring to *film noir* as a genre. To treat it as a genre is certainly tempting, since it simplifies the way in which it can be handled, even though it may never place the *film noir* within a specific semantical locus. Yet we must ground the term in some sort of adequate working definition if it is to warrant serious consideration as an object of either film or cultural history. While it sidesteps the semantical problem, a genetic definition creates a host of new ones. For one thing, the *film noir* cuts across many of the traditional genres: the gangster film (*White Heat*), the Western (*Pursued*), the comedy (*Unfaithfully Yours*); and this means we must create a genre out of pre-existing categories.

Though the classic gangster film preceded the *film noir*, there remain gangster films of this period that are quite clearly *noir* (*The Gangster*, 1947) and others that are clearly not (*Dillinger*, 1945). The same could be said for the suspense thriller (*Strangers on a Train* is, while *I Confess* is not). And this is equally true for the private eye, mystery or crime film—some are and some aren't. As a matter of fact, if one looks at the descriptions of these films in the trade journals of the period or speaks with some of the people involved in their production, one discovers rather quickly that the term *film noir* was then unknown in America and that the closest equivalent was "psychological melodrama (or thriller)." And perhaps this is the appropriate English term, since there is a psychological dimension and at least some aspect of crime (real or imagined) in every *film noir* that I have seen.

In his article, "The Family Tree of Film Noir," Raymond Durgnat perceptively attacks generic definition by demonstrating that *film noir*, unlike other genres, "takes us into the realms of classification by motif and tone." Durgnat then hastily arranges the *film noir* into eleven thematic categories, including over 300 titles as diverse as *King Kong* and *2001: A Space Odyssey*. From the standpoint of critical justification, however, his conception resolves nothing and creates more problems than it answers. Paul Schrader, in his "Notes on *Film Noir*," provides a way out by suggesting that *film noir* be conceived of as a specific period or cycle of films, analogous to the French new wave or Italian neo-realism: "In general, *film noir* refers to those Hollywood films of the 40s and early 50s which portrayed the world of dark, slick city streets, crime and corruption. *Film noir* is an extremely unwieldy period. It harks back to many previous periods..."

It is a period which at most lasted no longer than twenty years: from 1940 (*Stranger on the Third Floor*) roughly to 1960 (*Odds Against Tomorrow*). It is an unwieldy period because it was less self-conscious and articulated than, say, Italian neo-realism and because of the lack of precision with which it has been treated. Its extreme commerciality, particularly in the 1940s before theatre audiences dried up, meant that the *film noir* included large numbers of "B" films, which most scholars have refused to take seriously.

Film Noir is by nature time-bound, and it is this that makes modern "revivals," whether done in period (*Chinatown*) or not (*The Long Goodbye*), something other than what they pretend to be. But to place these films within a specific time period is not enough. Schrader was right in insisting upon both visual style and mood as criteria. Their so-called "expressionistic" style was quite literally a combination of impressionistic (i.e. technical effects) and expressionistic (i.e. mise-en-scene) techniques, which can be traced back to the period of German Expressionism. The infusion of this style into Hollywood film-making was due partly to the talents of the European emigrés and partly to the growth of the classic gangster and horror genres of the 1930s which called for such a style. But the unique development of this style in the film noir was most immediately due to *Citizen Kane*. Welles' film not only invigorated a baroque visual style which was later to characterise the pe-

Left, "The streets were dark with something more than night..." Edward G. Robinson in *Woman in the Window*

Right and below right: Gemanic angles and moods of *film noir*: Laird Cregar in John Brahm's *The Lodger*; Joan Crawford in *Possessed*.

Below, the prison as microcosm: Burt Lancaster in *Brute Force*.

riod, but also provided a new psychological dimension, a morally ambiguous hero, a convoluted time structure and the use of flashback and first person narration— all of which became film noir conventions. It is no surprise that Welles later made some classic films noirs (*The Stranger, Lady from Shanghai, Touch of Evil*) and some near misses (*Journey into Fear, Mr. Arkadin*) and provided a permanent blueprint for what might now be termed RKO noir. (Edward Dmytryk, who made *Farewell, My Lovely*, has reaffirmed the influence of Welles on the RKO "look"; appropriately, both he and Welles have acknowledged a debt to Murnau.)

Visual style rescued many an otherwise pedestrian film from oblivion. But it was not everything; nor was the presence of crime, in some guise, the fundamental defining motif. The 1940s saw the production of many routine thrillers which contained the requisite visual style yet fail as *film noir*. What keeps the *film noir* alive for us today is something more than a spurious nostalgia. It is the underlying mood of pessimism which undercuts any attempted happy endings and prevents the films from being the typical Hollywood escapist fare many were originally intended to be. More than lighting or photography, it is this sensibility which makes the black film black for us.

As Alfred Appel has noted in his book *Nabokov's Dark Cinema*: "What unites the seemingly disparate kinds of *films noirs*, then, is their dark visual style and their black vision of despair, loneliness and dread—a vision that touches an audience most intimately because it assures that their suppressed impulses and fears are shared human responses." This "black vision" is nothing less than an existential attitude towards life, and as Appel has indicated it is what unifies films as diverse as *The Maltese Falcon* (private eye), *Detour* (crime), *The Lodger* (period piece), *Brute Force* (prison film), *Woman in the Window* (psychological melodrama) and *Pursued* (Western).

In attempting to discuss some of the existential motifs in American *film noir*, I do not wish to tie myself too closely to the specific philosophy which evolved through the writings of successive generations of thinkers. Indeed, existentialism as a philosophical movement was largely unknown in America until after World War II, when the French variety was popularised by the writings and personal fame of two of its greatest exponents, Jean-Paul Sartre and Albert Camus. William Barrett, in his excellent book *Irrational Man* (1962), argues that initially existentialism went against the positivist bias of Anglo-American culture: "The American has not yet assimilated psychologically the disappearance of his own geographical frontier, his spiritual horizon is still the limitless play of human possibilities, and as yet he has not lived through the crucial experience of human finitude." If existentialism did gain a foothold in post-war America, it was only after this optimism had been successively challenged by the Depression; the rise of totalitarianism; the fear of Communism; the loss of insular security; and, finally, the tarnishing of the ideal of individual initiative with the growth of the technocratic state. Even French existentialism, so closely tied to the underground Resistance and prison camps, represented an earlier response to many of the same challenges of the integrity of self.

Existentialism is another term which defies exact definition. As a philosophical school of thought it has included both Christian and atheist, conservative and Marxist. For our purposes, it is best to view it as an attitude characteristic of the modern spirit, a powerful and complex cultural movement erupting somewhere on the edges of the Romantic tradition, and therefore a result of some of the same cultural energies which led to surrealism, expressionism and literary naturalism. Existentialism is an outlook which begins with a disoriented individual facing a confused world that he cannot accept. It places its emphasis on man's contingency in a world where there are no transcendental values or moral absolutes, a world devoid of any meaning but the one man himself creates. Its more positive aspect is captured in such key phrases as "freedom," "authenticity," "responsibility" and "the leap into faith (or the absurd)." Its negative side, the side to which its literary exponents are most closely drawn, emphasises life's meaninglessness and man's alienation; its catch-words include "nothingness," "sickness," "loneliness," "dread," "nausea." The special affinity of the *film noir* for this aspect of existentialism is nowhere better evidenced than in a random sampling of some of its most suggestive titles: *Cornered, One Way Street, No Way Out, Caged, The Dark Corner, In a Lonely Place*.

In *The Myth of Sisyphus*, Camus recognised that the confrontation of life's emptiness made suicide a dangerous and tempting escape. To withstand this temptation, Camus and Sartre offered a few alternatives: a stubborn perseverance despite the absurdity of existence; a recognition of the community of men; an obsession with social justice; a commitment to Marxism. In an early *film noir, I Wake Up Screaming* (1941), the ostensible heavy, police Lieutenant Ed Cornell, demonstrates just this sort of perseverance. While interrogating the sister (Betty Grable) of the murdered girl he worshipped from afar, he responds to her question ("What's the use of living without hope?") with the telling reply, "It can be done." Sensitively portrayed by Laird Cregar, Cornell is no lout but a skilled detective, a man of some taste and intelligence. He becomes the ironic victim of the perfidy of a girl unworthy of his love (Carole Landis) and of the unyielding demand for professional perfection placed upon him by the police department. Unlike most of Camus' heroes, Cornell yields to the temptation of suicide, but remains a pathetic figure capable of engaging our sympathies.

It would be untenable to assert that the American *film noir* was directly affected by the writings of the European existentialists, although after the end of the war there were a few films like *Brute Force*, which in its use of a prison as microcosm and in the fascist nature of its major antagonist indicates a familiarity with French existential novels. In any case, such attempts on the part of Hollywood to borrow directly from that European tradition would have been rare indeed, particularly in the 1940s. It is more likely that this existential bias was drawn from a source

Right, detachment: Bogart's Sam Spade sending Brigid (Mary Astor) "over" in *The Maltese Falcon*.

Left, passivity and neurosis: Robert Mitchum and Robert Ryan in *The Racket*.

Left, Hemingway's tough guys: Charles McGraw and William Conrad in *The Killers*.

Below, "Some day fate can put the finger on you...": Tom Neal in *Detour*.

much nearer at hand—the hard-boiled school of fiction without which quite possibly there would have been no *film noir*. Unfortunately, "hard-boiled" is but one more example of a popular term used rather ambiguously. It includes not only the writers of the *Black Mask* school, but also an extremely diverse group of major and minor talents: Hemingway, whom many consider to be the real father of the tradition; the pure "tough" writers like James M. Cain and Horace McCoy; and even the radical proletarian writers like B. Traven, Albert Maltz and Daniel Fuchs.[1] Scant critical attention has been paid to the literary rough guys, who have been forced to join the other "boys in the back room" (as Edmund Wilson once pejoratively termed some of them). Since they worked within narrow genres, set themselves limited goals and wrote fiction geared for a mass market, they lacked the elitist respectability of their famous Jazz Age predecessors. Although a few have recently come into their own, that they were taken seriously at all in the past was largely due to their association with the much brighter light of Hemingway's reputation and to the unique and almost symbiotic relationship which they had with the French existential writers. The very term *film noir* was coined in 1946 by the cinéaste Nino Frank from Marcel Duhamel's famous "Série Noire" book series.

Perhaps André Gide was not being completely candid when he surprised some American dignitaries at a party held during World War II by telling them that Dashiell Hammett was the one contemporary American novelist worthy of serious consideration, because he was the only one who kept his work free of the pollution of moral judgments. In any case, the virtue that Gide attributed to Hammett is present in his fiction, and the American intellectual community is no longer quite so willing to write off the adulation of their counterparts in France for such writers as some sort of foreign aberration.

It is not necessary to go further here in establishing connections between European existentialism and the hard-boiled literary tradition. If, as William Barrett suggests, existentialism is foreign to the generally optimistic and confident outlook of American society, then the vast popularity of the hard-boiled writers of the 1930s went far to "soften" this confidence and prepare audiences for a new sort of pessimistic film which would surface in the 1940s. Keeping in mind the debt to this literary tradition, here then are some of the major existential motifs of the *film noir*.

The Non-heroic Hero

The word "hero" never seems to fit the *noir* protagonist, for his world is devoid of the moral framework necessary to produce the traditional hero. He has been wrenched from familiar moorings, and is a hero only in the modern sense in which that word has been progressively redefined to fit the existential bias of contemporary fiction. For the past fifty years we have groped for some term that would more aptly describe such a protagonist: the Hemingway hero; the anti-hero; the rebel hero; the non-hero.

In one respect the Sam Spade of Huston's *The Maltese Falcon* (1941), as portrayed by Humphrey Bogart, is the least typical *noir* hero since he is the least vulnerable. Unlike Warner Brothers' first two attempts at the novel (1931 and 1936), this third is quite faithful to both the letter and the spirit of the Hammett original. The film's one unfortunate omission is the Flitcraft parable Spade tells Brigid O'Shaughnessy, for this is our only chance to peep into Spade's interior life. And what it reveals is that Spade is by nature an existentialist, with a strong conception of the randomness of existence. Robert Edenbaum sees Spade as representative of Hammett's "daemonic" tough guy: "...He is free of sentiment, of the fear of death, of the temptations of money and sex. He is what Albert Camus calls 'a man without memory,' free of the burden of the past. He is capable of any action, without regard to conventional morality, and thus is apparently as amoral...as his antagonists. His refusal to submit to the trammels which limit ordinary mortals results in a godlike immunity and independence, beyond the power of his enemies...[but] the price he pays for his power is to be cut off behind his own self-imposed masks, in an isolation that no criminal, in a community of crime, has to face."[2]

If the film's conclusion mitigates a little the bleak isolation of Hammett's Spade, it maintains the "daemonic" qualities of his nature through the sinister aspect of Bogart's persona, so apparent in his final confrontation with Brigid (Mary Astor). In Huston's ending, Spade's ability to dismiss the falcon, the one object of "faith" in the story, as "the stuff that dreams are made of" shows him to be more detached than almost any Hemingway hero. This stoic stance would be emulated, but seldom equalled, by many of the actors who dominated the period: by Bogart himself (*Dead Reckoning, Dark Passage*), followed in rapid succession by Alan Ladd (*This Gun for Hire, The Glass Key*) and a veritable army of tough guys—Edmond O'Brien, Robert Mitchum, Robert Ryan, Richard Widmark, Burt Lancaster, Kirk Douglas. By their physical make-up, their vocal qualities and their dress, as well as by the dialogue given them, these actors defined the tough guy regardless of whether they played detective or criminal. They also suggested varying degrees of vulnerability.

Critics have reminded us that the Hemingway hero is a person "to whom something has been done"; that most central to this hero is the loss, and an awareness of it, of all the fixed ties that bind a man to a community. This is an apt description of the *film noir* hero as well, and a real strength of Hollywood's studio system was to cast to type. Vulnerability and a sense of loss were suggested in Humphrey Bogart's lined face and slightly bent posture; in Alan Ladd's short stature and a certain feminine quality about his face; in the passivity and the heavy-lidded eyes of Robert Mitchum; in the thinly veiled hysteria that lay behind many of Richard Widmark's performances; in Robert Ryan's nervous manner. But this vulnerability was perhaps best embodied in the early screen persona of Burt Lancaster, whose powerful physique ironically dominated the cinematic frame. Unlike the expansive and exaggerated characterisations of later years, the Lancaster of the *film noir* kept his energy levels under rigid control, rarely extending himself and then only to withdraw quickly like a hunted animal. Fittingly, his first screen role was in the Robert Siodmak version of *The Killers* (1946) as the Hemingway character Ole Anderson who passively awaits death at the hands of the hired assassins. Throughout the 1940s Lancaster was adept at capturing the pathos of a character victimised by society (*Brute Force; Kiss the Blood Off My Hands*) or by a woman (*The Killers; Sorry, Wrong Number; Criss Cross*).

As the period progressed, *film noir* heroes seemed to become increasingly vulnerable and subject to pressures beyond their control. Bogart's roles moved from the lonely but impervious Sam Spade to the equally lonely but much less stable Dixon Steele of *In a Lonely Place*. The role of the detective shows the same sort of degeneration, and some succumbed to the corrupt world, becoming criminals themselves (Fred MacMurray in *Pushover*). This malaise is best seen in *The Dark Corner* (1946), whose detective Bradford Galt (Mark Stevens) strives to maintain personal integrity and hard-nosed style by mouthing the obligatory tough dialogue ("I'm as clean as a hard-boiled egg"). But it's not really enough, and Galt's angst is reflected in this cry: "I feel all dead inside...I'm backed up in a dark corner and I don't know who's hitting me!" Yet the typical *noir* protagonist wearily goes on living, seldom engaging in the kind of self-pity displayed by Dana Andrews' con man in *Fallen Angel* (1945) or his wayward cop in *Where the Sidewalk Ends* (1950).

The *mise en scène* of the *film noir* reinforced the vulnerability of its heroes. Although the habitat of the 1930s gangster was "the dark, sad city of the imagination," the gangster hero himself was generally well illuminated by a bright key-light, though his surroundings may have fallen off into darkness. Not so in the *film noir*. The hero moved in and out of shadows so dark as at times to obscure him completely; diagonal and horizontal lines "pierced" his body; small, enclosed spaces (a detective's office, a lonely apartment, a hoodlum's hotel bedroom), well modulated with some sort of "bar" motif (prison bars, shadows, bed posts and other furniture), visually echoed his entrapment. Small wonder that he found it hard to maintain any degree of rational control.

Alienation and Loneliness

The concept of alienation is crucial to most existentialists from Kierkegaard to Sartre. For them, man stands alone, alienated from any social or intellectual order, and is therefore totally self-dependent. We have seen how this alienation "works" for the private detective. By keeping emotional involvement to a minimum, the detective gains a degree of power over others but pays the price in terms of loneliness.

To a large degree, every *noir* hero is an alienated man. Even members of the police for or F.B.I. in the semi-documentary films are cut off from the camaraderie of their colleagues and forced to work undercover. The *noir* hero is most often "a stranger in a hostile world." In *Ride the Pink Horse*, the disillusioned veteran Gagin (Robert Montgomery) is referred to as "the man with no place," and he tells a local villager: "I'm nobody's friend." Even ostensibly happily married men (Edward G. Robinson in *Woman in the Window*, Dick Powell in *Pitfall*) become alienated from the comforts of home, usually for the sake of a beautiful woman. The homelessness of such characters as Harry Fabian (Richard Widmark) of *Night and the City* or Ole Anderson of *The Killers*, like that of an inhabitant of one of Robert Frost's bleakest winter landscapes, takes on almost cosmic dimensions. This estrangement is recapitulated in the *mise en scène*: bare rooms, dimly lit bars, dark, rain-soaked streets. In the shocking last sequence of *Scarlet Street*, the utter isolation of Chris Cross (Robinson) is underscored by means of an optical trick— all the people in the crowded street disappear from view, and we realise that for him they do not exist.

Sometimes the estrangement of the hero moves to even darker rhythms. Shubunka (Barry Sullivan), the title character of *The Gangster*, is reminiscent of Dostoevsky's underground man in his bitterness and the contempt he holds for his fellow men. In the prologue he tells the audience: "I knew everything I did was low and rotten. What did I care what people thought of me. I despised them." In the course of the film we find he despises himself almost as much; and at the end, betrayed by the one person he loved (Belita), he allows the syndicate figure who has wrested control of his rackets from him to shoot him down in the rain-soaked street. But before he dies, Shubunka delivers one of the most vitriolic speeches in the annals of *film noir*: "My sins are that I wasn't tough enough. I should have trusted no one; never loved a girl. I should have smashed [the others] first. That's the way the world is."

Even more misanthropic is Roy Martin (Richard Basehart), the elusive killer of *He Walked By Night*. A master of technology which rivals the police department's, Martin remains little more than a cipher and his motives for becoming a thief and a killer are unclear. Basehart's laconic performance contributed to this ambiguity (as, perhaps, do deficiencies of script and budget). Living alone in a darkened room in a typical Hollywood court, his only companion a small dog, he is literally the underground man, using the sewers as a means of travel and escape. Intelligent men like Shubunka and Martin are no mere victims of a slum environment; their criminality is rather the result of a conscious choice made sensible by the world they inhabit. For them, as for Sartre's characters in *No Exit*, "Hell is other people."

The major female protagonists of the *film noir* were no more socially inclined than the men. The "femme noire" was usually also a *femme fatale*, and a host of domineering women, castrating bitches, unfaithful wives and black widows seemed to personify the worst of male sexual fantasies. They were played with an aura of unreality by such actresses as Ava Gardner, Rita Hayworth or Gene Tierney, but perhaps most typically by Barbara Stanwyck and Claire Trevor. Even when the heroine was sweet and good (Ida Lupino in *On Dangerous Ground*, Joan Bennett in *The Reckless Moment*), she was for the most part a monad, unwilling or unable to avail herself of the benefits of society.

Existential Choice

The precipitous slide of existentialism toward nihilism is only halted by its heavy emphasis on man's freedom. In exchange for this benefit, the individual must be willing to cast aside the weight of outmoded beliefs in a tough recognition of the meaninglessness of existence. He must choose, in other words, between "being and nothingness," between the "authentic" and "inauthentic" life. The inauthentic life is the unquestioned one which derives its rationale from a facile acceptance of those values external to the self. To live authentically, one must reject these assurances and therein discover the ability to create one's own values; in so doing each individual assumes responsibility for his life through the act of choosing between two alternatives. And since man is his own arbiter, he literally creates good and evil.

For the most viable of the *noir* heroes this element of choice is readily apparent. The private eye exercises this choice in his willingness to face death,

Below: "Hell is other people..." James Mason in Max Ophuls' *The Reckless Moment*, a film in which *mise en scène* characteristically creates environment.

prompted only by a sense of duty towards rather dubious clients and a somewhat battered concept of integrity and professionalism. But what of the innocent victims, the fugitives from the law, and the criminals who often function as central protagonists? Existential freedom for them is much less apparent. Yet even the most victimised among them (like Edmond O'Brien in D.O.A. or Tom Neal in Detour) have some opportune moments to make choices which will affect their lives. With respect to the fugitives (John Dall and Peggy Cummins in Gun Crazy) and middle-class criminals (MacMurray in Double Indemnity), their choices appear more mundane than metaphysical and their acts less clearly rebellious against established conventions. Yet all are aware of these conventions, and their decision to disregard them indicates their willingness to live lives untrammelled by moral norms. They exist in a fluid world whose freedom is rather concretely embodied in sex, money, power and the promise of adventure. Thus, one may be motivated by the exhilaration of living dangerously (Gun Crazy), another by a desire to "beat the system" (Double Indemnity), others by a desire to break out of pedestrian daily routine and boredom (Robinson in Woman in the Window, Dick Powell in Pitfall, Van Heflin in The Prowler). Like Spade's Flitcraft, they can either fall back into the security of their former roles or make the leap into the absurd, take the gamble in which the stakes are their very lives.

Man Under Sentence of Death

Although many existentialists affirm that every act and attitude of man must be considered a choice, the existential attitude itself is not so much chosen as arrived at. Perhaps this is why the heroes of existential fiction are so perennially faced with the threat of imminent death; certainly such a threat forces the individual to re-examine his life. "The fable of the man under the sentence of death, writing to us from his prison cell or from the cell of his isolated self, is one of the great literary traditions." In a perceptive essay in Tough Guy Writers of the 30s, Joyce Carol Oates goes on to demonstrate the relevance of this undeniably existential situation to the fiction of James M. Cain, but its relevance to the film noir is equally apparent. Instead of writing his story, the hero tells it to us directly, and the combined techniques of first person narration and flashback enhance the aura of doom. It is almost as if the narrator takes a perverse pleasure in relating the events leading up to his current crisis, his romanticisation of it heightened by his particular surroundings; a wounded man dictating in a darkened office (Double Indemnity); an ex-private detective in a dimly lit car telling his fiancée about his sordid past (Robert Mitchum in Out of the Past); a prisoner in a cell about to be executed (John Garfield in The Postman Always Rings Twice); an accountant dying from the irreversible effects of an exotic poison, trying to explain his "murder" and the vengeance he has exacted for it to a police captain (Edmond O'Brien in D.O.A.). One hero, Joe Gillis (William Holden) of Sunset Boulevard, is even able to look back upon a life that has been completed, like a character out of Sartre's *No Exit*, beginning his story as a corpse floating face-downwards in a swimming pool.

Like the Hemingway hero, most *film noir* protagonists fear death but are not themselves afraid to die; indeed a good deal of what dignity they possess is derived from the way they react to the threat of death. That the way one dies is important is seen in Philip Marlowe's special admiration for Harry Jones (Elisha Cook, Jr.), the frightened little crook who takes the poison offered him with grim laughter rather than betray his girl friend (*The Big Sleep*). It is seen in the manner in which Cody Jarrett (James Cagney) in *White Heat* spits out: "I made it, Ma. Top of the world!" just before he ignites the gasoline tank on which he is perched. It is seen in the way the Swede spends those last lonely moments in his hotel room after his refusal to run (*The Killers*). The boxer in *Body and Soul* (John Garfield) puts it best when he tells the racketeer he has just crossed: "So what are you going to do kill me? Everybody dies."

Meaninglessness, Purposelessness, the Absurd

The meaninglessness of man's existence flows naturally from existentialism's emphasis on individual consciousness and its key denial of any sort of cosmic design or moral purpose. For Camus it involved a recognition of the "benign indifference" of the world, and ultimately a reclamation of a measure of dignity through the sheer persistence of living on despite life's absurdity. This sense of meaninglessness is also present in *film noir*, but there it is not the result of any sort of discursive reasoning. Rather it is an attitude which is worked out through *mise en scène* and plotting. The characters confined to the hermetic world of the films move to a scenario whose driving force is not the result of the inexorable workings of tragic fate or powerful natural forces, but of a kind of pure, Heraclitean flux. Look at the plot of almost any *film noir* and you become aware of the significant role played by blind chance: a car parked on a manhole cover prevents the protagonist's escape and he is shot down by police in the sewers (*He Walked By Night*); an accountant notarises a bill of sale and is poisoned for this innocent act (*D.O.A.*); a feckless youth is hypnotised into becoming the instrument of a murderer's devious plans simply because he accepted a cough drop in a crowded elevator (*Fear in the Night*, 1947; also *Nightmare*, 1956); a spinsterish psychology professor agrees to have dinner with one of her students and ends up killing him (*The Accused*). Such a list could go on endlessly, but these examples should indicate that such randomness is central to the *noir* world. The hero of *Detour* (Tom Neal) tells us: "Some day fate, or some mysterious force, can put the finger on you or me for no reason at all."

Chaos, Violence, Paranoia

The pre-existential world of the classical detective was ordered and meaningful; social aberrations were temporary and quickly righted through the detective's superior powers of deductive reasoning. A product of a rather smug Western society, such a world reflected a Victorian sense of order and a belief in the supremacy of science. The hard-boiled writers replaced this with a corrupt, chaotic world where the detective's greatest asset was the sheer ability to survive with a shred of dignity. Raymond Chandler described this world as a "wet emptiness" whose "streets were dark with something more than night." For most existentialists, the real world was equally inchoate and senseless. Sartre himself found the physical world, the world of things-in-themselves,[3] slightly disgusting and he associated it with images of softness, stickiness, viscosity, flabbiness. When, for example, Roquentin discovers existence in the experience of disgust in *Nausea*, it is a disgust engendered by the excessiveness of the physical world, represented by a chestnut tree with thick, tangled roots. For Sartre this world was disgusting precisely because it was too rich, too soft, too effusive; behind it lay the Jungian archetype of nature, the fertile female.

The *film noir* best expressed this effusiveness visually through a variety of techniques, the most important of which is the use of deep focus or depth-staging (here, perhaps, the primary influence of Orson Welles). As André Bazin pointed out, the use of this technique (as opposed to the shallow focus and "invisible" editing of Hollywood films of the 1930s) permitted the cinema more nearly to approximate the "real" world by allowing the spectator to pick and choose from a wealth of stimuli. Deep focus was an important element of the *noir* visual style until changing conditions and production techniques in the 1950s brought the *film noir* period to a close. In conjunction with chiaroscuro and other expressionistic touches, deep focus helped to create a cinematic world which in its own way embodied those very qualities—decadence, corpulence, viscosity—that Sartre found so disgusting in the physical world. It was a cinematic world that was dark, oppressive, cluttered and corrupt; characterised by wet city streets, dingy apartments and over-furnished mansions, but above all by an atmosphere thick with the potential for violence. In *T-Men*, for example, an undercover agent (Dennis O'Keefe) shares a nondescript hotel room with a couple of thugs, their virtual prisoner. In one scene, deep focus allows us to keep in view the threatening, brutal figure of Moxy (Charles McGraw) in the background shaving, while the agent is in another room in the extreme foreground, trying to read unobserved a note warning him to flee for his life. In this one sequence, the whole unstable and menacing world of the *film noir* is brilliantly caught.

Camus said that "at any street corner the absurd may strike a man in the face." Given the special ambience of *film noir*, the absurd often takes the form of an undercurrent of violence which could literally strike a man at any moment: a trench-

Left, "Everybody dies...": Burt Lancaster in *The Killers*.

Right, Edward G. Robinson in Scarlet Street: visual "echoes of entrapment" in the shadows and bars of the setting

Right, a Man under Sentence of Death: Henry Fonda as the self-imprisoned killer in *The Long Night*

Below, Mark Stevens in *The Dark Corner*: "...I'm backed up in a dark corner and I don't know who's hitting me."

coated figure beneath a street lamp; a car parked on a dark side street; a shadow hiding behind a curtain. The atmosphere is one in which the familiar is fraught with danger and the existential tonalities of "fear" and "trembling" are not out of place; even less that sense of "dread" which is taken to mean a pervasive fear of something hauntingly indeterminate. And just as existentialism itself was partly a response to a war-torn Europe, so too was the disquietude of post-war America (the Communist threat, the Bomb) reflected in the films' fear-ridden atmosphere. Finally, if the Jungian archetype of the female lurks behind Sartre's conception of the natural world, she is equally present in the image of the city conveyed in these films—the city, that is, which Jung himself characterised as a "harlot." For the *film noir* protagonist the city is both mother and whore, and the stylised location photography of such semi-documentaries as *Cry of the City* or *The Naked City* adeptly captures its essential corruption and oppressiveness.

Sanctuary, Ritual and Order

Set down in a violent and incoherent world, the *film noir* hero tries to deal with it in the best way he can, attempting to create some order out of chaos, to make some sense of his world. For the detective, of course, this goes with the territory, but it is attempted with an equal sense of urgency by the amnesiac (*Somewhere in the Night*), the falsely accused (*The Blue Dahlia*), the innocent victim (*D.O.A.*), or the loyal wife or girl friend (*Woman on the Run, Phantom Lady*). Given the nature of the *noir* world, the attempt is seldom totally successful, and convoluted time structures, flashbacks and plots that emphasise action over rational development do nothing to help.

The Hemingway hero may withdraw to the sanctuary of the country or a café; or he may lean heavily on the ritualistic aspects of sport or art as a way of assuaging his pain and finding some order in his life. The *noir* hero does likewise, but he has far fewer resources to work with. There is no "country" left,[4] only the modern wasteland of such cities as New York, San Francisco and Los Angeles. And art is no longer redemptive: it is a measure of the decadence and avariciousness of the rich (*Laura, The Dark Corner*), or an affectation of refinement on the part of syndicate chiefs (*The Chase, The Big Heat*) or the criminally insane (*The Unsuspected, Crack Up*). In any case, its healing powers are lost to artist (*Phantom Lady, The Two Mrs. Carrolls*) and detective (*The Big Sleep, Kiss Me Deadly*) alike. There are still a few restorative rituals remaining to the *film noir* hero, in particular the private eye: sometimes they are little things like rolling a cigarette (Spade) or pouring and downing a drink (Marlowe); sometimes bigger, like taking a beating or facing death. And in the hands of actors endowed with a special grace (a Humphrey Bogart or Dick Powell), such ceremonies as smoking or drinking take on sacramental overtones.

The only sanctuary left for the hero is his Spartan office or apartment room, and he goes back there for spiritual renewal just as surely as Nick Adams goes back to the country. This is why Sam Spade almost loses control when the police confront him in his own living quarters. When doomed men like Walter Neff in *Double Indemnity* (Fred MacMurray) or Al Roberts in *Detour* (Tom Neal) withdraw to a darkened office or a small diner, they are reminiscent of the older waiter in Hemingway's "A Clean, Well-lighted Place." They can use the quiet and solitude to try to order their lives (and note that Roberts does not want to talk or listen to the juke box); they are like artists trying to carve an aesthetic order out of the diffuse materials of existence. And what they have created is quite temporary, no more than a "momentary stay against confusion."

Given a rather broad range of heroes and situations in the *film noir*, it is of course always dangerous to generalise. I have tried in this article to avoid the facile generalisation, to take note of exceptions where they exist, and above all to remain faithful to the essence of the *film noir*. The period of the *film noir* was an extremely important one in American film history and had a profound effect on the later evolution of American cinema. It is of course impossible to do it justice in an article of this length. My rather narrow intention here has been to indicate the necessity of a critical reappraisal, following a lead established some years ago by Paul Schrader in the hope of opening up an approach to the subject which would free us of some of the semantical entanglements of the past.

Notes

1. Together with the "tough" writers, like Hammett, Chandler, McCoy and Cain, "proletarian" authors Fuchs, Bezzerides, Maltz and others were part of the literary exodus to Hollywood in the 1930s and 1940s. Many became friends or part of a radical colony there, but by and large the *films noirs* they were associated with exhibit more of an existential than a radical outlook (*Thieves' Highway* is a good example); a result no doubt of the political climate in America at the time.

2. "The Poetics of the Private Eyes," in *Tough Guy Writers of the Thirties*, edited by David Madden. (Carbondale, Illinois, 1968).

3. Sartre's particular dualistic system divides the world into two spheres: the objective, which exists quite apart from our minds, he termed "Being-in-itself"; the subjective, which is co-extensive with the realm of consciousness, he termed "Being-for-itself." It is the first that he found slightly repellent.

4. There are a few instances in which *films noirs* were not set in a city. But even here the setting does not prove to be any more redemptive: it is a swamp in *Gun Crazy*, a French province seething with repressed passions in *So Dark the Night*, unregenerate or oppressive Mexican towns in *Ride the Pink Horse* and *Touch of Evil*.

Above, a proletarian fatal woman Anna (Yvonne de Carlo) watches Steve Thompson (Burt Lancaster) spread mayonnaise on his sandwich in Siodmak's *Criss Cross* (1946).

Film Noir: A Modest Proposal

James Damico (1978)

Lamentably, the literature on *film noir*[1] is notable only for its skimpiness, but for an absence of any truly rigorous or meaningful examination of its subject. Beyond sketchy and perfunctory assumptions concerning possible political and social causes, the bulk of the literature is taken up with a generally undisciplined cataloguing of what individual authors consider the thematic and stylistic consistencies of those films they term FN.

More disconcerting than the meagerness of volume, to be sure, is the lack of depth. There is as yet no book-length study of FN in English and, as far as I know, only in French.[2] The commentary that does exist, moreover, is composed primarily of oblique analyses and passing acknowledgments of FN in survey works which take either a film historical or popular socio-psycho-mythological point of view; cursory and often euphemistic references to FN in overviews of the work of individual directors; and lastly, writings which, largely through emphasis on director, actor, screenwriter or source author, intend in some fashion to deal with the classification itself.

Books written for a broad public, such as Michael Wood's *America at the Movies*[3] and Barbara Deming's *Running Away From Myself*,[4] whose purpose is to examine film as a purveyor of popular myth and thus to suggest the cinema's social and psychological effect on and reflection of its audience, contain some pertinent notions about the social content of films in general and some perceptive insights into FN in particular—especially as to the cumulative meaning and effect of continuities of characters and situations from film to film. But they hardly take note of FN as a distinct entity and are obviously less interested in defining what distinguishes FN from other categories of film than in demonstrating how all films are alike.

Similarly, the popular film histories that recognize FN tend to accept extracinematic influences upon it as a given, or to treat the world as if it were merely a very large movie theater, as, for instance, Charles Higham and Joel Greenberg do in their sole attempt to situate FN in any context broader than other Hollywood films:

> A genre deeply rooted in the nineteenth century's vein of grim romanticism, developed through U.F.A. and the murky, fog-filled atmosphere of pre-war French movies, flowered in Hollywood as the great German or Austrian expatriates—Lang, Siodmak, Preminger,

Wilder—arrived there and were allowed more and more freedom to unleash their fantasies on the captive audience.[5]

This is dubious history from many perspectives, but in principle it is indicative of a prevalent attitude towards the formation of FN evident in presumably more sophisticated works such as Colin McArthur's generic study of the gangster film, *Underworld USA,*[6] and Lawrence Alloway's *Violent America*[7] (which is primarily concerned with proposing American films as a formulaic and iconographic art). Both have intelligent and useful things to say about their central subjects and about elements of FN, Alloway on the violence that is integral to the category and McArthur on its recurrent structures. But Alloway, for example, is willing to assert, without the slightest attempt at demonstration, that "the vernacular existentialism that thrived in violent movies of the later 40s deriv[ed] from the Resistance of Jean-Paul Sartre..." (p. 25); while McArthur, equally unhindered by documentation, rehearses what has become a litany as the generating causes of FN:

> ...the great crash on Wall Street in 1929, the Depression and the rise of Fascism in Europe can be seen to have influenced the American cinema in general in its production...However, this obvious interest in the workings of society was accompanied, indeed stimulated, by a general mood of fear and insecurity, by the feeling that the formerly rigid laws of politics and economics were dissolving and that the future involved only uncertainty. It seems reasonable to suggest the loneliness and angst and the lack of clarity about the characters' motives in the thriller. It seems reasonable, too, to suggest that its continuance into the post-war period was stimulated by the uncertainty of the Cold War, that its misogyny was connected with the heightened desirability and concomitant suspicion of women back home experienced by men at war, and its obvious cruelty was related to the mood of a society to whom the horrors of Auschwitz and Hiroshima and other atrocities of the Second World War had just been revealed (pp. 66-67).

Reasonable as suggestions, perhaps, but, like most of his colleagues in the field, the author goes on to adopt these bare contentions innocent of any proofs as the basis of a comprehensive understanding of the root causes of what amounted to a significant social phenomenon. This is either to thumb one's nose at rational investigation or to risk making the most egregious errors of misapprehension.

The same order of breezy assumption seems to have afflicted FN criticism from its beginnings. In an apparent effort to provide historical, political and economic background on Hollywood film production, Borde and Chaumeton, who otherwise concentrate on impressionistic and often provocative readings of films and film groupings over a considerable time span, are given to periodic, casual declarations of such sweeping character as, in the case of films like *This Gun for Hire* and *Murder, My Sweet,* "for reasons that seem financial, cinema was under total submission to literature" (p. 19); or that because "from 1939 on, the names of many Hollywood producers were found on the subscription list of *The Psychoanalytical Review*," the "cinema was not slow to profit from it" and to produce a cycle of films in which psychoanalysis figured in some manner (pp. 21-22). Though the subscription information is documented and thus at least constitutes solid data, it is hardly substantial enough to support the weight of the conclusion with which Borde and Chaumeton burden it.

The worst offender in this regard is Raymond Durgnat in his unfortunately influential article, "Paint It Black: The Family Tree of the *Film Noir*."[8] Certainly breezy and totally free of substantiation are such shot-from-the-lip, mentally convoluted Durgnatisms as: "Late '40s Hollywood is blacker than '30s precisely because its audience, being more secure, no longer needed cheering up" (p. 49); "American weakness in [film] social realism stems from post-puritan optimistic individualism" (p. 50); and Senator Joseph "McCarthy's impact forced *film noir* themes to retreat to the Western" (p. 52). Durgnat's most baneful influence, however, has operated not in this area, but with regard to a process of aesthetic analysis which seems to me to require a higher priority in the examination of FN than even the critical matter of the category's socio-historical contexts.

Nearly all of the literature on FN, and especially that which addresses the classification directly, though often explicitly remarking on the inherent dangers, ignores and inevitable risks foundering on the Scylla and Charybdis of the dual question fundamental to a complete understanding of the category: whether FN can be considered a genre, and if not, on precisely what basis does its cohesiveness as a category rest. Among those authors who openly confront the question, it is all likelihood FN cannot be a genre (one of the few but frequently advanced arguments being that FN operates transgenerically, it therefore cannot itself constitute a genre; not unassailable logic, which by analogy would preclude an orange from remaining an orange because it is also part of a tangerine). In any event, these authors continue, though obviously of some eventual significance, the question may conveniently be set aside to take up whatever particular interests prompted them to their own investigation of FN.

Yet it would seem to be self-evident that the foremost task of any inquiry into the category ought to be the identification of exactly what it is that causes films intuitively classed as FN to appear to share affinities; that the imperatives which attend the examination of an aesthetic artifact require first of all the meticulous description of the object itself—much as they do with regard to archaeological artifacts—in order to delineate similarities and congruities, as well as indications of dissimilarities, between it and other objects of its class; so that by this process, through the correlation of the results of the examination with available knowledge of the society involved, one is enabled to make reasonable assumptions concerning the relationship of such objects to the society of which they are an expression.[9]

But, perhaps because it is a difficult and laborious task to disentangle the many social and artistic influences and, in particular, the knot of crossbred film genre and types present in FN, the literature on the category for the most part hedges or blinks this primary question or, worse, claims to answer it with unrefined generalities and self-assuming definitions, such as those quoted above, either unburdened by any system of procedure, or employing, as Durgnat does with such assured abandon, a completely spurious methodology.

A simple, straightforward methodology, however, was proposed by Borde and Chaumeton early in the discussion of FN:

> Thus, the method [of examining FN] asserts itself: from as technical, as objective a basis as possible, to study the most prevalent characteristics of the films that criticism has termed *noir*; then to compare their qualities, to search for a common denominator and to define the unique affective attitude that the works of the cycle tend to bring into play (p. 5).

Even if one has basic objections to this schema (and its last element is clearly a problem), one must recognize its viability as a first step. Yet it remains a method unapplied to FN in any systematic way. Unhappily and precedentially, the first not to apply it were Borde and Chaumeton themselves.

Though their chapter headings imply a developmental, inductive approach ("Towards a Definition of the *Film Noir*," "Sources of the *Film Noir*," "The War Years and the Formulation of a Style (1941-45)," "The Great Era [1946-48]," etc.), what the authors do in fact is to begin by simply deducing recurrent thematic elements in FN (crime, psychological emphasis, violence, oneirism), which are general enough to encompass large blocs of films and which of course tend to be inclusive rather than exclusive; and then having established an entirely open structure, they proceed to a recitation of impressions of various films (some of which, as I have indicated, are most provocative), weighting their views along the way with pseudo-scientific data, such as I have quoted. Beyond this, they make some important distinctions between FN and those films which they find to be merely influenced by the classification, especially singling out police and detective "documentaries" and period or Gothic thrillers. But they add another category, "the psychological crime film,"[10] a vague, catch-all grouping, and in stressing its alleged distinctions from FN only succeed in confusing and blurring distinctions already made.

As adapted and supercharged by Durgnat (whose article draws directly upon Borde and Chaumeton), these difficulties of unrigorous, deductive methodology and amorphous categorization are employed to construct a Babeling Tower of arbitrary, inapposite and ill-defined FN classifications, whose main divisions—"Blacks and Reds" and "Hostages to Fortune," for example—are indistinguishable in order and precision from such subdivisions as "The Sombre Cross-Section," and which are composed of literally hundreds of supposed FN titles, from *Easy Street* and *King Kong* to *Whatever Happened to Baby Jane?* and *2001*. Clearly this is categorrhea, and though probably the result of Durgnat being the first to bring the topic before a significant English audience, the scope and persistence of his impact on subsequent criticism are in the end incomprehensible. (As recently as December, 1974, *Film Comment* arranged most, but not all, of Durgnat's nominated divisions, subdivisions and film titles into a two-page "chart," which understandably rather than abetting its systemization, only exposed its absence.) Yet, whatever the cause and despite its manifest failings, the precedent approach established by Durgnat out of Borde and Chaumeton has been incontestably pervasive.[11]

In consequence, what is revealed most conspicuously by a survey of the literature of FN is the urgent need at this point for a complete restructuring of critical approach and methodology; in effect, a new attack on the subject which would be specific rather than general, inductive rather than deductive, and investigatory rather than conclusive; in short, an examination of FN which is interested in working from the objects of study outward rather than in imposing assumptions upon those which suit such assumptions.

II

It does little to deny the need for an inductive methodology to accept from the outset that FN obviously constituted a particular artistic response to a particular set of social, historical and cultural conditions in a wartime and postwar America undergoing profound social and psychological changes. To understand that, after all, is to do no more than acknowledge the phenomenon.

But it remains a matter for individual, detailed demonstration as to what degree and effect the conditions that contributed to FN may or may not have included popular and personal reactions to the cumulative tensions of the Depression, the rise of fascism and the coming of war; the problems attending the end of the war, including the presumed general post-conflict letdown following the nation's psychological sacrifices in an apocalyptic event which in reality seemed to have changed little; indications of imminent additional wars; the returning veterans' various difficulties in readjusting to civilian life; the burgeoning availability of consumer goods after a period of relative austerity; and other possible generating causes and associated phenomena, including some not usually suggested in the literature on FN, such as the lack of efficacious religious faith or a societal system of agreed-upon ethical and philosophical values to which the population could repair in a time of extensive psychological stress, and the broad shift in the society from an objective to a subjective point of view—that is, from at least a significant concern with group reactions to universal conditions such as economic depression and war, to a growing focus on entirely individual responses to social stimuli.

The important point I wish to extract from this observation, however, is the manifest historical nature of the formation of FN, a point which not only Durgnat, with his all-inclusive approach, has blurred or missed. Though it is my intuition that FN is not a category which can enlarged to include an appreciable number of films before 1940 or after 1955, it again seems to be evident FN must be investigated in its original context—this historical period roughly bounded by the dates just given—and defined within that context as to its constituent elements before any assertions may be made about its development as a film category with no significant time limitations.

This matter is directly related to what has been referred to as the fundamental question to be confronted in the study of FN: whether or not it constitutes a genre and, if not, of what does its cohesiveness as a category consist. Robert G. Porfirio has suggested that Paul Schrader's view of FN as a "specific period or cycle of films" offers "a way out" of the problem of genre (p. 213), his idea apparently being that a genre cannot be, as Porfirio puts it, "time-bound." Stanley J. Solomon not only subscribes to this idea, but claims it as a major reason he undertook to write a study of film genres admitting only those forms which span the full history of cinema.[12] Yet this concept ignores simple aesthetic record and traditional theory. Taking the drama as an example, one can point to countless time-limited genres, from those of longer duration, such Greek tragedy and English miracle and morality plays, to the relatively short-lived Jacobean tragedy, Restoration comedy and French *drame à these*, to name just a few. Additionally, developments within the last century, as Rene Wellek and Austin Warren observe in their *Theory of Literature*, have increased the number and curtailed the life span of genres:

> With the vast widening of the audience in the nineteenth century, there are more genres...they are shorter-lived or pass through more rapid transitions. "Genre" in the nineteenth century and in our own time suffers from the same difficulty as "period"; we are conscious of the quick changes in literary fashion—a new literary generation every ten years, rather than fifty....[13]

Quite clearly, a genre may be bound by time, and rather narrowly at that.

Long considered a fixed and unassailable concept, genre has during the past 25 years come under such intense scrutiny and reevaluation that its very definability has been called into question. Wellek and Warren review at length the inherent difficulties in establishing standards for the recognition of a genre and for distinguishing it from nominal subgenres (pp. 222-27); while Northrop Frye speaks for the modern understanding when he say that "the theory of genres [is] an undeveloped subject in criticism."[14] Yet like Wellek and Warren before him, he proceeds to sketch out how one phase of the theory ought ideally to operate (to underline my ensuing point, I have substituted in brackets cinematic terms for the literary ones, "poem," "literary" and "literature"):

> In the first place, [the film] is unique, a techne or artifact, with its own peculiar structure of imagery, to be examined by itself without immediate reference to other things like it...In the second place, the [film] is one of a class of forms...With this ideal of external relations of a [film] with other [films], two considerations...become important: convention and genre.
>
> The study of genres is based on analogies in form...and has to be founded on the study of convention. The criticism which can deal with such matters will have to be based on that aspect of symbolism

> which relates [films] to one another, and it will choose, as its main
> field of operations, the symbols that link [films] together (pp. 95-96).

He goes on to explain that "symbol" as he uses it means a unit of communication,

> to which I give the name archetype: that is, a typical or recurring
> image. I mean by archetype a symbol which connects one [film] with
> another and thereby helps to unify and integrate our [cinematic]
> experience. And as the archetype is the communicable symbol,
> archetypal criticism is primarily concerned with [cinema] as a social
> fact and as a mode of communication. By the study of conventions
> and genres, it attempts to fit [films] into the body of [cinema] as a
> whole (p. 99).

In effect, this outline drawn from Frye, amended by the incorporation of word substitutions, comprises an elaboration of Borde's and Chaumeton's schema which I have suggested might form the basis of a reasonable methodology for the study of FN. With appropriate world replacements, the following statement from Wellek and Warren also echoes this schema:

> Modern genre theory...is interested...in finding the common
> denominator of a kind, its shared literary devices and literary
> purpose. (p. 225).

It is of course my intention by these correlations to postulate that a careful consideration of FN as a genre, modeled on a structure similar to Frye's which all but coincides with the inductive methodology previously set forth, would constitute not merely the most logical, but also the most expeditious and effective means of investigating FN at this time.

Though this directly opposes conventional wisdom in the area of FN scholarship, the objections raised in the literature to such a consideration have for the most part been based on an incomplete understanding of genre (e.g., Porfirio's misapprehension of its temporal limitations). As noted, one frequently cited impediment to FN being accepted as a genre is its transgeneric function; that is, its reputed participation in such amalgams as FN westerns, FN soap operas and FN gangster films. These dual forms may assuredly exist—we have Shakespeare's testimony that such mixing of genres is no modern development ("pastoral-comical, historical-pastoral, tragical-historical, tragical-comical-historical-pastoral"[15]), and we have present-day forms such as tragi-comedies, comedy-horror films and satire-soap operas (as in *Mary Hartman*). All of these hybrids, ancient and recent, blend two or more genres with varying degrees of artistic success. But what is patent, and germane to the issue here, is that none of them in doing so automatically disqualifies one of its elements from consideration as a separate authentic genre.

Once having accepted that a genre approach to FN has theoretical and practical underpinnings, the specifics of proceeding present some difficulties; but Wellek and Warren offer a principle that is useful:

> Genre should be conceived, we think, as a group of...works based,
> theoretically, upon both outer form (specific meter or structure) and
> also upon inner form (attitude, tone, purpose—more crudely, subject
> and audience) (p. 221).

The authors later define "structure" as "e.g., a special sort of plot organization" (p. 223). And then adjudging that the Gothic novel qualifies as a genre, they provide an analysis of it which has direct application to the question under consideration:

> ...there is not only a limited and continuous subject matter of
> thematics but there is a stock of devices (descriptive-accessory and
> narrative, e. g. ruined castles, Roman Catholic horrors, mysterious
> portraits, secret passageways reached through sliding panels,
> abductions, immurements, pursuits through lonely forests); there is,
> still further, a Knutswollen, an aesthetic intent, an intent to give the
> reader a special sort of pleasurable horror and thrill... (p. 223).

The typical FN projects precisely the same order of "limited and continuous subject matter or thematics" through a "stock of devices" both thematic and visual, and surely conveys an "aesthetic intent" to strike the audience with "a special sort of horror," if not exactly of pleasure, at the recognition of life's dark side. Further, as consistently as this inner form of "attitude, tone and purpose" may be traced from FN to FN, so even its outer form, a structure of a "special sort of plot organization"—though perhaps difficult to extrapolate into a generalized model of manageable size—may be delineated and expressed in as specific a form as Frye has done for one of the drama's oldest genres, Greek New Comedy (which he calls so conventionalized as to be a formula [p. 163]):

> Its main theme is the successful effort of a young man to outwit an
> opponent and possess the girl of his choice. The opponent is usually
> the father...[who] frequently wants the same girl, and is cheated out
> of her by the son...The girl is usually a slave or courtesan, and the plot
> turns on a...discovery of birth which makes her marriageable and
> marriage is the tonic chord on which [the play] ends.[16]

Such a model of FN plot structure and character type, which would affirm FN as an authentic genre, would of course have to be constructed and verified by a thoroughgoing inductive examination (the process to include, for example, in terms employed by Frye, Wellek and Warren, the detailed study of the "artifact" films individually, the identification of their "symbols" or "archetypes," and the search for "analogs" or "common denominators" among as many purported FN as possible). Though this process demands fare more time and study than I have as yet been able to devote to it, I believe I can suggest at least a rudimentary working prototype for such a model. It would run approximately as follows:

Either he is fated to do so or by chance, or because he has been hired for a job specifically associated with her, a man whose experience of life has left him sanguine and often bitter meets a not-innocent woman of similar outlook to whom he is sexually and fatally attracted. Through this attraction, either because the woman induces him to it or because it is the natural result of their relationship, the man comes to cheat, attempt to murder, or actually murder a second man to whom the woman is unhappily or unwillingly attached (generally he is her husband or lover), an act which often leads to the woman's betrayal of the protagonist, but which in any event brings about the sometimes metaphoric, but usually literal destruction of the woman, the man to whom she is attached, and frequently the protagonist himselff.

It should be emphasized that the purpose of such a model is not to describe a structure which exemplifies in precise detail every FN. There will naturally be many variations, substitutions, combinations, splinterings and reversals of constituents, depending upon psychological and aesthetic needs and audience acceptance. The aim is rather to describe a model which embodies the "truest" or "purest" example of the type. (Another of the many confusions about genre in FN literature is the lack of recognition that a genre has periods of birth, development, flowering, which presumably includes its purest examples, and even evolution into a new form of death. These periods in FN are clearly marked, as reflected in Borde's and Chaumeton's chapter divisions: birth around 1940; development and flowering from 1944 to 1948 or 1949; and transition from that point into an altered form which, depending upon one's understanding of FN, either ceases around 1955 or continues indefinitely evolving.)

What is significant about this suggested model is the number of films made in the period from 1944 to 1948 or 1949 and generally considered as FN that it does fit in detail: *Double Indemnity, The Woman in the Window, Scarlet Street, The Killers, The Lady from Shanghai, The Postman Always Rings Twice, Out of the Past, Pitfall, Criss Cross* come to mind. There are dozens more which incorporate only slight variations. In *The Strange Love of Martha Ivers*, for example, the protagonist doesn't comply with the fatal woman's request to murder her husband, but the result is the same. The fatal woman in *The Blue Dahlia* is the returning vet's unfaithful wife, and though it is rather him than the other man that she wishes to get rid of, at the film's conclusion both she and the second man are dead. A similar development is manifested in *Murder, My Sweet*, in which the fatal woman's connection with the other man, while important—it is he who kills her—is splintered into her general treachery towards all men and especially the protagonist. This concept seems to be a holdover from an earlier period. In essentially the same situation, the protagonist of *The Maltese Falcon*, though he is greatly attracted, "won't play the sap" and save the fatal woman from punishment; so he "sends her over," metaphorically killing her (an act that becomes literal in *Double Indemnity, The Postman Always Rings Twice* and *Out of the Past*). In the post-1949 transitional, perhaps "degenerate" stage of the form, one can see apparent mutations and collapsing of elements. In *In a Lonely Place* the fatal woman has become completely trustworthy, but many of her former characteristics and those of the other man appear to have been incorporated into the now intensely neurotic protagonist.

There is of course a multitude of other correspondences to be evaluated which will perhaps delimit, broaden or even invalidate this provisional model. Largely, these are composed of the "themes" and "motif" observers have noted in FN and claimed as one of the two means of interrelating the films of this type, and which include among other elements the pervasive atmosphere of corruption, crime, psychopathology and evil; the constant resort to gratuitous violence; the omnipresence of the returning veteran; the importance of the oneiric in structure and substance; and recurrent visuals.[17]

Additionally, there are numerous putative FN which seem at first to resist any accommodation with the proposed model. Many of these, it may be seen, simply do not fit into the category, or (as Borde and Chaumeton conclude about police "documentaries") are merely influenced by FN. Other films may be encompassed into a general model by understanding how elements have been altered and condensed or expanded. Tommy Udo in *Kiss of Death*, as an instance, can be seen as combining the masculine and feminine qualities of the other man and the fatal woman of the model, which suggests that it is perhaps this kind of configuration in FN that produces the gratuitous violence which marks the category.

But what I wish to underline regarding this model and the approach it represents is the process it provides by which the constituents common to a majority of the films intuitively grouped as FN may be isolated, objectified and their examination facilitated—even if provisional particulars of the model are later to be discarded in favor of more useful ones or even to pursue another but related method. Eventually, and most importantly, it is this kind of study which will not only elucidate this intriguing category of film and intensify an understanding of its aesthetic qualities, but which may as well establish a basis for the specific determination of the social, political and psychological root causes which gave rise to the phenomenon.

Short of this high aim, however, there certainly seems to be substantial and abundant reason to assume that FN may constitute a genre and to encourage an orderly and scrupulous consideration of the assumption.

Notes

1. Hereafter the designation FN will be used to denote the terms *film noir* and *films noirs*.

2. I except Amir Massoud Karimi's reproduced dissertation, *Toward a Definition of the American Film Noir* (1941-1949) (New York: Arno Press, 1976), which though helpful with certain antecedents, conceives of FN essentially as a branch of detective fiction. The French work is Raymond Borde and Étienne Chaumeton, *Panorama du film noir américain (1941-1953)* (Paris: Les Éditions de Minuit, 1955); translations from this volume are mine.

3. (New York: Basic Books, Inc., 1975).

4. (New York: Grossman Publishers, 1969).

5. *Hollywood in the Forties* (New York: A.S. Barnes and Co., 1968), pp. 19-20.

6. (New York: The Viking Press, 1972).

7. (New York: The Museum of Modern Art, 1971).

8. *Cinema*, Nos. 6 and 7 (August, 1970), pp. 48-56.

9. Auteurist and director-centered criticism has traditionally worked across the current of this kind of investigation, but this is less true of Alfred Appel, Jr., "The Director: Fritz Lang's American Nightmare," *Film Comment*, Vol. 10, No. 6 (November-December, 1974), pp. 12-17; and Peter Biskind, "'They Live by Night' By Daylight," *Sight and Sound*, Vol. 45, No. 4 (Autumn, 1976), pp. 218-22.

10. Approximately the term which Robert G. Porfirio endorses as the best English equivalent for *film noir*, in "No Way Out: Existential Motifs in the *Film noir*," *Sight and Sound*, Vol. 45, No. 4 (Autumn, 1976), pp. 212-17.

11. Even Paul Schrader's otherwise prudent "Notes on *Film Noir*," *Film Comment*, Vol. 8, No. 1 (Spring, 1972), pp. 8-13, lauds Durgnat's piece as "excellent," his work of classification as "thorough."

12. *Beyond Formula* (New York: Harcourt, Brace and Janovich, Inc., 1976).

13. (New York: Harcourt, Brace and Co., 1956), p. 222.

14. *Anatomy of Criticism: Four Essays* (Princeton, N.J.: Princeton University Press, 1971), p. 246.

15. "Hamlet," II. ii.

16. "The Argument of Comedy," in *Theories of Comedy*, ed. Paul Lauter (Garden City, N.Y.: Anchor Books, Doubleday and Co., Inc., 1964), p. 450.

17. The "visual style" so often reputed to FN (and the second means observers cite as correlating films classed in this category) is for me an extremely vexed question. I can see no conclusive evidence that anything as cohesive and determined as a visual style exists in FN. Assuredly, there is an emphasis on darkness and shadow, as there is in nearly all films of this period, but merely because an equal fashion for an emphatic brightness was manifested in a majority of Thirties films (whose subjects and outlook were similarly "bright"), a class of films blancs did not result. A visual style connotes a purposeful repetition from film to film of certain camera movements or angles: size of images; editing figures, devices or types; and/or a consistent movement of actors in relation to the camera. This is, after all, how we determine that Eisenstein's visual style differs from Welles'. No such patterns, however, are evident in FN. Its recurrent concentration on certain objects, types of faces, and perhaps settings, more nearly constitutes an iconography than a visual style.

Above, "just the facts, ma'am": L.A. police chief Bradley portrays himself in Eagle-Lion's B feature *He Walked by Night*, which Kerr believes "ironically" spawned *Dragnet* on television. (Jack Webb co-starred in the feature.)

Out of What Past? Notes on the B *film noir*

Paul Kerr (1979)

Ever since the publication of Borde and Chaumeton's pioneering *Panorama du Film Noir Américain* in 1955, there has been a continuing dispute about the genre's precise cultural sources and critical status.[1] In their attempts to provide *film noir* with a respectable pedigree, subsequent studies have cited not only cinematic but also sociological, psychological, philosophical, political, technological and aesthetic factors amongst its progenitors. What they have not done, however, is to relate these general—and generally untheorised—notions of "influence" to the specific modes of production, both economic and ideological, upon which they were, presumably, exercised; in this case, those structures and strategies adopted by certain factions within the American film industry over a period of almost two decades. Instead, these archaeologists of the genre have excavated a wide range of "ancestors" for *film noir*—the influx of German emigrés and the influence of expressionism; the influx of French emigrés and the influence of existentialism; Ernest Hemingway and the "hard-boiled" school of writing; Edward Hopper and the "ash can" school of painting; pre-war photo-journalism, wartime newsreels and post-war neorealism; the creators of *Kane*—Citizens Mankiewicz, Toland and Welles; the Wall Street crash and the rise of populism; the Second World War and the rise of fascism; the Cold War and the rise of McCarthyism. Finally, several critics have pointed, in passing, to a number of even less specific sources, such as general American fears about bureaucracy, the bomb, and the big city, as well as one or two more substantial ones, including the industrialisation of the female work-force during the war and the escalating corporatism of American capital throughout the 1940s.[2] However pertinent some of these suggestions, attempts to establish a "family tree" have usually revealed less about the formation of *film noir* in particular than about the poverty of film history in general. This article, therefore, is an attempt to refocus the debate on the specifically film-industrial determinants of the genre by concentrating on one important, industrially defined, fraction of it—the B *film noir*.

As I have indicated, most explanations have tended to credit either particular people (such as ex-employees of UFA and *Black Mask*) or events (the Depression and the war, for example) with the creation of—or, more accurately, a contribution to—*film noir*. Thus, in the first category, auteurists discuss the genre as if it were simply the chosen canvas of a few talented individuals, whether they were directors (Siodmak, Tourneur, Ulmer), writers (Chandler, Mainwaring, Paxton) or cinematographers (Alton, Musuraca, Toland). Similarly, genre critics generally consider *film noir* either in terms of its function as social myth or, more simply, as no more than a symptom of social malaise.[3] Borde and Chaumeton begin their chapter on sources with an account of *film noir*'s literary and cinematic precursors, so endorsing an evolutionary model of film history, but they go on to propose a much more interesting industrial origin in Hollywood's "synthesis of three types of films which at that time had developed such an autonomy that each studio had its own specialties from among them; the brutal and colourful gangster film, whose style carried over to other productions at Warner Bros.; the horror film over which Universal acquired a near-monopoly; and the classic detective film of deduction which was shared by Fox and Metro-Goldwyn-Mayer."[4] Having gone this far, though, Borde and Chaumeton fail to ask why such a synthesis should ever have taken place, if indeed it did. There are, I think, only two other theories which have been seriously put forward *vis-a-vis* the relationship between *film noir* and the film industry, both of which are equally untenable. The first argues that the genre was the cinema's unmediated reflection of an all-pervading postwar gloom and the second, that it was the expression of a community finally freed from its Depression duties as a dream factory by an audience that no longer needed cheering up.[5] In spite of their diametrically opposing views of postwar American "morale," both theories employ a conception of Hollywood as monolithic, its products either determined by American ideology or entirely autonomous of it.

Clearly, if we want to go on using the notion of "determination" rather than relying on the dubious concept "derivation," it is necessary to approach the classic base/superstructure formulation with some caution. Indeed, Raymond Williams has remarked that

> ...each term of the proposition has to be revalued in a particular direction. We have to revalue "determination" towards the setting of limits and the exertion of pressure and away from a predicted, prefigured and controlled content. We have to revalue "superstructure" towards a related range of cultural practices and away from a reflected, reproduced or specifically dependent content. And, crucially, we have revalued "the base" away from a notion of a fixed economic or technological abstraction, and towards the specific activities of men in real social and economic relationships, containing fundamental contradictions and variations and therefore always in a state of dynamic process.[6]

This article, then, taking its cue from the oft-cited specificity of *film noir* as a genre, will attempt to relate it not to the general American social formation (as some species of "reflection"), nor to a monolithically conceived film industry, but rather to particular, relatively autonomous modes of film production, distribution and exhibition in a particular conjuncture. What follows, therefore, is an exploratory rather than an exhaustive analysis of reciprocal relation which obtained between *film noir*'s primary determinants—the economic and the ideological. (The third determinant, at least in Althusserian terms, is that of the political, the effectivity of which with respect to the *film noir* would have to include the production code, the antitrust suits and the Hollywood blacklist. The political instance, for reasons of brevity, has here been subsumed within the other two categories.) This analysis attends in particular to the relatively autonomous and uneven development of the B *film noir*, a category constituted, I will argue by a negotiated resistance to the realist aesthetic on the one hand and an accommodation to restricted expenditure on the other. Of course, none of these terms—relative autonomy, non-synchronicity, realism (not to mention *film noir* itself)—is unproblematic; their employment here, however, is a necessary condition of any discussion which hopes to account for the existence of a genre at different times and in different places with a number of different inflections. The crucial theoretical formulation here is that of "determination" itself, since the identity of the infamous "last instance" though classically considered to be the economic will actually fluctuate, at least in the short term. Thus, in the long term, Hollywood's ideological and economic aims are complementary; the reproduction of the conditions necessary for continued cinematic production and consumption—in other words, the perpetuation of the industry. In the short term, however, these determinants may be less compatible, and it is the shifting balance of relations between the two which accords Hollywood's "superstructure" its relative autonomy from its economic "base." Furthermore, the economic or ideological space opened up for the American cinema in this way is in direct proportion to the urgency with which ideological or economic priorities in the industry are negotiated.

To take an example, Antony Easthope has argued that "in the early Thirties Hollywood production was determined ideologically or even politically rather than economically"[7] but his argument, like so many others, hinges on a reading of American history in general and not that of the film industry. In fact, it seems equally plausible—if equally schematic—to suggest that Hollywood's product was dominantly determined economically only in periods of economic crisis in the industry (like the early 1930s when several studios were actually bankrupted by a combination of reduced receipts and excessive capitalisation), whilst in eras of relative economic stability but marked ideological and/or political unrest (like the mid-1940s, when receipts rose to a new high but both international and industrial relations were of crucial importance) that product would have tended to be, primarily at least, ideologically determined. In modification of this latter formulation, however, it is necessary to add that low-budget and blockbuster film-making, neither of which was really established across the industry until the latter half of the

1930s—having their origins in precisely those economic conditions outlined above—might have been more vulnerable to economic imperatives ("masking" and "flaunting" their respective production values) than the admittedly slightly hypothetical "mid-budgeted" mainstream A products of the studios at that time. This privileging of the economic imperative on the B film, in a period of film history which was otherwise primarily ideologically determinate (at least until about 1947), might begin to account for the presence of several aesthetically (and therefore ideologically) unorthodox practices within the B *film noir*.

Towards a definition

Before a discussion of such suggestions can legitimately begin, however, some kind of critical consensus about those "practices" and the period in which they were pursued is needed. The authors of the *Panorama* focus their own analysis on those films produced between 1941 and 1953 but more recent critics have broadened these bounds somewhat to include films made from the beginning of the 1940s (and sometimes even earlier) until the end of the following decade. If we employ the more elastic of these estimates and allow an additional—and admittedly arbitrary margin at the beginning of the period, we may be able to reconstruct at least some of the industrial determinants of the genre. Furthermore, several critics have tried to demonstrate that *film noir* comprises a number of distinct stages. Paul Schrader, for example, has outlined "three broad phases" for the genre: the first lasting until about 1946 and characterised by couples like Bogart and Bacall and "classy" studio directors like Curtiz; the second spanning the immediate postwar years, when shooting began to move out of the studios and into the streets; and the third and final phase in which both characters and conventions alike were subject to extraordinary permutations. Perhaps film history will ultimately explain the industrial underpinnings of such "sub-generic" shifts as well as the primary determinants and eventual demise of the wider genre itself.[8] Until then, whether the period of *film noir* production is relatively easily agreed upon or not, the volume of that production is decidedly more difficult to ascertain. This is due, to some degree at least, to the primacy of the economic and relative autonomy of the ideological instances of the *film noir*. Equally important is its controversial status as a genre at all, since it is usually defined in terms of its style rather than—as most genres are—in relation to content, character, setting, plot. Further difficulties derive from its relative inaccessibility as an object of study: retrospectives are all too rare and there are still no book-length analyses of the genre in English—even the *Panorama* remains untranslated. *Film noir*, therefore, has still not received its due in terms of either critical or archival attention.

Despite such difficulties, it still remains possible to offer at least an outline of the genre's defining characteristics.[9] Primarily, *film noir* has been associated with a propensity for low key lighting, a convention which was in direct opposition to the cinematographic orthodoxy of the previous decade. In the 1930s the dominant lighting style, known as high key, had been characterized by a contrast ratio of approximately 4:1 between the light value of the key lamp on the one hand and the filler on the other. *Noir*, with a considerable higher range to contrasts, is thus a chiaroscuro style, its low key effects often undiffused by either lens gauzes or lamp glasses—as they certainly would have been in conventional high key style. Instead, *noir* sets are often only half or quarter lit, with the important exception of those brief sequences in the *"blanc"* (that is, "normal") world which are sometimes employed as a framing device at the beginning and end of the narrative. Otherwise, shooting tends to be either day-for-night or night-for-night and the main action has a habit of occurring in shadowy rooms, dingy offices, overlush apartments and rainwashed streets. In such settings both actors and decor are often partially obscured by the foregrounding of oblique objects—shutters and banisters, for instance, casting horizontal or vertical grids of light and dark across faces and furniture. Meanwhile, the arrangement of space within the frame is often equally irregular, both in regard to its occupation by actors and props as well as to the width and depth of focus. This can lead to a "discomposition" of the image (and consequent disorientation of the spectator) in terms of the neo-classical conventions of composition generally used and, indeed, reinforced by Hollywood. These kinds of disorientation can be accentuated by the use of "perversely" low and high camera angles (a perversity defined entirely in relation to contemporary realist criteria) and the virtual elimination of those other staples of realism, the establishing long shot and the personalising close-up. In fact, the latter is often used ironically in the *film noir* in soft focus treatment of male villainy (signifying feminine decadence) whilst women, the conventional "objects" of such attention, are often photographed in harsh, unflattering and undiffused light with wide angle distorting lenses. Such an emphasis on unconventional camera angles and lighting set-ups, however, is often achieved at the (literal) expense of camera movement and classical editing. A number of other realist conventions, including shot-reverse-shot alternation of points of view and the 180 degree rule, are also occasionally infringed by the *film noir*.[10] Finally there is a great deal of reliance on such fragmented narrative structures as the flashback, which an additional sense of inevitability to the plot and helplessness to characters. Hitherto, most definitions of the genre have more or less rested at this point, tend to ignore that plot and those characters. One recent critic, however, has assembled what he calls a "rudimentary working prototype" of characteristic content for *film noir* along the following lines:

> Either because he is fated to do so by chance, or because he has been hired for a job specifically associated with her, a man whose experience of life has left him sanguine and often bitter meets a not-innocent woman of similar outlook to who he is sexually and fatally attracted. Through this attraction, either because the woman

induces him to it or because it is the natural result of their relationship, the man comes to cheat, attempt to murder or actually murder a second man to whom the woman is unhappily or unwillingly attached (generally he is her husband or lover), an act which brings about the sometimes metaphoric but usually literal destruction of the woman, the man to whom she is attached and frequently the protagonist himself.[11]

This schematic summary of *film noir* will have to suffice for purposes here, if only as a result of the extremely tentative account of the genre's determination outlined below.

The coming of the B feature

The B film was launched as an attempt by a number of independent exhibitors to lure audiences back into their theatres at a time of acute economic crisis in the industry. Along with the double bill these independents had already—by the beginning of the 1930s—introduced lotteries, live acts, quizzes, free gifts and several other gimmicks in order to build up bigger audiences and, at the same time, keep those patrons they already had in their seats a little longer, so boosting box-office takings and confectionery sales whilst legitimising admission prices. The double bill, however, had the additional—and, as it proved, crucial—advantage of enabling independent exhibitors to accommodate their programme policies to the majors' monopolistic distribution practices (such as blind selling and block booking) and allowing them to exhibit more independent product at the same time. Of the 23,000 theatres operating in the United States in 1930, the five majors (MGM, RKO, Fox, Warners and Paramount) either owned or controlled some 3,000—most of that number being among the biggest and best situated of the first-run theatres; these 3.000 theatres, though comprising less than 14 per cent of the total number then in operation, accounted for nearly 70 per cent of the entire industry's box-office takings that year. This left the independents with some 20,000 theatres in which to screen what were either second-run or independent films. By the end of 1931 the double bill, which had originated in New England, had spread its influence on programme policy right across the country, establishing itself as at least a part of that policy in one-eighth of the theatres then in operation. In 1935, the last of the majors to adopt double bills in their theatres—MGM and RKO—announced their decision to screen two features in all but two of their theatres. By 1947, the fraction of cinemas advertising double bills had risen to nearly two-thirds. In normal circumstances, of course, any such increase in the volume of films in exhibition would have led to a similar increase in the volume of film production but this was not the case. Overproduction by the majors since the advent of sound had accumulated an enormous backlog of as yet unreleased material. It was not, therefore, until this reservoir of ready-made second features had been exhausted that it became necessary to set up an entirely new mode of film production—the B unit.

While those units within vertically integrated majors virtually monopolised the independent exhibition outlets a number of B studios established to meet the same demand were compelled to rely on the so-called States Rights system, whereby studios sold distribution rights to film franchises on a territorial basis. Lacking theatre chains of their own, several independent production companies were forced to farm out their product to a relatively unknown market. Monogram and Republic did eventually set up small exchanges of their own in a few cities and their main rival, PRC, even acquired some theatres of its own in the 1940s but the distinction between such venues and those owned by the majors should not be forgotten. Certainly, the producers of the B films themselves would have been acutely aware of the kind of cinemas in which the bulk of their products would have been seen and this may have been as influential a factor in B film production as the picture palaces were for the As. Mae D. Huettig,[12] for instance, has described how Los Angeles's eleven first-run theatres exhibited 405 films in the year 1939/40 of which only five were the product of independent companies, all but one of that five being shown at the bottom of a double bill. Wherever such double bills were programmed, however, few exhibitors could afford the rentals of two top quality (i.e. top price) products at the same time. The double bill, therefore, was a combination of one relatively expensive A film and one relatively inexpensive B, the former generally deriving from the major studios and costing, throughout the 1940s, upwards of $700,000 and the later being produced by low budget units at the same studios as well as by several B studios, at anything less than about $400,000.[13] In general, the A feature's rental was based on a percentage of box-office takings whilst the Bs played for a fixed or flat rental and were thus not so reliant on audience attendance figures at all—at least, not in the short term. In the long term, however, these B units would be compelled to carve out identifiable and distinctive styles for themselves in order to differentiate their product—within generic constraints—for the benefit of audiences in general and exhibitors in particular.

In most cases the B *film noir* would have been produced—like all Bs—on a fixed budget which would itself have been calculated in relation to fixed rentals. In illustrating the effects such economies exercised on these Bs I have restricted reference, as far as possible, to one large integrated company, RKO, and one small independent company, PRC.[14] At the beginning of the decade the budgets of RKO's most important production unit in the B sector were approximately $150,000 per picture; at PRC, several years later, most units were working with less than two-thirds of that amount. To take two examples: Val Lewton's films at RKO had tight, twenty-one-day schedules whilst Edgar G. Ulmer's at PRC were often brought in after only six days and nights. (To achieve this remarkable shooting speed night work was almost inevitable and Ulmer's unit used to mount as many as eighty different camera set-ups a day.) Props, sets and costumes were kept to a minimum except on those occasions when they could be borrowed from more expensive productions, as Lewton borrowed a staircase from *The Magnificent Ambersons* for his first feature, *The Cat People*. Nick Grinde, a veteran of B units in the 1940s, has described how a producer would resist charges of plagiarism on the grounds that "the way he will shoot it no one will recognize it for the same set. He'll have his director pick new angles and redress the foreground...[and]...will even agree to shoot at night..."[15]

Night shooting, of course, was an obvious and often unavoidable strategy for getting films in on short schedules as well as fully exploiting fixed assets and economising on rentals. (It also suited those employees who sought to avoid IATSE overtime bans.) Mark Robson, an editor and later director in Lewton's unit, has recalled that "the streets we had in *The Seventh Victim*, for instance, were studio streets and the less light we put on them the better they looked."[16] Similarly, expensive special effects and spectacular action sequences were generally avoided unless stock footage could be borrowed from other films. This "borrowing" became known as "montage" and involved the use of a "series of quick cuts of film," as Grinde has explained,

> You can't shoot a first-rate crime wave on short dough, so you borrow or buy about twenty pieces of thrilling moments from twenty forgotten pictures. A fleeing limousine skids into a street-car, a pedestrian is socked over the head in an alley, a newspaper office is wrecked by hoodlums, a woman screams, a couple of mugs are slapping a little merchant into seeing their way. And so on until we end up on a really big explosion.[17]

Not all such "thrilling moments" were "borrowed" from "forgotten pictures," however. Fritz Lang, for example, has noted that footage from *You Only Live Once* (UA 1937), including a classic bank robbery sequence, found its way into *Dillinger* (Monogram 1945).[18]

The exploitation of borrowed footage and furniture was only really possible as long as films were being shot inside the studios. Until the middle of the 1940s location shooting was extremely rare and even independents like Monogram and PRC had their own studio facilities. As fixed and variable costs began to escalate at the end of the war, however, production units were encouraged to go out on location and this practice was extended by the prolonged studio strikes of 1945-47. In 1946, the abolition of block booking encouraged the appearance of a number of small studio-less independent production companies and these also contributed to the "street" rather than "studio" look in the latter half of the decade. Constraints at both the production and distribution ends of the industry meant that the running length of Bs fluctuated between about fifty-five and seventy-five minutes; raw footage was expensive, audiences had only limited amounts of time and, of course, exhibitors were keen to screen their double bills as many times a day as possible. In 1943 the government reduced basic allotments of raw film stock to the studios by 25 per cent and once again it was the B units which were hardest hit. Consequently "montages" became even more common. Cast and crews on contract to B units were kept at a manageable minimum, so prohibiting plots with long cast lists, crowd scenes and complicated camera or lighting set-ups. Similarly, overworked script departments often produced unpolished and occasionally incoherent scripts. (Film titles were pre-tested with audiences before stories or scripts were even considered.) Despite such drawbacks, however, the B units, throughout the 1940s and as late as the mid-1950s, employed the same basic equipment as their big budget rivals, including Mitchell or Bell and Howell cameras, Mole Richardson lighting units, Moviola editing gear and RCA or Western Electric sound systems. Such economics as B units practised, therefore, were not related to fixed assets like rents and salaries but to variable costs like sets, scripts, footage, casual labour and, crucially, power.

RKO's production of *noir* B's seems to have been inaugurated in 1940 with the release of Boris Ingster's extraordinary *Stranger on the Third Floor*. The studio had emerged from receivership at end of the previous decade—a period of some prosperity for the other majors—to make only minimal profits of $18,604 in 1938 and $228,608 in 1939. In 1940 the studio lost almost half a million dollars and began to augment its low budget policy with B series like *The Saint* and *The Falcon*. It was not until 1942, however, when RKO plunged more than two million dollars into debt that the trend towards the B *film noir* became really evident. In that year, George Schaefer was fired as president and replaced by his deputy, Ned Depinet, who immediately appointed Charles M. Koerner—from RKO Theatres Inc.—as vice-president in charge of production. It was at this point that Val Lewton was brought to the studio to set up his own B unit. Within the limitations I have outlined, as well as the generic constraints of having to work in the "horror" category, Lewton's unit, and others like it, were accorded a degree of autonomy which would never have been sanctioned for more expensive studio productions.[19] At PRC the situation was rather different. The company had been formed in March 1940 by the creditors of its predecessor, the Producers' Distributing Corporation, and with the cooperation of the Pathé Laboratories. The new Producers' Releasing Corporation had five separate production units and the Fine Arts Studio (formerly Grand National). At first the emphasis was on comedy and westerns; PRC produced forty-four films, mostly in these genres, in the 1941/42 season. By 1942, however, PRC had acquired twenty-three film exchanges and with the replacement of George Batchelor by Leon Fromkess as production head, there was an increased diversification of product. While most units concentrated on comedies and musicals, others began to turn out cut-rate westerns and crime thrillers. It was also in 1942 that Edgar G. Ulmer began work for the studio. Allowed only about 15,000 feet per picture, Ulmer's unit, like Lewton's, economised with stock footage (as in *Girls in Chains* PRC 1943) and minimal casts and sets (as in *Detour* PRC 1946).

Artistic ingenuity in the face of economic intransigence is one critical commonplace about the B *film noir* (and about people like Lewton and Ulmer in particular). Against this, I have suggested that a number of *noir* characteristics can at least be associated with—if not directly attributed to—economic and therefore technological constraints. The paucity of "production values" (sets, stars and so forth) may even have encouraged low budget production units to compensate with complicated plots and convoluted atmosphere. Realist denotation would have thus been de-emphasized in favour of expressionist connotation (in *The Cat People* RKO 1942, for example). This connotative quality might also owe something to the influence of the Hays Office, which meant that "unspeakable" subjects could only be suggested—*Under Age* (Columbia 1941), although concerned with the criminal exploitation of young girls, could never actually illustrate that exploitation. Similarly, compressed shooting schedules, overworked script editors and general cost cutting procedures could well have contributed to what we now call *film noir*. Nevertheless, an analysis of *film noir* as nothing more than an attempt to make a stylistic virtue of economic necessity—the equation, at its crudest, of low budgets with low key lighting—is inadequate: budgetary constraints and the relative autonomy of many B units in comparison with As were a necessary but by no means sufficient condition for its formation. It was, I have suggested, constituted not only by accommodation to restricted expenditure but also by resistance to the realist aesthetic—like the B film generally, it was determined not only economically but also ideologically. For instance, the double bill was not simply the result of combining any two films, one A and one B, but often depended on a number of quite complex contrasts. *The Saint in New York*, for example, was billed with *Gold Diggers in Paris*, *Blind Alibi* with *Holiday*. According to Frank Ricketson Jr., the tendency of both distributors and exhibitors to ensure that

> Heavy drama is blended with sparkling comedy. A virile action picture is mated with a sophisticated society play. An all-star production is matched with a light situation comedy of no-star value. And adventure story is contrasted with a musical production.[20]

Initially, of course, B films had been little more than low budget versions of profitable A releases but as the industry was rationalised after the Depression this imitative trend was partially replaced by another differentiation. Thus, while early Bs had tended to remain in the least expensive of successful genres—westerns, situation comedies, melodramas, thrillers and horror films—the exhibitors themselves began to exert a moderating influence (by means of intercompany promotions like Koerner's within the integrated companies; by means of advertisements in the trade papers among the independents). By the end of the

1930s, therefore, double bills were beginning to contrast the staple A genres of that decade—gangster films, biopics, screwball comedies, mysteries and westerns—with a number of Poverty Row hybrids, mixtures of melodrama and mystery, gangster and private eye, screwball comedy and thriller (and later, "documentary" and drama). In part, of course, this hybrid quality is explicable in terms of studio insecurities about marketing their B products; nevertheless, the curiously cross-generic quality of *film noir* is perhaps a vestige of its origins as a kind of "oppositional" cinematic mode. Low key lighting styles, for example, were not only more economic than their high key alternatives, they were also dramatically and radically distinct from them.

Stylistic generation

In considering the concept of stylistic differentiation it is useful, at this point, to introduce the work of the Birmingham Centre for Contemporary Cultural Studies on "the process of stylistic generation."[21] Although specifically addressed to the "styles" adopted by such subcultural groups as Teds, punks and Rastas, this work seems to me to be applicable, with some reservations, to the style of the B *film noir*. Whether or not one can legitimately describe Poverty Row as a subculture is clearly a matter for serious debate but, until we have some kind of social history of Hollywood, a final decision on the matter is premature. Lacking such knowledge, it remains striking how appropriate some of the Birmingham conclusions are for the present study. In their analysis the authors make admittedly eclectic use of Levi-Strauss's concept of bricolage; but whereas Levi-Strauss is concerned with situations and cultures where a single myth is dominant, John Clarke concentrates on the "genesis of 'unofficial' styles, where the stylistic core (if there is one) can be located in the expression of a partly negotiated opposition to the values of a wider society."[22] (I will return to the notion of "negotiated opposition" later). Clarke proposes a two-tiered theory of stylistic generation, the first axiom of which states that the generation of subcultural styles involves differential selection from within the matrix of the existent and the second, that one of the main functions of a distinctive subcultural style is to define the boundaries of group membership as against other groups. I hope that the pertinence of these two axioms (the first "economic," the second "ideological") to the group which has designated the B *film noir* will become apparent. Clarke even goes on to discuss the process whereby such subcultural styles are assimilated into/recuperated by the dominant culture; a process which Raymond Williams refers to as "incorporation." The defusion and dilution of the B *film noir*'s unorthodox visual style within the aesthetic of the A film clearly fits this kind of pattern, with the most economically secure studios at that time—MGM, Fox and Paramount—tending to produce not only fewer films in the genre than their competitors but also more lavish ones like *The Postman Always Rings Twice*, *Laura* and *Double Indemnity*. Furthermore, it was Fox who was to launch and lead the break-away police procedural strand at the end of the 1940s, a strand which emanated from and to a certain extent replaced that studio's location-based *March of Time* series.[23]

Meanwhile, the monopoly structure of the industry—which had been initially, if indirectly, responsible for the B phenomenon—was being challenged. In May 1935 the Supreme Court voted to revoke Roosevelt's National Industrial Recovery Act (under which A *Code of Fair Competition for the Motion Picture Industry* had more or less condoned the industry's monopoly practices) on the grounds that it was unconstitutional. Opposition to motion picture monopolies was mounting, not only among the independent companies but also in the courts and even in Congress itself. Finally, in July 1938, the Department of Justice filed an Anti-Trust suit against the majors, United States versus Paramount Pictures Inc. et al., so launching a case which was to reach the Supreme Court a decade later. In the suit the majors were accused of separate infringements of Anti-Trust legislation but, in November 1940, the case was apparently abandoned; in fact it was merely being adjourned for the duration of hostilities, the government being unwilling to provoke Hollywood at a time when the communications media were of such crucial importance. The suit was settled out of court with the signing of a modest Consent Decree, the provisions of which included an agreement by the majors to "modify" their use of block booking, to eliminate blind selling and to refrain from "unnecessary" theatrical expansion. Most important of all the Decree's requirements, however, was the majors' agreement to withdraw from the package selling procedures which had compelled independent exhibitors to screen shorts, re-issues, serial westerns and newsreels with their main features. The last provision expanded the market for low budget production almost overnight. Whereas at the end of the 1930s there had been very few independent companies, by 1946 (the year in which block booking was finally abolished) there were more than forty. The Anti-Trust Commission never entirely dropped their case against Hollywood, however, and finally, in 1948, the five fully integrated companies were instructed to divest themselves of their theatrical holdings. Paramount was the first to obey this ruling, divorcing its exhibition arm from the production/distribution end of its business in late 1949. RKO followed in 1950, 20th Century-Fox in 1952, Warner Bros. in 1953 and MGM in 1959. Rather ironically, the divorce meant the demise of many independent studios which had thrived on providing films for the bottom half of the bill; quite simply, low budget productions could no longer be guaranteed fixed rentals in exhibition. Consequently, one of the first casualties of divorcement was the double bill. The majors cancelled their B productions and the independents were forced to choose between closure and absorption. In 1949 PRC was absorbed by Rank and transformed into Eagle Lion; the following year it ceased production altogether and merged with United Artists. In 1953 Monogram became Allied Artists Pictures Corporation and began to operate an increasingly important television subsidiary. Republic, whose staple product had always been westerns and serials, was finally sold to CBS in 1959 and became that network's Television City studio.

It was thus between the first filing of the Anti-Trust suit in 1938 and the final act of divorcement in 1959 that the B *film noir* flourished. Obviously, however, the trend towards media conglomerates and away from simple monopolies was by no means the only "political" determinant on cinematic modes in that period, a period which witnessed American entry into the war, the rise of McCarthyism and a series of jurisdictional disputes in the labour unions.[24] During the Second World War the international market for American films shrank drastically and the domestic market expanded to take its place. By 1941, the cinemas of continental Europe, where the majors had earned more than a quarter of their entire box-office in 1936, were no longer open to American distributors. Even in Britain, where most cinemas remained open throughout the war and where attendance actually rose from a weekly average of nineteen million in 1939 to more than thirty million in 1945, the Hollywood majors were unable to maintain even pre-war profits. The introduction of currency restrictions severely limited the amount that American distributors could remove from the country; thus, only half their former revenues—some $17,500,000—were withdrawn in 1940 and only $12,900,000 in 1941. Meanwhile, however, American domestic rentals soared from $193,000,000 in 1939 to $332,000,000 in 1946. By the end of the war, average weekly attendance in the US was back at about 90,000,000, its pre-war peak. As the majors' profits rose, the volume of their production actually fell: having released some 400 films in 1939 the big eight companies released only 250 in 1946, the balance being made up by a flush of new B companies. This geographically—but not economically—reduced constituency may have afforded Hollywood the opportunity to take a closer look at contemporary and specifically American phenomena without relying on the "comfortable" distance provided by classic genres like the western or the musical. That "closer look" (at, for instance, urban crime, the family and the rise of corporations) could, furthermore, because of the national specificity of its audience and as a result of the "dialectic" of its consumption (within the double bill) employ a less orthodox aesthetic than would previously have been likely.

The aesthetic orthodoxy of the American cinema in the 1940s and 1950s was realism and so it is necessary to relate cinematic realism to the *film noir*. Colin MacCabe has suggested its two primary conditions:

(1) The classic realist text cannot deal with the real as contradictory.

(2) In a reciprocal movement of the classic realist text ensures the position of the subject in a relation of dominant specularity.

These two conditions, the repression of contradiction and the construction of spectatorial omniscience, are negotiated through a hierarchy of narrative discourses:

> Through the knowledge we gain from the narrative we can split the
> discourses of the various characters from their situation and
> compare what is said in these discourses with what has been
> revealed to us through narration. The camera shows us what
> happens—it tells the truth against which we can measure the
> discourses.[25]

Elsewhere MacCabe has restated this notion quite clearly: "classical
realism...involves the homogenisation of different discourses by their relation to
one dominant discourse—assured of its domination by the security and
transparency of its image."[26]

It is this very "transparency" which *film noir* refuses; indeed, Sylvia Harvey has
noted that "One way of looking at the plot of the typical *film noir* is to see it as a
struggle between different voices for control over the telling of the story." From
that perspective, *film noir* represents a fissure in the aesthetic and ideological fabric of realism. Thus,

> Despite the presence of most of the conventions of the dominant
> methods of filmmaking and storytelling, the impetus towards the
> resolution of the plot, the diffusion of tension, the circularity of a
> narrative that resolves all the problems it encounters, the
> successful completion of the individual's quest, these methods do
> not, in the end, create the most significant contours of the cultural
> map of *film noir*. The defining contours of this group of films are the
> product of that which is abnormal and dissonant.[27]

Gill Davies, on the other hand, has suggested that such "dissonance" can quite
comfortably be contained by the "weight" of generic convention.

> The disturbing effect of mystery or suspense is balanced by
> confidence in the inevitability of the genre. Character types, stock
> settings and the repetition of familiar plot devices assure the reader
> that a harmonious resolution will take place. This narrative pattern
> pretends to challenge the reader, creates superficial disorientation,
> while maintaining total narrative control. Our knowledge of the
> genre (supported, in the cinema with the reappearance of certain
> actors and actresses in familiar roles) takes us through a baffling
> narrative with the confidence that all problems will ultimately be
> solved.[28]

In terms of *film noir*, however, I would argue that the "surplus" of realist devices
catalogued by Harvey and Davies indicates an attempt to hold in balance
traditional generic elements with unorthodox aesthetic practices that constantly
undermine them. *Film noir* can thus be seen as the negotiation of an "oppositional
space" within and against realist cinematic practice; this trend could only be
effectively disarmed by the introduction of a number of stock devices derived

from other genres (such as melodrama or the detective story). It is not an object of this article, though, to gauge the degree to which that resistance was or was not successful. Rather, its task is to begin to establish those historically contemporaneous strands of realism—Technicolor, television and the A film—against which any such resistance would necessarily have defined itself.

Television and Technicolor

In 1947 there were only 14,000 television receivers in the United States; two years later that number had risen to a million. By 1950 there were four million and by 1954 thirty-two million. In the face such swiftly escalating opposition and as a consequence of the impending demise of the double bill (in the aftermath of the Anti-Trust decision), several of the smaller studios began renting theatrical films for television exhibition and even producing tele-films of their own. Thus, in 1949, Columbia formed a subsidiary, Screen Gems, to produce new films for and release old films to the new medium. In 1955, the first of the five majors, Warner Bros., was persuaded to produce a weekly ABC TV series, to be called *Warner Brothers Presents*, based on three of that studio's successful 1940s features: *King's Row* (1941), *Casablanca* (1942) and *Cheyenne* (1947). It is perhaps worth pointing out that *Cheyenne* was the only one which lacked elements of the "noir" style and also the only one to enjoy a mass audience; indeed, it was ultimately "spun off" into a seven-year series of its own while the other two-thirds of the slot were quietly discontinued. In December of 1955 RKO withdrew from film production altogether and sold its film library to a television programming syndicate; two years later, the old RKO studio itself was in he hands of Desilu, an independent television production company owned by ex-RKO contract player Lucille Ball and her husband Desi Arnaz. In fact, Lucille Ball's comedy series *I Love Lucy* had been the first "filmed" (as opposed to live) series on American television; it was only dislodged from its place at the top of the ratings by another filmed series, *Dragnet*. The latter, characterised by high key lighting, sparse shadowless sets and procedural plots, was to provide a model for television crime fiction for more than two decades. It is particularly ironic, therefore, to note that *Dragnet* derived from a 1948 B *film noir* produced by Eagle Lion, *He Walked by Night*, a film which contains what is perhaps the most dramatically chiaroscuro scene ever shot in Hollywood. In 1954 Warner Bros. released a cinematic spin-off from the series, again called *Dragnet*, but this time without a trace of the stylistic virtuosity which had characterised its cinematic grandparent. (The fact that this film proved unsuccessful at the box office, far from invalidating my thesis about the relationship between television and the *film noir*, actually corroborates my account of the different "spaces" occupied by the discourse of realism in television and the cinema.) Very simply, the low contrast range of television receivers meant that any high contrast cinematic features (like films *noirs*) were inherently unsuitable for tele-cine reproduction.

If *film noir* was determined to any degree by an initial desire to differentiate B cinematic product from that of television (as A product was differentiated by colour, production values, 3D, wide screens and epic or "adult" themes), as, too, its ultimate demise relates to capitulation to the requirements of tele-cine, that "difference" can also be seen as a response to the advent of colour. The first full-length Technicolor feature, *Becky Sharp*, was released in 1935 (by RKO), and its director, Rouben Mamoulian—one of the few professionals in favour of colour at that time—has described in some detail the aesthetic consensus into which the new process was inserted:

> For more than twenty years, cinematographers have varied the key of lighting in photographing black-and-white pictures to make the visual impression enhance the emotional mood of the action. We have become accustomed to a definite language of lighting: low key effects, with sombre, heavy shadows express a somberly dramatic mood; high key effect, with brilliant lighting and sparkling definition, suggest a lighter mood; harsh contrasts with velvety shadows and strong highlights strike a melodramatic note. Today we have color—a new medium, basically different in many ways from any dramatic medium previously known...Is it not logical, therefore, to feel that it is incumbent upon all of us, as film craftsmen, to seek to evolve a photodramatic language of color analogous with the language of light with which we are all so familiar.[29]

Mamoulian's implicit appeal to a "logic of the form" might well have impressed some of the "creative" workers associated with A film productions but it is unlikely to have been heard sympathetically among employees of the Bs. Indeed, the advent of colour actually exacerbated the situation he had outlined: the Technicolor process demanded "high key effects, with brilliant lighting and sparkling definition" as a very condition of its existence. It is, therefore, hardly surprising that a cinema of "low key effects, with sombre, heavy shadows" flourished in counterpart to it. Furthermore, the films actually employing Technicolor were often characterised by exotic locations, lavish sets, elaborate costumes and spectacular action sequences (generally of the musical or swashbuckling variety) and so fell into an expanding group of "colour-specific" genres—westerns, musicals, epics, historical dramas, et cetera—leaving melodramas, thrillers, and horror to the lower budgets of black and white. Finally, in 1939 the really decisive blow for the industrial endorsement of colour was struck by unprecedented success of *Gone with the Wind*. However, wartime economic and technological restraint frustrated much further movement to colour for several years—as it also postponed the rise of television—and perhaps the very "dormancy" of the Technicolor phenomenon in those years encouraged those engaged in and/or committed to black and white to continue to experiment. If the war years saw no great increase in Technicolor features (from eighteen in 1939 to twenty-nine in 1945), the postwar period witnessed a rapid acceleration of colour production; in 1949 *Variety* confidently predicted that 30 per cent of all forthcoming features would be in colour and 15 July 1952 *Film Daily* announced that well over 75 per cent of features in production were shooting in colour.

At the other end of the colour quality spectrum, but perhaps equally influential on the *film noir*, was the development of a number of low budget, two-colour processes. In 1939, the first of these, Cinecolor, became available and the following year the first full-length Cinecolor feature—Monogram's *The Gentleman from Arizona*—was released. Costing only 25 per cent more than black and white stock and considerably less than Technicolor and with the additional advantage of overnight rushes, Cinecolor (and other "primitive" chromatic processes like it—Vitacolor, Anscocolor, Trucolor) naturally appealed to and was rapidly adopted by certain genres at the low budget end of the industry. By 1959, Allied Artists, Columbia, Eagle Lion, Film Classics, MGM, Monogram, Paramount, 20th Century-Fox, United Artists and Universal had all made some use of the process. Meanwhile, on the A front, Technicolor did have its disadvantages. For instance, because of the prism block between the back element of the lens and the film gates, neither wide angle lenses nor those with very long focal lengths could be accommodated by the new three strip cameras. Indeed, even the introduction of faster (black and white and colour) negative stock in 1938 was unable to produce any depth of focus without wide angle lenses and, for Technicolor, faster film necessitated stronger floodlighting throughout the late 1930s, the 1940s and into the 1950s; floodlighting which in turn made for a flatter image and a marked lack of contrast. For black and white, on the other hand, the introduction of faster film stock allowed a decrease in lighting levels and aperture openings commensurate with previously impractical chiaroscuro effects. Single source lighting became steadily more feasible and was attractively economic—cheap on both power and labour. Similarly, night for night shooting, which generally involved the payment of prohibitive overtime rates, was particularly applicable to B units which paid set rates for all hours worked.

Apart from colour, perhaps the most important technological development in the late 1930s was the introduction of a new range of Fresnel lenses which, for the first time, made it possible to place large diameter lenses close to a powerful light source without loss of focus. Consequently, spotlights began to replace key light functions. While colour stock still needed diffused high key lighting, the new fast black and white stock opened the way for smaller lighting units—such as Babys or Krieg Lilliputs—which permitted lower lighting levels. In 1940, small spotlights with Fresnel lenses and 150- or 300-watt tungsten incandescent bulbs began to outmode heavier, less mobile Carbon Arc lamps. The combination of swinging keys, lightweight spots and mobile military cameras made unorthodox angles possible but involved the erection of previously unnecessary set ceilings. It was for precisely this reason that Sid Hickox, Howard Hawks' cameraman on *To Have and Have Not* (1944),

> had a problem with his set ceilings: in wanting to hang the incandescent light low, he had to remove most of the ceilings, but the camera shooting from the floor would reveal the lights themselves. so he set up ready-made three quarter ceilings of butter muslin, just sufficiently dark to conceal the incandescents massed behind them, with the other incandescents only a fraction beyond the range of vision.[30]

There were also important developments in camera production in this period. The Mitchell BNC—produced in 1934 but not used in Hollywood until 1938—enabled synch-sound shooting with lenses of 25mm widths for the first time. The only new 35mm camera introduced in the 1940s in any quantity was the Cunningham Combat Camera, a lightweight (13 lb.) affair which allowed cinematographers to move more easily whilst filming and to set up in what would previously have been inaccessible positions. Even more appropriate for hand-held and high or low angle shooting, however, was the Arriflex, which was captured from German military cameramen. (The subjective camera opening sequence in Delmer Daves's *Dark Passage* in 1947, inspired by the previous year's *Lady in the Lake*, was shot with a hand-held Arriflex.) In 1940 the first practical anti-reflective coatings became available, coming into general cinematic currency after their use in *Citizen Kane*. These micro-thin coatings, knows as Vard Opticoats, together with twin-arc broadside lamps which were developed for Technicolor, minimised light loss at the surface of the lens (through reflection or refraction) and at the same time accelerated shutter speeds and facilitated the use of good wide-angle lenses—though once again only with black and white. So-called Tolandesque deep focus was therefore only technologically possible from 1938 when the new fast 1232 Super XX Panchromatic Stock could be combined with Duarc light, 25mm wide-angle lenses and considerably reduced apertures. Wide-angle lenses were extensively used thereafter until they were somewhat anachronised by the advent of wide screens in 1953 and the accommodation to television standards later in that decade. In the same way, the use of deep focus photography continued until it was necessarily abated by Hollywood's brief romance with 3D which lasted from 1952 until 1954. The first CinemaScope murder mystery—Nunnally Johnson's *Black Widow (1954)*—suffered from its screen size just as much as those 3D thrillers released at the same time—*I, the Jury* (1953) and *Dial M for Murder* (1954), all of which illustrate precisely how such processes militated against projects which might, only a few months earlier, have been *films noir*.[31]

This line of argument should not, however, be mistaken for a covert reintroduction of the tenets of technological determinism.[32] Indeed, these various "innovations" were all either side effects of the (profoundly ideological) desire for ever-increasing degrees of verisimilitude (Technicolor, Deep Focus) or were determined by a negotiated differentiation from and resistance to that realism (ex-emplified by the A film, by television and by Technicolor itself) in accordance with economic restraints. I would like, finally, to suggest that it was, specifically, the ab-sorption of a colour aesthetic within realism which generated the space which *film noir* was to occupy. Indeed, just as the advent of radio in 1924 had provoked a cinematic trend away from realism until it was reversed in 1927 with the coming of sound to the cinema, so while colour originally signified "fantasy" and was first appropriated by "fantastic" genres, it was too soon recuperated within the realist aesthetic. Compare, for instance, the realist status of black and white sequences in *The Wizard of Oz* (1939) and *If* (1969). The period of this transition, the period in which the equation between black and white on the one hand and realism on the other was at its most fragile, was thus the period from the late 1930s—when television, Technicolor and the double bill were first operating—to the late 1950s, when television and colour had established themselves, both economically and ideologically, as powerful lobbies in the industry, and the double bill had virtually disappeared. That period, of something less than twenty years, saw the conjunc-tion of a primarily economically determined mode of production, known as B film-making, with what were primarily ideologically defined modes of "differ-ence," known as the *film noir*. Specific conjunctures such as this—of economic constraints, institutional structures, technological developments, political, legal and labour relations—are central to any history of film; they represent the indus-trial conditions in which certain representational modes, certain generic codes come into existence. This is not to argue that cinema is somehow innocent of ex-tra-industrial determinants but simply to insist that Hollywood has a (so far un-specified) relative autonomy within the wider American social formation, however theoretically unsatisfactory that "relativity" remains. The point of this ar-ticle, therefore, has been to map out an influential fraction of that Hollywood ter-rain and, as part of that process, to challenge the conceptual catch-all of "mediation" with the concrete specificities of industrial history.

Notes

1. Raymond Borde and Étienne Chaumeton, *Panorama du Film noir Américain* (Paris: Les Éditions de Minuit, 1955). I use the term "genre" in this article where others have opted for "subgenre," "series," "cycle," "style," "period," "movement," etc. For a re-cent discussion of critical notions of (and approaches to) *film noir*, see James Damico *"Film noir*: a modest proposal" in *Film Reader* no. 3, 1978.

2. In an article on "Woman's place: the absent family of *film noir*" (in E. Ann Kaplan, *Women in Film noir* (London: British Film Institute, 1978, p. 26), Sylvia Harvey has de-scribed how "the increasing size of corporations, the growth of monopolies and the accelerated elimination of small businesses" all contributed to an atmosphere in which it was "increasingly hard for even the petit bourgeoisie to continue to believe in certain dominant myths. Foremost among these was the dream of equality of opportunity in

business and of the God-given right of every man to be his own boss. Increasingly, the petit bourgeoisie were forced into selling their labour and working for the big companies, instead of running their own businesses and working for themselves." Other genres have been analyzed in this way: for example, Will Wright's *Sixguns and Society* (Berkeley: University of California Press, 1975) treats the development of the Western as a (generically coded) reflection of the development of American capital.

3. This is not to deny the possible efficacy of such approaches, but rather to insist on their being predicated on the sort of industrial analysis attempted here.

4. Borde and Chaumeton's chapter on "The sources of *film noir*," translated in *Film Reader* no. 3, p. 63.

5. An example of the first is Paul Schrader, "Notes on *film noir*" in *Film Comment*. vol. 8, no. 1, Spring 1972, p. 11; of the second, Raymond Durgnat, "Paint it black: the family tree of *film noir*" in *Cinema*. nos. 6-7, August 1970.

6. Raymond Williams, "Base and superstructure in Marxist cultural theory," in *New Left Review*. no. 82, November-December 1973.

7. Antony Easthope, "Todorov, genre theory and TV detectives," mimeo, 1978, p. 4.

8. The poverty of film history already referred to is less material than conceptual. For a useful contribution to the historical debate see Edward Buscombe's "A new approach to film history," published with other papers from the Purdue University Conference in the 1977 *Film Studies Annual*.

9. Much of the stylistic detail in this outline is indebted to J.A. Place and L.S. Peterson, "Some visual motifs of *film noir*" in *Film Comment*. vol. 10, no. 1, January-February 1974.

10. For further examples of such infringements see Stuart Marshall, "*Lady in the Lake*: identification and the drives," in *Film Form*, vol. 1, nos. 1-2, 1977; Stephen Heath, "Film and system: terms of analysis," in *Screen*. vol. 16, nos. 1-2, Spring/Summer 1975; Kristin Thompson, "The duplicitous text: an analysis of *Stage Fright*," in *Film Reader*. no. 2, 1977; and idem, "Closure within a dream: point-of-view in *Laura*," in *Film Reader*. no. 3, 1978.

11. Damico, "*Film noir*: a modest proposal."

12. Mae D. Heuttig, *Economic Control of the Motion Picture Industry* (Philadelphia: University of Pennsylvania Press, 1944).

13. These figures are, of course, approximate—several of the smallest B companies actually produced films on budgets of less than $100,000—but they do at least indicate the degree of economic difference between the various "modes."

14. Producers' Releasing Corporation: for information on this see Todd McCarthy and Charles Flynn (eds.), *Kings of the Bs* (New York: Dutton, 1975); Don Miller, *B Movies* (New York: Curtis Books, 1973); idem, "Eagle-Lion: the violent years, " in *Focus on Film*. no. 31, November 1978.

15. Nick Grinde, "Pictures for peanuts," in *The Penguin Film Review*. no. 1, August 1946 (reprinted London: Scolar Press, 1977, pp. 46-7).

16. Mark Robson, interviewed in *The Velvet Light Trap*. no. 10, Fall 1973.

17. Grinde, "Pictures for peanuts," p. 44.

18. Peter Bogdanovich, *Fritz Lang in America* (London: Studio Vista, 1967).

19. For information on the Lewton unit see Joel Siegel, *Val Lewton, the Reality of Terror* (London: Secker and Warburg/BFI, 1972). For further detail on RKO see the special issue (no. 10) of *The Velvet Light Trap*. On production in general see Gene Fernett, *Poverty Row* (Satellite Beach, Florida: Coral Reef, 1973).

20. Frank Rickerson Jr., *The Management of Motion Picture Theatres* (New York: McGraw-Hill, 1938), pp. 82-3.

21. Stuart Hall and Tony Jefferson (eds.), *Resistance Through Rituals: Cultural Studies,* nos. 7-8, Summer 1975; reprinted London: Hutchinson, 1976.

22. John Clarke, "Style," in ibid., pp. 175-92.

23. Fox's *March of Time* series lasted from 1934 until 1953 and its photojournalistic aesthetic carried over into that studio's "documentary" fictions in the late 1940s. Similarly, MGM's series of shorts, *Crime Does Not Pay,* which ran from 1935 until 1948, also complemented Metro's own output in that genre.

24. For one account of the effect of these pressures on the cinema see Keith Kelly and Clay Steinman, "Crossfire: a dialectical attack," in *Film Reader* no. 3.

25. Colin MacCabe, "Realism and the cinema: notes on some Brechtian theses," *Screen,* vol. 15, no. 2, Summer 1974, pp. 10-12.

26. Colin MacCabe, "Theory and film: principles of realism and pleasure," *Screen,* vol. 17, no. 3, Autumn 1976, p. 12.

27. Sylvia Harvey, "Woman's place," p. 22.

28. Gill Davies, "Teaching about narrative," *Screen Education,* no. 29, Winter 1978/79, p. 62.

29. Rouben Mamoulian, "Controlling color for dramatic effect," in *The American Cinematographers,* June 1941, collected in Richard Kozarski (ed.), *Hollywood Directors 1941-1976* (New York: Oxford University Press, 1976) p. 15.

30. Charles Higham, *Warner Brothers* (New York: Charles Scribner's Sons, 1975) p. 157.

31. The major sources of technological history drawn on here are Barry Salt, "Film style and technology in the thirties," in *Film Quarterly,* vol. 30, no. 1, Fall 1976 and "Film style and technology in the forties," in *Film Quarterly,* vol. 31, no. 1, Fall 1977; and James Limbacher, *Four Aspects of the Film* (New York: Brussel & Brussel, 1968).

32. See, in this respect, Patrick Ogle, "Technological and aesthetic influence upon the development of deep focus cinematography in the United States" and Christopher Williams' critique of that article's elision of notions of ideology and economy. Both are anthologized in *Screen Reader, 1* (London: SEFT, 1977).

Above, "Pretty tie, expensive. I wish I could afford it." Inspector Burgess (Thomas Gomez) and another detective (Regis Toomey, right) mockingly question Scott Henderson (Alan Curtis) about his wife's death.

Phantom Lady, Cornell Woolrich, and the Masochistic Aesthetic

Tony Williams

Despite the conclusions of the Wisconsin-Madison neo-formalist school,[1] film noir still remains to be reckoned with as an important movement in Hollywood narrative both in terms of its stylistic innovations and subversion of patriarchal gender norms.[2] It is in the latter connection that the work of Gaylyn Studlar promises significant gains in its applications to film noir.[3] The aim of this paper is to apply Studlar's thesis to the writer Cornell Woolrich and Robert Siodmak's Phantom Lady (1944) noting both its relevance and the oppositions which the film text counters to a complete supremacy of the masochistic aesthetic's operations.[4]

Studlar's work questions the Freudian-Lacanian-Metzian theoretical hegemony of cinema spectatorship and "woman's place." In Freud's scenario the child renounces pre-Oedipal bisexuality and the mother as "love object" in order to submit to patriarchal Law and castration. However, Studlar emphasizes Gilles Deleuze's work on masochism, challenging basic Freudian tenets of sado-masochistic duality, to reveal a hitherto neglected "masochistic aesthetic" in the field of psychoanalysis. In contrast to sadism's elevation of the father, masochism promotes the mother in a particular textual fashion. A work such as Masoch's Venus in Furs contains a world that is "mythical, persuasive, aesthetically oriented, and centered around the idealizing, mystical exaltation of love for the punishing woman. In her ideal form, as representative of the powerful oral mother, the female in the masochistic scenario is not sadistic, but must inflict cruelty in love to fulfill her role in the mutually agreed upon masochistic scheme."[5]

This psychoanalytic model naturally challenges Laura Mulvey's visual pleasure argument which asserts that "male scopic desires must centre around control—never identification with or submission to the female."[6] Cinema spectatorship also becomes less of a predominantly masculine activity with its emphasis upon the sadistic male gaze. In Studlar's view, the spectator (male or female) regressed to the infantile pre-Oedipal phase, submitting to (and identifying with) the overpowering presence of the screen and the woman on it. Spectatorship and identification thus become a more complex process than in Mulvey's original formulation, having a bisexual component which has associations with the early phases of pre-Oedipal developments.

"Through the mobility of multiple, fluid identifications, the cinematic apparatus allows the spectator to experience the pleasure of satisfying 'the drive to be both sexes' that is repressed in everyday life dominated by the secondary process. The cinema provides an enunciative apparatus that acts as a protective guise like fantasy or dream to permit the temporary fulfillment of what Kubie describes as 'one of the deepest tendencies in human nature'; but like the wish and counterwish to fuse with or separate from the mother, the wish to change gender identity is also an ambivalent desire."[7]

Fulfillment of desire may also involve destruction, a fact true not just of films such as *The Devil is a Woman* but also of Cornell Woolrich novels such as *Waltz into Darkness*.

It is important to understand the masochistic phenomenon historically and not regard it in the same universal a-historic manner as Freud's original formulation of the Oedipus complex. Recent research has shown that masochism increased dramatically in the early modern period of Western culture that coincided with "increased emphasis on individuality."[8] Viewing several case histories Baumeister argues that "masochism is essentially an attempt to escape from self, in the sense of achieving a loss of high-level self-awareness."[9] Although he notes evidence of desires to escape sex roles,[10] enacting "fantasies that are radically divorced from normal reality,"[11] among predominantly upper socioeconomic white males, his findings have further implications. The masochistic scenario may illustrate a tendency of artist (as well as audience) to escape oppressive gender roles that western capitalist society has defined as "normal" in prescribing arbitrary definitions of "self." In the light of these important theories both the place of Cornell Woolrich and a 1944 film adaptation of one of his works merit close attention.

Author of *Phantom Lady* (under the pseudonym "William Irish") Cornell Woolrich (1904-68) is now recognized as an important force in the literary background of *film noir*, offering a significant alternative to the "hard-boiled" school of Hammett, Cain and Chandler with their emphasis on phallic pleasures of control and mastery.[12] In terms of recent critical investigations of "male hysteria" and gender construction Woolrich's work offers fertile territory. Recognizing the male hysteric tradition in both literature and film, Jonathan Rosenbaum comments that Woolrich "can give it a sexual undertone without ever making its meaning strictly gender-based as it is frequently in Poe and Hemingway, Sternberg and Peckinpah. His heroines tend to be phallic while his heroes often verge on being sissies and fear becomes the universal democratic place on which they can meet as equals."[13] Woolrich's fervent emotional style, his powerful heroines (such as Julie Killeen of *The Bride Wore Black* [1940] who reduces her male victims to states of pre-Oedipal passivity) and the frenzied amnesiac of *The Black Curtain* (1942) who has lost masculine control of his destiny, are dynamic figures in Woolrich's world but have not been depicted in American movies. Hollywood investment in patriarchal norms of gender construction may be a significant reason for this although, as we shall see, it cannot entirely suppress this alternative as in the case of *Phantom Lady*. In a recent article on Robert Siodmak, J.P. Telotte notes that "Siodmak's films appear almost classic texts for illustrating gender tensions that were surfacing in post-World War II America."[14] Although the film *Phantom Lady* came out in 1944 it is an anticipation of those subversive gender tensions which would emerge in *Out of the Past*, *Gilda*, *Criss Cross* and *Night and the City*. They are key texts in illustrating the insecurity of male control when attempts were made to reintroduce the pre-war patriarchal status quo. Writing of Siodmak's work (but in terms also applicable to *Phantom Lady*) Telotte notes of the director's male characters that "What finally makes Siodmak's world so disturbing though, is that his male characters, too, seem fluid, potentially phantoms, as if they, too, were infected by a contagious evaporation of the self."[15] This influence may be attributed to the work of Cornell Woolrich and the dominance in his writings of the masochistic aesthetic.

Studlar's description of masochism as an obsessive recreation of the movement between "revelation and concealment, appearance and disappearance, rejection and seduction" accurately resembles Woolrich's classic novels, especially *The Bride Wore Black* (1940) and *Black Angel* (1942), which contain worlds of "a sensual heterocosm in which the female is mystically idealized as the loving inflictor of punishment."[16] Both Woolrich and Edward Hopper were influenced by cinema in their respective artistic mediums.[17] There are many parallels between Studlar's research and the work of Woolrich which demand further investigation.

"If the male spectator identified with the masochistic male character, he is aligned with a position usually assigned to the female. If he rejects identification with this position, one alternative is to identify with the position of power: the female who inflicts pain. In either case, the male spectator assumes a position associated with the female. In the former, he identified with the culturally assigned feminine characteristics exhibited by the male within the masochistic scenario; in the latter he identifies with the powerful female who represents the mother of pre-Oedipal life and the primary identification."[18]

Woolrich has much in common with this scenario. Biographical research has revealed his mother fixation, bi-sexual tendencies and inability to follow the Oedipal trajectory of "normal" human development. His first, F. Scott Fitzgerald-influenced novel, *Cover Charge* (1927), introduced the passive male hero, often at the mercy of the powerful female, who would frequently appear in his later work. But his most powerful fiction appeared in the decade of *film noir*, the '40s, often in the "Black" series of novels. Most of his work was filmed within a year or so of its initial appearance either under his own name or his pseudonyms, William Irish and George Hopley.[19] Woolrich was often displeased with the film versions of his work.[20] One of his major works remains to be filmed while two appeared as films some 20 years after their initial appearance as novels.

	Cornell Woolrich	William Irish	George Hopley
1940.	The Bride Wore Black		
1941.	The Black Curtain		
1942.	Black Alibi	Phantom Lady	
1943.	The Black Angel		
1944.	The Black Path of Fear	Deadline at Dawn	
1945.			The Night Has A Thousand Eyes
1947.		Waltz into Darkness	
1948.	Rendezvous In Black	I Married a Dead Man	

The late appearance of *The Bride Wore Black* and *Waltz into Darkness* (Truffaut's *La Sirène du Mississippi*) as films is mysterious.[21] However, one reason may be the fact that the heroines of these works were such powerful threats to patriarchal ideology that they could not be successfully incorporated into the '40s norms of Hollywood gender representations. The only comparison is *Detour's* (1945) heroine (the appropriately named actress Ann Savage). Although we are familiar with the *femmes fatales* of *Murder My Sweet* (1944), *Double Indemnity* (1945), and *Out of the Past* (1948), all these pale into insignificance when compared to Julie Killeen and Bonnie. Both women are far too powerful to gain access even into the contemporary cracks within the dominant Hollywood ideology that made *film noir* possible.

Julie Killeen is a powerful avenging figure, able to disguise herself by embodying male romantic fantasies of the "ideal female" and eventually killing her victims after reducing them to positions of helpless dependency. Julie wreaks so much damage upon patriarchal order that even the traditionally imposed Hays Code ending of "punishment for her sins" would have appeared ludicrous. Bonnie in *Waltz into Darkness* is more of a castrating threat to male power than Julie.

Rendezvous in Black has never been filmed to date. Although it is a male re-working of *The Bride Wore Black*, its assault on patriarchal gender construction makes it too threatening. The avenging hero murders the wives and girlfriends of his victims in revenge for the death of his sweetheart. The novel makes clear his excessive over-idealization of his lost love and his collapse into male hysteria. Thus his ambivalent sexual nature, hysterical actions and passivity before death reveal him as another Woolrich male who does not operate according to the masculine action dynamics of the Law of the Father. The hero of *The Black Curtain* exhibits hysteria when he discovers that his amnesia has caused loss of masculine control in society. This dilemma was excellently acted by Cary Grant in the half-hour radio version.[22] In *The Black Angel*, a quiet housewife becomes an avenging female to save her husband. In one case her actions indirectly cause the death of one of Woolrich's recurrent male victims on the altar of romanticism. Like Julie, the heroine "becomes an idealized, powerful figure, both dangerous and comforting"[23]—a role which Carol Richmond of *Phantom Lady* plays, causing the death of two male victims. While Scott Henderson becomes passive and impotent on death row, Carol is active on his behalf, thus reversing the typical male-female trajectory. She turns from sweet secretary to threatening pre-Oedipal mother and sexually active *femme fatale*. Although *Deadline at Dawn* substitutes the symbolic function of the city expressing capitalist alienation for the powerful female as a main narrative device, the novel's heroine still has actively to urge her passive boyfriend to save himself from the accusation of murder. *Black Alibi* is a notable exception to Woolrich's other work but this may be due to the novelist's experimenting with the "sadistic" aesthetic in crime fiction. Another explanation may lie in the fact that the original short story revealed the hero as the perpetrator of the crime.[24] Although the novel made him innocent this initial narrative device may explain the virtual absence of the masochistic motif.

Woolrich may have influenced other films. Based on Steve Fisher's novel, *I Wake Up Screaming* (1941) modelled the psychotic cop Cornell on Woolrich. In what was possibly an inside reference to the real-life author, the film cast Laird Cregar as Cornell. Although his resemblance to Woolrich was non-existent (unlike the novel's description), the industry knew of Cregar's unhappy existence as a bi-sexual at the time.[25] Burt Lancaster's roles in Siodmak's *The Killers* (1946) and *Criss Cross* (1948) are undeniable echoes of Woolrich's doomed male victims of romanticism, especially in their respective manipulation by *femme fatales* Ava Gardner and Yvonne De-Carlo. Another example is Richard Widmark's performance in Dassin's *Night and the City* (1950). Before his death he collapses into the arms of Gene Tierney like a little boy before his mother.

Although modifying Woolrich's short story, Hitchcock's *Rear Window* (1954) preserved the hero's important role as well as developing the cinematic apparatus motif.[26] This also occupied an important element in *The Window* (1950) where a little boy observes a murder committed by two dark mirror image parental figures, watching a window as if viewing a cinema screen. The dark parents are the alter egos of his economically oppressed father and mother (Arthur Kennedy and Barbara Hale) turning to robbery, murder and prostitution to survive inside capitalism. It is not without significance that the biggest threat to the boy comes from the dark mother (Ruth Roman).

Woolrich's "fervent emotionalism,"[27] male passivity before either avenging female or dark universal malevolent powers, and the role of suspense (usually presented as a race against time as in *Phantom Lady*, *Deadline at Dawn* and *The Night Has A Thousand Eyes*)[28] are all integral components of the masochistic aesthetic. Louis Bernard's tortuous romanticism and passivity in *Waltz into Darkness* represents the imaginative masochistic desire for reunion with the mother. It is finally realized in that "kiss of farewell" when Bonnie changes from hostile oral mother into the good maternal spirit:

Their very souls seemed to flow together. *To try to blend forever into one.* [Italics mine] Then, despairing, failed and were separated, and one slipped down into darkness and one remained in the light.[29]

Bonnie thus represents that "dialectical unity between liberation and death, the bonding of Eros with Thanatos that places the former in the service of the latter."[30] She is the idealized mother to Louis's pre-Oedipal child.[31]

Like *Deadline at Dawn* and *Three O'Clock*,[32] *Phantom Lady* contains Woolrich's hysteric suspense formula of the race against time. It resembles a compulsive Freudian *fort/da* game in which death (and return to the womb) is the dominant motif. Deleuze's observations concerning the masochistic's suspension of the ultimate gratification of death, the obsessive return to the continuously re-enacted moment of separation from the oral mother, are all relevant to understanding Woolrich's technique in novels such as *The Black Path of Fear*.

Studlar's investigation of the masochistic aesthetic has certainly great relevance to the novels of Cornell Woolrich and the Dietrich/von Sternberg cycle of films.[33] But when we examine the film *Phantom Lady*, we find that the masochistic scenario is more in the nature of a crack within the dominant patriarchal ideology rather than an overpowering element in the filmic text. We must remember that every film is a complex of intersecting elements in potential competition with each other. Also it may be under the influence of social and historical factors that govern what may be adapted at any particular time. According to Frederic Jameson, a set of circumstances may circumscribe an area beyond which any text can not stray. Any given historical moment may foreground some generic possibilities and make others unlikely.[34] In the case of *Phantom Lady*, both the novel and film are lacking in comparison to *The Bride Wore Black*, *Waltz into Darkness* and *Rendezvous in Black* where the masochistic aesthetic is more fully realized. As well as the reasons listed above for the imperfect realization of Woolrich's subversive gender depictions on screen, we must remember the dominance of the Oedipal trajectory of classical Hollywood cinema in which the female becomes subjected to male control either by death or marriage.[35] At the climax of the film Carol is confined to the office and the offer of monogamy. However, enough remains of the masochistic model in the film to argue that the aesthetic, if not dominant, is there as a fissure, a gap in the ideology which permits the partial expression of the female voice. It exists as an alternative operation against patriarchal control of the text. Even if subdued at the climax, it is still there, attempting to strain against narrative bounds.

In both novel and film Carol Richmond fulfills the role of the oral mother threatening two males in her quest to save Scott Henderson from the electric chair. She intimidates the barman of the Anselmo by usurping that prerogative which Mulvey associates with male-dominated cinema—the sadistic power of the gaze. She pur-

sues him and causes his death in a manner reminiscent of Deleuze's description of
the "bad" pre-Oedipal mother:

> She appealed to them, self-possessedly but loudly enough to be
> heard, and the calm clarity of her voice stopped them all short.
> "Don't. Let him alone. Let him go about his business."

> But there was no warmth nor compassion about it, just a terrible
> steely impartiality. As if to say: Leave him to me. He's mine.[36]

In visually dominating the drummer, Cliff, by acting out the sexually powerful *femme
fatale* role Carol assumes the uterine mother's function with its associations of
prostitution.[37] This is excellently realized in that "jam session" sequence in the cellar
lit in the German expressionist manner in which Carol lords it over drugged
musicians. As in the Dietrich/von Sternberg films "the *femme fatale* does not steal
her 'controlling gaze' from the male, but exercises the authority of the pre-Oedipal
mother whose gaze forms the child's first experience of love and power."[38]

But the narrative cannot allow Carol's total dominance. In the last 10 minutes she
is reduced to the helpless position of the threatened, screaming female before her
last-minute rescue by Inspector Burgess, representative of the Law of the Father.

Below, "Kansas" (Ella Raines), standing at frame center, smoking, with her suit and hair emphasized
by a kick light, strikes a masculine and dominating pose over her jailed and passive boss (Alan Curtis).

Also, the male victims are figures whom the masculine audience can easily reject. They are not Robert Mitchum of *Out of the Past* nor Glenn Ford in *Gilda*. The audience is removed from them.

This explains Siodmak's transformation of Woolrich's "normal" murderous engineer, Lombard, into Franchot Tone's stereotyped Mad Artist, "complete with delusions of grandeur, symbolic migraine headaches, and overdone hand gestures."[39] He appears to owe more to Siodmak's German expressionist interests rather than the hard-boiled world of '40s *noir*. However, this change is easily understandable when we remember traditional concepts of masculine depiction in Hollywood cinema and its tendency to project unmasculine features of lack of control, impotence and emotionalism on to figures such as Elisha Cook, Jr. with whom the audience would find it impossible to identify.[40] Lombard's original engineer function is too closely associated with male control. The film thus seeks to make him different. However, in the novel he is one of Woolrich's doomed victims on the altar of romanticism. He exhibits qualities usually associated with stereotypical notions of the female and becomes a plaything for the whims of unseen, oral mother, Marcella Henderson:

> He'd spent most of his life around oil-fields in God forsaken parts of the world; and he hadn't had much experience with women. He didn't have any sense of humor about things like that. He took her seriously. And of course she liked that part of it all the better, that made the game more real.... After all, when a guy's that age, and not a kid any more, he takes it hard when you kick his heart around like that.[41]

Franchot Tone's Marlow is a Nietzshean mad artist. He is associated with modern art artifacts as well as a Van Gogh self-portrait. The film uses these tactics to remove him as a threat to typical definitions of the masculine. A mad modernist artist is less of a threat to gender stereotypes that a mad, masculine engineer.[42]

But although the masochistic aesthetic is not completely dominant either in novel or film enough traces remain of its presence as a subversive influence. Examination of both works reveals underlying tensions which are not completely recuperated despite attempts to do so.

The novel begins and ends with the male perspective. It opens with Scott Henderson. Three pages describe his attitudes before he notices the mysterious female. The novel ends with Inspector Burgess's final moral to the reunited couple, Scott and Carol: "If you've got to have a moral, I give you this: don't ever take strangers to the theatre unless you've got a good memory for faces."[43]

This resembles the classic detective fiction discourse in which everything is satisfactorily resolved by a controlling agent in the type of fiction associated with Conan Doyle, Agatha Christie and the "hard-boiled" school. It is an unsatisfactory climax to a novel which exhibits so many of Woolrich's better concepts—Scott's passivity before his fate, Carol's active control in trying to save his life by taking on female roles that are merely the construction of male fantasies,[44] and the bi-sexual implications of such role transferences. Carol is instrumental in trapping Lombard in the novel—"The best man of us all"—as Inspector Burgess describes her.

The film's opening scenes differ. From the close-up of her hat as the camera tracks out *before* Scott enters the bar Anne Terry's control over the male narrative (and Scott) receives emphasis. Anne refuses to give her name, thus rejecting male control of her identity. Scott's inability to learn her name is later ridiculed by the voice of the unseen District Attorney (Milburn Stone) at his trial.

Scott's return home further reveals his impotence before the dominant female presence. As he enters his apartment calling his wife, a cop (Regis Toomey) switches on the light. Inspector Burgess stands beneath Marcella's portrait with an accusing look on his face. The camera pans left in the next shot when Scott discovers Marcella's dead body. Acting as if malevolent agents of the dead Marcella, the cops stand cynically watching.

Marcella's portrait appears predominantly throughout the following interrogation. She dominates Scott in death as she did in life.[45] His masculine world of "Engineer" is undermined by Marcella's image controlling the frame. The camera pans right as he speaks of his marital difficulties whilst walking away from the picture. It pans left as Scott returns to his original position beneath Marcella surrounded by the two cops. As he begins to relate his evening's humiliation—"She just sat there and laughed. She kept laughing at me"—Marcella's portrait appears at a canted angle leftwards. Toomey is to the right of the portrait. He acts as chorus of the patriarchal

Below, "Franchot Tone's Marlow is a Nietzshean mad artist": he book-ends the smugness of Kettisha (Doris Lloyd) as they look over a sketch held by Kansas (Ella Raines).

world view—"Nothing makes a man madder than that!" The portrait also dominates the frame in the next shot when Scott tells of Marcella's refusing a divorce. Another cop makes the sardonic comment, "Making a patsy of you, eh?"

Thus the visuals explicitly associate the cops as Marcella's functionaries in reducing Scott into helpless masochistic passivity. The casting of Alan Curtis as Scott, an actor not particularly noted for predominantly masculine roles, reinforces this interpretation.[46] He breaks down like the traditional "hysterical female" after seeing Marcella's body carried out by uncaring medics.

The cops surround Scott on either side. A slow tracking shot begins until he becomes isolated in close-up. As the camera moves in it emphasizes Scott's passivity. The envious class-conscious cops make hostile comments about his clothes in a manner usually associated with male comments about female costume: "A very neat dresser, Mr. Henderson." "Yeah, everything goes together." "Pretty tie, expensive. I wish I could afford it." Finally, the scene (with its visual associations of rape) ends with Burgess noticing that Scott's tie does not match his suit. The appropriate tie is round his wife's neck.

In the next sequence we meet Scott's secretary, Carol, played by Ella Raines. If Alan Curtis was not sufficiently "masculine" to be a successful Hollywood hero, Ella Raines was conversely not sufficiently "feminine," so her career was relatively brief.[47] *Phantom Lady* was her most significant film. Carol is efficient enough to run Scott's office on her own. But she is under the dominance of patriarchal ideology. Scott's voice over the dictaphone giving her daily orders limits any possibility she may have of independent control in the masculine world of Scott Henderson Incorporated.

However, when Scott receives the death sentence Carol becomes an avenging female, pursuing the barman and drummer Cliff Milburn with the power of the gaze to gain information, thus usurping a traditional male prerogative. In the bar Carol is transformed by harsh *noir* lighting into both a Woolrich avenging fury and hostile oral mother figure. Changing into her "hooker" role she entices Cliff by manipulating his look for the purposes of her own control.

But the filmic text can only allow Carol so much latitude before two male forces of patriarchy intervene. The first is Inspector Burgess (Thomas Gomez) who offers his support. Thus, the power of the Law will eventually dominate the narrative until it rescues Carol after she has relinquished the power of the avenging female by collapsing into hysteria.

The second figure is Marlow who represents the dark forces of male chaos, an opposing figure to patriarchy-prescribed gender roles. Entering Cliff's room after Carol has fled, his speech not only reiterates the "mad artist" discourse by which the narrative can make him an "other" but also reveals his female perception. "She was magnificent. She loathed you but she went with you. She would have humiliated herself to make you talk."

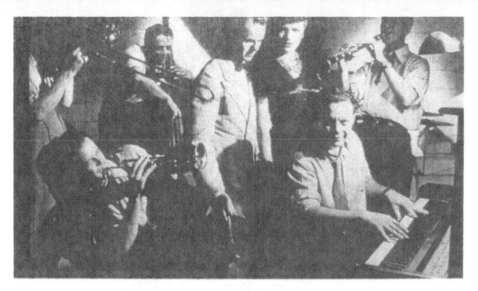

Above, Elisha Cook, Jr. and Ella Raines (center) at the jam session.

As portrayed by Franchot Tone, Lombard/Marlow is clearly a victim of socially restrictive gender definitions of male and female roles. Although the narrative attempts to depict him as a mad artist, an "other," it is clear that his insecurities in bearing an oppressive male role in capitalist society have overpowered him. Rejected by Marcella, he has psychotically erupted against an imagined threat to his socially constructed ego. Yet, Tone's performance contains a mixture of sympathy and pathos that clearly marks him as victim rather than monster. His act was the ultimate expression of male hysteria when his everyday "masculine" role became as impotent as that of Scott's before the cops. Like Scott he has clearly repressed "feminine" qualities which explode in murderous expression.

Up to Marlow's appearance Carol has occupied the role of the avenging Woolrich female. But the film's patriarchal narrative form can bear the strain no longer. A progressive subordination of her role begins until she is no longer the "threat" but "the threatened." She must lose all trace of her previous pre-Oedipal status by now occupying a subordinate position within the "sadistic" portion of the narrative in which she is threatened by Marlow until Inspector Burgess can successfully intervene.

When Carol eventually finds Anne Terry, the film clearly reveals that females are also *victims* of patriarchal ideology. After the death of her fiancé, Anne has collapsed into a nervous breakdown. She is as much a victim of romantic love ideology as is Lombard/Marlow. When Carol discovers her, Anne is living in her grandmother's house where she "had lived all her life." Dominated by the dead hand of the past, Anne tells Carol about her grandmother. "She was very happy here. She married the man she loved. I'll never marry." However, recognizing Carol's similar love (or entrapment) she gives her the hat needed for evidence before therapeutically breaking down in recognizing the death of her love.

After Inspector Burgess's rescue Carol once more occupies the subordinate secretarial role after Scott has seemingly resumed the boss demeanor. But although the film attempts to impose a "happy" ending by means of the classical Hollywood marriage motif,[48] the climax can be read in a much more subversive manner. Despite the film's ideological project of undermining Carol's dominant role by attempting to assert male control at the climax, both the opening and closing shots significantly operate against this. A tension is created in the overall structure impossible to recuperate successfully.

We remember that the film began with a close-up of Anne's hat. The enigmatic female, not the male (as in Woolrich's original), begins the narrative. At the climax Inspector Burgess and Scott await Carol. Both men leave as if nothing has happened. Scott tells Carol of the dictaphone messages awaiting her. Rescued from the electric chair he appears to show no gratitude to her. The formal boss-secretary relationship appears to resume as Carol presses the vocal instrument of male control.

Listlessly listening she hears Scott's marriage proposal. "You're having dinner with me tonight, and tomorrow night, and every night." The camera tracks in to a close-up as the message plays. It stops as the dictaphone needle sticks in the groove endlessly repeating "every night." An enigmatic look of pleasure emerges on her face in the final image.

Two interpretations are possible here. First, the climax represents the successful Oedipal project of subordinating the female to the male. As victim Carol takes pleasure in her own future oppression as both wife and secretary. But a second interpretation is also more likely. A contradiction certainly exists in the combination of needle sticking and a triumphant look on Carol's face. The dictaphone is symbolic of male control, a control that the film reveals as being non-existent in the cases of Scott, Marlow, the barman, and Cliff. Even Inspector Burgess admits his error about Scott's guilt to Carol mid-way in the film. We remember the powerful *femme fatale* role which she occupied in her pursuit of the guilty males. It is hard to believe that she will ever successfully settle down into the passive role of wife/secretary. The needle sticks on the words, "every night," the time in which Carol was at her most powerful. Carol's triumphant look may assert the latent presence of the "masochistic aesthetic" still awaiting another re-emergence in opposition to patriarchal power. The needle sticking opposes the male control triumph of the female outside the confines of the text. This scene anticipates those future victories of her sister "phantom ladies" in a later generation.

Notes

1. See David Bordwell, Janet Staiger and Kristin Thompson, *The Classical Hollywood Cinema: Film Style and Mode of Production to 1960* (New York: Columbia University Press 1985): pp. 74-77; Edward Branigan, *Point of View.*

2. For a relevant selection of work in this field see Raymond Borde and Étienne Chaumeton, *Panorama du film noir Américain* (Paris: Éditions d'aujourd'hui 1953; 1976 reprint); Raymond Durgnat, "The Family Tree of *film noir*," *Cinema* (Britain) 6/7 (August 1970): pp. 48-56; Paul Schrader, "Notes on *Film Noir*," *Film Comment*, 10.1 (January-February 1974): pp. 30-35; E. Ann Kaplan, ed., *Women in Film Noir* (London: British Film Institute 1978); Alain Silver and

Elizabeth Ward, *Film Noir: An Encyclopedic Reference to the American Style* (Woodstock, New York: The Overlook Press 1979); Jon Tuska, *Dark Cinema: American Film Noir* in Cultural Perspective (Westport, CT: Greenwood Press 1964).

3. Studlar's doctoral thesis (to be published this year [Editor's Note: 1988] by the University of Illinois Press) in its application to cinema deals exclusively with the Paramount Dietrich/von Sternberg films. For an outline of her position see Gaylyn Studlar, "Masochism and the Perverse Pleasures of the Cinema," *Quarterly Review of Film Studies*, 9.4 (January-February 1985): pp. 267-82; and "Visual Pleasures and the Masochistic Aesthetic," *Journal of Film and Video* 37.2 (Spring 1985): pp. 5-26. However, the findings are equally applicable to other areas of cinema such as *film noir*, horror and the musical. I am grateful to Professor Studlar for her suggestions in correspondence dated June 24th, 1987 and November 1st, 1987. See also Linda Bundtzen, "Monstrous Mothers: Medusa, Grendel and Now Alien," *Film Quarterly* 50.3 (Spring 1987): pp. 11-17; and Linda Mizejewski, "Women, Monsters and the Masochistic Aesthetic in Fosse's *Cabaret*," *Journal of Film and Video* 39.4 (Fall 1987): pp. 5-17.

4. This article is abased upon a paper delivered at the Mid-West Popular Culture Association Conference on October 16, 1987 at the Meramec campus of St. Louis Community College. I am grateful to the *CineAction!* editorial group for suggested revisions.

5. Studlar, *Masochism*, p. 267; see also Gilles Deleuze, *Masochism: An Interpretation of Coldness and Cruelty* (New York: George Braziller 1971).

6. Laura Mulvey, "Visual Pleasure and Narrative Cinema," *Screen* 16.1 (Autumn 1975): pp. 6-18. See also the criticism by D.N. Rodowick, "The Difficulty of Difference," *Wide Angle* 5.1 (1982): pp. 7-9.

7. Studlar, "Visual Pleasure and the Masochistic Aesthetic," p. 13.

8. See Roy F. Baumeister, "Masochism as Escape from Self," *The Journal of Sex Research*, 25.1 (February 1988): pp. 28-59, especially 51.

9. Baumeister, pp. 28-29.

10. Baumeister, p. 41.

11. Baumeister, p. 45.

12. On Woolrich as the real literary inspiration of film noir see Stephen Jenkins, "Dashiell Hammett and Noir: Out of the Vase?" in *Monthly Film Bulletin* 49, No. 586 (November 1982): p. 276. See also John Baxter, "Something more than night," *The Film Journal* 2.4 (1975): p. 9, who cites a passage from Woolrich's *The Black Path of Fear* (1944) as contributing towards noir lighting effects. This is also mentioned by Bordwell 77 who cites 1940s comic strips and German expressionist lighting techniques.

13. Jonathan Rosenbaum, "Black Window: Cornell Woolrich," *Film Comment* 20.5 (September-October 1984): pp. 36-38.

14. J.P. Telotte, "Siodmak's Phantom Women and *Noir* Narrative," *Film Criticism* 11.3 (Spring 1987): p. 2.

15. Telotte, p. 9.

16. Studlar, p. 8.

17. Woolrich briefly worked as a Hollywood screenwriter, taking the pseudonym of scenarist "William Irish" for four of his novels. See Francis M. Nevins Jr. "Introduction," Cornell Woolrich writing as William Irish, *Phantom Lady* (New York: Ballantine 1982): pp. ix-xiii. For one example of cinema in Woolrich see *The Black Angel* (New York: Ballantine 1982): p. 131. On Hopper's use of cinema see Erika L. Doss, "Edward Hopper, *Nighthawks* and *Film Noir*," *Postscript* 2.2 (Winter 1983): pp. 14-36.

18. Studlar, p. 14.

19. Hopley was Woolrich's maternal middle name. See Francis M. Nevins Jr. "Introduction," Cornell Woolrich writing as George Hopley, *The Night Has a Thousand Eyes* (New York: Ballantine 1982): p. xiv.

20. See the February 2, 1947 letter of Woolrich to Mark Van Doren concerning the filming of *Black Angel*. This was kindly reproduced for me by Mike Nevins.

21. For a description of the films and their flaws see Francis M. Nevins Jr. "Fade to Black," *The Armchair Detective* 20.1 (1987): pp. 39-51; "Fade to Black, Part Two," *The Armchair Detective* 20.2 (1987): pp. 160-175.

22. On the significance of Cary Grant in terms of bi-sexuality see Andrew Britton, "Cary Grant: Comedy and Male Desire," *CineAction!* 7 (December 1986): pp. 36-52.

23. Studlar, *Masochism*, p. 268.

24. See Francis M. Nevins Jr., "Introduction," Cornell Woolrich, *Black Alibi* (New York: Ballantine 1982): p. xi.

25. See Joel Greenberg, "Writing for the Movies: *Barry Lyndon*," *Focus on Film* 21 (Summer 1975): p. 48.

26. See Roberta Pearson and Robert Stamm, "Hitchcock's *Rear Window*: Reflexivity and the Critique of Voyeurism," *Enclitic* 7.1 (Spring 1983): pp. 136-45.

27. See Francis M. Nevins Jr. "Introduction," Cornell Woolrich, *Nightwebs* (New York: Harper & Row 1971).

28. *Phantom Lady's* chapters are all headed by the number of days or hours preceding Scott Henderson's execution.

29. Cornell Woolrich writing as William Irish, *Waltz into Darkness* (New York: Ballantine 1983): p. 319.

30. Studlar, p. 280.

31. See Studlar, p. 271 for an illuminating parallel to this scene in terms of the masochistic aesthetic.

32. See William Irish, *I Wouldn't Be in Your Shoes* (Philadelphia & New York: Lippincott 1943).

33. For some pertinent observations on the role of the masochistic aesthetic in the Paramount cycle see Florence Jacobowitz, "Power and the Masquerade: *The Devil is a Woman*," *CineAction!* 8 (March 1987): p.34.

34. Frederic Jameson, *The Political Unconscious* (Ithaca: Cornell University Press 1981): pp. 145-48.

35. The work of Raymond Bellour on classical Hollywood narrative is relevant here. For some qualifications to Studlar's work in terms of arguing for a sado-masochistic dialectic within

the viewing subject see Tania Modleski, *The Women Who Knew Too Much* (New York: Methuen 1988): pp. 9-13.

36. *Phantom Lady*, p. 110

37. Studlar, *Visual Pleasure*," p. 24, n. 13.

38. Studlar, p. 23.

39. Nevins, "Introduction," *Phantom Lady*, p. xiii.

40. For a significant article on this actor's function in *The Big Sleep* (1946) see Christopher Orr, "The Trouble With Harry: On the Hawks Version of *The Big Sleep*," *Wide Angle* 5.2 (1982): pp. 66-71.

41. *Phantom Lady*, p. 219.

42. On the cultural significance of this transformation in terms of contemporary attacks of modernism see Diane Waldman, "The Childish, the Insane and the Ugly: The Representation of Modern Art in Popular Films and Fiction of the Forties," *Wide Angel* 5.2 (1982): pp. 52-65.

43. *Phantom Lady*, p. 240.

44. The heroine's observations about Marty in *Black Angel* deserve quoting:

> Out of all the thousands and thousands of fine constructive women in this world, what evil star made him pick her out? What *got* him about her? Couldn't he see, couldn't he tell—?
> And the answer, of course, was self-evident. What gets any of us about any of them; what gets any of them about any of us? The image in our minds. Not the reality that others see; the image in the mind. Therefore, how could he see, how could he tell, how could he free himself, when the image in his mind all along, and even now, was that of a lovely creature, all sunshine, roses, and honey, a beatific haloed being, a jewel of womankind? Who would even strive to free himself from such a one? Watch out for the image in your mind." [p. 66]

Woolrich's ability to identify himself with both male and female positions receives classic exemplification here.

45. The role of the portrait is a special icon in *film noirs* such as *The Woman in the Window* (1944) and *Laura* (1945). For some relevant observations on this motif see Janey Place, "Women in Film Noir," E. Ann Kaplan, ed. *Women in Film Noir*, pp. 47-50. One recalls Keene's fascination with the portrait of the imprisoned Mrs. Paradine in *The Paradine Case* (1947) and the power exerted over Cregar's Cornell by Carole Landis's portrait in *I Wake Up Screaming*. For an interesting discussion of the former film in terms of male impotence and female ambiguity see Michael Anderegg, "Hitchcock's *The Paradine Case* and Filmic Unpleasure." *Cinema Journal* 26.4 (Summer 1987): pp. 49-59.

46. According to Ephraim Katz, *The International Film Encyclopedia* (London: Macmillan 1979, p. 293), he was originally a male model before entering films in 1936.

47. She was a joint discovery of Charles Boyer and Howard Hawks (Katz, p. 944).

48. See Janet Bergstrom, "Alternation, Segmentation, Hypnosis: Interview with Raymond Bellour," *Camera Obscura* 3/4 (1979): p. 88.

Above, Gail Russell as Jean Courtland and Edward G. Robinson as Triton in *Night Has a Thousand Eyes*.

John Farrow: Anonymous *Noir*

Alain Silver and James Ursini

Like many filmmakers who worked through the *noir* cycle, John Farrow's motion pictures melded seamlessly into the fabric of the classic period. In fact, his films were such an anonymous part of the total output of Hollywood in the 1940s and 50s that most film encyclopedias do not even list him. Andrew Sarris, who found room for John Brahm, Gordon Douglas, and even Burt Topper under the heading of "Miscellany" in *The American Cinema*, excluded John Farrow. Only half of the film references currently in print list Farrow; all include his daughter, Mia, and his wife, Maureen O'Sullivan. In some circles, Farrow is better-known as a Roman Catholic apologist, who wrote books on Thomas More and Father Damien's efforts with the lepers of Molokai.

Farrow directed nearly fifty features but only five *noir* films (or some might argue for six with the inclusion of the hard-boiled, supernatural melodrama *Alias Nick Beal*). This was a couple more than Joseph Losey or Max Ophuls, the same number as Robert Aldrich and Otto Preminger, and a few less than Joseph H. Lewis or Robert Siodmak. Like Siodmak at Universal and then Fox, Farrow's *noir* films were made within the studio system, first at Paramount and then at RKO. Farrow's cinematographers, John F. Seitz at Paramount, Nick Musuraca and Harry Wild at RKO, worked on other, better-known *noir* films, such as *Double Indemnity, Out of the Past*, and *Murder, My Sweet* respectively, and with better-known directors from Billy Wilder to Joseph von Sternberg. Most of Farrow's other collaborators, from screenwriters and composers to stars, worked on as many or more *noir* films, particularly actor Robert Mitchum.

I. The Paramount Films

As a contract director who theoretically worked on assignment, Farrow typifies how fully engaged America's film industry, as represented by the major studios, were in the *noir* cycle. Farrow's other pictures range from Westerns and war films to screwball comedies and costume dramas. His pre-*noir* work included the series detective feature, *The Saint Strikes Back* (1939) and the downbeat war adventure *China* (1943) starring Alan Ladd. Ladd also starred in Farrow's first *film noir*, *Calcutta* (1947), playing a Paramount equivalent of Bogart's Sam Spade in a plot

145

heavily derived from *The Maltese Falcon*: a cynical protagonist, the death of a partner, a duplicitous woman, smuggled jewels. After he beats a confession out of his dead partner's widow, Ladd's character turns her in with the sardonic admonishment: "You counted on your beauty with guys. Even ones you were going to kill."

Stylistically, Farrow favored occasional foreground clutter and wide angle close-ups as visual counterpoint. He was second to none of his contemporaries, not even Ophuls, in his passion for the long take and often staged entire sequences without a cut.[1] Farrow's films in the 50s ranged from the bizarrely plotted Western, *Ride, Vaquero*; the World War II drama starring John Wayne as a German freighter captain, *The Sea Chase*; and a post-*noir* melodrama of sexual paranoia and betrayal, *The Unholy Wife*.

After *Calcutta*, Farrow's *noir* pictures of the classic period at Paramount, *The Big Clock* and *The Night Has a Thousand Eyes* (both 1948), were produced back-to-back. Although the producers were different Farrow worked with essentially the same scenarist, cinematographer, costumer, sound recordists, art department, and composer on both pictures; and, although *The Night Has a Thousand Eyes* does have some location photography, he may well have shot both movies on the same sound stages. Narratively, both feature flashbacks from the point of view of a troubled protagonist.

The Big Clock uses a miniature, process photography, and optical effects to open with a low angle panning shot across a night skyline then to move into a building. A matte optical takes the camera past the letters that identify "Janoth Publications" and inside to a dark corridor, where a figure comes out of an elevator. As he does, he begins a tortured narration, wondering how he has ended up here, hunted, hiding in the darkness, how everything was different only "thirty-six hours ago," a phrase he repeats like a litany. An unbroken shot, typical of Farrow, follows him into the mechanism of a giant clock, around an interior catwalk then moves out of the clock to its exterior display of the date and time. A dissolve begins a flashback to a day-lit lobby, thirty-six hours before.

The narration and long take are combined to enhance suspense. The viewer knows that the figure (who names himself when he says, "Think fast, George!") is portrayed by Ray Milland, the star of the film, and thus the character with whom to identify. But the other items of *noir* style, the dark cityscape, the camera moves, the low-key sets, all these confuse and disorient the viewer. Point of view is established and expressed both in narrative terms as the character prepares to tell his story and in figurative terms as the audience coexperiences his tension and uncertainty.

Farrow stages the first scenes of the flashback, which will constitute most of the film, to counterbalance the tension-filled opening. In the busy, day-lit lobby, a guide drones on to a tour group about the big clock and the Janoth Building, which houses the publishing empire of its namesake, Earl Janoth. George Stroud, relaxed, smiling, crosses the lobby and, when a tourist asks the guide, "What if the clock stops?" George answers nonchalantly, "Oh, Mr. Janoth wouldn't allow that." As George rides the elevator up with other Janoth employees, the dialogue evokes the sense of everyday routine with its casual chit-chat punctuated by the attempt of a young visitor to make time with the elevator girl as she announces each floor. Ultimately she rebuffs him because "We are not allowed to speak to people in the elevator." As George adds again, "Mr. Janoth doesn't permit it."

Having established a more light-hearted or at least normal tone, Farrow reinforces it with a long take as Stroud enters the *Crimeways* bureau. Turning from a blackboard that reads "Crimeways Clue Chart" to the full-lit reception area and moving back with Stroud into his private office, the camera dollies and pans, as he passes and speaks to co-workers, tightening slightly with each movement until it frames him in medium close-up when he calls his home. The cut, which breaks the high-key elasticity of the image, is to his wife. Georgette Stroud mirrors George, in name and in framing. She does not believe that Janoth will permit him to leave for an extended vacation and belated "honeymoon" with their young son, also named George. On this first note of discord, there is a dissolve to a staff meeting which George must attend. Rather than a typical establishing shot, Farrow opens the scene with a tight close shot of Steve Hagen (George Macready), Janoth's executive assistant. Hagen's severe mien and harsh voice are an immediate contrast to the pleasant banter in the elevator and at *Crimeways*. The camera pulls back all the way to the other end of the table, reducing Hagen to a distant figure, as the clock sounds signaling the hour and all stand in anticipation. From this Farrow cuts to a high angle, as Janoth enters via a private elevator at the back of the conference room. In just two shots, the tone has shifted again. Acting and staging create an edgier atmosphere and a different stylistic undercurrent with the framing and angles. The camera follows Janoth all around the table as he makes a speech and asserts his control. Hagen's one line is delivered from the background. As Janoth comes around smoothly to the head of the table and questions one of the conferees, there is a cut. In the foyer a door opens and Stroud comes in. He disrupts the careful order of Janoth's world by coming late, and Farrow underscores that by timing the end of the long take to Stroud's entry.

Of course, Georgette is right. Stroud may be late for the meeting, a cardinal sin for Janoth, but with good reason: *Crimeways* has just tracked down and gotten an exclusive on a man named Fleming who has long eluded the authorities. Now Janoth wants George to stay in town to supervise this big story that will enhance the *Crimeways* circulation, but Hagen cannot convince him. "What does Janoth think I am," Stroud retorts, "a clock with rings and gears instead of flesh and blood."

In another sequence staged in a single take, Janoth comes down to see Stroud himself. He is not really interested in the *Crimeways* blackboard and "system of irrelevant clues." He glances at an odd painting in Stroud's office, sits, stands, circles, pats him on the back, offers a later, all-expenses-paid vacation to South America; but Stroud is unmoved. Despite Janoth's threat to fire and blackball him, he refuses to postpone his trip. In the context of *film noir*, this existential assertion seals Stroud's fate. After so much dialogue without a cut, the subconscious anticipation in a viewer again creates tension. Again a phone call motivates the cutaway, this time from Rita Johnson, a woman who claims to "know enough about Mr. Janoth" to control his behavior.

While it may predate the use of the term, Janoth himself is a classic "control freak"; and the clocks are the obvious symbols of that. His obsessive scheduling of his time down to the minute, his fastidious grooming, his inflected speech with syllables modulated like the swinging of a pendulum—these are all exaggerated traits, suggestive of a parody, even of a cartoon. There is an element of parody also in the way that representational reality is subtly questioned. Many aspects of the Janoth Building, the "big clock" itself being just one such item, are extremely stylized; the streamlined, moderne decor creates an atypical almost antiseptic atmosphere. The names of the various magazines of the Janoth publishing empire, *Crimeways, Artways,* etc., are as much about a distorted or manipulated reality, i.e., the "ways" of crime, art, etc., as they are about an objective reporting of facts. In a literal sense, the companies and the building are extensions of Janoth and his compulsive psychology. George Stroud's peril stems both directly and indirectly from the same troubled psyche.

This condition creates the twists most typical of *noir*. Stroud the narrator never realizes as he tells his story the real dimensions of his dilemma and how he himself has caused it. After being fired, Stroud's curiosity leads to a meeting with Rita Johnson. His drunken search with her for a "green clock" to irritate Janoth, which ends with a metal sundial, is self-defeating. Because of Stroud that implement, a symbol of the most primitive type of time keeping which is entirely abhorrent to his former boss, is near at hand in her apartment when Janoth is overcome with anger; and it becomes a murder weapon. As his discussions with his wife continue to reveal, Stroud's entire career has been spent under Janoth's control. He is trapped now, literally first inside Janoth's building and later within the confines of his clock; but figuratively Stroud is also trapped inside Janoth's head. When Janoth rehires George to find himself, it is the ultimate existential irony.

Even the comic relief provided by Elsa Lancaster as the zany artist Louise Patterson is part of the consistent ironic pattern of *The Big Clock*. Patterson's work is introduced anonymously long before she is, through a painting of two figures in Stroud's office. Not only does it clash somewhat with the imposed homogeneity of the building's offices, but it catches Janoth's eye when he tries to bully Stroud. Patterson herself is first seen, still unnamed, in an antique shop being outbid by a drunken Stroud for one of her works. As Janoth searches for the man that was with Rita Johnson, Patterson is summoned to sketch the purported killer. Realizing that Stroud is a collector of her work and not wanting to betray him, she

Above, *The Big Clock*: Stroud (Ray Milland) is reminded by his assistant Dan Tobin (Roy Cordette) that he owns a Patterson painting.

eventually produces an abstract sketch that, much to Janoth's exasperation, resembles a Lipchitz sculpture and two eggs.

Farrow's visual scheme complements the circular movement of the narrative. The oversized clock faces before which the actors posed for publicity stills are not actually in the picture; but the arcs and circles in which the characters move are. The figurative circle is closed the second time Stroud enters the clock in a repetition of the first scene. This time the camera follows Stroud out of the elevator in a tighter, medium close shot. Again he evades the guard, and without a cut another unbroken but different shot follows him inside the clock and up the short spiral staircase. The flashback never really ends as much as it merges back into the narrative and, since we have already heard what George is thinking, into itself through this overlapping action.

When George, having taken refuge in the big clock, inadvertently turns it off, Janoth and his associates in the building above notice that the office clocks have also stopped. "It's a mechanical thing!" Janoth exclaims after frenziedly shaking a desk clock; "It can go wrong." In Janoth's universe, where time, where all things are tied together in mechanized harmony, dissonance is anathema. Stroud knows that Janoth killed Johnson and has just used the library of phone books inside the clock to discover another key fact: that Janoth went to Hagen's after the murder.

When he elbows the clock switch shortly after this, it metaphorically underscores the turning point in the plot, the transfer of control from Janoth to Stroud. In the end, it is the loss of control which sends Janoth to his doom.

The concept of control is also a significant factor in *The Night Has a Thousand Eyes* which is based on a novel of the same name by Cornell Woolrich, whose fiction inspired a dozen *noir* films. Like most of Woolrich's work the story revolves around images of darkness and time, images which threaten to swallow up the main characters who are fighting desperately for their lives against these two inexorable forces. In this case it is a young girl, her father, and a haunted seer who predicts their doom and, in the film at least, his own.

In Farrow's rendering of this fatalistic piece, he and his screenwriters make several minor alterations and one particularly significant change. He shifts the focus away from the young girl, Jean Courtland, and her father. Instead, the narrative concentrates on the man, named Triton in the film, who sees visions of the future. This change brings to the foreground the supernatural and ironic aspects of Woolrich's story: the reluctant prophet whose life has been destroyed by his ability to see disaster but not to prevent it. Although Jean and her father are also haunted, they have only a few days of terror and anguish until it is resolved—by death in the father's case and by salvation, through Triton's actions, for Jean.

The audience's identification with Triton is established early in the film by having him narrate his pitiable fate to Jean and her boyfriend, Elliott Carson. Through flashback, a time distortion as typical of Woolrich in particular as it is of *noir* in general, Triton explains how a simple mind-reading act filled with "parlor tricks" turned into genuine instances of precognition. As his predictions proved more ac-

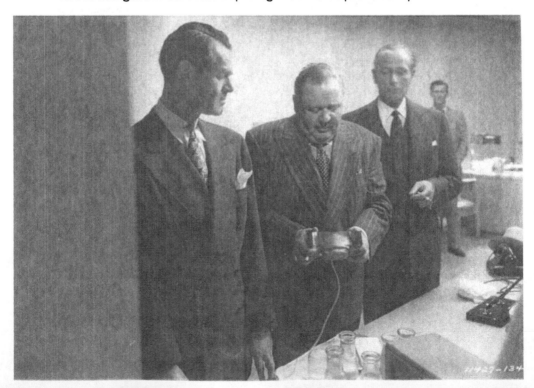

curate, Triton explains how he grew more and more guilty. The camera tracks around him, hunched over the table of the dimly lit, dingy bar, as he tells his story to the distraught Jean and her skeptical beau. Then it holds on a close-up of Triton as he confesses that "I had a crazy feeling I was making the things come true."

In order to test this "feeling," he decides not to tell the next person about the prediction and then to see if the event occurs. In yet another instance of a single take, Farrow's camera pulls back from Triton and a newspaper boy in a dark alley where rain pours down on them. Triton sees something in the boy's face but refuses to divulge the information. As Triton rushes away he hears the sound a car screeching to a stop, and as he turns back he is told that the boy has been hit by that very car. Here Farrow employs the long take not merely to enhance tension but also to have the unbroken image reinforce the sense of an unseen, metaphysical link between Triton and the boy.

Convinced that he can no longer control his fate, Triton retreats into a world of run-down hotel rooms and isolation. The camera pans across Bunker Hill and Angel's Flight, iconic settings in many *noir* films, to one of the area's seedier apartments where Triton has taken up residence. The use of practical locations in *The Night Has a Thousand Eyes* is limited to the sequences at Bunker Hill and the train yard. The effect is to add a graphic reality to Triton's self-imposed exile colored by the existing image of the neighborhood, where in Raymond Chandler's celebrated description "you could find anything from down-at-heels ex-Greenwich villagers to crooks on the lam." In this context, Triton buries himself alive, for as he says in voice-over, he was "living in a world already dead."

Triton does ultimately emerge from his "premature burial," to seek a final redemption. He is determined to save Jean, the daughter of his best friend and his ex-fiancée. The vision he has of her fate is delivered to him in bits and pieces: a flower crushed under a shoe, a sudden gust of wind, the talons of a lion, a broken vase, a voice saying "there's no danger now." But the most disturbing part of his vision is the one he sees in the mirror. In a three-quarter medium shot of Triton in double image, the audience witnesses his face turn to shock as he feels his side, looking for blood on his shirt. The scene is not subjectified. The audience does not see what he "sees" in his mind but is left to infer it from his face and actions.

Ultimately each of the images from Triton's vision, which he relates to others but which remain unseen to anyone but himself, are visually reified for the audience: a flower is crushed under a shoe; a vase does crash to the ground; a freak wind does blow open the curtains; and Jean does fall beneath the talons of a stone lion as she is attacked by the villain. Finally, Triton himself is shot in the side in saving Jean. As the camera pans around the baffled faces and down to the prone figure of Triton, the viewer realizes as do the characters that the parts of his vision were correct but not the whole, that it was not Jean's doom he saw but his own death and redemption through her. As in *The Big Clock* time is one of the crucial elements in this film as it was in the original novel. Triton would like to

Opposite, Janoth (Charles Laughton) shakes the stopped clock as his surprised employees look on in *The Big Clock*.

stop time, to hide from it so that he will no longer be tormented by these visions for which he has never asked. "Why was this gift given to me?" he complains to a pair of psychiatrists who have been summoned by the police to examine him.

Jean, too, wishes to stop time in order to avert the doom Triton has predicted: her death at night under the "thousand eyes" of the stars. In the first scene of the movie, Elliott finds her broken watch in the train yard. As he looks up, the camera assumes his helpless, low angle POV while he witnesses Jean's attempted suicide as she threatens to leap from the trestles above a moving train. She later says to him about time and the stars, whose shining she cannot stop, "At least I stopped it [her watch]." The flashback structure is, as noted, another effective means of

Below, Edward G. Robinson as Triton foresees his own death when he looks at himself in the mirror in *Night Has a Thousand Eyes.*

freezing and distorting time. All action in the present ceases as the narrator, dwelling on the details as if unwilling to return to the painful current reality, reconstructs his past. Although that past is filled with sorrow, it is a sorrow which can no longer touch Triton.

Like Janoth's $600,000 timepiece in *The Big Clock*, the grandfather clock in the Courtland house also is a key symbol. As 11:00 PM, the time Triton had predicted for Jean's "doom," draws closer, a series of close shots of Lieutenant Shawn and two-shots of Jean and Elliott are cut to the sound of the chimes. When nothing untoward occurs, the characters are relieved. The audience, however, has been put in a superior position and is aware of the irony of the scene: it is not really 11:00 PM. The time setting has been altered by an unidentified hand which moved the clock forward. As in *The Big Clock*, the control of time is tied to survival. Unlike it, Triton's transcendent awareness posits an even more compelling factor, a fabric of predetermined events which override everything else.

II. The RKO Films

In his first *noir* picture at RKO, *Where Danger Lives* (1950), Farrow creates a *femme fatale* unusual even for *noir*. Most of the cycle's "spider women" are heartless schemers empowered by a deadly eroticism, often deadly for themselves as well as their male victims. Margo, the heroine of this tale, is an out-of-control schizophrenic, who seems truly to believe in the fantasies she has concocted to ensnare her hapless lover, Dr. Jeff Cameron. In this she is unlike such classic *femme fatales* as the cold and cunning Phyllis Dietrichson of *Double Indemnity*, but anticipates a later, more conflicted heroine such as Diane Tremayne of Otto Preminger's 1953 *Angel Face*.[2]

The viewer's first close-up glimpse of Margo is from Cameron's point of view as he bends over her supine body and questions her regarding her attempted suicide. Her naked shoulders peek out seductively from beneath the hospital sheets. Her black hair frames her softly focused face like a demonic halo. His attraction is immediate as he sees in her both sexual object and damsel in distress. By the time she asks rhetorically, "Why should I live?" Cameron has already supplied an answer.

Margo is driven by an hysterical intensity which in turn drives all around her, including the submissive hero, into violence. Cameron's confrontation with Margo's husband (who she originally tells him is her father) is particularly illustrative. The scene is staged largely in three-shots which reify the triangular conflict of Margo, her husband (Lannington), and Cameron. When the fatal fight between Cameron and Lannington finally breaks out, it is instigated by another of Margo's hysterical fits. Cameron responds violently to her claim that her husband has ripped an earring from her ear and is consequently beaten over the head by Lannington. When he regains consciousness he discovers the husband dead and himself a fugitive.

The fight between Cameron and Margo's husband is only the beginning of Margo's control over Cameron. His association with Margo erodes his will as it sucks him into the back draft created by her frenetic energy. Only in a sleazy border-town hotel, where the concussion from his fight with her husband has left him drained and delirious, does he begin to sense the truth.

Jeff Cameron is among the most masochistic in a long line of pained *noir* protagonists.[3] In terms of Farrow's work, Cameron resembles George Stroud much more than Triton. The other link with *The Big Clock* is Maureen O'Sullivan as Cameron's girlfriend, Julie. As Georgette Stroud in *The Big Clock*, O'Sullivan's jealousy was never focused. When she came upon George with Rita Johnson, she momentarily suspected an affair. In fact, if there is a triangle in *The Big Clock*, it involves the Strouds and Janoth, whose desire to control has a definite sexual component. Julie is a more passive character than Georgette Stroud.

Even though it violates his medical oath, his code of morality, and common sense, Margo's sexual magnetism and control drag Cameron into a becoming half of a fugitive couple on the run to Mexico with a woman any trained doctor could plainly see is suffering from acute schizophrenia. The appeal this neurotic woman holds for him is two-fold: she is a dangerous and exciting object of desire who stimulates him from the first shots of her bare shoulders and sultry expressions. But more importantly, especially considering his profession, he sees her as a fulfillment of his messiah complex. Or as Lannington says when they first meet, "...a clinging vine brings out your protective side." Lannington's words are visually complemented by a two-shot a few minutes later in which Margo clutches him desperately and whispers in his ear, "How much I need you now."

As Margo alternates between loving partner and ruthless exploiter, Cameron grows weaker and weaker, bodily and mentally. His physical decline is an exter-

It is interesting to note that Charles Laughton's portrayal of Janoth carries the same homosexual undertone as many of his other roles. His relationship with Steve Hagen is not overtly sexual, but the staging and interaction of the characters creates an innuendo, as in the still at left. Obviously, in 1947 only the suggestion was possible. In the recent remake of *The Big Clock*, *No Way Out* (1987), the new version of the Hagen character is more explicitly gay. But the Janoth character is not, the Stroud character is unmarried, and the sexual triangle is refocused on both men's involvement with the Johnson character.

Above, Jeff and Margo (Robert Mitchum and Faith Domergue) on the run in *Where Danger*

nalization of his psychic/spiritual wound. As his strength diminishes, hers grows. Like a dominatrix or an emotional vampire the *femme fatale* feeds off the weakness of her victim. Margo hectors him constantly to keep moving towards "freedom" and the Mexican border by saying, "If you love me, you'll make it," even though she realizes his paralysis and possible death is imminent. In a seedy motel on the border Cameron and Margo await a "coyote" who will conduct them across the international line. A neon sign flashes into the dimly lit room. In one long take the camera locks onto Margo at her most frenetic, pacing the room as Cameron writhes in pain in the foreground. Gradually she reveals the truth about herself, that she was under psychiatric care, that she actually murdered her husband. Cameron crawls around the room in anguish, only to collapse as she attempts to smother him with a pillow. To the end Margo is consistent in her inconsistency.

As a limping Cameron pursues her, Margo sees him from her hiding place in a produce truck. Farrow's staging underscores the twisted relationship between the two. The injured Cameron staggers along a line of porch posts, clinging to them as he pursues the source of his pain. An extreme low-angle frames Margo as she slips from the truck and holds her in a medium close shot as she pulls out a pistol. Even after she shoots him, the masochistic Cameron keeps coming. Margo flees but is brought down by a police bullet.

In her final reversal, she clears Cameron of the murder of her husband. While clinging to the chain-link fence, she defiantly delivers her own epitaph: "Nobody pities me."

The practical night exteriors in *Where Danger Lives*, such as the border town, are a departure from the studio work of the Paramount films. As with Bunker Hill in *The Night Has a Thousand Eyes*, the dingy border town where Jeff and Margo take temporary refuge provides a graphic context for Cameron's fall: from manors to shacks, from doctor to transient on the lam.

Like *The Night Has A Thousand Eyes*, *His Kind of Woman* (1951) is set almost entirely at night. As a result it is on a literal level Farrow's most oppressively dark *noir* film. Both in Los Angeles where the film opens and in Mexico where the action is played out, the terrain is also severely restricted. The protagonist, Dan Milner, is a small-time gambler, who is being set up to have his identity stolen by a brutal syndicate boss named Ferraro. En route to a Mexican resort to wait for instructions he meets a singer, Liz Brady, posing as heiress Lenore Brent heading for a rendezvous at the same resort with movie star Mark Cardigan, who will eventually intervene to save Milner.

The convolutions of the narrative of *His Kind of Woman* culminate by balancing and intercutting comedy that verges on slapstick, as Cardigan leads his unlikely band of rescuers against Ferraro's ship, with the graphic violence of Milner's prolonged beating and torture. First Milner is whipped with the buckle end of a belt and thrown into the steam-filled engine room; then Ferraro revives him to point a gun between his eyes while he murmurs, "Wake up, little boy, I want you to see it coming." Finally he is held down for a fatal injection. The editing scheme creates a pattern of abrupt shifts in narrative tone and content. From Milner doubling over under vicious body blows the cut is to a hapless Cardigan standing in the sunken bow after his boat has foundered from an excess burden of men and guns and quoting from *The Tempest*: "Now would I give a thousand furlongs of sea for an acre of barren ground." From this comic aside, the scene on the boat resumes with the bare-chested Milner struggling against a half dozen hands as the deadly, glistening needle draws nearer to his skin.

On the one hand, Farrow's staging isolates and to some degree exaggerates familiar icons of *film noir*. There are complex group shots as when Ferraro's men bring Milner in. The scene is composed initially with Ferraro reclining on a sofa so that the crime boss's rim-lit face seems to float at the bottom edge of the frame, then restructured with a wide-angle lens so that when he sits up Ferraro's face becomes an oversized silhouette in the right foreground. There are also dramatic extreme close-ups like that of the needle containing an overdose of anesthetic. On the other hand, there are the elaborate comic scenes with Cardigan which range from his melodramatic declaration as he locks Liz/Lenore in a closet ("If I'm not here by Wednesday, chop that door down") to his absurd posturing before his "volunteers": "Survivors will get parts in my next picture."

The juxtaposition satirizes and debunks the conventionally "serious" events aboard the yacht. Still, rather than undercut the stereotypical reality of the leering Ferraro obsessed with liquidating the "welsher" Milner, Krafft, the ex-Nazi surgeon, or the simple-minded, brutal thugs, Cardigan's comic antics concentrate narrative tension and viewer apprehension on those sequences with Milner. Ferraro and his minions become less real characters than the embodiment of the impersonal peril that has threatened Milner through out the film. Each cutaway to Cardigan reemphasizes the illogical chaos of Milner's situation and prolongs his ordeal in a manner suggestive of the hazards and incongruities of the *noir* universe.

In a sense, *His Kind of Woman* deals only in archetypes of the *noir* world. There are a series of ambiguous characters and events such as the songstress Liz Brady "playing" the role of the heiress Lenore Brent and the insecure Mark Cardigan unable to escape his film star persona. Casting Vincent Price in the role of the would-be classical actor trapped in a career as a movie star overtly plays with the audience's genre expectations for comic effect. Using Jane Russell as Liz/Lenore subtly does the same thing. Many other characters are drawn with touches of parody. Some are visual: Krafft wears dark glasses while he plays chess with himself. Others are verbal, as when the dispassionate Thompson proclaims himself "ignorant and happy to be that way." All these figures are clustered around the central, prototypically *noir* conflict between Milner, the aimless, laconic "hero," and Ferraro, the determined, rapacious crime boss.

Actually, Milner is uncertain for much of the film whether his suspicions are justified. He knows that something is being done to him; but, surrounded by an unrelenting, literal, and metaphorical darkness, he cannot perceive what it is or by whom. Although Ferraro is physically absent through most of the narrative, he is represented in every threatening or apprehensive moment coexperienced by Milner and the viewer. Appropriately, Raymond Burr as Ferraro is introduced first, shortly after the film begins. His is a bulky figure in a white suit slowly striding forward into the foreground of a medium shot.[4] The close-up that ends the shot is back-lit to reveal eyes flashing in a somber visage and stylized to underscore his archetypal menace. Milner, as portrayed by Robert Mitchum, is an equally exaggerated characterization: weary, sardonic, but critically unaware that the components of a fateful plot, which will ensnare him and compel him into action, are already in motion. In a mise-en-scene that combines long takes with compositions in which wedges of light and bizarre shadows clutter the frame and distract the viewer, Milner is the only predictable element, he is the only emblem of stability, however uncertain. Milner's introduction in the late night diner is fully as stylized as Ferraro's. He explains to an acquaintance behind the counter that he is out of money and has just spent thirty days on a county road gang for vagrancy. The counterman gives Milner a free meal; but then he stands with his back to the gambler and the occasional glances over his shoulder creates a distance and suggests his inability to understand Milner's life-style—a style that types the gambler, despite his constant weary smile, as a friendless loner. The suggestion that Milner inhabits the *noir* underworld is reinforced in the next sequence. First a long shot isolates Milner on a dark street, where he climbs a set of wooden steps to a cheap second-floor apartment. Inside Milner finds three men waiting. In the course of a long take Milner dismisses their accusations of reneging on a bet. Then, after telling them it would "be nice if you guys cleaned up this mess before you got out of here," he snubs out a cigarette in the palm of one of the men. The sustained shot is broken as Milner falls out of frame under the fists of the other two.

Milner's self-destructive defiance is symptomatic of his world-weariness. The opening is just the first of many beatings he will endure during the course of the film. Ferraro's man calls with his proposition. Milner offhandedly tells him, "I was just getting ready to take my tie off... wondering whether I should hang myself with it." For all his postures of fatigue and weariness, Milner is most at home in the *noir* underworld. Clearly the white-walled, expensively furnished home he visits to hear Ferraro's offer makes him uncomfortable, As he discusses the proposition in a sustained three shot, Milner paces back and forth, finally slumping against a Greek-styled column and remarking on the offer, "I'm not knocking it, man, I'm just trying to understand it." For Milner, who understands the complexities of odds, "something for nothing" is a puzzle. He moves through Mexico like a som-

Below, Milner and Liz/Lenore (Robert Mitchum and Jane Russell) at the Mexican resort.

nambulist in search of a waking reality. There is some degree of that reality to be found, but only in money and in sexuality as represented by Liz. At that, Milner's relationship with sex and money is somewhat eccentric. He jokingly remarks to the vacationing financier that he buries his money in the ground. When Liz drops by his room late at night, she finds him ironing currency: "When I have nothing to do and can't think, I always iron my money." Clearly, Milner is not avaricious; he could easily fleece a vacationing financier but restricts himself to helping a young husband win back what he has lost. Nor is he as likely to inflict violence as to endure it. Cardigan makes the equation of violence with sexuality by telling Milner, after both men catch sight of Liz/Lenore, that "I've got a little Winchester I'd like you to try. If it feels right to you, I'll let you use it." Milner refuses to equate her either with violence or with money.

Although he is clearly drawn to Liz/Lenore, her claim to being wealthy is not enticing to him. It is her off-screen voice that draws him around the bar at the cantina where the choker close-ups of both of them, suddenly inserted as he watches her sing, suggest an immediate fascination with her. There is also an indication of an underlying sexual tension between them in their initial conversation after Milner buys her champagne; but their awkward movements when they find themselves together in the plane to the resort reinforce the sense of a mutual reluctance toward a precipitous intimacy. Nonetheless, Liz is more real for Milner than any of the film's other characters. The only day scene, which occurs midway through the narrative, features Milner with her at the resort's private beach. Ultimately her presence provides a serio-comic counterpoint to the darker elements. "What do you press when you're broke?" she asks Milner: "When I'm broke, I press my pants.". This kind of banter permits sequences of relative verisimilitude that contrast with Milner's other encounters. In terms of *film noir* conventions, because Liz/Lenore is his kind of woman, Milner's relationship with her, despite its sexual tension, is crucial to his survival. He survives; and the tension is finally dissipated in the film's last shot, the comic sexual metaphor of an iron burning Milner's pants while he and Lenore embrace.

Notes

1. That Farrow's staging was somewhat atypical is reflected in this anecdote from the assistant director on *California*: "We had a three-day shooting schedule for something in a saloon. Farrow had a camera that roamed all over the set.... We rehearsed for the first two days, and the front office had a fit. They said, 'When the hell are we going to get any film?' Everybody was panicky, because there was nothing shot and there was nothing in the can. Farrow told them that we would stay on schedule. In about the second-and-half day, he had three days worth of work done—all in one shot." [Joseph C. Youngerman, *My Seventy Years at Paramount and the DGA*, (Directors Guild of America, 1995), p. 60.]

2. Cf. Richard Lippe's comments on this in the following essay, pp. 133-34.

3. Cf. Tony Williams' comments on the masochistic aesthetic in the preceding essay.

4. Cf. Robert Smith's comments on Burr in his essay on Anthony Mann, p. 191.

Above, Diane (Jean Simmons) blocks the path of Frank (Robert Mitchum) in *Angel Face*.

At the Margins of *Film Noir*:
Preminger's *Angel Face*

Richard Lippe

I have greatly admired *Angel Face* for a long time and had often considered writing on the film but when it came to doing so, I realized that I couldn't account for various aspects of it which seemed relevant to its over-all conception. It has been only recently that I have begun to think that I could produce an interpretation of the film that did justice to its complexity. In this paper, I am not attempting to offer a reading of the film that pretends to explain what the film is about in any sort of all-encompassing manner. Aside from my concern with Preminger's critical reputation, my intention is to discuss certain thematic and stylistic aspects of *Angel Face* that I think are of particular importance to my perception of the film.

*   *   *

Otto Preminger was proclaimed an auteur by the *Cahiers du Cinéma* critics in the '50s and promoted as such in the early '60s by the original *Movie* critics. By the mid-'60s, the popular press had adopted the notion of the director as auteur/artist although it tended to disregard the underpinnings of the auteur theory. While there was a superficial acceptance of the theory, journalistic critics continued to concentrate on the film's subject—they never grasped the principle that what gives the auteur's film distinction isn't the subject matter itself but how the director regards it. This was particularly evident in their responses to Preminger's films. In the early to mid-60's Preminger undertook several "big" subject projects based on best-selling novels and the resulting films were, for the most part, judged largely on the literary status of their source materials. That Preminger's mise-en-scene often produced complex attitudes toward his material was ignored; instead, the films were criticized for their commercialism which was taken as an indication of Preminger's vulgar sensibility. On his part, Preminger refused to make apologies and, as a result, the reviews became increasingly hostile. And, eventually, Preminger himself was under attack; like Hitchcock, he had created a somewhat outrageous media persona to promote his films, but whereas the press delighted in Hitchcock's various self-promotional strategies, Preminger was accused of using tactics to gain the public's attention. Gradually,

161

Preminger lost his battle with the critics and lost his public as well. Driven by the press from the blockbuster novel, he took refuge in eccentric treatments of already idiosyncratic subject matter (*Skidoo*; *Tell Me That You Love Me, Junie Moon*).

Preminger's critical reputation, at least outside France, has always stood on the superficially more modest (i.e., low budget) black/white films of the '40s and early '50s. As a result of the present backlash, even these have largely fallen into neglect. The rehabilitation of Preminger's obviously more problematic late work has yet to be undertaken and seems to be not so impossible a task as is generally assumed. Meanwhile I want to examine one of the most remarkable of the earlier films, *Angel Face*, which, in fact, I feel to be no less ambitious, scarcely less eccentric in relation to the norms and no more understood than the late films.

Angel Face (1952) is the last film Preminger made before establishing himself as an independent producer-director; the film also marks the end of his association with the *film noir* which began with *Laura* and includes *Fallen Angel*, *Where the Sidewalk Ends* and *The Thirteenth Letter*. But with the exception of *Laura*, there has been almost nothing written on these films although they are often cited, *Angel Face* in particular, in discussions of the *film noir* cycle. For that matter, critics writing on Preminger, many of whom consider *Angel Face* one of his most provocative and enigmatic films, have been reluctant to deal with it in detail and attempt to define what the film actually does by falling back on what became the clichés of early Preminger criticism: "objectivity" and "neutrality." I want to argue that what has been mistaken for neutrality is in fact an unusually sophisticated complexity of attitude. But before elaborating, I want to consider the early auteurist position on Preminger and the film.

Jacques Rivette, in his article "The Essential,"[1] a typically esoteric and mystifying piece of *Cahiers du Cinéma* criticism, acknowledges that the film related to a Preminger thematic but evades the implied promise of pursuing this in favour of using the film as a pretext for pursuing the mirage of the cinematic "essential," a favourite project of the early auteurist critics but extremely dubious in relation to the impure nature of an art form that derives from other art forms. In Rivette's estimation, *Angel Face* is an "...utterly enigmatic film..." and, as such, characteristic of Preminger's cinema of which he says, "In the midst of a dramatic space created by human encounters he would instead exploit to its limit the cinema's ability to capture the fortuitous (but a fortuity that is willed), to record the accidental (but the accidental that is created) through the closeness and sharpness of the look; the relationships of the characters create a closed circuit of exchanges, where nothing makes an appeal to the viewer" (p. 134). Rivette's description of Preminger's approach to his subject is highly perceptive but what is perhaps most intriguing is that the observation could have been just as easily made about an early '50s Rossellini film like *Voyage to Italy*. There are, of course, many points at which these two filmmakers don't intersect; what connects Preminger and Rossellini, it seems to me, is that both are employing formal strategies which counter certain rules of the classical cinema. In Rossellini's work, these challenges are direct and radical; Preminger, on the other hand, produces these strategies while remaining within the bounds of classical style, continually pushing against those bounds, emphasizing certain of the devices it makes available while virtually eliminating others. The neglect of Preminger by the semiotic school may be accountable for by that school's preoccupation with the typical and the representative and its tendency to reduce classical cinema to a more or less constant set of narrative patterns and stylistic devices. Preminger's cinema, in its stylistic and thematic idiosyncrasy, resists reduction to the "typical."

In "From *Laura* to *Angel Face*,"[2] Paul Mayersberg begins by noting that in Preminger's contract films there is a "...preoccupation with the personality of women...." Although there are numerous later Preminger films that are centrally concerned with women's identity and experience (e.g. *Bonjour Tristesse*, *Exodus*, *Bunny Lake Is Missing*, etc.),[3] Mayersberg primarily restricts himself to the early films because his concern is to illustrate that, while these were studio assignments, they display stylistic and thematic consistency. And it is for this reason that Mayersberg is interested in the films' female characters, whom he reads as the means by which Preminger imposes his thematic concerns on the material. Hence, for Mayersberg, *Angel Face* is Preminger's most fully realized study of the obsessive personality. But, in Mayersberg's schema, it doesn't really matter whether or not the character who embodies the thematic is female or male. Nevertheless, Mayersberg's article is of interest, aside from his tracing of Preminger's thematic concerns, in that it perhaps inadvertently acknowledges the extent to which Preminger's cinema is woman-centred. Aside from Molly Haskell, who, in *From Reverence to Rape*,[4] includes Preminger along with Ophuls, Sirk and Lubitsch as directors whose achievements are often underrated because the critics don't take the work of a "woman's director" seriously, there seems to have been no critical investigation of Preminger's work in relation to the melodrama and/or the woman's film. While such films as *Laura*, *Fallen Angel* and *Angel Face* have the necessary characteristics to be identified as belonging to the *noir* genre, these films also are through a combination of subject and treatment, a complex genre mixture. *Fallen Angel*, for instance, has a hero who is positioned between two women who represent, respectively, the active/sexual and the passive/non-sexual. This pattern is found in numerous *noir* films, but in *Fallen Angel*, its relation to the melodrama is explicit.[5] *Fallen Angel* is, in its triangular relationship which pivots on the hero's choice, a male-centred melodrama in the tradition of a film like *Sunrise* to which it bears comparison. Although both films employ male and female archetypes, in *Fallen Angel* these images are neither aligned with nor reduced to elemental forces within nature. Instead, the identities of the film's central protagonists are shown to be the result of a social system that encourages patterns of domination and/or exploitation between the sexes. In the film, it isn't evil but economic forces that have made Linda Darnell greedy and Dana Andrews desperate. And, although Alice Faye, as the "good" woman, functions as Andrews' salvation, the film also suggests that her motives include freeing herself from the repressive social and sexual conditions of her small town existence. *Angel Face*, on the other hand, has strong affinities to the woman's film; more specifically, as the film's central female protagonist is obsessed, it belongs to what has become, since the early '40s and the introduction of psychoanalysis into popular culture, a sub-genre of the woman's film. The film links a woman's destructive behaviour to madness, but unlike such films as *The Dark Mirror*, *The Locket* and *Possessed*, *Angel Face* doesn't deal with psychiatry or provide an explicit psychoanalytic explanation to account for its heroine's illness. In this respect and others, i.e., the heroine's strong attachment to her father, the film has parallels to *Leave Her to Heaven*, which is another film, like those mentioned above, that belongs to both the *noir* and the woman's film genres; but, although *Leave Her to Heaven* is of considerable interest in that Stahl's direction and Gene Tierney's persona work to undercut the film's ideological project of making the Tierney character and her demands monstrous, the film lacks *Angel Face*'s systematic analysis of gender and class relations.

In discussing the way in which Preminger's films work, Mayersberg says that Preminger "...detaches the spectator to a degree and allows him to judge the characters for himself." In part, this claim is based on the fact that Preminger is a mise-en-scene filmmaker who tends to avoid using montage to construct "meaning" for the viewer through cutting to a specific object, gesture, detail, etc. But the claim is also based on the assumption that Preminger himself has an "objective" attitude toward his material. Mayersberg implies this when, after analyzing a sequence from *Daisy Kenyon* to illustrate Preminger's approach and how it functions, he says: "It is, in effect, part of Preminger's detachment, because as a style it does not force an attitude or an emotional experience on the spectator. The spectator, like the camera, *arrives* at the experience. Then the camera moves on and the experience is modified and enriched: the moments become functions in a total development" (p. 16). As with Rivette, Mayersberg's project is to argue that Preminger's sensibility, which is expressed through his mise-en-scene, is highly attuned to the medium and its potential to record, in the Bazinian sense, the more intangible aspects of human behaviour and interaction. For these critics, Preminger's supposed "detachment" affords him the means to comment on the "human condition." But, on the contrary, while Preminger uses mise-en-scene to produce a critical distance from his subject, he doesn't exist outside of or transcend the concerns of his films: he is deeply implicated in the films' thematic. Similarly, Preminger's films often contain characters who are ambiguous in their behaviour but the films don't express an impartial attitude to the characters and their situations.

Although cultural politics shaped auteur criticism to a degree, this criticism, which has been invaluable to the development of a critical/theoretical rethinking of the cinema, was, for the most part, as the introduction of the concept of ideology into film criticism has shown, non-political. Despite the various arguments put forth against authorship, it remains, I think, a significant element in critical discipline. To recognize that specific cultural, social and historical factors contribute to the construction of an individual, the work s/he produces and its reception is crucial; but it is also important to recognize that human intelligence and creativity exist.

Angel Face,[6] unlike Preminger's other contract films, wasn't a Twentieth Century-Fox production; the film was made at RKO which, at the time, was owned by Howard Hughes who requested Preminger's services because he wanted a director who could work quickly under pressure. In his autobiography,[7] Preminger says that Hughes' primary reason for making the film was to pique Jean Simmons, with whom he was having conflicts. Simmons had 18 working days left to her contract and Hughes was determined to get another film out of her. To obtain his commitment, Hughes agreed to Preminger's demands, which included a new script by writers of his choice and with whom Preminger worked. In effect, Hughes gave Preminger almost total freedom to do as he wanted with the project.

While there seems to be a more or less agreed critical consensus about *film noir* conventions, critical emphasis tends to vary as to what constitutes a *noir* film: iconography, visual style, narrative structure, protagonists, thematic concerns, the historical moment are, among others, variables in how these films are to be read. In narrative structure, *Angel Face*, for instance, doesn't employ such "typical" *noir* conventions as voice-over narration or the flashback which are predominantly associated with the central male protagonist; and the film isn't centred on a male's investigation of a woman to ascertain her guilt or innocence. On the other hand, the film is typical in having a transgressive woman and, thematically, deals with obsessive behaviour and alienation. By the time *Angel Face* was made, Robert Mitchum had become one of *film noir*'s leading icons; but the casting of Jean Simmons, who had been recently imported from England where she specialized in playing innocent but victimized heroines, is equally important to the film. Simmons' Diane, despite having certain features in common with the typical *femme fatale*, is far removed from this model. Preminger was, as Robin Wood has pointed out,[8] the first director to provide her with a characterization that fully utilized the innocent/sexual tension underlying Simmons' persona. In this respect, it is instructive to compare *Angel Face* to *Where Danger Lives*, another Hughes-produced *film noir* of the early '50s, in which Mitchum is also attracted to and becomes involved with an unstable woman who, it is gradually revealed, is homicidal. In John Farrow's film, Faith Domergue primarily exists to endorse the film's misogyny and complacent cynicism toward heterosexual relations which is what, in effect, the typical *film noir* is in great part about. *Where Danger Lives* is representative of the worst aspects of the tradition; in contrast, *Angel Face* is an example of a progressive usage of its conventions and thematics.

Gender and Power

As I said, Diane has features that relate her to the archetypal *femme fatale* of the *film noir*—she manipulates and eventually murders to get what she wants. But Diane differs in that her concern isn't gaining the power money accords, she already has access to this kind of power, and there is no ambiguity about her commitment to Frank [Robert Mitchum], as she, before and after the trial, wants to testify to his innocence. On the narrative level, what motivates her behaviour in an obsessive attachment to her father and a pathological hatred of her step-mother. The latter Diane justifies through her perception that Catherine [Barbara O'Neil] has destroyed her father's initiative to pursue his career as a writer. In effect, Diane is maintaining that Catherine has emasculated her father; but, as the film reveals, Charles [Herbert Marshall] is more or less contentedly indulging his cultural interests while living off his wife's money. If he harbours any resentment toward Catherine, it seems to be the product of his disdain for her middle-class sensibility. In contrast to her father's passive character, Diane's is

Below, Frank (Robert Mitchum) and Diane (Jean Simmons) with her "masculine" sports car.

active. Although she is ultra-feminine in appearance and works to reinforce gender roles (in her relations with her father, Diane is both an ideal daughter/child and comforting mother figure), Diane displays, in various ways, an identification with and understanding of the masculine identity. For instance, Diane's sports car associates her with risk-taking and adventure, and, to Frank, both Diane and her car are equally attractive. But, more tellingly, in her handling of Frank and Mary [Mona Freeman], whom she perceives as a rival, not unlike Catherine, whom she must eliminate, Diane knowingly plays on Frank's fears of being entrapped within domesticity. In the initial café scene, after Frank has telephoned Mary, Diane questions whether he's reporting in to his wife. Having spent the evening with Frank, Diane, the following day, meets with Mary, using the pretext that she wants to help the two financially, to undermine Mary's confidence in Frank. Later, when Diane and Frank again meet at the café, she implies that Mary's possessiveness prevented her from being receptive to the offer. To Frank's "Look, I'm a free agent," Diane replies, "...but you know what girls are." Clearly, Diane isn't speaking as a representative member of her own sex here but is, instead, alluding to her and Frank's mutual understanding of "what girls are" like. While giving Frank the impression that he is taking control of the situation, it is, in fact, Diane who is in control.

To both Diane and Frank, control is a major concern, for Diane it is linked to the possession of an individual, but for Frank it is a guarantee of his masculine identity. While there are numerous *films noirs* in which the lead male protagonist acknowledges his loss of control, which is often attributed to Fate, Frank, crucially, never fully perceives the possibility of this happening to him. The reason he doesn't, as the film makes clear, is bound up to a belief in male superiority. This is most evident in his treatment of Mary; although he quickly abandons her, he expects Mary to take him back when he's through with Diane. With Diane, Frank is more tentative in his actions, in part, because he knows there is more at stake. Then, too, Diane alternates in presenting herself as an innocent child seeking paternal approval and a sexually adult woman who wants him as her lover.

In *Angel Face*, there is an intimate relation between control or the loss of control and entrapment and, although the film doesn't make this perception gender-specific, it does suggest that it is an issue of particular importance to the male's identity. For instance, when Frank enters the Tremayne household as a chauffeur, he is already aware that Catherine, through her money, controls Charles but he is also confronted by the Japanese servant complaining that his wife, having become influenced by American habits, is trying to dominate him. Later, as Preminger indicates, Frank begins to sense Diane's control; he cross-cuts scenes of Diane with her father in the main house and scenes in which Frank, in his quarters, anxiously watches from the window and, then, with the realization that Diane isn't going to come, makes an attempt to telephone Mary to assert himself.

The film's central metaphor for the control/entrapment opposition is the car. As I mentioned, on the one hand, Diane's sports car associates her with masculinity; but, on the other, Frank sees Diane and the car as a means to fully regain his masculine self-image. (He was a professional racer before World War II.) To Frank, the car represents an image of phallic potency but, within the film's context, it increasingly becomes identified with his entrapment. Although Frank has been aware that Diane wants Catherine dead, it isn't until the murder (and, significantly, the murder weapon is Catherine's car) that he senses the possible threat she poses to his masculinity. (In *Angel Face*, in contrast to a typical *film noir* pattern, e.g., *The Postman Always Rings Twice*, *Double Indemnity*, the woman doesn't need the man to help her commit the murder.) It is at this point that Frank attempts to disengage himself from Diane but the murder, in fact, leads to their marrying. After the trial, Diane gives Frank a potential access to the car when she bets it against Mary's taking him back; Mary, in refusing to do so, rejects his notions of masculine privilege. In the film's climactic sequence, the car becomes the site of Diane's control and Frank's entrapment. Diane, in offering to drive Frank to the bus station, seems to think that there is still a chance that she can convince him to stay. It isn't until Frank's shout, as he's opening the champagne, of "Watch it," as Diane steps on the gas, that Diane makes the decision to kill Frank and herself. The enraged look on Diane's face on hearing his command is similar to her look after Frank slapped her in their initial meeting. In that encounter, Diane returned the slap. Here, her instantaneous decision to kill them is her intuitive reaction to his assumption of a masculine prerogative that excludes any sense of her autonomy or individual identity.

Undoubtedly, *Angel Face* has one of the most devastating endings in the entire history of cinema. In part, the ending's impact is attributable, as it has been previously in the Catherine/Charles car scene, to the horrific manner in which the characters meet their death; but the impact also stems from the unexpectedness of Diane's action—arguably, the viewer, not unlike Frank, hasn't contemplated the possibility. (Although the viewer is provided with indications of how and when Catherine and Charles will be killed, the action, in its abruptness, is equally startling.) There are other *films noirs*, i.e., *Double Indemnity*, *Out of the Past*, in which, by the film's conclusion, the central couple is dead. But, in these films, although the victim-hero is fatally shot by the woman and he, in turn, precipitates her death, in *Angel Face* Frank isn't given this final assertion of his control over the woman. Also, Frank lacks the pessimistic romanticism often associated with the *noir* victim-hero who, through his death, achieves, as in *Out of the Past*, a degree of tragic nobility. In fact, when compared to the typical *film noir* male, Frank has nothing that connotes a "glamorous" identity: he isn't, for instance, in an ambiguous position to the criminal world and the law nor is he, for that matter, guilty of committing a crime of any sort. (Diane's attorney, Fred Barrett [Leon Ames], comes closest to being a male criminal figure in the film.)[9] Then, too, it isn't Fate, which is never a factor in Preminger's films, that leads Frank to his death but, as I said, the conviction that his masculine identity secures him a controlling position in gender relations. On the other hand, Frank, more characteristic of the typical *film noir* male, tends to project his distrust of the feminine and a woman's wants onto the women herself. Pointedly, in respect to this, when Diane, who has given him no reason to doubt her love, says, "Do you love me at all? I must know," he responds with "I suppose it's a kind of love...but, with a girl like you, how can a man be sure?"

Women and *Film Noir*

Although each of the three female protagonists of *Angel Face* relates to images of women associated with the *film noir*, Preminger doesn't provide these characters with the conventional identities that these types suggest, in each case subtly qualifying and undermining the spectator's expectations.

1. Diane identifies Catherine as a domineering, mean-minded woman who takes pleasure in humiliating her father and denying her wants; but Catherine, as she's presented, doesn't fulfill the bitch image Diane has assigned her. If Catherine denies Diane, as she does in deciding against financing Frank's sports car garage project, it is because she's trying to contain Charles' indulgence of her: in the scene which immediately follows Catherine's interviewing Frank about his plan, she, after attempting to telephone her lawyer about the project, is confronted by Charles who offers a perfunctory expression of his affection and then informs her that she's getting a $300 bill for a dress he thought Diane should have. The scene, in addition to foregrounding Charles' cynical attitude towards his financial dependency, suggests that Catherine has cause to reprimand him. The scene also suggests, as does an earlier, intimate scene between Charles and Diane in which they jokingly dismiss the seriousness of Catherine's near asphyxiation, that Charles tends to promote a sex and class (Catherine's bourgeois identity vs. the "aristocratic" refinement Diane is seen as sharing with her father) barrier between the two women. As Catherine isn't the monstrous woman Diane claims, her death is neither deserved nor gratifying. It isn't until she's killed her that Diane comes to this realization and recognizes that Catherine, too, loved Charles.

2. In its Diane/Mary opposition, *Angel Face* employs the archetypes of the "bad" and the "good" woman; in the *film noir* cycle, the opposition occurs perhaps most notably in Jacques Tourneur's *Out of the Past* in which the sexual Kathie/Jane Greer is contrasted to the innocent Ann/Virginia Huston who unconditionally commits herself to the film's hero, Jeff/Robert Mitchum, providing understanding, support and love. In Preminger's film, Mary, in various ways, contradicts the Ann stereotype. Unlike Ann, for instance, Mary is, as the film implicitly conveys, when she, in her slip, is unperturbed by Frank's unexpected arrival at her apartment, a

sexualized woman. Clearly Mary isn't in the tradition of the chaste virginal type most classically exemplified by Janet Gaynor in *Sunrise*. And, as is made explicit, in her rejecting of Frank, she refuses to passively accept his unwillingness to make a commitment. When he attempts to return, Mary, after informing Bill [Kenneth Tobey] that she wants to speak for herself, says: "...I want a marriage and not a competition. I want a husband and not a trophy that I have to defend over and over again." In a sense, Mary, in this scene, voices what Diane comes to feel about Frank's assumption of his independence. Although Mary and Bill can be taken as the film's "good" couple, *Angel Face*, doesn't, in actuality, construct the conventional polarization of the two couples.

3. As I have indicated, Diane has certain characteristics which type her as a *femme fatale*; but, when compared to the archetypal transgressive woman of the *film noir*, Diane appears highly unconventional. Briefly to recapitulate: although she manipulates Frank, her motive isn't that he provides a means to her gaining power. What Diane wants is Frank's love; as with her father, Diane has made a total commitment to Frank, and at no point in the film does she betray him. Diane doesn't implicate Frank in her plans to kill Catherine and, after the deaths, she twice tries (in the second instance, Diane thinks that she may have already lost Frank) to testify that she alone was responsible for the killings. Uncharacteristically, in *Angel Face* it is Diane and not Frank who is the more vulnerable of the couple. Although Preminger makes Diane's vulnerability apparent in several scenes between her and Frank before the deaths of Catherine and Charles, it is after the trial sequence that he fully develops this aspect of her identity. Having returned to the Tremayne house, Diane, after telling Frank that she regrets what she's done, tries to explain herself and why she had wanted Catherine dead. While Diane's explanation doesn't adequately justify her actions, it is a genuine attempt on her part to make Frank understand her present and past feelings—to Diane's plea that he grant her a degree of forgiveness, Frank responds with indifference. But Diane's vulnerability is most strikingly depicted in the scenes in which she, after Frank has left her for Mary, wanders through the house entering Charles' room, then Frank's (I discuss these sequences in more detail later). In terms of the film's plot, these sequences aren't necessary, but they are crucial to Preminger's conception and sympathetic portrayal of Diane. Although Preminger doesn't employ technical devices to produce a viewer identification with Diane (in the above-mentioned scenes, there are, for instance, no POV shots of the objects Diane associates with the presence of the two men). Preminger constructs, through narrative and characterization, a woman-centered *film noir* that sustains (unlike *Leave Her to Heaven*, in which Tierney's suicide is followed by a lengthy amount of footage devoted to the restoration of the "good" couple) its commitment to the woman who, ostensibly, is the film's *femme fatale* figure.

In Preminger's film, a reason why Mary and Bill don't become the alternative "good" couple is that Diane and Frank aren't the typical "bad" couple of the *film noir*. In their first meeting, Frank slaps Diane because she's hysterical; seemingly, what impressed Diane about Frank and prompts her to follow him, is his ease in taking control, his masculine display of authority. On the other hand, Frank's attraction to Diane is more obvious: her aggressiveness is a challenge, she's beautiful and rich. While Frank, at one point, tells Diane that they don't belong together because of their different social positions, Diane, for Frank, holds a fascination because of her class privilege. Although Diane is associated with aggressive sexuality and crime she isn't so much corrupt as spoiled and, consequently, she isn't even capable of corrupting Frank; she knowingly uses her access to money to keep Frank's interest, but he is no less guilty, fully realizing the financial potentials she offers him.[10] The union of Mary and Bill can be read easily enough as the film's restoration of "normality," but in this case normality is defined as the absence of

Below, Barrett (Leon Ames, left), Diane (Jean Simmons), and Frank (Robert Mitchum) await the verdict at their murder trial.

desires beyond the most commonplace and material; and, significantly, after the deaths of Diane and Frank, the film does not re-introduce Mary and Bill. Instead, the film's final shot is the arrival of the taxi-cab to pick up Frank, the driver blowing his horn to summon his fare from an empty house whose occupants are all dead. The shot symmetrically echoes the opening (the ambulance, driven by Frank, arriving at the house at night): one of the bleakest and least reassuring instances of closure and the "restoration of normality" in the entire Hollywood cinema.

Preminger and mise-en-scene

Given that *Angel Face* is a *film noir* the viewer would be led to assume that the film's identification figure is to be the lead male protagonist. (This is reinforced in the casting of Robert Mitchum who has top-billing in the film's opening credits.) As the initial scenes of *Angel Face* are centered on Frank's experiences, it seems that we are being encouraged to take him as our identification source; and, with Frank, the viewer is placed in relation to a disorientating situation in entering the Tremayne house. After leaving Catherine's bedroom, Frank and Bill are seen in a medium long shot walking down the stairs; as Bill exits the frame screen right, Frank's attention is drawn screen left towards an off-screen space in which someone is playing a piano. As Frank continues to look screen left and gradually walks in that direction the camera begins to pan left keeping him in the frame. Frank and the camera keep moving until Diane, sitting at the piano, is also in the frame. What is important here is that Preminger doesn't cut to Diane which would have suggested a POV shot from Frank's perspective; instead, by constructing the two-shot through camera movement to introduce Diane he discourages viewer identification with Frank and, simultaneously, her objectification.

I am not suggesting that the above-mentioned two-shot in itself prevents any further possible viewer identification with Frank. But it does initiate a detachment from Frank which is crucial to the film's concerns. In fact, up until Diane's killing of Catherine and Charles, Frank remains the more accessible of the two lead protagonists. To an extent, we are sharing his orientation towards Diane; this occurs because Preminger doesn't give us full access to either the intentions behind her actions or her machinations: perhaps the most extreme example of the latter is that Preminger withholds the information that Diane has tampered with Catherine's car to transform it into a murder weapon. On the other hand, Preminger, through his close-ups of Diane, when she's playing the piano, produces a certain intimacy between her and the viewer which has no equivalent elsewhere in the film; although, paradoxically, with these close-ups, Diane is arguably at her most impenetrable. Prior to her killing of Catherine and Charles, Preminger allows for an ambiguous attitude on the viewer's part towards Diane but, in its aftermath, she becomes, although now a murderess, the emotional centre of the film. Diane and her situation become increasingly poignant while Frank, in his response to her, becomes increasingly unpleasant. The sequences in which Diane wanders the house are exemplary here: there are no POV shots, and Preminger keeps her in long shot throughout until the final track-in to medium shot. The sequence described below is preceded by Diane's wandering from Catherine's room to Charles' which she enters pausing at his chess board and picking up one of the pieces. Diane then proceeds to Frank's quarters initiating a two shot sequence: the first shot begins with Diane entering the quarters and glancing around; she then lifts up the cover of a suitcase to see if it's empty, goes into an adjoining room and fondles a shirt on the bureau, returning to pick up Frank's sports jacket which she caresses; she then moves towards a window bench at which she and Frank had previously sat, pauses and exits the frame as the image fades indicating a time lapse. With a fade-in, the camera moves right from the window and tracks in towards Diane who is sitting in an armchair with Frank's jacket wrapped around her. She stares into space until she hears the sound of a car arriving at which point she gets up and exits the frame. *Angel Face*, among other things, illustrates that the viewer identification process is much more complicated than it is often assumed to be.

Throughout the film, Preminger's highly complex mise-en-scene is everywhere evident: for instance, the film's control/loss of control motif is visualized in his handling of the first murder sequence which is prefaced with a shot of Diane dropping an empty cigarette packet off the cliff on which the Tremayne house stands. The sequence itself begins with a shot of Diane at her bedroom window looking down at the pavement area and garage below; in addition to alluding to the height indication of the previous shot, it suggests that Diane presumes that she has control over what is about to happen. Preminger also introduces viewing height through a camera movement which begins as a tracking shot of Catherine and Charles as they move toward and then get into the car; as Charles closes Catherine's car door and exits the frame to get to his door the shot continues and the camera cranes up and tracks forward to frame in close-up the shift lever which Catherine has just placed in the drive position. While Diane thinks she has complete control, she doesn't know that her father will also be in the car. In the shot immediately preceding the murder scene, Diane sits down at per piano and begins to play; after the long shots of the car plunging down the cliff, Preminger dissolves back to Diane who, still playing the piano, maintains her illusion of control.

In *Angel Face*, there are more than 30 dissolves, the amount being, I think, as uncharacteristic of a Preminger film as it is of the typical classical Hollywood film. What these dissolves impart to the film is a degree of lyricism which is taken up in the piano music associated with Diane; like Diane's music, the dissolves function as counterpoint to the film's eruptions of violence which are particularly abrupt and brutal.

Conclusion

With *Angel Face*, the viewer is confronted by an extremely complex tangle in which class and gender concerns are pointedly raised: on the one hand, there is Diane's class privilege and, on the other, Frank's gender privilege. Contrary to Mayersberg's contention, Preminger isn't neutral either in his attitude towards his material or in his presentation of it. What his distanciation provides the viewer with is the opportunity to reflect on the concerns he is dealing with. This is altogether different from claiming that Preminger is objective in treating his subject. Mayersberg, in the *Movie* of 1962, presented this alleged "objectivity" on the level of the individual; its function was to leave the spectator free to judge the motivations and actions of the characters. But Preminger's attitude to his characters is, as I have tried to show, neither neutral nor undefinable (however complex); the function of the distance upon which his mise-en-scene insists is to allow us to pass beyond personal motivation to the awareness of the web of class and gender positions within which they struggle.

Notes

1. Jacques Rivette. "The Essential", *Cahiers du Cinéma. The 1950s* Vol. 1, Ed. Jim Hillier. (Routledge Kegan Paul, 1985): pp. 132-135.

2. Paul Mayersberg. "From *Laura* to *Angel Face*." *Movie*, No. 2 (September 1962): pp. 14-16.

3. *Bonjour Tristesse* is a fascinating companion piece to *Angel Face*. In *The Films in My Life* (Simon and Schuster, 1975), François Truffaut backhandedly suggests that Françoise Sagan used *Angel Face* as her inspiration for her celebrated novel.

4. Molly Haskell. *From Reverence to Rape.* (Penguin Books Inc. 1974): p. 159.

5. Contrary to those critics who claim that the *film noir* and the melodrama are polar opposites, I see them as complementary genres as both are centrally concerned with gender relations and particularly the entrapment thematic.

6. Set in Beverly Hills, the film begins with ambulance drivers, Frank/Robert Mitchum and Bill/Kenneth Tobey, answering a call from a hill-top mansion where Catherine Tremayne/Barbara O'Neil has almost been asphyxiated by gas in her bedroom. Mrs. Tremayne thinks someone tried to murder her but her husband, Charles/Herbert Marshall, discounts the possibility, insisting it was an accident. About to leave the house, Frank finds Diane Tremayne/Jean Simmons in the living room playing the piano; when he tells her that Mrs. Tremayne, her stepmother, will survive, she becomes hysterical. Frank and Bill return to the hospital and Diane follows in her sports car. At a nearby cafe, where Frank is attempting to call his girlfriend Mary/Mona Freeman, Frank and Diane meet again. Frank cancels his date with Mary and takes Diane out. Diane tells Frank that she and her father are very close much to the annoyance of her stepmother. Later, she offers Frank a live-in job as the family chauffeur suggesting that Mrs. Tremayne might help finance his plans to start a sports car garage. When Mrs. Tre-

mayne withdraws her support, Diane says she did so to spite her. Soon after, Diane claims that Mrs. Tremayne tried to asphyxiate her but Frank finds the story highly suspect. Diane, sensing that Frank is becoming uncomfortable with his situation and intends to leave, convinces him to stay until she can sell her jewels which will give them the money to buy a garage business and start a new life together. In actuality, Diane has decided to make another attempt at murdering her stepmother: when backed out of the family garage, Mrs. Tremayne's car is positioned near the edge of a steep drop-off; Diane removes a mechanism from the car so that it remains in reverse when Mrs. Tremayne puts the car shift into the drive position and steps on the gas. Although Diane's plan succeeds, she inadvertently also kills her father who was a passenger in the car.

An insurance investigation leads to the conclusion that the car was tampered with. As Frank is a mechanic and Diane's suitcase was found in his room, they are charged with murdering the Tremaynes to get Mrs. Tremayne's money. After recovering from the shock of her father's death, Diane tells her attorney, Fred Barrett/Leon Ames, that she alone was responsible for the deaths. Barrett, thinking that the admission will raise issues about Diane's mental state and, more importantly, tie up the estate which she inherits, argues that a confession at this point would be taken as an attempt on her part to protect Frank. Intending to exploit the jury's sentimental notions regarding young lovers, Barrett has Frank marry Diane before the trial. Through a combination of insufficient evidence and Barrett's manipulation, Frank and Diane are acquitted. After a return to the Tremayne house, Diane tells Frank that she regrets what she's done; she also says that her love for her father blinded her to the fact that Catherine also loved him. But Frank offers her no compassion; he informs Diane that he wants a divorce and intends to return to Mary. Telling Frank that Mary, unlike herself, couldn't love a man who might have murdered, Diane bets her sports car against Mary's taking him back. Since Frank's rejection, Mary has become involved with Bill and, when Frank confronts her with his return, she rejects him on the grounds that she no longer wants to compete for his affections. Diane, thinking that she may have lost Frank, goes to Barrett to make an official statement wanting both to clear Frank's name and appease her guilt. Barrett says that her confession is now pointless and advises that, if she persists, her sanity will be questioned. When Frank returns Diane's car, he tells her that he's going to Mexico. She offers to drive him to the bus station. With both in the car, Diane throws the car shift into reverse and backs it off the drop-off, killing Frank and herself.

7. Otto Preminger. *Preminger: An Autobiography* (Doubleday & Company, Inc. 1977): pp. 123-126.

8. Robin Wood. *The International Dictionary of Films and Filmmakers: Volume III Actors and Actresses.* (St. James Press, 1986): pp. 576-577.

9. Barrett is also associated with the control/loss of control motif in his threatening Diane that she will wind up in a mental institution if she persists in wanting to confess to the killings.

10. In this respect, the Catherine/Charles and Diane/Frank relationships reflect each other.

Above, Burt Lancaster as the Swede and Ava Gardner as Kitty in a scene from her flashback in *The Killers*.

The Killers: Expressiveness of Sound and Image in Film Noir

Robert G. Porfirio

> In cinema I find the best way of approaching the crime film is to let your audience in on the secret. Not to ask them who did it, but rather to let them follow the story line from one character's point of view.
>
> Robert Siodmak[1]

As an illustration of some definitive aspects of *film noir*'s visual style and their relationship to narrative structure *The Killers* (1946) is altogether fitting. First, this film drew its inspiration from a short story by Ernest Hemingway, the acknowledged "father" of the "hard-boiled school" of fiction which provided *film noir* with its most notable literary antecedent. Second, the film's director, Robert Siodmak, was a major contributor to the *noir* cycle (with at least ten entries by my reckoning) and was one of a group of Germanic emigrés who came to America and infused Hollywood with expressionistic proclivities. Despite an ostensible antagonism between the "realistic" impetus of the hard-boiled tradition and the "formative" tendencies of expressionism, Siodmak was exemplary in the way he worked within the Hollywood system to synthesize such contradictory strands into a fabric which could be perceived as homogenous. For the *noir* cycle, this would lead to the rise of the semi-documentary *film policier* beginning with *T-Men* and culminating, outside the cycle, with the highly popular TV series *Dragnet*. Siodmak's own *Cry of the City* (1948) provides an important line between the "closed" form of the early studio-bound *noir* films and the "open" form of the later police thrillers shot on location (cf. my entry in *Film Noir: An Encyclopedic Reference to the American Style*.)

Siodmak's *noir* films can provide us with numerous instances of the expressive use of sound and images, perhaps none more telling than those which eliminate the use of diegetic dialogue. Of course, the "jam session" from *Phantom Lady* (1944) comes quickly to mind since it stands out as a startling visual expression of Cornell Woolrich's own fear-ridden vision. Yet the two se-

177

quences from *The Killers* discussed below are perhaps more worthy of our attention because they owe less to the "influence" of their literary author and are less extrusive to the narrative body of the film: the robbery at the Prentiss Hat Co. looks forward to the motifs of the "caper" film just as the attempt of the two killers to execute Riordan at the Green Cat nightclub looks backward to the *Phantom Lady* "jam session" in its concatenation of jazz, sexuality, and the threat of violence. Although the emotional impact of each varies somewhat, both reflect the formative desire of the implied author, in this case Siodmak, to affect an audience through a variety of stratagems. These include the sequence shot, i.e., an entire sequence photographed in one unbroken shot; montage; and a heterogeneity of visual conventions.

The Sequence Shot: Spatial and Temporal Articulations

Contrary to critics who assert that the *film noir* eschewed the "realism" of the long take and highly mobile camera in favor of an editorial formativeness, both were well within the cycle's repertory. Of course, when the long take entailed intricate trucking movements (as opposed to depth-staging only), the time and expense involved therein forced many more modestly budgeted (or "talented") productions to "get by" with the formative effects of *noir* lighting and editing. Yet, post-war Hollywood had an impressive arsenal of new equipment at its disposal and an array of styles as varied as Welles' and Minnelli's from which to draw, so a consistent if conservative deployment of these techniques was to be expected, at least until the advent of wide-screen created new demands. The *film noir* was as sensitive to these techniques as any genre,[2] although one is hard pressed to detect there the "liberating" camera of the Hollywood musical or the "inquiring" one of neo-realism. As it had with deep focus, the *film noir* assimilated the moving camera and the long take into its own closed form, controlling diegetic space in an architectonic manner (like any of the planned and edited sequences of Hitchcock) that ideally provides the viewer with a metonymic "lock" on its hermetic world. Simply put, the expressive components of the moving camera and long take draw the audience into a pre-determined reading of the scene.

I have chosen to illustrate this effect with the robbery sequence from *The Killers* (1946). There are a number of cogent reasons for selecting this example. Critics have often cited this film for its dark fatalism and closed form, qualities usually attributed to the compelling influence of director Robert Siodmak and his cinematographer Elwood Bredell. Of course, the producer, Mark Hellinger, and the studio, Universal, were familiar with Siodmak's "Germanic" sensibilities through his past work. Since a fluid camera was never Siodmak's "signature," it is not surprising that critics have chosen to describe the film's "brooding fatalism" in terms of its constrained visuals and fixed camera. Thus, *The Killers* offers a fairer test of the impact of the certain visual expressions than the work of directors such as Welles or Ophuls, whose careers have always been associated with more conspicuous technique including long takes and elaborate camera moves. And while the robbery sequence is not the only instance of elaborate camera movement in *The Killers*, it is an exceptional example in that it involves not merely a long take but a sequence shot, the two-minute length of which rivals those of Welles. Indeed this instance maintains precisely those unities of time and space that have caused the sequence shot to be extolled as a "realist" technique par excellence, but here those unities camouflage a highly contrived camera movement that controls the off-screen space with a closed form and that substitutes a formative manipulation of mise-en-scene for the temporal plasticity of traditional editing. Finally, this sequence has seldom been acknowledged as the effective "germ" of a subsequent type of caper film, one which used the *plein air* setting of a studio exterior to achieve the "look" of the semi-documentary. As such, it is a telling example of the *noir* cycle's unique synthesis of "realism" and expressionism.

The reader should remember also that the robbery itself is part of an overall narrative structure that estranges the viewer from its actions. The script of *The Killers* develops through flashbacks to a remote diegetic past. This particular flashback begins after the viewer witnesses the assassination of its most sympathetic participant, Ole Anderson (Burt Lancaster), at the film's beginning. This mode of enunciation is made even more alienating through the monotonous narration of an unenthusiastic insurance executive named Kenyon (Donald McBride), who is forced to read an old newspaper account of the affair although he has scant interest in reopening the case. Since all of the "normal" diegetic sounds that might be associated with the robbery have been eliminated in favor of McBride's voice and Miklós Rózsa's subdued background score, the scene is articulated through some of the conventions of the documentary, which audiences associate with "detachment." This detachment is enhanced by the objective persuasion of the crane-mounted camera which sweeps down from its initial imperious position (**Figure 1**) to bring the participants into close visual range. This position is held very briefly (**2**) before withdrawing for the action of the robbery itself (**3** through **8**). Such codes of expression combine to dissipate much of the tension implicit in the immediacy of the spatio-temporal order of the sequence shot.

Initially the camera does no more than to reaffirm the narration establishing the site of the robbery as the Prentiss Hat Co. (**1**) before descending in a rightward arc to reveal the gang entering the factory disguised as workers (**2**), a ploy which the narrator has already informed the audience was woefully easy for them to effect. However, after the camera moves back up and over the

fence to pick up each member of the gang as he enters the industrial area (**3**), it
begins to anticipate the action, tracking towards the paymaster's building even
before the four robbers make their own move towards it (**4**). On the other
hand, the narrator, droning on about the details of the robbers' plan and its
execution, occasionally falls behind the visual revelations of those events.

The calculated nature of the visuals is quite apparent once the men enter the
building (**4**), for the camera swings in a leftward arc up the side wall and positions itself outside the windows of a second floor office. Once there, it simply
waits for the gang to arrive upstairs and come within view. The whole robbery
is presented from this vantage point (**5**), while the voice of the narrator provides the audience with unseen details. After this short interval, the camera
again "beats" the men back down to ground level and pauses until they have
time to catch up as a slow-moving vehicle arrives to cover their getaway (**6**).
The camera then trucks backward and begins to ascend, as the gang hurries to
the cars parked outside in the street (**7**). The camera continues to rise, finally
reaching a much higher and wider angle for the sequence's conclusion. This final vista permits the viewer a privileged position, somewhat removed from the
violent action of the climax. At the same time, it provides the necessary space
for a rigidly controlled mise-en-scene to simulate the aleatory: as the gang
leader's dark coupe, pursued by a guard on foot, makes its escape in one direc-

Above, **Figures 1** (left) and **2** (right); below, **Figures 3** (left) and **4** (right).

tion (**8**, right foreground), the other two cars proceed in the opposite direction; and the first, a light coupe in the left background, is barely able to maneuver around a truck which is pulling out into the street. The second car, a dark sedan (middle of **8**), is forced to turn around and go the other way. As the guard redirects his attention towards it, he is shot in the ensuing exchange of gunfire.

All of this action is presented from an "omniscient" perspective, looking down from the camera's final position above the action. This position perfectly reinforces the clinical detachment of the narrator as he describes the confrontation, first identifying the guard by name, even giving his address, and then offhandedly remarking that "he fell to the ground with a bullet in the groin... and is now in the Hackensack hospital where doctors say he will probably recover." Such a detached attitude towards violence is typical of *noir*; and the clipped tone of McBride's comments anticipate the perfunctory epilogues of television shows like *Dragnet*, where the fates of the police and criminals alike receive the same impersonal descriptions.

The formative and architectonic nature of this sequence shot, as part of a *film noir*, reinforces the underlying concept of a chaotic universe, prone to unexpected and deadly eruptions of violence. The chance nature of who is

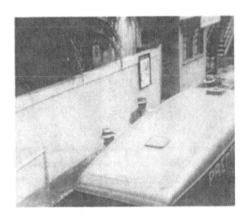

Above, **Figures 5** (left) and **6** (right); below, **Figures 7** (left) and **8** (right).

harmed and who escapes unscathed creates a narrative tension which the dynamic of the sequence shot sustains and enhances. Perhaps the simplest way to isolate the *noir* implication of such a staging in *The Killers* is to compare it with the "robbery" in De Sica's *Bicycle Thief* or one of the riot scenes in *Medium Cool*. In those instances, a very different manipulation of the diegetic space creates a very different attitude towards the aleatory.

Intra-sequence Editing: Formative Functions of Sound and Image

The gunfight sequence in the Green Cat nightclub not only mixes diverse visual techniques but synthesizes these with a complex number of aural elements, both motivated and unmotivated.

This sequence is part of a larger segment set in the Green Cat during which Kitty Collins (Ava Gardner), seated at a table with insurance investigator Riordan (Edmond O'Brien), reveals to him in a flashback "all she knows" about the hat company robbery and her part in it. As the film's *femme fatale*, Kitty is its principal locus of moral ambiguity; and the Green Cat, as an obvious metaphorical extension of Kitty (who is of Irish origin and has a feline name), is invested with an aura of eroticism and danger. This places it at the center of other narrative ambiguities, which the gunfight underscores but does not resolve. In an earlier scene, under pressure from Riordan over the telephone, Kitty had suggested the Green Cat as a rendezvous point. Riordan had wisely declined in favor of a more neutral and public location. Yet after meeting her and escorting her into a cab, Riordan curiously decides to go with her to the Green Cat. The cutaways explicitly suggest that they are being tailed by a short, sinister man (Ernie Adams, whose frequent casting in such parts makes him something of an icon for the audience). He, in turn, is followed by Al (Charles McGraw) and Max (William Conrad), the two killers from the opening segment.

The association of the Green Cat with Kitty's sexual power is reinforced by a long dissolve which moves from a romantic flashback between her and Ole back to the nightclub. Further links to this romantic moment are created metaphorically by the burning candle on the table between Kitty and Riordan and the motivated romantic melody being performed by the club's piano player. Riordan's remark about her tale of infidelity is "I would have liked to have known the old Kitty Collins." After this line, a cut to Kitty's approximate POV reveals the presence of the short man at the bar. In an "orthodox" dialogue sequence, the cut back to Kitty reveals a change in demeanor, as if she were reacting to noticing the man. She asks to leave and suggests that Riordan take her to his hotel room. But the shot from Kitty's point of view is not a traditional one. Kitty is seated and the last part of her conversation with Riordan is shot in slightly low angle medium close-ups. The shot of the bar is from a slightly high angle. Moreover, the camera is angled towards the street-side wall of the night-club, against which Kitty is seated, and photographs the bar with a statue of a green cat (or at least, one presumes it is that color, from the establishment's name if not from the black-and-white image) in the foreground. Such an angle could hardly be Kitty's literal point of view. Kitty never actually turns her head towards the bar but only shifts her eyes in that direction. In addition, the cat statue suggests her figurative presence in her own POV, somehow impelling the sinister man's actions.

The narrative information easily combines with this mysterious behavior by Kitty to sustain her identification as the *femme fatale* for the viewer. This paradigm is further extended as, exactly on Riordan's line to Kitty, "Too bad it had to catch up with you now," the nightclub pianist segues into a "boogie" jazz riff. Its insistent rhythm has associations of disquietude and sexual energy. A low angle shot of Kitty standing next to Riordan as she suggestively asks him to "wait here for me" while she goes to "powder her nose" is the last "normal" moment before the killers go into action.

The sequence of their attack begins with a cut to a wider shot, taken from behind the bar (**Figure 9**). The camera dollies to the left, then pans left with Kitty and pauses as she goes into the ladies' room before continuing in a left-

Above, **Figures 9** (left) and **10** (right); below, **Figures 11** (left) and **12** (right).

ward arc ending on the entryway to the club. During this pan, the slightly dissonant jazz riff picks up tempo and volume, as it blends with the cacophony of environmental sounds—people talking and laughing, etc. Another subtle
revelation, hard to pick out in the camera move, is that the sinister man is no
longer at the bar. At this point, the soundtrack is the perfect cue for the
viewer's disquietude with its ambivalent connotations: the sexual innuendo of
the jazz confirms Riordan's attraction to Kitty, while the dissonance reaffirms
her negative attributes, and the ironic (that is, unknown to Riordan) element of
danger in the sinister man. What is more, as the killers now appear in the entryway, an extra-diegetic element is added. The non-motivated underscore
swells with Miklós Rózsa's "killers' motif" (which is essentially the first four bars
of the theme from the series *Dragnet*), the meaning of which has been palpably
inscribed on the audience in the film's opening segment. The slow, steady repetition of this motif in counterpoint with the jazz riff begins to mask the sounds
of the nightclub. An anticipatory tension is generated by the overdetermined
status of the sound track throughout this sequence; and this is matched by a di-
versity of visual techniques which so alternate point of view and so control diegetic space that the heterogeneous signifiers are given the semblance of
"wholeness."

Above, **Figures 13** (left) and **14** (right); below, **Figures 15** (left) and **16** (right).

To begin, when Al enters the club followed by Max (**Figure 10**), the camera is stationary. This permits Al to escape the visual field and exit frame right. Subsequently, however, the camera pans to the right to follow Max, reversing itself along the same arc used to follow Kitty. In so doing it recovers lost space and terminates in a position which recaptures Al and "fixes" him to the bar (11). At this point, the controlled objectivity of the camera motivates a cut to a subjective shot, taken from the approximate point of view not of Al (in the foreground of 11) but of Max (in the mid-ground of 11) and revealing Riordan alone at the table (12). The denotative effect of this virtual shot/countershot is to indicate that Max is aware of Riordan but not vice versa, as Riordan is glancing down at the tabletop. Although the next shot of Max is head on, from a position in front of the bar (13), it is too close to Max to suggest Riordan's POV. Riordan is therefore outside the frame but still perilously within Max's visual field. The premeditated, objective stance of the camera is reaffirmed a moment later when a waiter comes around the bar and the camera is pushed back and pans slightly left as he walks down the bar, turns to pick up a drink, and then exits the frame. The waiter's natural actions have shifted the perspective of the frame so that other patrons along the bar are now visible; and as the waiter leans back, he opens a space for one of these patrons to turn towards camera. This man is Sam Lubinsky (Sam Levene), a retired policeman who is assisting Riordan's investigation. Lubinsky's expression reveals little; but his gaze is directed to a point which suggests a congruence with Max's look. This carries the strong connotation that Lubinsky is aware of Riordan's exposed posture, perhaps even part of a some plan to protect him. His immediate gesture—placing his hand beneath his coat for an instant—is to check for his gun. In an earlier scene, Lubinsky had kidded Riordan when the latter "lost" his gun. When Lubinsky now glances towards the opposite end of the bar (14), the camera pans off to the right and reframes on a medium long shot of the killers. Camera movement here transforms diegetic space by changing an objective shot to a semi-point of view, as the movement off Lubinsky's look onto the other two men implies that he is aware of the two killers. This is in spite of the fact that the narrative has not made it clear that either Lubinsky or Riordan "objectively" know who these men are. These shifting perspectives which combine to focus on both meaningful (Max, Riordan, and Lubinsky) and non-meaningful (the waiter) characters require the viewer carefully to read each shot and camera move and create a tension between objective and subjective information. This tension is also articulated in the intensity of the frenetic jazz piece and the legato of its musical counterpoint. As these subsume the realistic background noise, the "objective" reality of the associated images is further compromised.

The frequency and volume of the "killers' motif" increase again with the next cut, a long shot of Al and Max maneuvering at the bar from an "impossible" angle over Riordan's left shoulder, physically impossible because he is seated directly in front of some wooden wall paneling and a mirror (**Figure 15,** compare with **Figure 12**). The mirror had been particularly noticeable behind Riordan as he talked with Kitty before her flashback. Its slight tilt forward created an oddly distorted background behind his close-ups which literally "mirrored" but were different from the action behind her. Although they faced each other as they spoke, Kitty herself was not visible in that mirror. Now the camera is suddenly positioned on the other side of that mirror; and the rimlit seated figure of Riordan in the foreground has no depth, so that the low angle of his silhouette appears unnaturally high and graphically detached from the action. At the top of the frame a ceiling piece almost makes it seem as if Riordan is watching the killers prepare to attack though a window or a two-way mirror.

Manipulated in this manner, the traditional semi-subjective purview of the intended victim and the heightened music serve to increase viewer agitation, regardless of whether one "identifies" with Riordan or not. This tension is finally relieved by the gunfight itself. It begins with a slight downward tilt of the camera; then as the shot is held stationary the killers draw their guns. Riordan overturns the table and ducks for cover; in fact, he literally disappears from the frame. As the killers open fire, the music is so dominant that the gunshots and screams of the patrons can hardly be heard. There are more shots than visible muzzle blasts and Max winces in pain. Only at this point does a cutaway show Lubinsky firing away at the two men from the side. The cut back to the master reveals Al doubling over from a wound; he falls as Lubinsky enters this shot and moves up to him. Then in a semi-reverse, gun in hand, Riordan suddenly leaps up from behind the table. While the viewer may wonder if Riordan got off any shots, he moves quickly to the ladies room to discover that Kitty has gone out the window.

The visual confusion of the gunfight is accompanied by an interplay of diegetic and non-diegetic aural effects. At the first gunshot, the jazz riff terminates. In the motivated context—a flurry of gunshots—the club pianist might well be likely to stop playing. But the brass and strings play chords on the underscore which onomatopoeically mimic the muted sounds of the shots and the onlookers' screams. When the shooting subsides, the score briefly restates the "killers' motif" then segues to a "chase" theme as Riordan rushes to the ladies' room. Riordan is nonplused to discover that Kitty is missing, which perpetuates the implicit narrative "gaps" or confusion of the previous scene. Was Lubinsky's presence at the Green Cat part of a plan and were the identities of the killers known beforehand? Is this why Riordan surprised Kitty by deciding to take her there? If so, then why did he let her have a chance to escape? Was he disarmed by her fatal charm? Did Kitty signal or receive a signal from the sinister man, who in turn slipped out to cue the killers? The conclusion of the film, in which the remainder of the original robbery gang is killed off and Kitty is presumably arrested, does not resolve these ambiguities. Rather it expressively overcomes them through the structure of false homogeneity. This structure positions the viewer carefully within its chain of signifiers and by manipulation of sound and image, as Borde and Chaumeton first suggested, "make the viewer co-experience the anguish and insecurity which are the true emotions of contemporary *film noir*."[3]

Notes

1. Robert Siodmak, "HOODLUMS: the Myth...," *Films and Filming*, Vol. 5, no. 9 (June, 1959), p. 10.

2. As I suggested in my essay on "Existential Motifs in the *Film Noir*," it may be misleading to refer to *film noir* as a genre. Since part of what this brief piece is meant to illustrate is the influence of style in defining specific meaning in an individual film and in defining groups of film that share a common style, such as *film noir*, I use the term *genre* here in its broadest sense of a "sort" or specie of film, not in the common and more restricted usage implying a group of films defined outside of style by narrative structures, icons, etc.

3. See above, "Towards a Definition of *Film Noir*." p. 25.

Above, Dennis O'Keefe and Marsha Hunt in *Raw Deal*.

Mann in the Dark:
The *Films Noir* of Anthony Mann

Robert E. Smith

The career of Anthony Mann breaks into three relatively distinct periods. From his directorial debut in 1942 with *Dr. Broadway* until *Side Street* in 1949, Mann confined himself to a series of inexpensively made films which run the gamut from atmospheric *noirs* to lightweight musicals. Then, from *Devil's Doorway*, *The Furies* and *Winchester '73* (all in 1950) until *Man of the West* in 1958, he explored the psychological and physical terrain of the West with notable detours to the psychological war genre (*Men in War*, 1957), the Erskine Caldwell South (*God's Little Acre*, 1958), and a return to the B-format of the earlier years (*The Tall Target*, 1951). Mann's pointed use of landscape and decor in the 1950s films led naturally into the epics with which he ended his career. The grandiose commercial motivations of Mann's producer Samuel Bronston, and the nature of the genre, cannot obscure the spectacular tableaux and heroic imagery of *El Cid* (1961) and *The Fall of the Roman Empire* (1964). After the commercial failure of the sumptuous *The Fall of the Roman Empire*, Mann ended his career with *The Heroes of Telemark* (1965) and *A Dandy in Aspic* (1968) in both of which he abandoned the virtually mythological settings of the works which immediately preceded them.

Mann's reputation today is based primarily on the Westerns of the 1950s. This West which Mann created and explored is a land of interiority externalized in the form of the landscape. The psychological dramas of James Stewart, Robert Ryan, Gary Cooper, Victor Mature and many others are mirrored in the torturous wilderness through which they make their physical and metaphorical passages. Mann's classical familial antagonisms, father against son, brother against brother, allow for the channeling of protean emotions. Hero and villain are at the mercy of passions molded by events of the inescapable past. The characteristic love/hate rapport of charming "villain" and near-psychotic "hero" indicates the greatest danger for the Mann protagonist is the possibility of becoming completely what he so closely resembles, the Mann villain. The morally complex interrelationship of hero/villain, which is partially accountable for the remarkable intensity of his films, has at its roots the *films noir* of the 1940s. The darker side of human nature, the interiority of these earlier, psychologically troubled characters, is the determining force in Mann's noirs. We see the director striving for the depth and complexity of characterization he ultimately achieved in the great films of the 1950s.

The protagonists of the earlier noirs are not the flawed, intensely human hero/villains we see time and again in the Westerns. The conditions of poverty row: hurried production schedules; relative lack of writing and acting talent; cheapness of the physical settings and the conventions inherent in B-genre films all mitigate against the duality of characterization present in the later works. A similar, though less marked, departure from the protagonists of the Western occurs in the epics where the conventions and necessities of the genre point to character achieved, at least partially, through the spectacle. In both instances (poverty row and multi-million dollar spectacular) Mann attempts to deepen characters through his masterful visual style. Lighting, composition, camera angles and cutting are extremely well calculated in the early works, marking the director's exploration of every possibility inherent in the medium. His approach is largely successful, resulting in the clever transcendence of conventional material and inferior performers. The decisive protagonist of these Mann noirs is the ambience of darkness and pain, the visually suggested pessimism which is as tangible as the frequency of physical and moral confrontation between and within protagonists.

Mann fully utilized the iconography of film noir, iconography which in part developed from his own films. The dark underside of urban life provides the milieu. From the colorful characters of Dr. Broadway to the fully realized protagonists of Raw Deal and Side Street and even to the denizens of that most bizarre of French Revolutions in Reign of Terror (1949), shadowy darkness is the common stylistic determinant. Action generally occurs at night. Typically, isolated sources of light are bare light bulbs, deserted street lamps, flashlights, candles and matches. Elaborate shadow patterns fracture this light. Venetian blinds, the characteristic source of shadow in film noir, refracts light on faces and objects into many planes of light and dark. This world of black and white values (perhaps gray would be a closer approximation of the moral stance of Mann's "heroes" in this period) is reflected in extreme contrasts in black/white imagery. The thematic determinant is an evil which reaches everywhere. The blackness which envelops, indeed smothers, Mann's noirs is the tangible reflection of the ever present despair of lost hopes and entrapment, insured by the black soul of a psychotic universe.

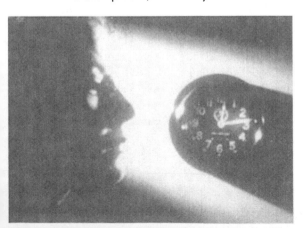

Left, long shadows and depth of field, Claire Trevor and a wall clock in Raw Deal.
Opposite right, the hulking figure of Raymond Burr in Raw Deal.

Mann uses the icons of *film noir*—guns, dark staircases, neon-lit hotel rooms, bars, deserted streets, etc.—but their primary distinction lies in the baroque photography which captures and places them in context. John Alton shot five Mann films (*T-Men, Raw Deal, Reign of Terror*, the 1949 *Border Incident* and, a year later, *Devil's Doorway*). Alton's unique lighting style and experimental bent suited Mann very well, though the director's visual style is quite consistent from the Alton films to those shot by less distinctive cinematographers. A favorite Alton technique frequently employed in the Mann films is to dispense with lighting from above altogether, using only lateral illumination. The consequent reduction in light intensity greatly lengthens and accentuates shadows, resulting in a very dramatic lighting scheme of small points of illumination, around which strikingly deep shadows fall. Large portions of the mise-en-scene are thereupon drenched in darkness, lit just enough to vaguely distinguish whatever objects might be there. Often the only source of illumination will be the studio's artful and often poetic approximation of natural light, such as the moonlight which shines through the Venetian blinds of Marsha Hunt's bedroom in *Raw Deal* or the light of the street lamp which dimly illuminates the nightclub finale of *Railroaded* (1947).

Hand in hand with Mann's dramatic lighting is his tendency to employ bizarre camera angles. The world depicted in these films is off balance, a nightmare approximation of everyday reality much more than a naturalistic one, and the instability of characters in precarious situations is ably suggested through the strikingly off-balance angles Mann employs. The most unnatural camera setups are generally saved for moments of high tension and big action set-pieces. The murder of Dan Duryea in *The Great Flammarion* (1945) is one such instance. As the pace of the cutting quickens with shots alternating between prospective victim, killer, and instigator, the camera positions become progressively more unstable. The angles and pacing here and in similar situations throughout Mann's early films, through this instability, suggest an uneasy atmosphere of malevolence and the rejection of conventional expectations for virtue triumphant in an ordered world.

The gangsters and psychos of Mann's poverty row films look forward to the Robert Ryans and John McIntires of the Westerns. These earlier *noir* villains are the central ingredient in the bleak world of Mann's films. Typically, low wide-angle shots provide the visual correlative for these often psychotic villains. In *Raw Deal*, Raymond Burr is frequently shot from the waist up, his bulk totally filling the frame, ominously looming over the action. Similarly, John Ireland in *Railroaded* is frequently, and dramatically, shot from below and in darkness, stressing his dangerously unstable

nature as well as his control over the events of the film. Darkness, and Mann's choice of bizarre and unstable camera angles are responsible for the ominous connotations associated with the Ireland character far more than any of the obvi- ous, though effective, things the actor is given to do.

The wide angle lenses developed through the 1940s were also utilized by Mann. Looming low angle photography is characteristic from the start of his ca- reer. The addition of wide angle lenses allowed Mann to enlarge the depth of field while often maintaining the ominous camera placement. This leads to some strik- ing crowd effects in *Border Incident* and alienating urban images in *Side Street* (1949), both photographed primarily (or most memorably) at dusk. Extreme high angle shots of city streets emphasize the dehumanizing, dwarfing scale of the ur- ban milieu in *Side Street*, while the terrifying potentialities of the cultivator in *Bor- der Incident* are enhanced through the use of a wide angle lens which distorts the size and consequently the frightfulness of the machine as it almost literally eats its way through the screen and into the audience. Through the use of these various lenses Mann was also able to stress the importance of objects by placing them very close to the camera while at the same time maintaining the action deeper within the frame. An exceptional example involves the black book around which the action of *Reign of Terror* revolves. It looms enormously large in the extreme foreground of a series of key shots as a peasant family is interrogated about its whereabouts deeper within the frame. Similar experiments with objects and cam- era placement encompassing an extreme field of vision are notable in the Alton films. Alton's experimental tendencies and talent make his work with Mann among the most interesting and valuable of the period. Nevertheless, Mann util- ized the possibilities of the wide angle lens in most of his post-1947 *noirs*.

The *noirs*, both prior to and after the pivotal *T-Men* (1947), are notable for their romantically fatalistic atmosphere and imagery. Mann's collaboration with Al- ton and the superior scripts he was offered after he joined Eagle-Lion in 1946-47 resulted in films which are more successful than any of his previous work. The vil- lains, particularly in the earliest films, lack the ambivalence of the later heavies. Raymond Burr, a notable Mann psychopath, functions most successfully when the film preserves an imagistic and narrative consistency. In *Raw Deal* (1948), which never deviates from its nightmarish mise-en-scene of pain-filled, shadowy dark- ness reinforced by fatalistic narration, the powers of underworld king Burr ap- proach the omniscient. He sees into everything, reaches everywhere and leaves no avenue of escape in the film's stylistically and thematically closed universe. *Raw Deal* becomes, through its intensity, a manifestation of bleak destiny. *Desperate* (1947), with a similarly cast Burr, provides considerable contrast. Here the care- fully created atmosphere is frequently undermined by the intrusion of home-life scenes, wedding parties, local color and sympathetic lawmen. Mann has little in- terest in all of this (at least in *Desperate*'s *noir* context of entrapment and pain); consequently, the young protagonists' scenes together, which establish the milieu, are painfully cloying. It is only when husband and wife are finally and inevitably sucked into this world's common denominator of chaos and pervasive evil that the film begins to function successfully. With so many avenues of escape open to the protagonists, leading to changes in tone and atmosphere, Burr's villain loses the all-encompassing power that he possesses in *Raw Deal*. Perhaps Mann's intention was to enrich the film through contrast; unfortunately, at this stage of his career, he was unsuccessful.

Mann's early career reflected the studio-imposed variety of material characteristic of fledgling directors in Hollywood's B-units during the 1940s (and any other time). Unable to choose his scripts or mold them by working on the screenplays, Mann was forced to transform often unsuitable material into personal expression through his style. These experimental years were ones of much testing of stylistic ideas and the development of what was from the start a rather intuitive ability to use the camera dramatically. Mann experimented with virtually every technical possibility appropriate to his material and the dictates of his dark personal vision (which meshed fortuitously with the demands of the *noir* genre). A gradual simplification of technique developed after Mann left the Bs in the early 1950s. After the tragic, poetically dark *Devil's Doorway* and the spectacularly baroque *The Furies*, Mann began a series of comparatively austere films with James Stewart, which are imagistically striking but far less exuberantly baroque.

Below, *T-Men*: undercover agent Genaro (Alfred Ryder, right) is cornered by the gun-wielding Moxie (Charles McGraw) while his partner O'Brien (Dennis O'Keefe, left) must watch helplessly.

Dr. Broadway provided Mann with the opportunity to transform Damon Runyo-nesque material, revolving around a conventional B-mystery plot, into a study of atmosphere and nuance. Dramatically lit, big standing sets and Mann's adroit pac-ing give the film an expensive look not accounted for by the budget. The quaintly colorful characters are less noteworthy than the urban nightmare Mann evokes through his style. *Dr. Broadway* provides the milieu Mann would build upon in his most successful early films. Gone, however, in later works, would be the genial and loyal "Apple Annies," frog-voiced shoe-shine boys, phony blind men and watchful hobos. The dark mysterious decor and the feel of the omnipotent dan-gers of the city would remain. A different breed of "colorful" characters would in-habit it, far less genial and far less loyal than the denizens of Mann's first film.

Strangers in the Night (1944) marks a relatively important step in the develop-ment of Mann's abilities. The striking photography of Republic's house cinematog-rapher Reggie Lanning is as lush and expressive as that of Alton. What Lanning's style lacks in experimentation is more than made up for in richness and fullness of the deep focus mise-en-scene. Mann utilizes Lanning's abilities (and the plush pro-duction values) to create his first visually lavish production. Curtains rippling in the wind, darkened glistening staircases, shadowy decor shot from daring angles, and the large close-ups which dramatically punctuate the film are beautiful to look at and constitute the visual high-water mark in Mann's career until *T-Men*. Mann at-tempts, partly through the expressive use of this highly textured mise-en-scene, to create characters of real psychological depth, ones who suffer from the same imbalance of mind and spirit that later afflict Barbara Stanwyck (*The Furies*), James Stewart (*The Naked Spur*, etc.), and Gary Cooper (*Man of the West*). The charac-ters and their psychoses often veer into overstatement and parody (especially the totally lifeless relationship of "goody-goody" hero/heroine), denoting the fact that Mann was simply not proficient enough at this point, particularly in the molding of dialogue and situations, to carry off such an ambitious psychological undertaking.

By *The Great Flammarion* (1945), Mann had begun learning the process by which unlikely material could be molded into something personal or, failing that, at least somewhat subversive. The all-bad girl format, the mirror image of the equally popular innocent-wife-driven-insane-by-diabolical-husband, becomes the basis for a sporadically effective and generally entertaining melodrama. The re-sources of Republic provide for a number of extensive tracking shots into a thea-ter and around the perimeter of an orchestra pit. Characters are framed with precision and incisiveness in the course of these tracks, establishing more com-plex relationships than the screenplay indicates. The plotting of Mary Beth Hughes vis-à-vis Erich Von Stroheim and other of her victims takes on the conventional, as well as unexpectedly subversive and humorous connotations, again provided al-most wholly by Mann's choice of camera placement and angle. Hughes sizing up her next victim in a portentous low-angle shot or scheming in two-shots is under-cuttingly amusing as is the devastating image of pretentious Erich dancing around a

Above, Mary Beth Hughes (right) and Erich Von Stroheim as *The Great Flammarion*.

hotel room on the wings of love. The many shots accentuating the kinkiness of Stroheim, such as the close-up shaving of his head, provide for additional amusement at the expense of the screenplay's more lofty aspirations. The big setpieces, Dan Duryea's and Hughes' deaths and the opening sequence, are far more seriously approached and very well calculated in terms of camera movement, elaborate cutting (generally on one-shots) and angling.

Strange Impersonation (1946) is surely one of the cheapest films ever made by an important artist (always excepting Edgar G. Ulmer, of course), and the most impoverished film of Mann's career. Somewhat more in keeping with the director's inclinations than was *The Great Flammarion*, it lacks the focus and stylistic intensity which would really begin to appear with *Railroaded* in 1947. The story of a woman research scientist who tries her own experimental anesthetic with horrifying and surreal results, the film points the way to what would be Mann's forte during this period: a nightmare landscape of pain, trapped characters and vicious, unscrupulous villains. The overstated and coincidence-prone material and silly screenplay and performances frequently bog down the film, but often *Strange Impersonation* is reflective of Mann's *noir* preoccupations. A down-and-out alcoholic who robs the heroine and leads to the "strange impersonation" and the milieu of neon-lit streets, punk hustlers, and double-dealing "friends" are realized by the director with economy (enforced) and conviction. The clever ending which reveals

Above, Sheila Ryan and John Ireland in the nightclub scene from *Railroaded.*

that it was all a dream is a disappointment, dissipating the nightmare just as it was becoming consistently oppressive. A rather conventional lighting scheme, primarily white with little in the way of textured high contrast black/white patterning is another flaw of the film, probably due to the very short shooting schedule.

Desperate (1947), which follows the impersonal but graceful *The Bamboo Blonde* (1946) marks another step in Mann's progression toward the creation of a consistent *noir* milieu. A young couple try to escape from both the law and the mob, from which there is no escape. Raymond Burr as the crime king-pin contributed the first of his two memorable Mann performances. Beautifully realized sequences, such as the beating of Steve Brodie (administered by Burr's stooges under a wildly dramatic swinging light bulb which throws patches of black over the decor and characters) with crosscut shots of Burr photographed from an extreme low angle, cannot fully justify the inconsistencies of the film. Shots of the couple escaping at dusk over the farm hills are also quite evocative and effective in setting the mood of desperation the film strives for. The hellish world of the criminals is, characteristically, far more strikingly presented than the pallid and colorless young couple. Normalcy is a condition which rarely intrudes, at least successfully, on Mann's bleak vision.

Moral culpability on the part of the hero (or heroine in this case) and interaction between the opposing sides begins to emerge, if haltingly, in *Railroaded* (1947). Violent and bizarre, with protagonists caught in a nightmare, *Railroaded* is more consistent than earlier Manns, though it is hampered by impoverishment and inferior performances. The relationship between unpleasant hood John Ireland and Sheila Ryan (the basic plot has her attempting to clear her brother) assumes more complex connotations as the film progresses. Unfortunately, Mann was unable to completely develop the emotional and sexual attraction between the two suggested by the film's frequent two-shot format. Nevertheless, *Railroaded* is the first more or less consistent example of the baroque stylistics (particularly in the lighting, in this instance) Mann would employ on his subsequent B-films.

Mann's first film produced at Eagle-Lion Studios, *T-Men* (1947) was also his first film with John Alton. *T-Men* goes beyond the consistency of *Railroaded*, maintaining a mature, unselfconscious stylistic sureness mirroring the first good script from which the director had worked. Treasury agents tracking down an unscrupulous counterfeiting ring provides the foundation for characters who are much more real than any which preceded them. The relationship of the agents and their wives is developed with economy through detail and careful and pointed framing within shots. Within the suspense context of the narrative, relationships are developed with a considerable amount of intimacy and tenderness. The result is the first instance of audience concern for Mann protagonists. Also within this context are a number of bravura passages such as a steam bath murder and the exciting finale on board a darkened ship, which are not only highly effective, but far more carefully integrated into the overall formal structure of the film than anything comparable in earlier Manns. From this point on the director's films would be characterized by a greater stylistic consistency and a more careful and assured working out of relationships than we find in the previous films. The formal command previously developed is henceforth refined and combined with much more attention to the psychological makeup of the characters. More than stylistic showpieces, these later films are involved with the relationships of real people in difficult situations.

Raw Deal (1948) exemplifies Mann's mastery of both style and feeling. Photographed by Alton, the film is resplendent with velvety blacks, mists, netting and other expressive accessories of poetic *noir* decor and lighting. One of the most visually stylish and striking of Mann's early films, *Raw Deal* is also one of the most fatalistic. The lighting scheme, preponderantly dark, ably suggests the milieu of lost chances so central to the director's intentions. Claire Trevor's narration, spoken with world-weary and resigned inflection, sets the tone for the drama of

Dennis O'Keefe, Marsha Hunt, and Raymond Burr. O'Keefe, a good-hearted, small-time crook, and his adoring girl Trevor on the run from both police and Burr's double-crossing mob form the basic plot line. Hunt as representative of the outside world serves to demonstrate to O'Keefe what he has missed and can never have. There are many emotional crosscurrents as relationships between the three develop and pull at the empathies of the viewer, all in a fatalistic context reinforced by dark, claustrophobic images. Hunt's naive illusions are shattered in the course of the trio's escape and are replaced by a more realistic conception of people and actions. The denouement in Burr's apartment shows the arch criminal as paranoid maniac. The confrontation of criminal and loser ends the film in the primal manner of the familial Westerns, with the exception that here the hero is not reborn out of the death of his alter-ego. Low angle shots and close-up two-shots in murky half-darkness provide the stylistic context for this ultimate confrontation which ends in flames and death for both men, confirming the expectations created by the visual tone of the film and Trevor's narration.

After the attention to character displayed in *Raw Deal*, *Reign of Terror* might seem to be somewhat uncharacteristic if not outright disappointing. *Reign of Terror* is much more of a stylistic tour de force accentuating action and excitement than

Below, a B *femme fatale*, Pat (Claire Trevor) reclines while talking to Joe (Dennis O'Keefe) in *Raw Deal*.

a film of carefully realized characters and relationships. Everything in the film is sacrificed to speed and thrills. One breathless escape or fight leads immediately to another in seemingly endless profusion. Conspirators, revolutionaries, maniacs, those of pure heart (Robert Cummings) and damsels in distress (lovely Arlene Dahl) populate this most bizarre and baroquely shot of French Revolutions. Mann compensates for the lack of gripping protagonists with a dazzling stylistic command. The most unusual camera angles, extremes of lighting, camera movements and cutting create a crazily inclusive world divorced from the "real" one in which amazing amounts of well-staged and calculated action can occur almost constantly. From the highly exciting pacing and sureness of action and the stylistic command evident in the visuals, *Reign of Terror* must surely be judged a success. A film without real characters, unless its unique style be judged a protagonist, *Reign of Terror* can be seen as a stylistic watershed summing up everything the director had learned about the possibilities of the camera to that time. In this respect it is quite similar to his even more baroque *The Furies* (1950) where psychological intensity as well is explored.

The unusual union of period setting and *film noir* which characterizes *Reign of Terror* is echoed in Mann's last foray into the *noir*, *The Tall Target* (1951). Dark, sinister lighting and tight camera work are used in this mystery dealing with an attempted assassination of President Lincoln. Borrowing from Hitchcock's suspense techniques, Mann's film is more of an experiment in compressed time and setting than a completely satisfactory character study, in that respect also similar to *Reign of Terror*. We see the detailed mechanics of intrigue, entrapment and the race against time, sometimes at the expense of the people who are enacting the complex movements of the narrative. A lack of commitment strangely permeates the film, which Mann made for the opportunity it gave him to experiment with self-imposed structural and stylistic limitations. The feeling of a backward glance hangs over *The Tall Target* in a way quite foreign to the dynamic and vital *noirs* of the pre-Western years.

1949 marks the last year of Mann's association with the so-called poverty row studios. He had worked his way up through Republic, PRC, Eagle-Lion, and the B-units at Paramount and RKO. With the exception of *Dr. Broadway* and *Stranger in the Night*, which benefit from expensive looking sets, all of these films are quite inexpensive. Often the physical impoverishment is so evident as to become a distinctly depressing hindrance; one can do only so much by cutting down revealing lighting before the entire image fades away. There is no doubt that *Strange Impersonation, Railroaded* and *Desperate* would have been better had the director had more time in which to realize his ideas. Mann's stay at Eagle-Lion, from *T-Men* on, marks the real turning point in his career. Finally given the necessary physical resources, talented collaborators (Alton, his performers), and good genre scripts, Mann immediately began to realize more personal and successful films. *T-Men* had been noticed critically, and *Reign of Terror* was one of the largest financial successes in the short but respectable history of Eagle-Lion. As a result Mann began to be noticed. MGM signed the director after *Reign of Terror* and set him on the upward road first to respectable middle budget A-films and eventually to some of the biggest budgeted films in history.

Taking John Alton with him, Mann made *Border Incident* at MGM on an obviously greatly augmented budget. Extensive location shooting, large crowds of extras, and relatively important studio performers mark the more notable departures from previous films. That MGM's 25th anniversary fell in 1949 is perhaps the reason for the plushness of the film. The illegal smuggling and exploitation of Mexican farm workers into Southern California (and their subsequent murder when returning to Mexico) is the subject of *Border Incident*. George Murphy and Ricardo Montalban represent their respective governments' attempts to break up the ring. *Border Incident* is notable for the same chasm between good and evil that would remain constant, though later enriched by ever deepening ambiguity, throughout Mann's career. Quicksand pits, death marches through strikingly shot rockscapes, carefully calculated and timed for suspense searches and escapes culminate in the extraordinary cultivator sequence, which benefits from Alton's use of wide angle lenses. The unexpectedly graphic demise of Murphy leads into the exposure of the smugglers and the end of this somber film.

The film with which Mann ended the decade of the 1940s, *Side Street*, combines typical Mann stylistics with the most complexly developed male/female relationship in any of his films up to this time. Something of a companion piece to Nicholas Ray's magnificent first film, *They Live By Night*, *Side Street*'s milieu is the honestly felt concept of the urban nightmare. Weakness is the motivation for Farley Granger's thievery. His attempt to return stolen money comes too late as once again, both mob and police chase him through the city. For all its expected violence and the presence of Mann's psychopaths, *Side Street* has a gentler, more humane atmosphere than the director's previous work, no doubt due to the development of the Granger/O'Donnell relationship. Weakness, not greed, is the cause of Granger's action and from that point on events far beyond any individual's control push him. The lyrical love scenes, which are unfortunately rare (Cathy O'Donnell's part is rather small) blunt the bleakness of the milieu and the protagonists' lack of options. Ultimately, however, the couple is boxed into a corner from which there is no escape. Though the end is optimistic the general feeling of desperation and tragedy is similar to that of other, lesser Mann *noirs*. *Side Street*, in the maturity of its relationships and refinement of technique, marks the apogee of this period in Mann's career. Shot with much less flourish than the earlier films, *Side Street* is also notable for its beautifully written, well-motivated and acted characters. Mann lets them speak for themselves without the—in this case unnecessary—support of baroque stylistics. Alton's work is as incisive as ever, his wide, very high angle car chase through the deserted Wall Street section of New

York being a particularly striking example of the masterful wedding of style and meaning which was to be henceforth a primary characteristic of Mann's work.

Anthony Mann's *films noirs* can be seen as a testing ground out of which the director emerged a fully matured artist. These inexpensive, quickly made films were, in this respect, experiments which allowed Mann to exercise his directorial muscles. The B atmosphere was freer and more conducive to experiment and innovation than the far more costly, and consequently conservative, milieu of big budget film-making. Mann not only acquired an intimate knowledge of every facet of film-making, he was also able to exercise far more control over the style and construction of his films than were many far better established big budget studio directors. Certainly one of the most gratifying aspects of the Bs is the personal control a few talented artists were able to exercise over the stylistic totality of their films because of their "unimportance," cheapness and speed of their work. Mann, Ulmer, Joseph H. Lewis and later Gerd Oswald and Phil Karlson exercised more personal control over their films than did the Henry Kings and Clarence Browns of the big studios who were at the mercy of powerful producers and stars.

Though in fact the B *noirs* did provide this invaluable training, they constitute something far more creative and important than a mere apprenticeship. Mann's progression leads from uncertainty and stylistic inconsistency to mastery of every nuance of style and feeling. His post-1947 *noirs* stand independently as fully realized works of popular and personal art. *Raw Deal*, *Border Incident* and *Side Street* among other, slightly lesser achievements, are works of complex character relationships, reflective of an equally complex stylistic matrix. The moral ambiguity of protagonists and their lack of options in a mise-en-scene of darkness and desperation-filled instability are Mann's means, and simultaneously the tangible visual expression of his philosophy. The director's grim vision lurks in every shadow, kiltered dramatic close-up and act of psychotic violence. These *noirs*, which so succinctly combine powerfully stated personal vision, characters of depth, complex moral relationships and classically constructed narrative structures, constitute a distinct and successful chapter in the career of a master of modern cinema.

Above, Harry Fabian (Richard Widmark) is comforted by Mary (Gene Tierney).

Expressionist Doom in *Night and the City*

Glenn Erickson

A thin white silhouette of a man stumbles over the masonry rubble of a collapsed wall and rushes forward into a huge frozen close-up, sweating, panting for air, his eyes fixed in a rictus of anguish. This is Harry Fabian, at the end of his rope, pursued in a twilight of ruined buildings and narrow streets, desperation defining his every move—a rat in a maze lined with razor blades.

Were I asked to offer a title for the *film noir* that best exemplifies the textbook definitions of the *noir* sensibility, I would nominate Jules Dassin's *Night and the City* (1950). I can think of no other title that better satisfies the formal criteria of the *noir* movement, and, as a personal choice, no other that delineates the *noir* universe so immediately for the uninitiated viewer.

In its welter of hysteria and brutality, deceit and despair, *Night and the City* is a graphic showcase of the style at its most extreme. Its visuals are the most alienating and baroquely expressionistic of any *noir* film this side of Orson Welles. Its defeated and crazed characters move through a story line consisting almost exclusively of deceptions and fatally closing traps. Its resolution implodes into a bleak world view of near-cosmic fatality. Even in 1950, when grim subject matter, oppressive violence, and downbeat endings had become fairly common, *Night and the City* must have packed a heavy *noir* punch.

The director Jules Dassin was blacklisted in Hollywood and like a number of other *Noir* directors spent the rest of his career in Europe. *Night and the City*, his last American film, is set in London, which seems an apt choice for such a strong proponent of "the American Style": the film itself seems to be a fugitive from McCarthyism. Other *noir* films have been set in England, but none make as much of the locale as does *Night and the City*. Being a city that had taken real punishment from the war with its economic chaos and its rubble in the streets looking all the more baroque set against the older architecture, bombed-out London has an advantage over Los Angeles,. One of the more subversive elements of classic *noir* films is their use of expressionistic visuals to impose a second reality, an "underworld night land" over the normal, affluent, official face of American complacency, to reveal the rot and soullessness beneath the postwar success machine. *Night and the City* has the advantage of starting with a setting where these conditions are clearly already manifest: the soullessness doesn't have to be established. In this London underworld of street beggars, seedy club touts, and petty criminals the situation appears to be well matched to the grotesque visual setting. London also serves for *Night and the City* the same function Berlin performed for Lang's *M*; its *Three Penny Opera*-style criminal society would not have translated well to American streets, as witness the Joseph Losey remake of *M*. Finally, the London location would indicate the elevation of the "American" *noir* from a specific locality to a universal plane. Perpetually pursued, Harry Fabian is not running in the alleys of some vague Everytown. The blasted metropolis through which he flees resembles nothing so much as the surreal domain of Cocteau's *Orpheus*, "La Zone," a mythical limbo somewhere beyond reality.

Night and the City is populated with characters whose alienation is both implied and explicit. Mary (Gene Tierney) and Harry Fabian (Richard Widmark) are presumably both American expatriates down on their luck, he reduced to touting for the crooked nightclub where she pushes watered-down champagne with her songs. Mary is weary but honest, too exhausted to consider a way clear from her predicament. Their neighbor Adam Dunn (Hugh Marlowe) is an effete artist whose romantic interest in Mary is not helped by his accurate verbal assessment of Harry. Adam's irrelevance is augmented by the omission of several scenes in Jo Eisinger's original script (probably excised for time constraints) which would have depicted him as a more determined romantic alternative for Mary. The hugely obese nightclub owner Nosseross (Francis L. Sullivan), for all his riches, is a prisoner of his obsession with his faithless wife Helen (Googie Withers), a mania expressed through his fetishistic pawing of the plastic-wrapped fur with which he has tried to purchase her. Success atop this underworld brings only disillusion and distrust, and the vain wish to control others. Helen's own desperation to escape her marriage to the cloying, repulsive Nosseross has twisted her into a perpetual harpy-like rage.

At the low end of the scale in this bizarre world is the army of paupers on the street, fake cripples and phony blind men organized into a Kurt Weill-like legion of beggars. They seem everywhere underfoot, peering from the corners like Tod Browning's *Freaks*, a living testament to the dehumanization of society, midway toward becoming the troglodytic Morlocks of H.G. Wells. At the high end is Kristo (Herbert Lom), the kingpin of organized wrestling, an oily mobster who is realistic, businesslike, and ruthless. With his predatory solicitors, he inspires doglike devotion from thugs like "The Strangler" (Mike Mazurki), a professional wrestler willing to murder in the mere hope of pleasing his "master." It is perversely appropriate that Kristo is the only character to evince commitment to a traditional value. He reveres his father, the wrestler Gregorius (Stanilaus Zbyzsko); but not his father's art, Greco-Roman wrestling, whose great formal beauties are lost on a public desensitized by Kristo's brutal commercial wrestling empire.

This is the world, full of grotesques and predators and pathetic monsters, in which Harry Fabian has set his ambitions. Harry himself is a source of discomfort for the viewer because, as portrayed by Richard Widmark, he remains a character with whom it is easy to identify even as he moves from one totally unlikable act to another. Stealing from his girlfriend, touting for Nosserosses' club, playing the "comer" for all concerned, Harry turns his plaintive whine—"I just want to be somebody" (predating *On the Waterfront*, by the way)—into the logical end of ambition: Horatio Alger evolved into a selfish creep. Harry's urge to get rich quick, live "a life of ease, Mary," is his curse. He's a talented, bright young man putting his energies into his own destruction. "Always the wrong things," weeps Mary. "Harry's an artist without an art," observes Adam. Harry's mad dash to deceive both his enemies and his friends and somehow bluff together his own racket can lead only to tragedy. His character, unlike the relative Everymen of other *noir* films whom Destiny might push to the brink of some desperate act (as in *Pitfall* or *Pushover*), starts at desperation and quickly crosses the line into hysteria. Harry is not tempted to trespass; he's frustrated by not being able to move fast enough, not being able to keep all of his suckers conned at any given time. Even Darryl F. Zanuck, the studio head under whom *Night and the City* was produced, understood the perverse appeal of the unethical Harry Fabian character. His notes to the Jo Eisinger script prompted not the commercial compromises usually associated with front office changes but a revised beginning that jettisoned Eisinger's soft introduction of the Fabian character, in which he did magic tricks and played the wistful dreamer, in favor of getting right to the point. Fabian is immediately caught rifling Mary's purse and has to wheedle his way off the hook. Harry Fabian likely represents the acting highlight of Richard Widmark's career. Poised between the caustic horror figure, Tommy Udo, of *Kiss of Death* and the not particularly compelling heroes of his later starring roles, Widmark's constantly ranting performance never seems out of control, not even when he's screaming in tears in confrontations so hypercharged that the film frame seems ready to explode. Along with James Cagney's Cody Jarrett in *White Heat*, Widmark's Fabian is among the most unstable, apocalyptic characters in *film noir*.

Assessing creative contributions to this unique film produces some interesting surprises. The elegantly crafted Eisinger screenplay, from the source novel by Gerald Kersh, contains all of the verbal nuances of the finished film and includes the more notable lines of dialogue, such as the aforementioned and frequently quoted remark about an "artist without an art." For the most part, the social agenda of Eisinger's script is expressed in the characters and events themselves and not in Trumbo-esque "position speeches." One deleted script scene, had it been included, would have made an unsubtle religious comment: Harry is shown hiding in a bombed-out church whose senile former sexton thinks Harry is a burglar come to steal the long-absent holy artifacts. In his pathetic state of denial, the sexton believes his church to be intact and functioning in this Godless city.

Above, Francis L. Sullivan as the obese and unattractive Nosse-ross, "lurks above the Silver Fox nightlcub [like]...a spider in its lair."

Eisinger's cool vision describes the narrow streets and has quick delineations of extreme compositions; but what the script cannot convey is the striking visual element of *Night and the City*. This grips the viewer from Harry's first high-angled long shot and never lets go. The overall look of the film is arguably the most baroquely styled of the classic *noir* period. Welles' *Touch of Evil* is a *noir* film whose visual components integrate more levels of thematic complexity. The stark visuals here make their bleak point with a more dreamlike single-mindedness.

The extreme chiaroscuro lighting schemes of *Night and the City* define the psychological entrapment of its inhabitants. Like abstract magnetic waves bending around astronomical bodies, *Night and the City*'s distorting effects increase when in proximity to its most bizarre characters. Nosseross, already filmed with wide lenses that exaggerate his mass, lurks above his Silver Fox nightclub in a glass-paned cage whose bars throw broad web-like patterns across ceilings and walls. The effect is of a spider in its lair, counting money poked in through trap doors. At other times the cage-like lighting scheme suggests Nosseross' own egocentric dementia, his psychic isolation from the rest of humanity. Elsewhere the lighting distorts with other connotations. In Beggar's Lane the smoky, pit-like darkness says more about class oppression in a capitalist society than any subversive speech. In the ring/arena of Harry's gymnasium the harsh, overhead lighting of the big wrestling match between Gregorius and The Strangler creates an overexposed look that transforms their combat into a clash between giant, pallid gods.

But the most memorable visuals in *Night and the City* are the nightmarish exteriors seen as Harry Fabian scrambles through the London lanes and across the vacant rubble-strewn lots left over from the bombings of W.W. II. The cinematographers seem determined to carry the night-for-night location trend of the late Forties to new heights of creativity. A typical set-up is a shot featuring Fabian entering frame over a wall in the far background, making his way forward through crumbling ruins, and ending several seconds later in a choking close-up as he searches for a new avenue of escape. Whether back-lit and silhouetting Harry over a carpet of damp-lit paving stones or side-lit and highlighting a forest of fragmented walls and torn fences, these night scenes invariably maintain focus from a couple of feet away from the camera to infinity. Many scenes are shot in the just-prior-to-sunrise "magic hour," resulting in sky backgrounds with just enough detail to make these scenes appear suspended in time between day and night. Selective spotlighting of features in the shattered landscape transform ordinary brick lots into a minatory dream world. It is interesting to note the cumulative effect of these scenes in contrast to the similarly photographed night exteriors of Carol Reed's *The Third Man*. Reed's nocturnal Vienna has its menacing aspect but retains a fairyland beauty, a decorative irony, that suggests the elegant decadence of Harry Lime's guiltily divided city. Dassin's stark London has none of these reassuring qualities; it's just plain damned.

"You've got it all—but you're a dead man, Harry Fabian." As Fabian's doom approaches, the expressionistic devices of *Night and the City* are marshaled with operatic precision. The command to "Get Harry Fabian!" is circulated throughout the city and depicted in a breathtaking single-take shot filmed from the interior of a moving car spreading the word from corner to corner across several city blocks. Harry's every possible ally denies him. Bookies and beggar-masters turn him away, until he is left to face a fatal dawn with the sun seen rising through a bridge aswarm with Kristo minions determined to win the price on Harry's head. Harry's rejection of Mary's maternal offer of help is the act of a man so tired of running he

no longer wants to live. The shocking bleakness of his final choice, to turn his own destruction into another shabby "deal," provides the irony for one of the darkest finales in *film noir*. In the naked light of day, Harry achieves a perverse state of grace and becomes, not an outlaw hero, but just another ragged man racing toward his own oblivion.

Right, "another ragged man racing toward his own oblivion," Harry Fabian, crossing the "rubble-strewn lots."

Above, an *homme fatal*. Ralph Meeker as the narcissistic Mike Hammer kisses Velda (Maxine Cooper).

Kiss Me Deadly: Evidence of a Style

Alain Silver

At the core of *Kiss Me Deadly* are speed and violence. The adaptation of Mickey Spillane's novel takes Mike Hammer from New York to Los Angeles, where it situates him in a landscape of somber streets and decaying houses even less inviting than those stalked by Spade and Marlowe in the preceding decades of Depression and War years. Much like Hammer's fast cars, the movie swerves frenziedly through a series of disconnected and cataclysmic scenes. As such, it typifies the frenetic, post-Bomb L.A. with all its malignant undercurrents. It records the degenerative half life of an unstable universe as it moves towards critical mass. When it reaches the fission point, the graphic threat of machine-gun bullets traced in the door of a house on Laurel Canyon in *The Big Sleep* in the 40s is explosively superseded in the 50s as a beach cottage in Malibu becomes ground zero.

From the beginning, *Kiss Me Deadly* is a true sensory explosion. In the pre-credit sequence, a woman stumbles out of the pitch darkness, while her breathing fills the soundtrack with amplified, staccato gasps. Blurred metallic shapes flash by without stopping. She positions herself in the center of the roadway until oncoming headlights blind her with the harsh glare of their high beams. Brakes grab, tires scream across the asphalt, and a Jaguar spins off the highway in a swirl of dust. A close shot reveals Hammer behind the wheel: over the sounds of her panting and a jazz piano on the car radio, the ignition grinds repeatedly as he tries to restart the engine. Finally, he snarls at the woman, "You almost wrecked my car! Well? Get in!"

As in Aldrich's earlier *World For Ransom*, the shot selection and lighting provide immediate keys to the style, to *film noir*. But in *Kiss Me Deadly*, the opening dialogue between Hammer and Christina is the significant component in establishing another sort of hero: one that is sneering, sarcastic, and not really a hero at all.

HAMMER	Can I have my hand back now? (Pause.) So, you're a fugitive from the laughing house.
CHRISTINA	They forced me to go there. They took away my clothes to make me stay.
HAMMER	Who?

CHRISTINA	I wish I could tell you that. I have to tell someone. When people are in trouble, they need to talk. But you know the old saying.
HAMMER	"What I don't know can't hurt me"?
CHRISTINA	You're angry with me aren't you? Sorry I nearly wrecked your pretty little car. I was just thinking how much you can tell about a person from such simple things. Your car, for instance.
HAMMER	Now what kind of message does it send you?
CHRISTINA	You have only one real lasting love.
HAMMER	Now who could that be?
CHRISTINA	You. You're one of those self-indulgent males who thinks about nothing but his clothes, his car, himself. Bet you do push-ups every morning just to keep your belly hard.
HAMMER	You against good health or something?
CHRISTINA	I could tolerate flabby muscles in a man, if it'd make him more friendly. You're the kind of person who never gives in a relationship, who only takes. (sardonically) Ah, woman, the incomplete sex. And what does she need to complete her? (mockingly dreamy) One man, wonderful man!
HAMMER	All right, all right. Let it go

What kind of man is Mike Hammer? *Kiss Me Deadly*'s opening dialogue types him quickly. Christina's direct accusation of narcissism merely confirms what the icons suggest about "how much you can tell about the person from such simple things": the sports car, the trench coat, the curled lip, the jazz on the radio. Aldrich and writer A.I. Bezzerides use the character of Christina to explain and reinforce what the images have already suggested, that this is not a modest or admirable man.

The dialogue also reveals that Hammer knows exactly who he is and the image he presents: "What kind of message does it send you?" It sends the one Hammer wants to send, a message which Christina, the "fugitive from the laughing house," can discuss directly. This is a first hint of what will be something of a role reversal in the way men and women speak. The older male characters, the Italian house mover and Dr. Soberin, will use figurative images and make mythical allusions, rather than speak directly about people and objects. The younger women, Christina, Velda, and even Carver, usually say what is on their minds.

The dark highway of the opening is a kind of narrative limbo: the elements of the plot have not yet been brought into line, let alone focused. Certainly, contemporary viewers brought with them expectations about character and plot both from the underlying novel and from the conventions of *film noir*. The opening selectively underscores aspects of those expectations while withholding detail. Visually, the discussion of the "laughing house" and Hammer's materialism is shot entirely in a medium two shot of Christina and Hammer, either from the front or rear, in the cockpit of his car. The viewer is not distracted from the character interaction, in which Hammer "loses" the verbal sparring: he is effectively "put down" by Christina until he must tell her to "let it go." *Kiss Me Deadly* has no clearly defined landscape at this point to use as a textural reinforcement. The countryside and the rural gas station are all unidentified settings. They are open, shadowy, and, even within the fringes of the station's neon lights, menacing. Generically this last trait primes the viewer for Christina's murder under torture and Hammer's near death.

In terms of subject/object tension, the Aldrich/Bezzerides conception of Hammer is both more objective and "anti-Spillane." Spillane's use of first-person prose is certainly in the hard-boiled tradition.

> All I saw was the dame standing there in the glare of the headlights waving her arms like a huge puppet and the curse I spit out filled the car and my own ears. I wrenched the car over, felt the rear end start to slide, brought it out with a splash of power and almost ran up the side of the cliff as the car fishtailed. The brakes bit in, gouging a furrow in the shoulder, then jumped to the pavement and held. Somehow I had managed a sweeping curve around the babe.

This offhanded objectification of women is in play from the novel's first paragraph. This attitude along with Spillane's lurid sadomasochism and his rabid anti-Communism in the shadow of McCarthy are legendary. From the opening Aldrich and Bezzerides take the events and little else. Spillane's recurring protagonist, Hammer, provides the predetermined viewpoint of the narratives. Hammer's deprecations and wisecracks in the novel are not detached or objective descriptions of people and events and are part of his "color." Aldrich and Bezzerides abandon most of this also or rather, in Aldrich's preferred method, they "stand it on its head."

Of the opening dialogue only one line—"They forced me...to make me stay."—is from the novel. But much more is changed than just the words. In terms of plot, elements such as the Rossetti poem or the radioactive "great whatsit" are inventions of the filmmakers. Among the characters, Nick the mechanic is wholly original. In terms of attitude, Hammer becomes a grinning predator, the antithesis of Chandler's urban knight and with survival instincts sharper even than Sam Spade's. Even Spillane's Hammer has some glimmer of sympathy for a "damn-fool crazy Viking dame with holes in her head" and follows the trail of those who tried to kill him, out of simpleminded outrage at their misdeeds: "I wouldn't need to look at their faces to know I was killing the right ones. The bastards, the dirty, lousy bastards!" The film Hammer is incorporated into a more sophisticated system that combines the undertone of *film noir* with Aldrich's moral determinism. While Hammer wants to know "what's in it for me," all around him crime breeds counter-crime, while thieves and murderers fashion the implements of their own destruction.

For Spillane, Hammer's very name revealed all: a hard, heavy, unrelenting object pounding away mindlessly at social outcasts like two penny nails. The filmmakers refine this archetype slightly: Hammer does think, mostly about how to turn a buck. Christina is arguably the most conventionally "sensitive" of the picture's characters. She reads poetry and, although mockingly, lyricizes her own predicament. It is not without irony that she is the "loony," the one institutionalized by society, yet quickest to penetrate Hammer's tough-guy pose. In that first scene, she helps to reveal that the hero of the film *Kiss Me Deadly* is closer to other characters in Aldrich's work than to Spillane's. He inherits the cynical greed of Joe Erin in *Vera Cruz* and anticipates the transcendent egomania of Zarkan in *The Legend of Lylah Clare*. As Ralph Meeker's interpretation propels Hammer beyond the smugness and self-satisfaction of the novel into a blacker, more sardonic disdain for the world in general, the character becomes a cipher for all the unsavory denizens of the *noir* underworld.

The informal inquiry into Christina's death by the unidentified government agents expositionally establishes that Hammer's professional as well as personal conduct is unscrupulously self-seeking: "Who do you sic on the wives, Mr. Hammer?" Throughout much of the scene, Hammer is framed in the shot's foreground, sullenly staring at a blank wall off camera, ignoring the baiting remarks. His snide retort—"All right. You've got me convinced: I'm a real stinker."—is effectively true. Because the committee members have made more than a few gibes about Hammer, his response does not yet alienate the viewer. But a dichotomy between audience and the "hero's" viewpoint is building, is creating a subject/object spilt which runs counter to the first person elements of the novel. Hammer first asks, "What's in it for me?" as he speaks to Pat Murphy in the corridor after the inquiry. That utterance completes the character composite: Hammer is certainly not like Callahan in *World for Ransom*, not another selfless "Galahad" as he begins a quest for "something big," for the private eye's grail.

Hammer *is* a quester. He is not an outsider in the *noir* underworld or any equivalent of a mythic "other world." If this is a foreign or alien milieu, Hammer is at home there. For Hammer, the dark streets and ramshackle buildings are a questing ground which is conspicuously detached from the commonplace material world. Deception is the key to this world. Deception not detection is Hammer's trade. His livelihood depends on the divorce frame-up and the generally shady deal. Deception is Lily Carver's game also, from the false name she assumes to the vulnerable pitch of her voice to the pathetic way she brings her hand up against her face like a wing of Christina's dead canary. Failure to deceive is what costs Christina and others their lives.

This deception and uncertainty, as in most *noir* films, lay the groundwork for *Kiss Me Deadly*'s melodramatic tension. The plot-line has all the stability of one of Nick's "Va-va-voom's," so inversion becomes a constant; and subsurface values become central concerns. In this milieu, the first "torpedo" set to go off when a car key is turned necessarily posits a second rigged to explode at a higher speed. From the viewer's objective vantage, the shift from one level of appearances to another is occasionally discernible. An early example is the transformation of the sensual Carver, first framed behind a bed post and swinging a hip up to expose more of her leg through the fold of the terry cloth robe, then becoming shrill and waif-like for Hammer's benefit. Usually, though, the viewer is also deceived.

For those on a quest in the *noir* underworld, instability is the overriding factor and disjunction is the rule. The sensational elements in *Kiss Me Deadly* follow this rule. The craning down and the hiss of the hydraulic jack as the screaming Nick is crushed under the weight of a car; the pillar of fire that consumes Lily Carver; the eerie growl of the black box; even a simple "Pretty pow!" as Nick jams a fist into his open palm—these random acts have no organizing principles. They transcend context to deliver a shock that is purely sensory. Still they fit homogeneously into the generic fabric and the subversive whole of the narrative.

Most of *Kiss Me Deadly*'s visual devices are derivations from the generic styles of Aldrich's prior work in *World For Ransom* or *Vera Cruz*: high and low angles, depth of field, constriction of the frame through foreground clutter. The long take or sequence shot, however, is used more extensively and more specifically than before. There are four examples of it in *Kiss Me Deadly*, all of which might be classed as interrogation scenes: Pat Murphy's first visit to Hammer's apartment, and Hammer's questionings of Harvey Wallace, Carmen Trivago, and Eddie Yeager. The specifics of the shots vary, from the slow traveling into close shot during the brief discussion with the truck driver, Wallace, to the elaborate tracking and panning in Hammer's apartment, shifting characters front to back and left to right in an uneasy search for equilibrium. In no sequence shot does Hammer get answers to everything he asks; yet each takes him to the brink of some discovery.

More than anything else these shots serve as a sort of punctuation in the narrative line. In the scenes with Trivago and Yeager especially, the sustained camera seems to externalize a reflective pause. Hammer only half listens in these scenes, wandering about and sampling Trivago's wine and spaghetti or, with Yeager, glancing over at the sparring match. They also create visual pauses at odd intervals. While they diminish tension on the one hand by preserving a level of stasis or consistency, barring the cut and the extreme angle, they reinforce it on the other, playing first with the viewer's expectancy of the cut and then with the interior movements of the camera. As the possibility of a change in angle is removed only for a set period that cannot exceed the length of the sequence, so the pause is a baited one, barely allowing Hammer and/or the audience time to "catch their breath."

As in *World for Ransom*, the trap is a part of *Kiss Me Deadly*'s figurative scheme. Again, its constructs are primarily visual. But the elaborate "capture" of Callahan in the earlier picture is distilled down to single shots in *Kiss Me Deadly*. For example, in the high angle long shot of Hammer outside Lily Carver's room, the dark foreground of stairway and balustrades are arrayed concentrically about Hammer's figure and seem to enclose him. Usages such as this contribute to *Kiss Me Deadly*'s figurative continuity of instability or inversion and the lurking menace, all set up in the opening sequences.

What most distinguishes *Kiss Me Deadly*'s figurative usage from that of earlier and many later Aldrich films is the added dimension of an explicit, aural fabric of allusions and metaphor. The Christina Rossetti poem, "Remember Me," is a recurrent example. Other background sounds are keyed to character. The Caruso recording with which Carmen Trivago sings is the Flotow opera, *Martha*. Another classical piece plays on the radio in Christina's room as the manager remarks,

Below, Lily Carver (Gaby Rodgers) reads "Remember Me" to Hammer (Ralph Meeker).

"She was always listening to that station." A prize fight is being broadcast in the background when Evello and Sugar Smallhouse are killed.

While these sounds may not be as fully incorporated into the narrative structure as the poem is, all provide immediate textural contrast if not subsidiary meaning. The sibilant tone of Evello's gasp as he is killed echoes the hiss of the car jack in Nick's murder. As tropes both recall in turn the equation of vitality with a "deep breath" made by the old mover. The play of sounds and meaning can create other anomalies. For instance, at one point Velda approaches Mike asking, "But under any other name, would you be as sweet?" and he, not paying attention to her, says, "Kowalski." On one level, all these can be appreciated as textural noise or *non sequiturs*. On another, they are conscious metaphors and puns.

As with Callahan, "chance" is a factor. As Hammer says, "If she hadn't gotten in my way, I wouldn't have stopped." Velda's statements about the "great whatsit" and "the nameless ones who kill people" reinforce the sense that the vagaries of chance or destiny, a word which the mythically-minded Dr. Soberin would likely have preferred, are an underlying constant. Soberin himself is one of the most consciously allusive characters in Aldrich's films. He brings up the notion of rising from the dead after Christina expires: "Do you know what that would be? That would be resurrection." He mentions Lazarus again during a conversation with Hammer. The old moving man also speaks of "the house of my body" that can only be left once. These concepts run parallel to Hammer's own search for meaning in the cryptic pentameter of the Rossetti poem: "But when the darkness and corruption leave/A vestige of the thoughts that once we had."

Myth becomes a surface value entirely in the case of the "great whatsit." What Pat Murphy utters—a "few, harmless words...just a bunch of letters scrambled together, but their meaning is very important.... Manhattan project. Los Alamos. Trinity."—are as much words to conjure with as Soberin's pedantic analogies. Soberin's references to Lot's wife and "cerberus barking with all his heads" are too archaic and unfrightening to keep Gabrielle/Lily Carver from opening her own Pandora's box. In the final analysis, the "great whatsit" contains pure phlogiston. The quest for it becomes the quest for the cleansing, combustible element, for the spark of the purifying fire that reduces the nether world of *Kiss Me Deadly* to radioactive ash.

As modern myth, as anti-myth (discussed in more detail in the Addendum), and/or as *film noir, Kiss Me Deadly*'s narrative outlook is equally somber. "A savage lyricism hurls us into a world in full decomposition, ruled by the dissolute and the cruel," wrote Borde and Chaumeton in *Panorama du Film Noir Américain*, then "to these savage and corrupted intrigues, Aldrich brings the most radical of solutions: nuclear apocalypse."[1] *Kiss Me Deadly* is also a key to the development of Aldrich's visual style. In this "apocalyptic" context, the choices of angle, framing, staging, lighting, and all the other elements which constitute a visual style are all in play in a particularly expressive way.

Above, **Frame 1**

Above, **Frame 2**

Above, **Frame 3**; below, left and
right **Frames 4 and 5**

Nine Elements of Style in *Kiss Me Deadly*

[Based on an outline developed with Janey Place]

1. Angle. A low angle point-of-view shot, such as that of the feet of Hammer's captors (see **Frame 9**), also functions to withhold critical information—the faces of the men—and to have the viewer co-experience Hammer's mental note-taking of his only clue: the style of Soberin's shoes. Framing works with the choice of angle in that, objectively, both the fact of the viewer empathy with Christina, who the dialogue reveals has just been tortured to death, and the position of her white, lifeless legs in the center of the frame draw attention away from the aspect of the dark shoes in the surrounding foreground.

This low angle is "motivated," that is, the camera is placed on the floor to simulate Hammer's semiconscious sprawl. In contrast, the ground level medium shot when Sugar interrupts Hammer's examination of the shoes in Evello's bathhouse (**26**) represents a director's and not a character's point-of-view. That angle similarly restricts the visual information which the viewer receives (how Hammer renders Sugar unconscious remains an off-screen mystery), while the tilt upward combines with a shorter focal length lens to distort perspective and exaggerate the magnitude of Sugar's fall.

The tilted angles in the hospital room (**10, 11**) alternate between directorial and char-

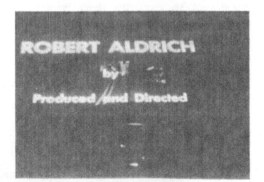

acter point of view. As a disembodied voice calls Mike's name, the sequence begins with an optical device used over a shot of Velda and the nurse. A rippling effect through an image from the character's point of view is a convention for awakening from a dream or returning to consciousness. The tilting off from horizontal approximates the imbalance which Hammer experiences as he comes to; but that tilting is carried over into a shot which includes Hammer (10). The shift between "first person" and "third person"—the scene ends in the former mode (11)—serves to objectify the unusual angle. As first-person usage and its conventions are undercut, the split between Hammer's viewpoint and that of the narrative is accentuated.

The use of an extreme high angle or overhead, as in Hammer's first visit to Carver's apartment (19), even more significantly restricts the reading or denotation of a shot. Because it shifts away from connotations of either dominant force or point of view, which may be present in a low or eye-level setup, such a shot moves towards an omniscient perspective. By association, by interaction with the shot's material content, this shift can cause the viewer to sense, subconsciously at least, that he or she is looking down on the scene from a deific or deterministic vantage.

The most frequent use of other than eye-level camera placement in *Kiss Me Deadly* is the slight high and low angles which clarify interpersonal relationships. In certain medium close two shots, the camera aiming down at

Above, **Frame 6**

Above, **Frame 7**

Above, **Frame 8**; below, left and right **Frames 9** and **10**

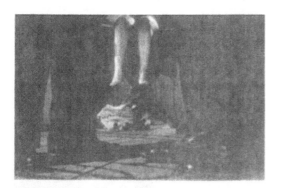

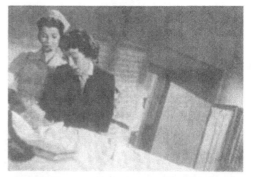

Above, **Frame 11**

Above, **Frame 12**

Above, **Frame 13**; below, left and
right **Frames 14 and 15**

Nick (**14**) or at the morgue attendant over
Hammer's shoulder implies that he intimidates or controls them to some degree.
When Velda comes to Mike's apartment, the
more extreme angle over him down at her
(**47**) is appropriate to the degree in which he
dominates her. Even as he looks away from
Velda in her own bedroom (**32**), Hammer
still dominates. Conversely, the very similar
shots aimed upwards at Carver (**35**) or Pat
Murphy (**39**) or over Carver at Hammer (**34**)
all reverse that effect to suggest a weaker
position on his part. Angle combines with
framing and/or cutting for enhanced effect.

2. Framing. The recurrent use of objects
and faces in the foreground of various shots,
either as indeterminate shapes or held in
focus by depth of field, creates a visual
tension. These elements both conceal a
portion of the rear ground and compete with
more "significant" content for viewer
attention, as with Christina's legs, mentioned
above (**9**). Conversely, the severe cropping
in a close shot of a battered Ray Diker (**17**)
at his front door or a medium shot of Carver
aflame in the beach house (**44**) concentrate
viewer attention by forming a kind of natural
iris. The first shot of Hammer (**3**) framed off
center against the night sky anticipates more
severe manipulations.

On a connotative level, the foreground
clutter of the stairs, banisters, and corridors
present in high angle long shots of both
Hammer alone (**19**) and later with Carver
(**28**) occupies a larger portion of the frame
relative to the smaller human figures. Rather

than forming simple black wedges, they have a textural presence made up of highlights and a confusion of angular shapes. The characters at frame center thus appear caught in a tangible vortex or enclosed in a trap.

The shot of Hammer at Soberin's feet (**48**) is a telling transliteration of the novel which relies on framing, decor, mise-en-scene, and the association of sound and image for its full effect. Spillane wrote. "They had left me on the floor.... Something moved and a pair of shoes shuffled into sight so I knew I wasn't alone." In the film, Hammer is unconscious and in the shot, so that it cannot be subjective. Instead of being on the floor he lies on a bare set of bed springs suggestive of a cold, metallic decay. The shoes are below. While Soberin's stentorian voice drones on about resurrection, the springs cast a maze of shadows enmeshing his feet and Hammer's face in the same tangled web.

3. Mise-en-scene. The staging of the elements in a shot or the *mise-en-scene* combines with framing and depth of field to further define Hammer's relationship to his environment and other characters. He has a tendency to stare off towards a point outside the frame. Instances vary from the three shot in the morgue to the interview by federal investigators after the accident (**12, 13**) or when he awakens Velda after learning of Nick's death (**32**). All suggest a high degree of alienation. His inability to look at people at critical times contrasts with his professional but manic interest in examining the fixtures of a strange room, as when he goes to

Above, **Frame 16**

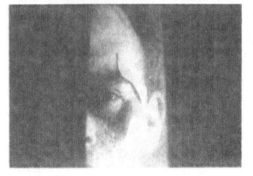

Above, **Frame 17**

Above, **Frame 18**; below, left and right **Frames 19 and 20**

Above, **Frame 21**

Above, **Frame 22**

Above, **Frame 23**; below, left and right **Frames 24 and 25**

Christina's (**18**) or interviews Carmen Trivago (**27**), pausing in the latter instance to sample wine and sniff spaghetti but seldom glancing at the other person in the shot. Hammer is not only estranged from his environment but alienates others with his deportment, as in Velda's emotional outburst about the "great whatsit" when he tells her of Nick's death then sits sipping milk on her couch.

The choice of setting and the use of real locations reinforce this sense of alienation. The general decay of the city coupled with specific usages such as the flashing street lights and isolated gas station (**6**) create, as mentioned earlier, an overtone of lingering menace. The pan up from the street lights is to Ray Diker's decrepit Victorian house perched on a dark hill. The departure from the gas station leads to death for Christina.

Other usages comment metaphorically on the confusion of identities. The mirrors and panning movement when Hammer visits Velda in her exercise room create a complex of confusing doppelgängers. As the shot opens, the viewer sees two sets of figures as Hammer steps into the room. The pan reveals that neither set was "real" and displaces them with the actual people reflected in still another mirror (**21**). Even as Velda elaborates figuratively on the possible consequences of his investigation and speaks of a "thread" leading to a "rope" by which he might well "hang," she spins around on the pole. The mise-en-scene, her action and the

setting, actively undercuts the surrounding reality.

At least one identity-transfer, that of Hammer and Christina, which is suggested narratively by their interaction in the first scenes, is elaborated upon by the staging. Specifically, the X-shaped pose which Christina assumes as she flags down Hammer's car (**1, 2**) is recalled in the painted figure seen on the wall of her room when Hammer examines it (**18**). That figure, bisected by the lamplight, is reflected in turn in the later image of Hammer tied to bed at Soberin's beach house (**33**).

Hammer's answering machine, which was a very unusual device in 1955, is part of his dissembling lifestyle. When he first listens to playback from the wall-mounted, reel-to-reel tape recorder, Hammer stands leaning against the living room wall (**49**). He and the machine are on the right and left of a medium shot with his shadow between them. The machine becomes a second shadow, another self, an embodiment of the mechanistic, emotionless aspect of Hammer's psyche. The framing and mise-en-scene reinforce this relationship. In a later scene, when Murphy comes to Hammer's apartment, Hammer is in the left background in front of the machine. (**50**). With his coat off, the gray tone of Hammer's shirt and the device behind him blend, so that it appears perched on his shoulder or even growing out of it.

On a less symbolic level, much of the mise-en-scene simply adds a layer of distracting action behind that in the foreground. The

Above, **Frame 26**

Above, **Frame 27**

Above, **Frame 28**; below, left and right **Frames 29** and **30**

Above, **Frame 31**

Above, **Frame 32**

Above, **Frame 33**; below, left and
right **Frames 34 and 35**

use of depth of field to keep the sparring and shadow boxing in the background in relative focus as Hammer interviews Eddie Yeager (**24**) injects a constant, unsettling motion into the shot which could reflect the inner disturbance of both men, just as the sudden droop of Yeager's cigar conveys his dismay at the mention of Evello's name. When Hammer walks over to the side of the gym to make a call, the shadow of a large bag swaying on a rear wall in the center of the shot (**25**) perpetuates the distraction.

4. Lighting. All the shadows, whether in the gym, more obviously in the shot of Soberin's shoes, or more subtly in the shadow cast over Hammer's face when he stops at the roadblock (**5**), are stylistic corroborations of Velda's sense of impending danger. Other elements of lighting function similarly. The low light on Hammer and Christina conform to a convention of visual expression which associates shadows cast upward of the face (**8**) with the unnatural and ominous, the ritual opposite of sunlight. The low light when Carver opens the box of radioactive material (**43**) is, most appropriately at that moment in the film, hellish. Her demonic aspect as she screams anticipates her immolation by Soberin's "brimstone."

Side light is used conventionally to reflect character ambivalence. For example, in the low angle medium close shot of Hammer looking down at Nick's body (**31**). Framed against a night sky, Hammer is both literally and figuratively isolated in surrounding darkness. The half of his face cast in shadow is

emblematic of an impulse to abandon the search generated by the sudden death of his friend, an impulse which accounts for the sense of loss and indecision that he manifests in the remainder of the film.

Lighting combines with framing to create the constricting wedges and trap-like arrays of foreground material mentioned above. In the hard shadow line which cuts across the top of the frame and obscures Hammer's face in his first visit to Carver's apartment (**20**), it functions independently of framing to instill a sense of peril and comment on the interaction of characters and objects. The lamps which form a dark triangle behind Carver, as she prepares to open the "great whatsit" (**41**), define visual geometry that is deterministic in implication: i.e., her head is "directed" to align itself with the apex of the triangle.

5. Depth of Field. The presence of depth in the medium close two shot of Hammer and Yeager permits a distracting rear ground which draws attention away or externalizes character emotion. A more "active" use of depth is found in the close two shot of Christina and the gas station attendant (**7**). Because his profile is present in the left foreground, he is not only more noticeable than the boxers in the gym but he severely restricts the amount of the frame in which she can move. As such he externalizes, even as he exchanges pleasant words with her, the pervasive sense of constriction which she experiences as a fugitive.

Above, **Frame 36**

Above, **Frame 37**

Above, **Frame 38**; below, left and right **Frames 39** and **40**

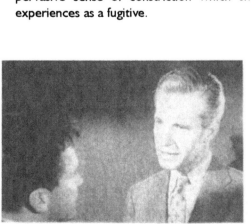

Above, **Frame 41**

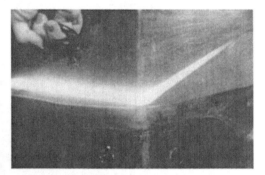

Above, **Frame 42**

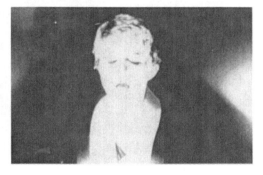

Above, **Frame 43**; below, left and
right **Frames 44 and 45**

The depth of field in Hammer's first call on Carver situates him by the door while she reclines in the near ground holding a gun on him (**20**). Despite the potential for violence expressed by the gun, the angle (low) and the deep focus define a large field in which Hammer can move back and forth. Unlike other objects or clutter in the foreground, Carver's head and the three bars in the bed frame work against each other. The center bar separates her both from Hammer and from her gun, which she holds awkwardly. The left bar cuts into her head. The right bar completes a rectangle in which Hammer, posed comfortably with his hands in his pockets, is alone with the gun but not threatened by it. Lacking constriction, he can come forward out of the shadows to smile at Carver from the edge of the bed and establish his dominance over the scene.

Conversely, the lack of depth caused by a long focal length lens when Hammer is followed by an unidentified man (**16**) intensifies the sense of isolation and real danger implicit in the lonely street at night. Detached from the rear ground, which is both out of focus optically and blurred by the panning movement following him down the sidewalk, Hammer cannot flee into the surrounding decor but is held in the shallow plane of the lens and must turn to face his assailant who is photographed in that same plane.

6. Opticals. The most unusual optical device in *Kiss Me Deadly* is the title sequence. Over a shot of Hammer and Christina in his car, the main title ("DEADLY/KISS ME"), cast

names, and technical credits all appear and move across the screen from top to bottom, stacked to be read bottom line first, like signs painted on the roadway (**4**). Superficially, the confusion of titles with road signs is little more than gimmicky; but the dual inversion of conventional titles, which is justified as a gimmick, is also appropriate to the kind of unnatural or otherworldly events which follow in the film.

Most of the transitions in *Kiss Me Deadly* are accomplished by fades or direct cuts. The dissolve from Hammer looking out the window of his apartment to him kissing Velda in the center of the room is unusual for two reasons: it overlays two shots taken from the same camera position, outside the window (**15**) which Hammer's POV reveals is on an upper floor; and it represents a kind of projection/wish fulfillment in which a character imagines or anticipates an event and the dissolve reveals what he was anticipating.

7. Camera Movement. Camera movement, both traveling and panning, figures in many of the sequences already discussed, such as the mirror shot of Hammer and Velda or the attack on Hammer in the street. Occasionally, the camera will move sideways "under" an establishing shot to introduce objects into the foreground and restrict the open area of the frame, for example, the bed post in Carver's room. At other times, as with the sequence shot of Hammer's interview with the truck driver, Wallace, the camera moves slowly inwards, reducing the dimensions of

Above, **Frame 46**

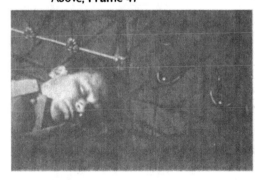

Above, **Frame 47**

Above, **Frame 48**; below, left and right **Frames 49** and **50**

the frame around the characters and intensifying its "closure" or constriction (**25**) even as the duration of the shot adds tension. An even more dynamic usage is the boom down towards Nick as he is crushed, in which the viewer becomes an active participant in his murder, by literally being in the position of the car as it kills him.

8. Duration of Shot. Various aspects of the three sequence-shot interviews with Wallace, Eddie Yeager, and Carmen Trivago have already been mentioned. As discussed earlier, the withholding of a cut in each sequence introduces a tension between the viewer's expectation of a "normally" occurring cut and its absence, so that when the withheld cut finally arrives subconscious tension is released. Even shorter shots, as when Carver shoots Hammer and he slowly twists and falls (**40**), can be slightly "abnormal" as Aldrich holds the angle for a few extra beats.

In the scene with Trivago, sequence-shot tension is accentuated both by the literal violence of the events when Hammer breaks his record to extort information and the frenetic motion of the continuous traveling back and forth in his long, shallow room. Even while the shot is held, the image changes as characters reposition themselves; and clutter such as Trivago's clothes on a line (**27**) impinges and recedes in the foreground. In the scene with Yeager, the sequence shot binds together a number of "individual" shots (**23, 24, 25**) linked by traveling and panning and each affected by its respective framing, lighting, depth, etc.

9. Montage. As with duration of shot, montage is primarily a binding mechanism in *Kiss Me Deadly*, joining or opposing other elements of stylistic expression for a compound effect. A simple example that epitomizes the most basic power of montage as posited by Kuleshov is found in two shots from Hammer's questioning of the morgue attendant. As the man reaches down to put the key he found in Christina's body back into a desk, Hammer slams the drawer shut on his hand (**51**). The shot is powerfully violent in itself, even though neither man's head or shoulders is visible. Aldrich cuts to a close-up of Hammer grinning (**52**), and in a single shot captures all the sadistic impulses of Spillane's character. To the silent evocation of abstract meaning which Kuleshov defined, Aldrich adds the additional dimension of sound, so that Hammer grins not just at the sight of the morgue attendant's crushed hand but at his screams and whimpers as well. Later Aldrich combines an insert (**42**) and a sound effect to transform the "great whatsit" into a living, growling beast.

While angle creates the basic meaning in the shot of Carver aimed upwards

Below **Frames 51 and 52**

over Hammer's shoulder (**35**), montage intensifies it when it is intercut with a shot of Hammer aimed down over Carver's shoulder (**36**). As in his interview with the federal men (**12, 13**); his discussion with Velda (**32**); and the other instances already described, in this latter shot Hammer looks away distractedly. This reverse not only reveals his expression but elaborates the force of Carver's dominance or direction of Hammer at that point in the film, a force which links the two separate shots. As an overlay (**46**) reveals, the shot of Pat Murphy over Hammer (**39**) is composed identically to that of Carver over Hammer. It defines a similarly dominant moment and is complemented by and intercut with another angled shot of Hammer over Murphy's shoulder.

There are many "normal" reverse shots in *Kiss Me Deadly*, such as the cut from Christina facing the oncoming headlights (**1**) to behind her (**2**), where the context is highly charged. At other times a shift of angle from high to low may merely accompany a simple change in camera position as with Hammer's interrogation (**12, 13**). Even more severe shifts in angle occur in the intercuts as Hammer discovers the "great whatsit" in a locker (**37, 38**) and as he and Carver hurry away from her building (**29, 30**). These extreme high/low shifts compel the viewer to reread the shot and create a visual undercurrent of rupture and instability.

As many of these examples demonstrate, the interaction of montage and angle, framing and staging, lighting and depth of field create a multiplicity of stylistic expressions. In the sequence shot in the gym, eight of the nine elements of style contribute towards the totality of literal and figurative meaning:

1. Angle: The sequence shot opens with an eye-level view of a man punching a bag, follows a figure who crosses the shot to a stairway, and then tilts down to a high medium shot of Hammer coming up. It levels off again as Hammer reaches the top of the stairs and remains at eye-level for the remainder of the shot (**22**). The angle shifts at the beginning to disorient the viewer, which in turn subtly connotes, even in broad daylight and in a large room full of other people, the instability and menace all around.

2. Framing: The framing adjusts to follow Hammer in the beginning, then is balanced in the two shot with Yeager (**23**). Hammer is on the left when he places a call later (**24**), so that the shadow of the bag can occupy the center of the shot. Hammer is the narrative center and mostly the visual center. But other people and objects distract from that and reduce his implicit control over past, present, and future events.

3. Mise-en-scene: Yeager begins the interview with a smile on his face and his cigar pointed upwards. His expression sours and the cigar drops down when Hammer mentions Evello's name. The presence of numerous others in the background raises the noise level and distracts visually from the principals who are static in the foreground (**23**). The subtle chaos again bespeaks an underlying instability and loss of control.

4. Lighting: Full light is used throughout the section with Yeager, but many dark areas and a bright spot formed by the street door below accompany the high angle of Hammer on the stairs (**22**). The full-lit background combines with mise-en-scene and depth of field to permit the distraction in the two shot (**23**). A separate key light casts the shadow on the wall during Hammer's phone call.

5. Depth of Field: There are three instances: in the high angle of Hammer (**22**) allowing him to be recognized while still near the bottom of the stairs; in the two shot (**23**) keeping the rear ground fairly well-defined; and in the phone conversation picking out sharp shadows on the wall behind.

6. Opticals: The fade which concludes the sequence shot is followed by a shot of Evello's pool, revealed when a woman in a black bathing suit walks away from the front of the camera.

7. Camera Movement: Tilting, panning, and traveling are used as Hammer moves up the stairs and into the gym. The shot remains static for some time as he speaks with Yeager, then a side-traveling follows him to the phone.

8. Duration of Shot: The sequence shot serves to concentrate and reinforce the tension and character interaction created by the other elements. This is particularly true given the amount of movement and re-framing and refocusing in the shot, all of which add to the difficulty of using one take for the entire sequence. Each element of movement works with the lack of a cut to enhance the tension.

9. Montage: None in this sequence shot, opened and closed by a fade.

Addendum

Since this article first appeared twenty years ago, *Kiss Me Deadly* continues to be one of the classic period's most discussed films. In the "Postface" of a new printing of their text, a decade after Paul Schrader called it "the masterpiece of *film noir*,"[2] Borde and Chaumeton wrote: "1955, the end of an epoch. *Film Noir* has fulfilled its role by creating a particular disquiet and providing a vehicle for social criticism in the United States. Robert Aldrich gives this happening a fascinating and shadowy conclusion, *Kiss Me Deadly*. It is the despairing opposite of the film which, fourteen years earlier, opened the noir cycle, *The Maltese Falcon*."[3]

One of the most discussed aspects of *Kiss Me Deadly* is its ending, which the filmmakers themselves referred to as "Let's go fission."[4] Borde and Chaumeton were a bit more effusive when they spoke of "savage lyricism" and "nuclear apocalypse." Before going further, it should be noted that unfortunately both the 16mm prints and the video version of *Kiss Me Deadly* are missing scenes no. 305 and 307.[5] As I mentioned in the third edition of *Film Noir: An Encyclopedic Reference to the American Style*, some commentators most notably Jack Shadoian in *Dreams and Dead Ends* and J.P. Telotte in *Voices in the Dark*, have questioned whether Mike and Velda stumble into the surf. Shadoian even suggests that since many of Raymond Durgnat's recollections are wrong, so is his version of the ending.[6] Telotte does not know "whether such accounts indicate the existence of an alternate ending for the film or simply represent the kind of creative recollection—prodded by wish fulfillment—that often marks film commentary."[7] One might wonder why any commentator would "wish" for Velda and Hammer to survive. Certainly audience expectations might be for that survival; but in terms of narrative irony, it would seem most apt for Hammer to witness the apocalypse which he and others have wrought [see Aldrich's remarks below].

Even critics who accept the existence of this ending have further compounded the problem by such assertions as "the studio added a final shot still there in some prints showing Hammer and Velda standing amid the waves."[8] Here Robin Wood suggests that Aldrich did not want these two cuts in the finished picture. In a more recent book Edward Gallafent asserts that a "gesture to the benign couple remains in some prints."[9]

These shots should be in all the prints, and Aldrich never regarded them as any sort of gesture. While they had never seen a complete print, Edward Arnold and Eugene Miller asked Aldrich about the ending, and he replied, "I have never seen a print without, repeat, without Hammer and Velda stumbling in the surf. That's

Below, Hammer (Ralph Meeker) follows the old mover (Silvio Minciotti) to the doorway of 325 Bunker HIll, where Mr. and Mrs "Super" (James McCallian, Jesslyn Fax)

the way it was shot, that's the way it was released; the idea being that Mike was left alive long enough to see what havoc he had caused, though certainly he and Velda were both seriously contaminated."[10] Viewers of the laser disc of *Kiss Me Deadly* can catch a glimpse in the theatrical trailer included at the end of the disc of one shot of Mike and Velda in the surf as the house explodes.

In comparing *Kiss Me Deadly* with Fritz Lang's *The Big Heat*, Robin Wood remarks that "the sledgehammer sensibility that is both the strength and weakness of *Kiss Me Deadly* prohibits any nuance."[11] Even Andrew Sarris' early assessment suggests an uncontrolled atmosphere: "Aldrich's direction of his players generally creates a subtle frenzy on the screen, and his visual style suggests an unstable world full of awkward angles and harsh transitions."[12] Wood's critique may reflect the same ambivalence towards Aldrich's authorial consciousness and/or political correctness as Raymond Borde had when he questioned Aldrich's beliefs in 1956: "We've been discouraged so often that we are wary of American liberals. Like most left of center Americans Aldrich can evidently deceive us from one day to the next."[13] Borde's concern about being deceived did not diminish his enthusiasm for *Kiss Me Deadly* as expressed in *Panorama du Film Noir Américain*. In 1968 Sarris also believed that *Kiss Me Deadly* was a "most perplexing and revealing work...a testament to Aldrich's anarchic spirit."[14]

Whether Aldrich or A.I. Bezzerides were leftists, anarchists, or any other type of "ist" outside of the context of the films themselves seems less of a concern for more recent commentators. Perhaps this is because *Kiss Me Deadly* typifies those rare films which transcend critical modalities. Borde and Chaumeton, Schrader, Durgnat, Sarris, Wood, and scores of other critical writers all agree on the merits of the film. Structuralist, formalist, feminist, auteurist, and Marxist critics alike have all found something to admire in it. A quarter of century apart, Borde and Wood both remark on how Aldrich transformed Spillane's solipsistic and reactionary novel into something remarkable. Whether or not *Kiss Me Deadly* does anticipate the freeform narratives of the New Wave or, it could be argued, the self-conscious stylistic de-constructions of later Godard, it is undeniably multi-faceted and complex in attitude.

For many observers the mixture of *film noir*, McCarthyism, and "va-va-voom" has, to use Sarris' celebrated analogy from *The American Cinema*, caused a confusion between the forest and the trees. Borde sensed it when he wrote that "on the extreme right, certain imbeciles have identified this *thriller* as the quest for the Grail."[15] Shadouin may not have been aware of Borde's assertion but was reacting to my comment [see p. 212 above] when he wrote that "Hammer is the inheritor of a superfluous culture and a superfluous role, a modern, ironic Galahad whose quest leads him to a fire-breathing atomic box."[16] Telotte takes up this issue and ultimately concludes that "like Perceval, Mike fails as a quester."

As I suggested twenty years ago, *Kiss Me Deadly* obviously *is* a quest for a *noir* grail. Whether or not Hammer "fails" as a quester is less important than the quest itself. From his name to his survival of the assault to his ability to overcome Evello's thugs, Hammer clearly has, as Shadouin notes, mythic qualities; but in myth some protagonists succeed and others fail. Aside from the question of "Subject/Object split and First Person Usage," which was a sub-head in the *Film Comment* article, my other context in originally writing that Hammer is not another Galahad but is a quester was Aldrich's *World for Ransom.*[17] In that film Julian March, the principal antagonist, actually says to the white-suited hero Mike Callahan: "You shouldn't play Galahad. You're way out of character." Ignorant of more distant past behaviors to which March may be referring, the viewer has only seen Calahan shelter a woman who betrayed his love and risk his life for the good of society. The irony in Marsh's comment is that for Calahan "playing Galahad" is not

Below, a modern "knight" or "Galahad" at work: Hammer (Ralph Meeker) grapples inelegantly with Charlie Max (Jack Elam).

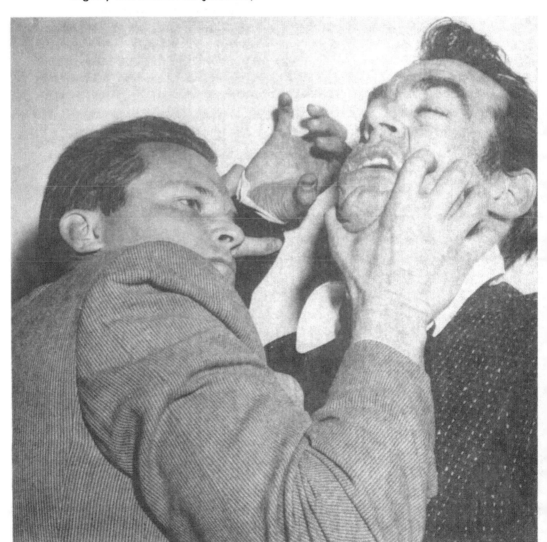

"way out of character." Superficially, that same irony does not apply to Hammer and his "what's in it for me?" attitude in *Kiss Me, Deadly*. What is actually in play in *Kiss Me Deadly* is not a standard archetype but a part of process that social historian Mike Davis describes as "that great anti-myth usually known as *noir*."[18] Hammer is indeed an "anti-Galahad" in search of his "great whatsit," a perfect colloquialism to stand in for and parody the fabled concept of a Grail. Wood calls Christina's perception of Hammer's narcissism at the beginning of *Kiss Me Deadly* "abrupt and rhetorical." But in an anti-mythic structure, a classic invocation of the epic hero, like Virgil's "Of arms and the man I sing" must be transformed into an antiheroic equivalent, something like: "You're the kind of person that has only one true love: you." This tension between myth and anti-myth, between hero and antihero, is one key to *Kiss Me Deadly* and the root of the complexity which Wood finds lacking. Hammer is a radically different character than many who preceded him in *film noir* and in Aldrich's work as well. For Aldrich, who often spoke of turning concepts on their heads, Hammer is the consummate anti-idealist.

Most recent commentaries beginning with Telotte have refocused on narrative issues. A simple example is a recent essay by R. Barton Palmer which consists mostly of plot summary (but, at least, he gets the ending right). Palmer's other comments, such as calling Hammer a "knight" because "he proves vulnerable to the desperation of ladies in distress" or saying "real locations...do not seem night-

Opposite, Hammer (Ralph Meeker) and Christina (Cloris Leachman) in a (pick one or more) threatening/non-threatening environment full of sexual repression/misogyny/homophobia. Actually in the cockpit of his sports car next to a gas pump, all of which are open to interpretation.

marish,"[19] are puzzling. Palmer does call Aldrich "perhaps the most political of *noir* directors."[20] This runs slightly counter to Gallafent's assertions about Aldrich's intentions. Gallafent explores the history of Spillane's prose and the evolution of Aldrich's assessment of his work through interviews; but he never cites Aldrich's most direct statement on the film's "sex and violence."[21] Gallafent characterizes "the release of massive physical violence"[22] in the scene where Hammer beats up a pursuer as an expression of Hammer's sexual frustration. In fact, complete with obscure allusions to the work of Douglas Sirk, Gallefent tries to make the entire narrative revolve around sexual frustration. One hesitates to think what unprecedented orgasmic connotations Gallafent might derive from the final explosion.

Still other commentators have taken analysis of the components of sex and violence much further than Gallafent. For one critic Hammer's violent beating of that same pursuer is an example of his repressed homosexuality in a film full of masculinized women and phallic symbols that is ultimately "homophobic as well as misogynistic."[23] Carol Flinn searches not for a great whatsit but for "feminine sexuality which displays itself so lavishly across this and other examples of *film noir*."[24] In considering "aural signifiers" Flinn raises several points. For instance, her mention of Christina's labored breaths at the film's beginning being "closer than they ought to be" and creating "a break in cinematic verisimilitude"[25] suggests one aural equivalent to the unusual visual elements in *Kiss Me Deadly*. Other subtle effects, such as dog barking outside Christina's house that seems to foreshadow Soberin's reference to "Cerberus barking with all his heads," understandably go unnoticed; but many obviously unusual sound elements, like Mist's loud snoring or Evello's literal expiration or even the growl of the box itself, are inexplicably overlooked amid discussions of dialogue and music.

Despite these wide-ranging critical excursions, one never gets the sense that the depths of *Kiss Me Deadly* have been fully probed. Certainly *Kiss Me Deadly* ranks with the most important examples of *film noir* by any director. It has the menace of *Night and the City*, the grim determinism of *Out of the Past*, the cynicism of *Double Indemnity*, the reckless energy of *Gun Crazy*, and the visual flourish of *Touch of Evil*. Its focus on the underlying sense of nuclear peril that haunted the end of the *noir* period could not have been more apt. If *Kiss Me Deadly* also reflects such contemporary issues as McCarthyism and moral decline, those, too, are part of the fabric of *film noir*.

As it happens, Aldrich's early career as assistant director and director coincides with the beginning and end of the classic period of *film noir*; and he would revisit many of the *noir* cycle's themes. sometimes accompanied by A.I. Bezzerides, in later films. But as a symbol of what *film noir* epitomized or of the powerful, malevolent forces lurking in the Aldrich/Bezzerides vision of the modern world, nothing would ever loom larger than a mushroom cloud over Malibu.

Notes

1. Raymond Borde and Étienne Chaumeton, Panorama du Film Noir Américain (Paris: Les Éditions de Minuit, 1983), p. 277.

2. See reprint above, p. 61

3. Borde and Chaumeton, p. 277.

4. Robert Justman, *Kiss Me Deadly* Shooting Schedule, November 23, 1954, p. 5.

5. A.I. Bezzerides, *Kiss Me Deadly* screenplay, p. 130. Bezzerides wrote:

   305 BEACH - VELDA AND MIKE

   Velda helps Mike and they run through the darkness which is stabbed by sharp flickers of light. Now, as they COME CLOSER TO CAMERA, there is a tremendous explosion. Light gushes fiercely upon them. and they stop, turn.

   306 ON BEACH COTTAGE

   It is a boiling ball of fire.

   307 ON BEACH - VELDA AND MIKE

   As he holds her, to protect her from the sight. Debris from the shattered house falls hissing into the sea behind them.

   FADE OUT:

   <u>THE END</u>

   1st A.D. Robert Justman refers to these two scenes as "Der Tag." In the actual film, through an optical effect the title, "The End," emerges and is brought forward out of the bright white flames engulfing the house (scene 306) and remains superimposed over Velda and Mike in the final shot (scene 307).

6. Jack Shadouin, *Dreams and Dead Ends. The American Gangster/Crime Film* (Cambridge, Massachusetts: MIT Press, 1977), pp. 349-350.

7. J.P. Telotte, *Voices in the Dark. The Narrative Patterns of Film Noir* (Chicago: University of Illinois Press, 1989), p. 213.

8. Robin Wood, "Creativity and Evaluation: two film noirs of the '50's," *CineAction!*, No. 20/21 (November, 1990), p. 20.

9. Edward Gallefent, *"Kiss Me Deadly"* in *The Book of Film Noir* (New York: Continuum, 1993), p. 246.

10. Edwin T. Arnold and Eugene L Miller, *The Films and Career of Robert Aldrich* (Knoxville, Tennessee: University of Tennessee Press, 1986), p. 246.

11. Wood, p. 19.

12. Andrew Sarris, *The American Cinema* (New York: E.P. Dutton, 1968), p. 85.

13. Raymond Borde, "Un Cinéaste Non-conformiste: Robert Aldrich." *Le Temps Moderne* (May, 1956), p. 1684.

14. Sarris, p. 84.

15. Borde, p. 1688.

16. Shadouin, p. 273 and in Note 13, p. 350.

17. In fact, the outline of nine elements of style originally produced with Janey Place was designed around examples found in *World for Ransom*. *Kiss Me Deadly* was substituted at the request of *Film Comment*.

18. Mike Davis, *City of Quartz* (New York: Vintage, 1992), p. 37.

19. R. Barton Palmer, *Hollywood's Dark Cinema. The American Film Noir* (New York: Twayne, 1994), p. 95/p. 96.

20. Ibid., p. 104.

21. Aldrich's reply to attacks by the Legion of Decency and other appeared as "Sex and Violence Justified" in *America*, No. 92 (May, 1955).

22. Gallafent, p. 242.

23. Robert Lang, "Looking for the 'Great Whatzit': [sic] *Kiss Me Deadly* and Film Noir" *Cinema Journal*, Vol. 27, No. 3 (Spring, 1988), p. 33.

24. Carol Flinn, "Sound, Woman, and the Bomb," *Wide Angle*, Vol. 8, Nos. 3/4, 1986, p. 116.

25. Ibid., p. 122.

Below, in a publicity pose that would have done Spillane proud, a sneering Hammer (Ralph Meeker) menaces a trussed-up Lily Carver (Gaby Rodgers). The pose suggests he is about to put the barrel of his gun in her mouth.

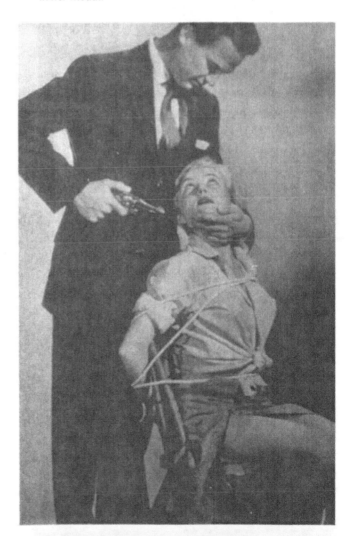

Above, Elliott Gould as Philip Marlowe sits on a jailhouse floor in *The Long Goodbye*. Below, Robert Culp as the world-weary Frank Boggs in his untidy office in *Hickey and Boggs*.

The Post-*Noir* P.I.:
The Long Goodbye and *Hickey and Boggs*

Elizabeth Ward

Film noir has often used the character of the male private investigator to illustrate the alienated and paranoid nature of men in postwar America. As detectives these men become involved in dangerous situations that they feel compelled to control and change while attempting to reestablish morality in a world that appeared to ignore it. After the classic period of *film noir*, the private detective still remained an occasional protagonist in a traditional mystery film. Only a few times in the post-*noir* era of the 1960s and 1970s did filmmakers evoke the *noir* sensibility through the "p.i." Two prominent examples from the early 1970s are *Hickey and Boggs* and *The Long Goodbye*. Both share a self-consciousness of the history of *film noir*. The former film, written by Walter Hill who went on to write and direct many other post-*noir* films, has two protagonists and a convoluted plot line that recalls elements of the caper film and the gangster genre. *Hickey and Boggs* co-stars Bill Cosby and Robert Culp (who also directed), played against the personas established in the *I Spy* television series. *The Long Goodbye* based on a novel by Raymond Chandler and adapted by Leigh Brackett and director Robert Altman was the second post-*noir* incarnation of Chandler's universally recognized character, Philip Marlowe. The earlier *Marlowe* (1966) was cast according to type with James Garner in the title role systematically, and somewhat unimaginatively, recalling the earlier portrayals of Marlowe by Dick Powell, Robert Montgomery, and Humphrey Bogart. By using Elliott Gould as his Marlowe, Altman cast strongly against type. As with *Hickey and Boggs*, part of the underlying irony of the *The Long Goodbye* is that in the early 1970s the classic p.i. such as Marlowe is a human anachronism.

While the detectives of *Hickey and Boggs* share the independent spirit of their earlier counterparts, they differ in the extent to which they can control their situation. Through ten years, the *film noir* protagonist had steadily lost any ability to effect change in a modern world, and this increasing powerlessness is a correlative of diminishing social morality. This powerlessness is sardonically expressed by Frank Boggs when he says, "I gotta get a bigger gun. I can't hit anything." His revolvers, small and large, are trademarks of his profession, icons that recall the

237

"gats" and "roscoes" of a more colorful era. As symbols of both his personal power and genre identity, they are nothing compared to the modern arsenal of weapons possessed by the gangsters and the political guerrillas, who annihilate each other with carbines and high-caliber automatic rifles at the film's climax. Hickey and Boggs are too small, too unimportant, to control anything.

Even the film's plot only marginally involves them. The cache of stolen cash hidden from the syndicate by a Latino convict named Quemondo and his wife Mary Jane is the real cause of all the film's action. Hickey and Boggs are initially hired by Leroy Rice, a crooked lawyer trying to find the cache, merely as unwitting decoys. Eventually Rice and his Black Panther-like partners just want Hickey and Boggs out of the way. There is also a trio of syndicate "soldiers" on the trail of the money. When they murder Hickey's wife in an attempt to frighten the detectives away from continuing their investigation and to avenge Boggs' killing of their associate in an earlier shoot-out, it is more of a professional than personal act.

In one sense Hickey and Boggs are the film's protagonists by default. They are after all the title characters and because the film's events are seen and/or evaluated mostly from the point of view of these down-at-the-heels private detectives, the film *Hickey and Boggs* is more a character study than a narrative thriller. In the beginning, the behavior of the syndicate killers is mechanical and psychopathic; but in certain ways their peculiar code is a counterpart to Hickey and Boggs' fallen romanticism. By the end, the last survivor, the feeble-minded, strong-arm man, enraged at the killing of his partners, attacks Hickey for emotional reasons. Hickey and Boggs themselves seem to alternate in their desire for money and revenge. At the end Hickey is forced to the realization that vengeance is futile. He had previously complained that "there's nothing left of this profession, it's all over. It's not about anything." But Boggs, the dissolute believer in a bygone heroism, seemed to understand their existential dependence on this profession and insists it is important to "try and even it up, make it right." As the smoke clears over the carnage and destruction of the final scene, Hickey again asserts, "Nobody came, nobody cares. It's still not about anything." Boggs wearily replies, "Yeah, you told me."

As if to epitomize the underlying disorder of the modern society, all of the sequences involving the search for the missing money in *Hickey and Boggs* take place during broad daylight. It is events in the private lives of the detectives that take place at night. Contrary to any heroic iconic archetype, even that of the hard-boiled p.i., these men are not strikingly handsome or romanticized loners but weary, displaced persons. Hickey's nighttime arrival at the home of his estranged wife scares and angers her. Her off-handed complaint that she is not running a boarding house, captures the transitory nature of Hickey's lifestyle. Boggs is an alcoholic, who spends his off hours in bars, where he watches television commercials and broods about his ex-wife. His fixation on her leads him to frequent the sleazy nightclub where she works as a strip teaser. Her mockery psychologically castrates him. This is a severe statement about the place of men in the world that is as a dismal as any from the classic period of *film noir*. Both of these men are adrift, alienated from their environment and their families, clearly out of any mainstream lifestyle. They are superfluous figures, wandering through the urban landscape.

Instead of the anonymity provided in many *film noir* by crowded city streets, much of the action *of Hickey and Boggs* occurs in large areas of unoccupied public space. The violence that takes place in a deserted stadium, ball park, neighborhood park, and coastal beach underscore the sense of decay of social strictures. It sets the same tone as many classic *film noir* by suggesting that society has lost control on the subversive and antagonistic forces within it. The sheer firepower of the final shoot out verges on satire as the gangsters' helicopter gunship shoots a Rolls Royce full of holes. The absurdity of the gangsters and Panther clones slaughtering each other in this sequence also recalls a similarly extravagant moment as the unstable "great whatsit" explodes at the end of *Kiss Me Deadly* (1955). In a closing, sardonic variant of the old-fashioned happy ending the detectives walk off into the sunset, together but not side-by-side. Hickey and Boggs are the only survivors; but they have survived only because they are unimportant.

Like *Hickey and Boggs*, *The Long Goodbye* is as much about friendship and betrayal as it is about violence and murder. P.I. Marlowe's primary purpose is to clear his friend's name and to help a woman find her disturbed husband, whom he believes she loves very much. As in *Hickey and Boggs*, there is a vicious gangster, Marty Augustine, looking for the person who took his money. The mystery that ensnares the characters is something that Philip Marlowe stumbles upon. He does not wish to unravel it but cannot help doing so. The 70s Marlowe is a man lost in a world he does not understand. Rather than facing the fact that his profession is "not about anything anymore," Marlowe constantly attempts to convince himself that each antagonizing incident is "O.K. with me"; but obviously it is not. All film Marlowes carry the baggage of Chandler's literary urban knight, a man who lives by a code as rigorous as that of chivalry. For such a man, nothing is as it seems and nothing is right. As Chandler himself wrote in his oft-quoted essay, "The Simple Art of Murder": "But down these mean streets a man must go who is not himself mean, who is neither tarnished nor afraid.... The detective in this kind of story must be such a man. He is the hero; he is everything.... The story is this man's adventure in search of a hidden truth." Because he is such a man, Marlowe can ignore the whacked-out girls next door or the rude market clerk, but he cannot ignore what he supposes is a convenient frame-up of his friend and, finally, he cannot be indifferent to his friend's exploitation of his trust. When Terry Lennox tells him, "But that's you, Marlowe... you'll never learn, you're a born loser," Marlowe righteously kills him, because Terry is wrong. Marlowe is a loner but not a loser. He lives in a world of other values "neither tarnished nor afraid."

Given Chandler's chivalric attitude towards women, it is ironic that *The Long Goodbye* depicts a considerable amount of violence towards them. Women, too, are murderously beaten like Sylvia Lennox, casually struck like Eileen Wade, and even willfully disfigured like Augustine's girl friend. For Marlowe this is the ultimate in savagery. The first thing Marlowe notices about Eileen Wade is the bruise which she tries to hide with her long blond hair. When Marlowe touches it gently, she politely ignores his concern. He admires her stoicism and, correspondingly, she admires the loyal friendship he has shown Lennox. Marlowe and Eileen Wade greatly resemble each other, which is a considerable departure from Chandler's novel, wherein Eileen is a *femme fatale* and murderess. In the film she, like Marlowe, tries to hide her alienation. But her method is to hide behind a facade of cheerfulness and beauty. She attempts to conceal her bruised face, a symbol of her internal suffering. She also conceals her belief that her husband murdered Sylvia Lennox. She knows Roger Wade is capable of extreme violence when drunk, for she bears the mark of it; but she cannot betray him. Conversely, she shares Marlowe's inaccurate conviction that Terry Lennox is incapable of murder. Marlowe and Eileen work at cross purposes to achieve the same goal, neither realizing that the goal is worthless. From the endistanced perspective of the disaffected 1970s, this is the additional irony that filmmakers Altman and Brackett have imposed on Chandler's character.

Even in a post-*noir* context, *The Long Goodbye* evokes the emotions of a mainstream *film noir*. The powerlessness of its independent protagonists, Marlowe and Eileen Wade, to untangle a moral dilemma in a modern, corrupt world make them prototypically *noir*. While Marlowe may not verbalize his sense of anachronistic despair as directly as Hickey or Boggs, he shares their ability to endure physical and emotional punishment. As a p.i. Marlowe is expected from genre convention to understand and discern a solution to this puzzle; but even the police know more than he does.

Unlike the attitudes of the police conveyed in *film noir* of the classic period, the "modern" corruption of the police in *The Long Goodbye* is not caused by individual ambition and greed but by overload and burn-out. All the police want is their paperwork completed, a murder confessed, and a suicide certified by the proper official. They crave simple solutions regardless of conflicting facts because they lack energy and time to explore alternative answers. While Chandler's novels use the police as identifiable personalities and antagonists, Altman makes the police relatively anonymous and surly, interchangeable and unimportant. A policeman's face is never lingered upon in the film without a distracting element occurring simultaneously. When Marlowe is interrogated at the station, he is the center of the frame while the police circle about him like gnats firing questions. All the while Marlowe plays with the inky smears left by the fingerprinting procedure. He does this while looking at his reflection in a two-way mirror, as if to demonstrate his contempt for the police authorities he knows are watching on the other side of the glass. Later, when he confronts the police face to face at the scene of Wade's suicide, Marlowe drunkenly waves a wine glass in their faces while they exhibit little expression.

Altman uses glass throughout the film as a fragile and reflective prop to express the illusory nature of clarity and appearances. Just as the plot will reveal that Lennox has deceived everyone and that Roger Wade, for all his rowdiness, directed his murderous violence inward, even simple textural details are not as they seem. The Wades' beach house is made almost entirely of glass. While Roger and Eileen stand inside and watch Marlowe out on the beach, Roger condemns the detective as an ignorant slob. A few minutes later, Marlowe watches the couple argue fiercely, and his image is placed between the two of them in the window's reflection, suggesting that he brought them back together and that he may have to protect each one from the other. Marlowe's quizzical look indicates that he isn't sure what to do. Later, Marlowe and Eileen argue over dinner inside, while outside, visible through a window, Roger commits suicide; but their plain view of his action does not make them able to help him. Marlowe again watches through the window while the gangster Augustine intimidates Eileen; but is unable to make a clear connection between the two until he sees her leave Augustine's building. The undraped picture windows in the gangster's office do not hinder Augustine's attempt to get at the truth and would not hold him back from killing Marlowe, even though literally anyone passing by could watch the crime. But the city is silent and indifferent. As Augustine's girl friend is carried out screaming and bleeding profusely, the neighboring girls are too self-engrossed to notice her plight. Malibu neighbors crowd around the scene of Roger's suicide with the tinkling wine glasses they have carried from their parties. In The Long Goodbye, Altman adds society's conscious indifference to the long list of alienating elements that comprise film noir.

This social indifference is at the heart of the post-noir films of the 1970s. It is the reason that the profession of Marlowe and of Hickey and Boggs is "not about anything anymore." In a world where no one cares, men with a code are out of place. Hickey and Boggs come to admire Quemondo and Mary Jane for trying to beat the odds. The shot of their bodies lying peacefully in the sand reflects that sentiment. It is that same sentiment which compelled Marlowe to suffer brutalization and almost be killed rather than betray his friend Terry. In the end it is that same sentiment which makes Marlowe react so violently to Terry's perfidiousness. For Marlowe his act is not about revenge. Like Boggs, he acts out of a motive that is "about making it right."

Above, Johnny (Glenn Ford) in the arms of Gilda (Rita Hayworth).

Film Noir, Voice-Over, and the Femme Fatale

Karen Hollinger

The period of the 1940s was the golden age of filmic first person voice-over narration, which involves an overt act of communicating a narrative to an audience by a recognized speaker in a film. Most commonly after an initial presentation of a narrating situation in which we see the narrating character begin to tell the story, the film moves into flashback sequences that visually portray the recounted events. We, as viewers, intermittently hear the narrator speaking within the film although we no longer see the narrating situation; thus, the voice seems to come from a time and place distinct from the visual portrayal of events. The first person narrator also plays a part in the story told and refers to him or herself as "I." This type of narration can be distinguished from the third person narrational mode, which involves a narrator who plays no part in the film's diegesis except to narrate the story from the perspective of an uninvolved observer.

By the 1940s the voice-over technique had found wide acceptance in various types of Hollywood films. Critics point especially to its use in popular 40s genre films: war films, semi- or pseudo-documentaries, literary adaptations, and *films noirs*.[1] The unique quality of the use of first person voice-over in *films noirs* and its connection to the films' investigation of their female characters, however, deserves further analysis.

In contrast to *films noirs*, other 1940's genres use voice-over primarily to accentuate the verisimilitude of and to increase audience identification with their narrators' stories. Voice-over is used in war dramas, for instance, to increase viewer identification with the films' heroic soldier protagonists. Semi- and pseudo-documentaries, like war films, employ voice-over—most often in the third rather than the first person—to add credibility to their stories. In films adapted from literary sources, the voice-over is most often associated with a recreation of the original novel's authorial narrational voice. Thus, the voices-over employed in these films are associated with authority, heroism, and power—either authorial, narrative, or both.

Films noirs, however, do not attempt this association; instead, they most often contain weak, powerless narrators who tell a story of their past failures or of their inability to shape the events of their lives to their own designs. Eric Smoodin, for instance, argues that voice-over in *film noir* represents an aberrant use of the technique, standing in stark contrast to its use in other classical Hollywood films.[2] Smoodin's characterization of *noir* voice-over narrators as aberrant fits well with established views of *film noir* as a deviant genre within the classical Hollywood tradition. *Films noirs*, for instance, commonly are seen as "maladjusted" texts that reflect "the dark side of the screen," the ideological contradictions, disequilibrium, and disturbing imbalance characteristic of the World War II and post-war periods.[3] Because *noirs* reached their peak of popularity during and after the war, wartime social turmoil has largely been seen as responsible for their "deviant" nature.

A close analysis of first person voice-over *noir* films, however, yields a number of salient features which their simple categorization as aberrant classical Hollywood reflections of wartime and post-war angst elides. First of all, the genre's use of first person voice-over occurs within a configuration that commonly involves a confessional/investigative mode. The voice-over penetrates into the past of a central male character as well as into this character's psyche in order to arrive at a fundamental truth that is seen as causing an individually and/or socially abnormal or destructive situation. This confessional/investigative arrangement is also typically tied to a vaguely psychoanalytic situation, a Freudian "talking cure" of sorts in which the confessing narrator is somehow relieved of guilt or anxiety by arriving at a sense of truth through confession. In *film noir*, first person voice-over narrators, in fact, frequently offer their confessions to patriarchal authority figures within the film text or to the film audience itself who seem to be asked to grant a kind of absolution and to act as a curative force.

Interestingly, what the confessing male narrators of these films search for in their past experiences or psychological condition is a revelation that involves the truth not so much about masculinity but rather about femininity. Like Freud, these films seem to be concerned with ascertaining "what the woman wants," finding the essential nature of female difference, which often is symbolized in female sexuality—as it is also for Freud. Femininity thus becomes the ultimate subject of the film's discourse. Michel Foucault argues in *The History of Sexuality* that Western society has attempted to control sex by putting it into a discourse which connects it with a search for truth. According to Foucault, this search for the truth of sexuality while seeming to reveal sexual truth, really acts only to mask, deny access to, and assert power over it. The confession is merely one procedure that has been developed for telling a "truth" about sex, which, in fact, masks the very nature of sex itself.[4]

Indeed, the male confessors of *film noir* do seem determined to probe femaleness in order to capture a hidden "truth" which is the key not only to female but to male nature as well. But like Foucault's conception of the ultimately unrevealing truth of Western society's discourses on sexuality, the truth about women uncovered in *film noir* often fails to reveal real gender difference or even really to imagine this difference at all. At the same time, the very project of these films, their repeatedly unsuccessful attempts to probe the nature of sexual difference, foregrounds a societal failure to resolve the contradictions inherent in conventional configurations of sexuality and gender difference.

Approached from a psychoanalytic perspective, the male confessing/investigating figures of *film noir* and the paternal figures who often listen to their stories consistently try to interpret the meaning of femaleness by male standards—from the point of view of the phallus. In these terms, femaleness is always judged as excess or lack from the perspective of male normalcy. The difference is reduced to one of degree, not kind, and the different truth of woman is elided in favor of the single phallic truth of man with the woman becoming either more or less than the male norm. In this phallic economy, femaleness becomes simply insufficiency or excess in comparison to maleness, and real difference is masked under a discourse that approaches understanding only of this limited conception of truth. In this way, the films can soothe castration fears that the notion of sexual difference might raise in the male spectator and that the advances of women out of the home and into the work place exacerbated in 1940's society. By eliding difference, the films can create a unified male spectator untroubled by contradictions within his society that are symbolized in the films by female otherness.

In this sense, *films noirs* serve a very conservative ideological function, yet their repeated use of first person voice-over narration also opens up, within the films, points of resistance to this ideological conservatism. At first glance, the *noir* voice-over seems to do exactly the opposite, to establish within the text a single overriding male narrational perspective that appears to dominate all other textual elements. As the films progress, however, this single, dominating point of view does not hold, and the films begin to fracture.

Voice-over creates this fragmenting effect by establishing within the film a fight for narrative power as the narrator struggles to gain control of the narrative events recounted. This battle between the narrator and the film's flashback visuals leads to an extreme tension between word and image. It has been argued that voice-over narration in *film noir* implicates the spectator completely in the perspective of the film's male narrator and leads this implicated spectator to join with the narrator in his condemnation of the film's major female character, the dangerous and often deadly femme fatale. Mary Ann Doane, for instance, sees the *noir* voice-over as embedding the figure of the femme fatale in the narrative's metadiegetic level, framing her speech within an overpowering masculine discourse in order to withhold from her access to narration and grant the male narrator control of both her words and image.[5]

While one can point to those characteristics of *noir* first person voice-over which attempt to subject the female image to male narrational power, this power is not nearly as complete as Doane suggests. As a number of feminist critics have suggested, women in classical Hollywood films have been positioned as objects of spectacle, fixed and held by the male gaze.[6] The femme fatale of *film noir* is clearly yet another female object of spectacle, defined by her dangerous, yet desirable sexual presence, but she is an object with a difference. Female characters in classical Hollywood films are traditionally portrayed as weak, ineffectual figures safely placed in the fixed female roles of wives, mothers, or daughters and desperately in need of the male hero's affection and protection. *Films noirs* release the female image from these fixed roles and grant it overwhelming visual power. The iconography of the femme fatale grants these beautiful, provocative women visual primacy through shot composition as well as camera positioning, movement, and lighting.

The freedom of movement and visual dominance of the femme fatale admittedly is presented as inappropriate to a "proper" female role and as igniting sinister forces that are deadly to the male protagonist. Narratively, this dangerous, evil woman is damned and ultimately punished, but stylistically she exhibits such an extremely powerful visual presence that the conventional narrative is disoriented and the image of the erotic, strong, unrepressed woman dominates the text, even in the face of narrative repression.[7]

The male voice-over in *film noir*, while it may attempt to control the female image, serves instead to pit the femme fatale's dominant visual presence against the

male voice, thereby foregrounding ideological battles raging in the 1940s in regard to women's appropriate social role. This situation of embattlement is exacerbated by the voice-over's fragmenting effect with regard to spectator positioning. Susan Lanser, writing on first person narration in literature, and Ellen Feldman, working with its use in film, suggest that various stages of surrogate positioning exist between a narrator or central character and the text's implied author and implied reader/spectator.[8] In *films noirs*, the relationships among the implied spectator, voice-over narrator, and the agency of the implied author are inscribed in the text in a way that triggers what can be termed a proliferation of point of view, a divorce of the narrator's, implied author's and implied spectator's positions.

Often, within a narrated work a narrational hierarchy is established in which one perspective—either that of the narrator, implied author, or implied spectator/reader—comes to dominate and enclose all others or the three perspectives merge into a unified whole. In *film noir* a narrational hierarchy fails to establish itself and a proliferation of point of view dominates the texts. While first person voice-over can act as an authoritative evocation of the power of the text's implied author, when it is combined with certain elements in *film noir* (the confessional mode, investigative and psychologically penetrating narration, the flashback structure, and most notably the investigation of the femme fatale) it loses control of events, which seem inevitably to escape the voice-over narrator's power. As a result, sound becomes dislocated from image, the gap between the planes of the narrative widens, establishing a narrational hierarchy becomes difficult, and finally point of view fragments. Situated within these gaps and torn by this fragmentation, the spectator is placed in a position from which he or she judges between what is shown and the narrator's account of it, attaining a distance from the narrative that allows for meaning to be perceived not as a static quantity to be passively grasped as the single ideologically "correct" position but rather as a battleground for competing perspectives.

Throughout the period of the 1940s, voice-over *noir* texts evidence such extreme tendencies to fragmentation and proliferation of point of view that any attempt to resolve their investigations of their female characters are rendered hopelessly inconclusive. The following examination of four prominent voice-over *noir* films demonstrates how the structural aspects of the texts have a resulting effect on spectator positioning that encourages a perception not only of the text's structural contradictions but also of a social failure that lies beneath them—a failure even to begin to comprehend a female nature that because of women's changing societal roles seems to have appeared unfathomable.

Laura (Preminger, 1944) is a case in point. The film might at first glance seem aberrant in the *noir* canon. Unlike other *noir* narrators, Waldo Lydecker (Clifton Webb), the film's first person narrator, does not fall victim to the evil designs of an ambitious femme fatale; instead, he reveals himself to be her psychopathic attempted killer. He sets out to murder the film's heroine on two separate occa-

Opposite, McPherson (Dana Andrews) stares at the portrait of Laura (Gene Tierney).

sions when she determines to break his hold on her by forming an attachment to
another man. Yet, in spite of Lydecker's differences from the conventional *noir*
narrator, the effect of his voice-over is indicative of the pattern characteristic of
other *noir* films. His narration encompasses a significant amount of the first half of
the film when he is involved in a struggle with Detective McPhearson (Dana Andrews), who is investigating the possible murder of Laura Hunt (Gene Tierney).
Lydecker's voice-over is part of his attempt to impose upon McPhearson and on
the spectator as well—since his first narrative presentation is addressed directly
to the audience and his second to McPhearson—his interpretation of Laura's
character and of his involvement with her. According to his account, he always
demonstrated and continues to feel only a fatherly concern for her welfare.

Suddenly, in mid-film, Lydecker's voice-over disappears. This loss of narration
has a significant effect on spectator positioning within the text's structure.
Lydecker sets himself up as an initial object of spectator identification. He also ties
himself to the implied author of the work by announcing at the beginning of his
narration his literary pretensions; he tells us that he was just about to begin a
written eulogy for Laura when he was interrupted by McPhearson's arrival to
question him about her possible murder. Thus, when his position as a spectator
surrogate is repudiated by the loss of his narration and the final revelation in the

Below, while bathing Waldo Lydecker (Clifton Webb) tells the story of Laura's life to Det. McPherson (Dana Andrews) in *Laura*.   Opposite, Lydecker faints when Laura (Gene Tierney) turns
out to be alive.

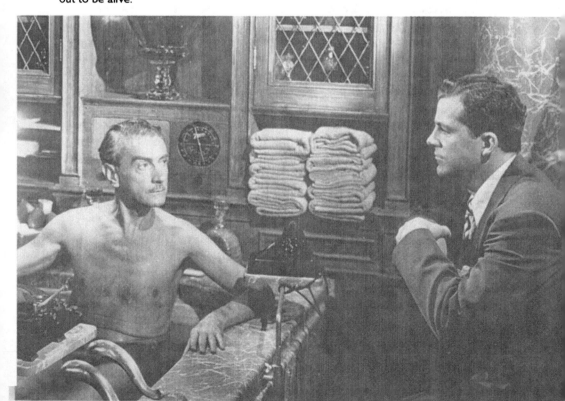

film's closing scenes that he is, in fact, a murderer, the effect on the spectator is devastating. The film cannot effectively provide another object of viewer identification to replace him. McPhearson would be the logical choice. He serves as the center of the investigation after Lydecker's narration disappears and acts as the film's hero, saving Laura from Lydecker's second murder attempt in the film's closing scenes. Significantly, however, he never assumes the role of narrator.

In this way, the film is very different from the novel on which it is based. *Laura* by Vera Caspary establishes single unified narrational control even in a multiply narrated work.[9] The novel contains several narratives, each of which is presented by a different narrator: Waldo Lydecker, Detective McPhearson, Laura's fiancé Shelby Carpenter, and Laura Hunt herself all provide accounts of Laura's attempted murder. In the novel, however, McPhearson writes a concluding statement in which he identifies himself as the overriding authorial presence in the text. He explains in this conclusion that he accumulated and organized the various narratives. This narrational control is never replicated in the film; instead, the spectator is placed in a position characterized by a complex oscillation between identification with the villain/narrator's position and that of the investigating hero. The film's attempts at its conclusion to realign the spectator with legal authority through an identification with the figure of McPhearson are, thus, seriously compromised.

As a result of this disorienting narrational structure, the film fails to investigate adequately the character of its major female character. It attempts to do so by alternately presenting her through Lydecker's voice-over narration as a possible murder victim or a cold-blooded murderess. McPhearson also sets out to investigate her, yet as the film progresses, his investigation is transformed into an investigation of Lydecker. Laura remains an enigma throughout: Lydecker's attempts to narrate her story end in the sudden disappearance of his voice-over, and McPhearson's investigation brings him only to Lydecker as her attempted murderer. Laura herself remains a mystery, her unknowable nature symbolized by her portrait which hangs prominently over the fireplace in her apartment, overlooks much of the action, and eventually leads McPhearson to become obsessed with her. Like the image in the portrait, Laura presents a beautiful, fascinating surface, but one impenetrable to investigation.[10]

In contrast to *Laura*, other *noirs* with voice-over narration hold more closely to the formula of the *noir* hero as the victim, rather than the attempted victimizer, of the dangerous femme fatale. *Gilda* (Vidor) and *The Postman Always Rings Twice* (Garnett), both released in 1946, have criminal narrators who are presented as victims of the machinations of female characters. *Gilda* provides another instance of lost narration similar to that found in *Laura*. It begins, as Richard Dyer points out, as Johnny's story.[11] Johnny Farrell (Glenn Ford) tells in voice-over of his involvement with his male mentor Ballin (George Macready) and Ballin's wife Gilda (Rita Hayworth). Yet, Johnny's voice-over serves primarily to inform the spectator of his negative assessments of Gilda's character and of his disdain for her, rather than to tell us much about Johnny himself. In addition, Johnny's perspective is so immersed in a narrative progression that calls all of his judgments into question that it is difficult to view his commentary from anything but a critical perspective. Johnny, in fact, seems totally unable throughout the film to comprehend the true nature of his feelings for Gilda. The visuals show repeated instances of their mutual attraction, but his voice-over tells only of his disdain for her. For instance, as he contemplates his feelings at one point in the film he comments in voice-over: "I hated her, so I couldn't get her out of my mind for a minute." This remark seems more a product of frustrated sexual attraction than of disdain. Johnny's voice-over also seems curiously unaware of his feelings for Ballin. The film, through the narrative presentation of the strong attachment between the two men, hints at a homosexual involvement between them that Ford later indicated was obvious to the actors as they fashioned their roles.[12] Yet, Johnny's voice-over totally ignores this aspect of his sexuality.

The film also fails to place Johnny's narration within an introductory or concluding narrating situation. It begins with Johnny's voice-over imposed over the visual depiction of his initial encounter with Ballin. As the narrative progresses, Johnny, as narrator, periodically interjects comments over the action, but his narration suddenly disappears as conflicts are resolved at the film's conclusion. Johnny's voice-over is not only abruptly terminated, completely unmotivated, and stemming from an indefinite time and place of narration, but it is also curiously tied to the emotions and reactions of his character in the flashbacks rather than to those of his narrating persona, who is recounting the story in the past tense. Thus, the voice-over is tied to the conflicts that dominate the text until its conclusion rather than to the attempts at resolution that are made in the film's closing segments.

These concluding attempts at resolution are imposed upon the narrator by an authoritative listener/interpreter, who suddenly appears at the film's conclusion to provide both the narrator and spectator with a suggested interpretation of events. A detective who has been investigating both Johnny and Ballin steps in to analyze Johnny's behavior toward Gilda and advise him of the proper attitude he should adopt toward her. As the detective sees it:

> It's the most curious love-hate pattern I've ever had the privilege of witnessing and as long as you're as sick in the head as you are about her, you're not able to think of anything clearly... How dumb can a man be? I'd hate to see you break down and act like a human being. Gilda didn't do any of those things you've been losing sleep over, not any of them. It was just an act, all of it, and I'll give you credit. You were a great audience, Mr. Farrell.

This interpretation provides Johnny with crucial insight into his past behavior and empowers him to go to Gilda, confess his love, and beg her to take him back. Yet, Johnny as voice-over narrator never recognizes this insight. Not only is his narration tied to his feelings of disdain for Gilda, but by the film's end, the voice-over has completely disappeared. While the detective's perspective seems to offer the implied author's interpretation of events, it cannot provide the spectator with complete involvement in this point of view because it is not accepted or endorsed by Johnny's voice-over.

The film's attempts to explicate the nature of its femme fatale are seriously undermined by this failure. As Foster Hirsch notes, *Gilda*'s ending seems forced.[13] It is tacked on to a text that condemns its femme fatale so strongly through Johnny's narration and the visual presentation of her sexual seductiveness (for example, her "Put The Blame on Mame" musical number) that the film's final recognition of her as a "good woman," an innocent victim of the sinister designs of the evil Ballin and the unfounded suspicions of the self-deceived narrator, rings false.[14] The film's voice-over narrator never seems to determine the true nature of Gilda's character, and this failure renders all attempts to resolve other narrative conflicts inadequate. In its conclusion, the film projects its evil completely onto the character of Ballin, a "foreigner" connected with a Nazi tungsten cartel, and exonerates its American characters, Johnny and Gilda. Yet, the voice-over technique and its failure to close off the questions concerning Gilda's character or to validate completely either Johnny's voice-over perceptions of events or his final non-voice-over insights call this attempted resolution into question. Again, the character of the film's femme fatale is left unresolved and uncontrolled.

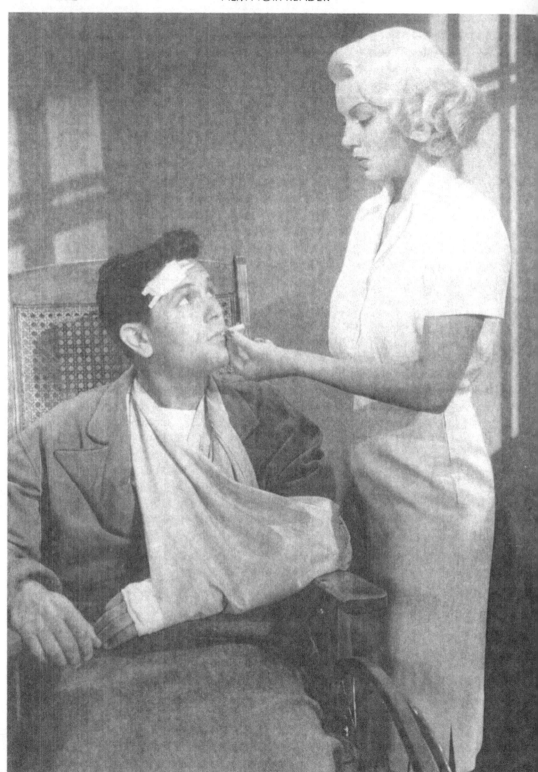

The operation of fate in *The Postman Always Rings Twice* serves a purpose very similar to that of the lost voice-overs in *Laura* and *Gilda*. It prevents the film from centering its point of view on its central character's perspective and from resolving its textual conflicts successfully. *Postman* ends with a concluding frame in which the narrator/protagonist proclaims to the audience his belief that fate has taken a hand in engineering his destruction. This fatalistic notion of human destiny seems intended to eradicate all social contradictions raised in the film. The narrator's problems are said to stem not from his inability to find a satisfying place in the social structure but from a malign fate that directed his life to destructive ends. Frank Chambers (John Garfield) declares at the film's conclusion that his unjust conviction for the murder of his lover Cora (Lana Turner) represents divine retribution for their earlier murder of her husband. Yet, throughout the film, Frank's voice-over describes his situation differently. He still views events as out of his control, but he describes himself as trapped not by fate or divine retribution but by Cora's sexual hold over him. As he puts it, "She had me hooked, and she knew it." Cora is presented as responsible for encouraging Frank's sexual desires for her, and thus deliberately luring him into a relationship with a married woman that leads him to murder.

The concept of fate is used very differently in the 1934 James M. Cain novel upon which the film is based.[15] While the film attempts to replicate very closely the novel's first person narration, it does so in a way that destroys the book's identification of its implied author's perspective with a fatalistic notion of human destiny. In spite of the novel's first person narration, its implied author's point of view is clearly delineated from its central character's. Frank's character in the novel, like his filmic counterpart, is driven by a malign fate, but he is completely unaware of this aspect of his situation. The conviction that it is the operation of fate that engineers Frank's doom is aligned in the novel not with Frank's perspective on events, but with the implied author's.

In the film, Frank's final declaration of the divine retribution he sees worked out through his punishment identifies the concept of fate strongly with his individual perspective on events at the moment of his execution, rather than with that of the implied author. The limited nature of this perspective is accentuated by its last minute expression in the concluding frame, by the visual presentation of the unwise decisions made throughout the film by both Frank and Cora as they act to engineer their own destruction, and by Frank's feelings expressed earlier in the film's voice-over narration that he was trapped by Cora's sexual allure. In the novel, the concept of fate permeates the whole structure of the work. It is not expressed as a final judgment by the narrator; instead, it seems intimately connected with the implied author's overriding perspective.

The use of first person narration in the film, rather than drawing together the implied spectator's and implied author's positions through the intermediary perspective of the narrator or uniting them in contradistinction to the narrator's posi-

Opposite, Cora (Lana Turner) helps an injured Frank (John Garfield) with his cigarette in *The Postman Always Rings Twice.*

tion, acts, instead, both to implicate the spectator into the narrator's perspective and at the same time to call this perspective into question. The sudden revelation of a priest in the closing frame as a hidden narratee further disorients the viewer who had previously identified with the addressee of Frank's narration. In the novel, the text is clearly signaled as Frank's written account of the murder which he gives to a priest for possible publication after his execution. He does not narrate this account to the priest as he does in the film; rather, it is always intended for the reader's consumption.

Postman, like other *noirs* that use voice-over narration, expresses much more ambiguity in its narrational strategy than is found in its novelistic source. Rather than achieving centralization of point of view through the dominant perspective of a single character or of the implied author in contradistinction to this character, the film defuses point of view, separating the implied spectator's position from both that of the narrator and the implied author. Hence, the film fails to achieve the unification of point of view found in the novel.

This fragmented point of view structure leaves the film's investigation of its femme fatale unresolved in a way that it is not in the novel, where Cora and Frank are both portrayed as puppets of a malign fate. In the film, Frank's narration seems hopelessly confused as to Cora's role in bringing about his doom. We never know for sure if we are to hold her responsible for having trapped him in a web of uncontrolled female sexuality or if fate trapped them both in its inexorable grip and divine retribution punished their sins. As a result, the nature of Cora's character is left enigmatic and unresolved.

In contrast to *Postman, The Lady From Shanghai* (Welles, 1948) attempts to envision a more positive fate for its narrator. Like other *noirs* employing the voice-over technique, however, it also sets out to connect its flashback visuals to its voice-over narration by extending the narrative battles for control of events within the flashbacks out into the narration. This extension calls its attempts at positive resolution into question. In *The Lady From Shanghai,* Michael O'Hara (Orson Welles) tells the story of his involvement with the beautiful femme fatale Elsa (Rita Hayworth), her evil lawyer husband Arthur Bannister (Everett Sloane), and her lover George Grisby (Glenn Anders). As Michael describes them, they are "a pack of sharks mad with their own blood, chewin' away at their own selves."

Michael allows himself to get involved with this sinister group through what he describes as his own stupidity and his intense attraction to the beautiful Elsa. He confesses in voice-over just before we see the flashback presentation of his initial meeting with Elsa:

> When I start to make a fool of myself, there's very little can stop me. If I'd known where it would end, I would have never let anything start. If I'd been in my right mind, that is. And once I'd seen her...once I'd seen her, I was not in my right mind for quite some time.

While he admits that his involvement with these evil characters involved him in a murder plot, he eventually claims to have escaped their designs. Yet, he can never fully exonerate himself from his involvement with the evil they represent. As he puts it at the end: "I'd be innocent officially, but that's a big word—innocent. Stupid's more like it." In his final dialogue with Elsa as she lies dying, he condemns her for having attempted to "deal with the badness and make terms" with it. Michael proposes that he'll never "make terms" with evil again. Elsa in response expresses her cynical belief that one cannot win in a struggle with evil, and he retorts, "But we can't lose either, only if we quit." He then leaves her to die alone.

Michael's final actions indicate that he has won his battle by extricating himself from involvement with the evil that Elsa represents, but he does so only by callously abandoning her in her dying moments, ignoring her pleas for him to stay. Additionally, as he leaves her, Michael's voice-over narration reaffirms the ongoing nature of his struggle:

> Well, everybody is somebody's fool. The only way to stay out of trouble is to grow old, so I guess I'll concentrate on that. Maybe, I'll live so long that I'll forget her. Maybe, I'll die tryin'.

As his voice-over narration demonstrates, Michael's battle seems far from over.

While this battle is extended into the narration by Michael's final proclamation that his struggle to extricate himself from Elsa's influence continues, the spectator is not implicated in Michael's perspective by this extension. In comparing the film to the novel upon which it is based, *If I Die Before I Wake* by Raymond Sherwood King, it becomes clear that the novel more strongly encourages its reader to adopt its first person narrator's perspective than does the film.[16] The novel's narrator, like his filmic counterpart, is a common man trapped in a web of conspiracy and murder that he has great difficulty even understanding. Yet, the film's Michael O'Hara focuses repeatedly through his voice-over narration on his stupidity in having gotten involved with Bannister and Grisby and in having fallen so completely under Elsa's spell. The novel's protagonist/narrator, on the other hand, constantly reminds the reader that he was trying desperately throughout his experiences to comprehend the exact nature of the intrigue surrounding him.

The narrator of the novel might never fully gain control of events, but his expressed desire to understand what is going on around him, rather than constantly reiterating his inability to do so, connects his perspective to that of the reader who is also trying to learn the significance of events. The film's emphasis on Michael's stupidity and complete enthrallment by Elsa's beauty have the opposite effect. While the spectator is trying throughout the film to comprehend the nature of the conspiracy surrounding Michael, Michael himself seems unable to distance himself enough from events to achieve any comprehension of their significance. As a result, the spectator's adoption of his perspective is significantly reduced.

The novel also connects its narrator's perspective with that of the work's implied author much more strongly than the film does by having the text conclude with the supposed place of its authorship. The narrative ends with an inscription from Tahiti. In this way, it becomes a personal account that connects its narrator strongly with its implied author. The film also attempts to make this connection by having its star, Orson Welles, also function as its director, but the connection is incomplete because Michael O'Hara with his prominent Irish brogue and repeated attestations to stupidity seems very different from Welles' boy genius persona. The emphasis on the characterological status of the narrator interferes with his identification with the implied author.

Because the film fails to achieve unification in its point of view structure, it cannot resolve the issue of the nature of its femme fatale. Elsa is characterized as a beautiful, enigmatic woman with a mysterious past that is never fully revealed. In the book, while she is initially an enigmatic figure, any mystery associated with her is eventually resolved. The narrator discovers that she is an ex-chorus girl who married Bannister for his money, and in the end a detective involved in the case describes her as the "cleverest, most cold-blooded murderess that he ever heard of."[17]

Below, Bannister (Everett Sloane) questions Elsa (Rita Hayworth) in *The Lady from Shanghai*.

While the novel's narrator seems to accept the detective's final characterization of Elsa as evil, in the film Michael never fully comprehends Elsa's enigmatic nature. While she does implicate him in a sinister murder conspiracy, her involvement is complicated by indications that she is really as much a victim of Bannister and Grisby's evil designs as Michael is. Described by Michael as a "sleeping rattlesnake," Bannister is clearly portrayed as an evil figure whose physical deformity symbolizes a twisted inner nature. It is not completely certain, however, whether Elsa partakes of his evil or has merely been victimized by it.[18] As Bannister prepares to shoot her, he makes an intimate connection between them: "Course killing you is killing myself, but, you know, I'm pretty tired of both of us." Yet, Michael's final words to Elsa do not portray her as inherently evil but only as having foolishly attempted to compromise with evil:

> You said the world's bad, and we can't run away from the badness, and you're right there, but you said we can't fight it. We must deal with the badness and make terms, and didn't the badness deal with you and make its own terms in the end, surely.

The film's extension of its narrative battles out into its narration lead yet again, as in other voice-over *noirs*, to its failure adequately to resolve the question of Elsa's true nature. This irresolution places viewers in a position that reduces their unification with narrational and implied authorial perspectives. A sense of closure at the film's end is thus minimized in favor of a recognition of the conflicts and contradictions inherent in the text. In spite of attempts at resolution, the spectator cannot help but question the concluding notion that Michael could successfully divorce himself from evil in a society that seems to validate the actions of the sinister lawyer Arthur Bannister and ally them with the allure of Elsa's captivating beauty, nor are we even sure that Elsa's beauty should be seen as aligned with or abused by that evil. What we are left with is a feeling of irresolution.

In conclusion, *films noirs* with first person voice-over narration attempt to forge a connection between their flashback visuals and voice-over narration by structuring their texts as narrative battles that extend out into the narration itself. This strategy prevents them from achieving the sense of narrative resolution and unification of point of view that the films' seek at their conclusions. The disruptive potential of the voice-over technique and its complicating effect on the investigation of female sexual difference in the films are too strong to allow attempts at closure to have their desired effect. Since *noir* films focus so strongly on the investigation of their female characters, their failure to resolve the issue of female sexual difference in any satisfying way calls attention to the instability in regard to women's social positioning that characterized the period of the 1940s. The ideological irresolution that dominates the films speaks of a society torn between challenges to its patriarchal social structure and conservative support of the existing status quo. The films' fragmented nature encourages a questioning of social norms that is muted but never completely shut down at the film's end by an attempted reso-lution of conflict.

These films, therefore, cannot be explained away so easily as aberrant repre-sentatives of a classical narrative form that employs them merely as safety-valves for wartime angst, alienation, and discontent, nor can they be seen as raising problems inherent in the social structure only to close them off by final narrative resolution and unity. They are structured, instead, as scenes of battle between conflicting aspects of their social milieux. The embattled narrational and resulting ideological structure that the voice-over technique and the unresolved issue of fe-male sexual difference create within the texts points to the conflicted nature of the *noir* genre in its response to social contradiction and societal change. Specifi-cally in regard to their presentation of women, they strongly represent through their narrational structure the inability of a patriarchal society not only to answer the question of "what the woman wants," but even to understand it.

Notes

1. Sarah Kozloff, *Invisible Storytellers: Voice-Over Narration in American Fiction Film* (Ber-keley: University of California Press, 1988), 34.

2. Eric Smoodin, *Voice-Over: A Study of the Narration within the Narrative* (Dissertation, University of California, Los Angeles, 1984), 152.

3. Richard Maltby, "*Film noir:* The Politics of the Maladjusted Text" *Journal of American Studies* 18 (1984), 73-87; Foster Hirsch, *Film Noir: The Dark Side of the Screen* (New York: Da Capo Press, 1981).

4. Michel Foucault, *The History of Sexuality. Volume I: An Introduction,* trans. Robert Hurley (New York: Random House, 1978), 53-55.

5. Mary Ann Doane, *The Desire to Desire: The Woman's Film of the 1940s* (Bloomington: Indiana University Press, 1987), 54-55.

6. See, for example, Laura Mulvey, "Visual Pleasure and Narrative Cinema" *Screen* 16 (1975): 6-18; and Mary Ann Doane, "Woman's Stake in Representation: Filming the Female Body" *October* no. 17 (1981): 23-36.

7. Janey Place, "Women in *Film Noir*," in *Women in Film Noir,* ed. E. Ann Kaplan (London: British Film Institute, 1980), 35-54.

8. Susan Sniader Lanser, *The Narrative Act: Point of View in Prose Fiction* (Princeton: Prince-ton University Press, 1981); Ellen Harriet Feldman, *The Character-Centered Narrative: A Comparative Study of Three Films Structured According to the Organizing Perspective of a Single Character* (Dissertation, New York University, New York, 1981).

9. Vera Caspary, *Laura* (Boston: Houghton Mifflin, 1942).

10. For another reading of Laura which sees it as much more uncomplicatedly in accord with patriarchal norms see Kristin Thompson, "Closure within a Dream: Point-of-View in Laura" *Film Reader* 3 (1978): 90-105. Maureen Turim, *Flashbacks in Film: Memory and*

Above, Lydecker (Clifton Webb, center) watches McPherson (Dana Andrews, left) shake hands with Shelby Carpenter (Vincent Price) while Ann Treadwell (Judith Anderson) also looks on in *Laura*.

History (New York: Routledge, Chapman, and Hall, 1989), 185-186, presents a short, but useful, analysis of the complexities involved in Lydecker's narration; and Eugene McNamara, *Laura as Novel, Film, and Myth* (Lewiston, New York: The Edwin Mellen Press, 1992) discusses at length the novel, film, the film's production, and its reception.

11. Richard Dyer, "Resistance Through Charisma: Rita Hayworth and Gilda," in *Women in Film Noir*, ed. E. Ann Kaplan (London: British Film Institute, 1978), 93.

12. Dyer, 99, note 3.

13. Hirsch, 188.

14. For other readings of Gilda that focus on the film's portrayal of Gilda's character, see, for instance, Dyer, in Kaplan, 91-99; and Mary Ann Doane, "Gilda: Epistemology as Strip Tease" *Camera Obscura* 11 (1983): 6-27.

15. James M. Cain, *The Postman Always Rings Twice* (New York: Random House, 1934).

16. Raymond Sherwood King, *If I Die Before I Wake* (New York: Simon and Schuster, 1938).

17. King, 295.

18. Other feminist critics, ignoring the ambiguities in her portrayal, have read the film as an unequivocal condemnation of Elsa as an evil character. See, for example, E. Ann Kaplan. *Women and Film: Both Sides of the Camera* (New York: Methuen, 1983), 60-72; and Lucy Fischer, *Shot/Countershot: Film Tradition and Women's Cinema* (Princeton, N.J.: Princeton University Press, 1989), 32-49.

Above, Steve Cochran as Bill and Ruth Roman as Catherine, the proletarian fugitive couple in *Tomorrow Is Another Day*.

What Is This Thing Called *Noir*?

Alain Silver and Linda Brookover

> Of course, I'm not talking about commonplace affairs, planned out
> and prudent, but of an all-consuming passion that feeds on itself and
> is blind to everything else: of Mad Love. This love isolates the
> lovers, makes them ignore normal social obligations, ruptures
> ordinary family ties, and ultimately brings them to destruction. This
> love frightens society, shocks it profoundly. And society uses all its
> means to separate these lovers as it would two dogs in the street.[1]

In motion pictures the epitome of *amour fou* or "mad love" has most been
associated with couples on the run. These fugitive couples were outcasts and
outlaws, hunted and hopeless, and usually dead or dying at the film's end. As a
sub-genre, the "fugitive couple" film has a long history from D.W. Griffith's *Scarlet
Days* in 1919 to 1994's *Natural Born Killers* or *True Romance*. But even admitting
such modern variants as *Thelma and Louise*, there are still only a score or two of
pictures that fit this type. Many if not most of these were made as part of the
classic era of *film noir*, in a fifteen year span from *You Only Live Once* (1937) to
Where Danger Lives (1952). Both the obsessive character of *amour fou* and the
alienated posture of the fugitives in relation to society as a whole are prototypical
of the themes of *film noir*.

In his survey of *noir*, "Paint It Black," Raymond Durgnat gives a thumbnail sketch
of the fugitive couples under the heading "On the Run": "Here the criminals, or
the framed innocents are essentially passive and fugitive, and, even if tragically or
despicably guilty, sufficiently sympathetic for the audience to be caught between,
on the one hand, pity, identification and regret, and, on the other, moral condemnation and conformist fatalism."[2] As usual, Durgnat's prose is so densely packed
that it masks the shortcomings of his analysis. What permits, even compels,
viewer pity or identification with the innocent and guilty is the nature of most fugitive couples' love: obsessive, erotically charged, far beyond simple Romanticism.

I. The Innocent

"Teach me how to kiss."

Since *film noir* is as much a style as it is a genre, the manner in which the wild passion of the fugitives is portrayed is more significant than the plot points which keep them on the run. Some of these lovers are little more than children, like Bowie and Keechie in Nicholas Ray's *They Live by Night* (1947) or the high school girl and her simple-minded, ex-convict pen pal in the recent *Guncrazy* (1992). In their naiveté, typified by Keechie's request to Bowie to teach her how to kiss, both films recall Fritz Lang's seminal couple in *You Only Live Once*.

Lang's narrative focus in *You Only Live Once* is typical of his deterministic world view and, like his earlier *Fury* (1936), is as concerned with the outrage of the unjustly punished as with the fugitive couple. The director's naturalistic staging relies on the conventions of casting and the innate audience sympathy for stars Henry Fonda and Sylvia Sidney to maintain identification with a fugitive couple irrevocably at odds with the forces of law and order. As Eddie Taylor is released from his third term in prison, he is greeted at the gate by his fiancée, Jo Graham. Eddie promises her that he is through with crime; and he marries her, settles down, and takes a job as a truck driver. Yet after a local bank is robbed and an employee killed, Eddie becomes a prime suspect. Although innocent, he is arrested, convicted on circumstantial evidence, and, in view of his past record, sentenced to death. Not only is Eddie Taylor thus rapidly overwhelmed by the fateful forces of the film's narrative, but Lang accents his harsh determinism in *You Only Live Once* with an accumulation of chance encounters and telling images, culminating when the truck used in the robbery, evidence which could prove Taylor's innocence, slips silently beneath the surface of a pool of quicksand. That image becomes a metaphor for the luckless Taylor, slowly and helplessly drowning under the weight of circumstantial events. Ultimately, because Lang is, in Andrew Sarris' words "obsessed with the structure of the trap,"[3] the fateful turn of events is more important than the reasons for Eddie and Jo's devotion to one another.

Henry Fonda's interpretation of Taylor contains residues of hope and idealism which are almost incongruous in a man thrice-imprisoned by society for his past criminal acts. Nonetheless this outlook would become prototypical of later characters in the same predicament as Eddie. Whereas Lang's *Fury* concentrated on the question of mob psychology and recruited such stereotypes as the gruffly authoritarian sheriff, the politically motivated governor, and even the righteously liberal district attorney to probe that psychology, Lang does not elect to dramatize many of the possible parallel events in *You Only Live Once*.

As the title suggests, the individual protagonists, Eddie and Jo, and their one life are the major concern. On the date set for his execution, Eddie is sent a message that a gun has been hidden for him in the prison hospital. By the act of slitting his wrists, he has himself admitted to the hospital, finds the gun, and, holding the prison doctor as a hostage, demands his release. Both Eddie and the warden are unaware that the actual robber has been captured and that a pardon is being prepared for Eddie. When this word arrives and the warden announces it to him, Eddie assumes that it is merely a ruse. He refuses to give up and impulsively shoots the chaplain who bars his way.

As *You Only Live Once* is more subjective than other of Lang's films, so is its direction keyed to the emotions of Eddie and Jo. In the opening sequences, a series of elegiac details establish Eddie and Jo's romantic dependence on each other, culminating as they stand in the evening by the frog pond of a small motel where Eddie explains to Jo that the frogs mate for life and always die together. Even as they feel secure in themselves, the motel manager is inside searching through his collection of pulp detective magazines under the harsh glare of his desk lamp. When he finds several photos and a story on Eddie's criminal past, Lang underscores the irony first with a shot of a frog jumping into the pond and diffracting Eddie's reflection in the water. Then comes a view of a dark, vaporous swamp where the truck that could prove Eddie innocent of a crime of which he is not yet aware sinks into the quicksand. Although the frog pond scene could have either ridiculed the naiveté of Lang's characters or awkwardly stressed their lowly social status, Lang's staging and cutting makes it a simple, evocative metaphor for the entire narrative. As with Fonda's optimism, this elegiac moment is also a stylistic proto-

Below, Jo (Sylvia Sidney) goes to meet Eddie (Henry Fonda) on the day of his release in *You Only Live Once*.

type for the treatment of a young and innocent couple on the run that endured throughout the *film noir* cycle.

When Jo, now pregnant, joins Eddie after his escape, the audience must expect that, for this couple as it would be for numerous later fugitives in *film noir*, the only way to freedom is through death. After their baby is born and entrusted to Jo's sister, they drive toward the border to escape. At a roadblock a flurry of gunfire forces them to abandon the car and flee on foot. A few yards from freedom, both are shot, Eddie falling last while he carries the already mortally wounded Jo in his arms. Despite the non-realistic, quasi-religious conceit, reworked from Lang's *Der Müde Tod* (1921), of having the dead chaplain cry out "Open the Gates" in voice-over, the final shot of his couple through the cross hairs of a police sniper's gun scope is an image that is both characteristically *noir* and surprisingly modern. Thirty years later Arthur Penn went a little further when he staged a realistic end-ing to *Bonnie and Clyde* (1967) by having them and their car perforated by scores of bullets. Of course, Penn's film purported to be the saga of the real Bonnie and Clyde. Lang's fugitive couple was merely inspired by those actual killers on the run.

They Live by Night shares an elegiac aspect with *You Only Live Once* in its contrast of the lovers' feelings with the insensitivity of the world around. In a way Nicholas Ray's film is something of a fable. Its characters with their odd-sounding names— Bowie, Keechie, T-Dub, Chicamaw—exist in a world of grubby garages and cheap

Below, the staging and framing reinforces the dominance of T-Bub (Jay C. FLippen, left) and Chicamaw (Howard Da Silva) over the young couple, Bowie (Farley Granger) and Keechie (Cathy O'Donnell) in Nicholas Ray's *They Live by Night*.

motels, cut off from the mainstream, from the ordinary, in an aura of myth. As its fugitive lovers are little more than children, the *noir* ironies of *They Live by Night* are reinforced even more strongly than in *You Only Live Once* by the very youth and innocence of its "outlaw" protagonists.

As the brief prologue explains, Bowie and Keechie are not just "thieves like us." That is not why society isolates them. As an early writer on Ray's work suggested "by their very simplicity and their desire for happiness, they are isolated, exposed to the hatred of a culture which would destroy that which it no longer possesses: purity in its desires."[4] That may seem an oversimplification; but Bowie, at least, really is too naive to survive. It is not merely that he is just a "kid"—the nickname which the press gives him to add color to their depiction of his flight—playing at being a man. It is because his lack of sophistication permits real criminals like T-Dub and Chicamaw to take advantage of him. How else but through his naiveté could they persuade Bowie that the only way to clear himself of an old criminal charge is to get money for a lawyer; and how else to get money for a lawyer than by helping his friends to rob a bank! Even Keechie's common sense cannot save Bowie from his own ingenuousness. She may help by removing him from the influence of T-Dub and Chicamaw; but the couple cannot remove themselves from the constraining influences of society itself. It surrounds them. Like the doorbell of the wedding broker that plays an off-key wedding march, while he hawks a "deluxe ceremony including a snapshot of the happy couple," the real world touches them with its cheapness and insensitivity. It entices them with the hope of escape like the bungalow of a backwoods motel where they find temporary refuge.

In the end, Bowie is guilty and he must die. But unlike Eddie Taylor, in Ray's hands, Bowie's fate seems less a question of implacable destiny than simple mischance. The fact that Keechie survives creates an alternate prototype for the ending of a fugitive couple drama. The Christmas tree and the small presents they leave behind when they must flee their bungalow are icons of hope and kindness that help sustain Bowie and Keechie in their brief time together.

It could be argued that the poignancy of the relationships in both *You Only Live Once* and *They Live by Night*, linked to life-mates in the animal world or wedding chapels and Christmas trees, may seem more romantic than *noir*. What is darkest about these movies, particularly in the context of mainstream Hollywood, is that one or both halves of each couple perish. Obviously one of the motivating factors is the straightforward concept of moral retribution, of the need that is both abstractly dramatic and backed by the dictates of the Hollywood production code for the guilty to die. It is by emphasizing the innocence of their protagonists—literally for Eddie who is not guilty of the crime for which he is condemned and emotionally for Bowie who is ensnared by the older, duplicitous criminals—that filmmakers such as Lang and Ray make these films even darker and firmly imbed them into the *noir* cycle

More "upbeat" examples of the fugitive couple plot in *film noir* could be the Douglas Sirk/Sam Fuller *Shockproof* (1949) or *Tomorrow Is Another Day* (1951, directed by Felix Feist the scenarist/director of the manic *The Devil Thumbs A Ride* four years earlier). Both of these couples survive, but the *noir* sensibility of these pictures is sustained through *amour fou*. Like *You Only Live Once*, both feature protagonists who have already been convicted of a crime when the narrative opens. *Shockproof* adds the element of the "rogue cop" in the parole officer whose obsessive love drives him to flee with a women parolee accused of murder. *Tomorrow Is Another Day* goes even farther. The prospective couple are a bizarre admixture of innocence and depravity. The man, Bill (Steve Cochran), has grown up in prison convicted for a murder committed under the influence of an uncontrollable temper while still a youth. Paroled as an adult, he is sexually inexperienced. As portrayed by Cochran, better known for such supporting roles as the gangster who cuckolds Cagney's Cody Jarrett in *White Heat*, Bill has a physical maturity which belies his stunted emotional growth. The woman, Catherine (Ruth Roman), who becomes the object of Bill's obsessive love is a taxi dancer/prostitute. Again the element of the rogue cop is introduced, this time when a detective, who is himself in love with the woman, sexually assaults her and is killed. Like most of Hollywood's fugitive couples, including Eddie and Jo and Bowie and Keechie, the lovers of *Tomorrow Is Another Day* are proletarian. As with the couple in *Shockproof*, who find work in an oil field, Bill and Catherine seek refuge in the anonymity of migrant farming.

In the end, the subtlest irony of both *Shockproof* and *Tomorrow Is Another Day* is that neither of these couples take charge of their own destiny and create their own salvation. Rather they survive because they are both exonerated by their victims. For many fugitive couples, particularly in the context of *film noir*, the emotional sustenance which may be derived from any hope of escape or the kindness of strangers is secondary to their own obsessive love. When *amour four* is as

Buñuel suggested an all-consuming passion, every action—hiding out, stealing money, killing interlopers—is a desperate attempt to remain at large where that passion may be sustained.

II. The Guilty

> "We go together. I don't know how. Maybe like guns and ammunition go together."

Although it was made just two years later, *Gun Crazy* and its couple are far-removed from the innocence of *They Live by Night*. When Clyde first shows Bonnie his gun in Arthur Penn's film, she casually fondles the barrel. As a sexual metaphor such a staging pales in comparison to the meeting of the lovers in director Joseph H. Lewis' *Gun Crazy*. The first shot of Annie Laurie Starr, the sideshow sharpshooter of *Gun Crazy* (originally released as *Deadly is the Female*), is from a low angle as she strides into the frame firing two pistols above her head. Bart Tare accepts her open challenge to a shoot-off with anyone in the audience; and soon he and Laurie are firing at crowns of matches on each other's head. The sequence ends with an exchange of glances between the two. Laurie, the loser, smiles seductively. Bart, the victor with his potency established, grins from ear to ear.

This is merely the first meeting. Bart gets a job with the carnival, and from then on, Laurie wears her beret at an angle, her sweaters tight, and her lipstick thick. When a jealous sideshow manager fires them both, Laurie tries to convince Bart that there is more money to be had by staging shooting exhibitions in banks rather than tents. When he hesitates, she sits on the edge of a bed, demurely slips on her stockings, and issues her ultimatum: take it or leave me. Bart capitulates.

The aura of eroticism which Lewis builds so intensely into the first part of *Gun Crazy* is, albeit 1950 vintage, anything but subtle. As Borde and Chaumeton enthusiastically noted back in 1955, "*Gun Crazy*, we dare say, brought an exceptionally attractive but murderous couple to the screen."[5] The physical aspect of the lovers does much to influence the viewer's perception; and the performance of the actors can sustain or counteract the visual impression, often assisted by the physical details of costuming and make-up. Catherine in *Tomorrow Is Another Day*, for instance, appears, in all senses of the word, "guiltier," with blonde hair, heavier make-up, and the gaudier clothes of her profession. As a plainly dressed brunette, her image is entirely different. Fred MacMurray's sneer as Walter Neff and Barbara Stanwyck's brazen, square-shouldered sexuality are keys to their outlook in *Double Indemnity*. Their underlying emotional estrangement is reinforced by the mise-en-scene. Two typical moments are found in the often reproduced scene stills of the couple side-by-side in a market but not facing each other [see p. 34] or her hiding behind his apartment door [see p. 64]. How would the audience

Opposite, parole officer Griff Marat (Cornel Wilde) interviews a new parolee, Jenny Marsh (Patricia Knight) in *Shockproof.*

Above, a publicity pose of Frec MacMurray and Barbara Stanwyck in *Double Indemnity.*

perceived them if they had acted and been posed throughout the film, as they did in the publicity still reproduced above?

Because they are an "attractive couple," because, as Bart puts it, they go together explosively like guns and ammunition, the intensity of the budding *amour fou* of the couple in *Gun Crazy*, is immediate and overt. His companions on the carnival outing cannot help but sense it, as does the sideshow manager, who hires Bart nonetheless. While Laurie's passion is less obvious at first, she not only marries Bart, but pins her hopes on him. At that point, the full madness of *amour fou* is ready to erupt.

As *Gun Crazy* progresses the lovers' continued physical attraction is keyed, for Laurie at least, to the excitement of their crime spree. Laurie tells Bart that she gets afraid and that is why she almost shoots down innocent people. Her real feelings are most clear in the celebrated long take during a small-town bank robbery. With the camera in the back of a stolen Cadillac for the entire sequence, Bart and Laurie drive in dressed in Western costumes, ostensibly to be part of the town's festival. The suggestion, of course, is that they are throw-backs to another era, desperadoes of an ilk closer to Jesse James or Belle Starr than Bonnie and Clyde. While Bart is inside the bank, Laurie uses her charms to distract and knock out a policeman who happens by. The encounter has agitated and thrilled her. As they race off, she looks back, her hands around Bart's neck as if to embrace him. In that sustained, breathless glance, backwards towards the camera, her smile is unmistakably sexual.

By more contemporary standards, the mere innuendo of sexual pleasure from a criminal act may seem rather tame. But the staging of the scene in *Gun Crazy*, the tightly controlled perspective from the back of the car and the entire sequence

Opposite, Annie Laurie Starr (Peggy Cummins) and Bart Tare (John Dall) in their final escape attempt in *Gun Crazy.*

shot without a cut, creates a tension for the viewer that is subtly analogous to the couple's. The release of the tension as the sequence ends is keyed to Laurie's expression. What is building, to use more contemporary terminology, is an addiction. Laurie's addiction to violence, initially motivated by the desire for "money and all the things it will buy," is now the need for an adrenaline rush. In feeding her habit, Bart is a typical co-dependent. Unlike earlier fugitive couples, who flee to save themselves from unjust accusations, Bart and Laurie choose to become criminals. As they come to depend more and more on each other, the process of *They Live by Night* is reversed. Rather than being innocents whose total, platonic interdependence becomes a sexual relationship, Bart and Laurie's purely physical attraction becomes an emotional connection.

Appropriately then, the emotional climax of the picture follows immediately after their last job together. Laurie had planned for them to separate and rejoin later to throw off any pursuers. They drive to where a second car is waiting and start off in opposite directions. Abruptly and at the same moment, they veer around and rejoin each other. Like Buñuel's archetypes, Lewis' couple stand embracing each other in the street and figuratively serve notice on society that they will not be separated. After this declaration of *amour fou*, that they will perish is a given. They die together, he shooting her in a last, perverse act of love.

III. The Ones Who Got Away

> "You'd do the same for me, Doc, wouldn't you? I mean if I got
> caught, wouldn't you?"

Both film versions of *The Getaway* (1972 and 1994) star actors who are real-life married couples with established screen personas. Jim Thompson's laconic bank robber, Doc McCoy, is portrayed by Steve McQueen and Alec Baldwin, actors who share strong teeth and gritty expressions, and usually evoke expectations of heroic actions in the viewer. Both versions are adapted from Thompson's novel by Walter Hill, whose other neo-*noir* work, such as *Hickey and Boggs* and *The Driver*, also features hard-bitten professionals living on the fringes of society in the *noir* underworld. As directed by Sam Peckinpah, the earlier version with McQueen has a harder edge. The supporting players are nasty, garrulous, and otherwise unattractive in line with Peckinpah's naturalist bent and, of course, given to offhanded and extreme violence. The Baldwin Doc is on the one hand beefier and sports flashier dental work, but on the other hand has a more romantic regard for his lifestyle and his wife. In the various adapters' hands, the novelist's usual assumptions about the sordidness of crime and its corrupting influence on the criminal's will, became instead a story of betrayal and redemption, of self-righteous violence and paranoiac romance. Still as a narrative of *amour fou* and the fugitive couple, the two versions of *The Getaway* provide an expressive link to the films of the classic period of *film noir*. In a sense, just as *You Only Live Once* anticipated much of what would befall the fugitive couples of the 1940s and 50s, *The Getaway* films put a 70s and 90s spin on the plot with the most obvious difference being, as the title indicates, that these couples are the guilty ones who get away.

One of the supporting heavies in *The Getaway* (1994) remarks to Doc: "You got a smart little woman there... you taught her real well. She figures we do most of the work and you get most of the cash." One of the consistent aspects of both versions, which is certainly retrograde given the societal conditions of the 1990s despite being co-scripted by a woman, is that Carol's position as the film opens is subservient to Doc. Obviously couples portrayed in the classic period of *film noir* reflected the patriarchal prejudices of American society. Still, from *You Only Live Once* to *Tomorrow Is Another Day*, the outlook and fictional experiences of the couples injected a more egalitarian tone. In *The Getaways*, both Carols use their sexuality to control their husbands' fates. Ironically, the liberating power of the women's sexuality, which literally gets Doc out of jail, is psychologically imprisoning for Doc. His reaction when he learns of Carol's infidelity is understandable in a patriarchal context and certainly in terms of *amour fou*.

As with the male actors, the screen personas of the respective Carols, Ali MacGraw in 1972 and Kim Bassinger in 1994, "glamorize" the character. The title sequence of the latter version exemplifies this. Compared to the introduction of the MacGraw Carol as she visits Doc/McQueen in prison, the Bassinger Carol is first seen at target practice. A slow motion, extreme close-up of a finger pulling a trigger injects a note of genre awareness that verges on parody. The actors' names are superimposed as the frame widens via a zoom back to reveal the muzzle flash and recoil of the shots and a cutaway reveals tin cans jumping as they are hit. Doc and Carol are first seen in a two shot. She wears a sleeveless turtle neck under a black halter top, the lines of which mirror his shoulder holster. The first shot of her alone is as she fires a smaller caliber handgun. She wants the .45, but a smiling Doc asserts that "It's mine." Her answer—"but I want it"—effectively summarizes the dynamics of their relationship. The associations of gunplay and sexplay develop naturally from the staging and statements ("We go together...like guns and ammunition...") of more than forty years earlier in *Gun Crazy*. Not only does the 90s Doc have the big gun that Carol wants, but he struts around displaying it tucked into his waistband.

In contrast, the opening of the 1972 version focuses on Doc already in prison. Carol is first seen in the form of two snapshots taped to the wall of his cell. Moreover Peckinpah unabashedly puts forth his typical naturalistic metaphors. The first shot is of a kneeling doe, followed by a stag. From this, there is a pan up to reveal a prison watch tower. Finally a long shot of sheep zooms back to reveal rows of cell blocks. Over this noise from the prison textile mill fades in. The isolated male and female animals prefigure Doc's overwhelming sense of sexual repression. The machine noise; Doc upsetting chess pieces and his opponent's remark, "Oh, man, it's just a game"; the destruction of the match stick bridge—all this overt symbolism establishes a deterministic undertow; and even though the machine noise stops with marked abruptness when Doc is released, this undertow will grip

Below, Carol and Doc (Ali MacGraw and Steve McQueen) on the run in *The Getaway* (1972).

Peckinpah's fugitive couple unrelentingly. Throughout the film, other elements from Lucien Ballard's flat lighting scheme to the clipped dialogue delivery reinforce the realism. In the escape from the bank robbery, a crossing guard stops Doc and Carol's car. The red, hand-held "Stop" sign which she holds up for them to see is a typical expression of *noir* fatalism always threatening to capsize a scheme that goes back to the grind of the starter motor in *Double Indemnity*. For Wilder and Chandler adapting Cain, the engine finally starts. For Peckinpah and Hill interpreting Thompson, the delay creates a moment of chaos and violence which the characters must stoically endure.

While the narrative events of both *The Getaways* are closely aligned, the tone of Peckinpah's violence is markedly different. His car chases are full of odd angles and cut points. The sound effects complement the lighting, they are muted and hollow. For Peckinpah, violent action is a transcendent activity. The slow motion and other stylistic manipulations create a distorted perspective for the viewer that is meant to be roughly equivalent to the temporal and sensory distortions which real violence imposes on its participants. Roger Donaldson, the director of the 1994 *The Getaway*, stages and edits the same action sequence in a more standard way, which, although the viewer/camera rides in the careening vehicles with the fugitive couple, has a depersonalizing effect.

Both films have the parallel plot line of the two-timing accomplice, Rudy, who kidnaps a veterinarian and his wife to help him track the couple. Rudy's seduction of the wife and the cuckolded vet's suicide also provide an ironic counterpoint to Doc's sense of betrayal because Carol bought his freedom with sexual favors. The 1994 Carol is slightly more emphatic when she asks "You'd do the same for me, wouldn't you, Doc? You'd humiliate yourself for me?" As a "90's woman," Bassinger's Carol not only wants the biggest gun, she wants to control her own destiny. MacGraw's Carol winces when she shoots people; but she does shoot them. When Bassinger expertly plays the dumb decoy or runs interference for her husband's scam from the driver's seat, it belies her ability to drive, shoot, and even throw a punch like a man. In this sense, she is closer to Annie Laurie Starr.

Outside the darker context of the classic period, both *The Getaways* offer a detached perspective on the questions of the fugitive couple, *amour fou*, and what is this thing called *noir*. If the moral issues at stake—trust, fidelity, family values, and self-esteem—are subsumed within the action, then why are the McCoys the ones who get away? Perhaps it is precisely because moral values are at stake. In the 50s, neither the deadliness of the female, which the original title of *Gun Crazy* proclaimed, nor the overpowering impulse of *amour fou* could permit Bart and Annie to run off together without pointedly getting married. Unlike most of the fugitive couples of the classic period, the McCoys are already married and already criminals when the films begin. No matter that they rob and kill, the film McCoys are faithful to each other in the truest sense. The Carols "expiate" their infidelity by killing Benyon. Doc accepts the overriding loyalty betokened by her "betrayal" and

Opposite, Carol (Ali MacGraw) is slapped by Doc (Steve McQueen), angry over her infidelity.

finally realizes that he would do the same for her. The graphically overt sex scenes, iconically reinforced in both versions because the viewer knows that the actors are actually married to each other, make the McCoys more real and less *noir*.

Is it still that same *amour fou* which so discomfits society? In the films' last sequences, the couples ride off to safety in Mexico in a dilapidated pick-up truck with an old geezer/guru of morality. In the 1972 version, that figure sums it up as, "Thats the trouble with this Goddamned world, no morals! Kids figure if they ain't living together, they ain't living." The 1994 old philosopher is a widower but he knows that if his wife were alive today he would be going "nowhere but home. Its a tough haul sometimes, but well worth it. I think the most important thing in life is something you've got to give to each other." In the 90s, that's *amour fou* and the pop version is the end-title song lyric: "Now and Forever, I will be your man."

Even if it were not in the aftermath of *Wild at Heart* and *True Romance* or in the same year as *Natural Born Killers*, this sentiment might seem old-fashioned; and, to the extent that the *noir* outlook and/or mad love are the conceits of past times, it is old-fashioned. The emotions of the fugitive couples may be extreme, perhaps even unreasonable, but not irrational. They understand the perils of obsessive love, but cling to each other anyway. Some might say they are too violent in their *amour fou*, too imbalanced. Others might agree with Buñuel that "the real monsters are those men and women incapable of loving too much."[6]

Notes

1. Luis Buñuel quoted in Giuseppe Lo Duca, *L'Érotisme au Cinéma* (supplement), Montreuil: Edilu, 1968, p. 44.

2. Reprinted above, p. 45.

3. Andrew Sarris, "The American Cinema," *Film Culture*, No. 28 (Spring, 1963), p. 14.

4. François Truchaud, *Nicholas Ray*, Paris: Editions Universitaires, 1965, p. 17.

5. Reprinted above, p. 21.

6. Lo Duca, p. 94.

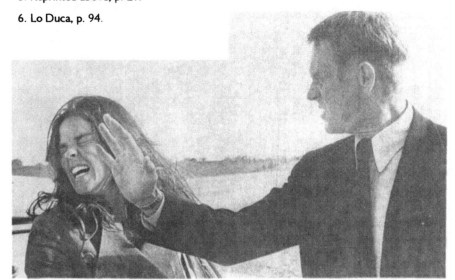

Above, Dr. Richard Kimble (David Janssen) hopped a lot of freight trains on *The Fugitive* series.

Angst at Sixty Fields per Second

James Ursini

Over the last four decades there has been a growing body of critical literature on the subject of *"film noir"*: from Borde and Chaumeton's seminal analysis *Panorama du film noir américain* (1955) through *Film Noir: an Encyclopedic Reference to the American Style* (first edition: 1979) to a virtual plethora of contemporary articles heralding a revival of the *noir* style in the movies of the 80s and 90s, all categorized under the neologism *"neo-noir."*[1] But amongst all these books and articles few have given any space to the *noir* style on television.[2]

On one level this disregard for television *noir* is understandable. Critics and filmmakers alike have always considered television the poor step-child of the cinema, particularly in the early days of the medium. Television was and is still viewed, not unjustly, as a kind of electronic vampire sucking its ideas from the marrow of other media: chiefly, the movies and classic radio (*Dragnet, Ozzie and Harriet, Gunsmoke, Richard Diamond*, etc.) Only recently has the relationship begun to change and become more reciprocal, primarily due to the influences of the fractured style of MTV and the series of movie remakes of episodic TV (e.g., *The Beverly Hillbillies* [1993], *The Fugitive* [1993], *The Flintstones* [1994], etc.).

To aggravate further TV's devalued status, television shows are shot at such a rapid pace and on such minuscule budgets compared to the average film that quality seemed to be of secondary concern to the auteurs of the medium. To add artistic insult to injury, advertisers control the medium so completely that they can effectively dilute whatever radical ideas or techniques might blossom in the brains of the artists behind the shows. Safe bourgeois values most often emerged victorious by the final frames no matter what had preceded. Controversial subjects like drug addiction, sex, corruption in American institutions, violence in American culture had to be soft-pedaled in order to gain the omnipotent advertiser's imprimatur. This was particularly daunting in the early days of television when single advertisers often sponsored individual shows such as Procter and Gamble's *Johnny Staccato* or *The Alcoa Hour*.

Finally, there are the physical limitations of the medium itself. No matter how arduously filmmakers might work to make their products visually stylish and dramatically intense, they were still faced with a basically low-definition electronic medium flashing by at sixty fields per second onto a relatively small box in the home of a viewer easily distracted by the interruptions of family, phone, and refrigerator. All this is a far cry from the dark, womb-like theater where all distractions are purposely filtered out to guarantee as complete a suspension of disbelief as possible. This physical limitation inherent to the medium is felt even more strongly in a *noir* TV piece which often depends heavily on chiaroscuro lighting for its effect. On television, unfortunately, low-key lighting still often reads like mud.

Episodic television, the focus of this article, still has an additional drawback: lack of closure. Because the main characters are carried over from week to week, the fatalistic resolutions of such classic *film noirs* as *The Killers* (1946), *Criss Cross* (1949), *DOA* (1950), *Out of the Past* (1947), or *Kiss Me Deadly* (1955) must, by necessity, be eschewed by the creators of TV *noir*. Instead the viewer witnesses a race to resolve all the complexities and anxieties of the story by the end of the thirty- or sixty-minute episode. The result can be contrived and overly moralistic, driven by the bourgeois values forced on TV by advertisers and the networks' codified "Standards and Practices."

Even if one accepts all these negatives as givens—-and it would be difficult to argue with most of them even today in a more high tech environment (high-definition TV, wall-size monitors, etc.)—there are two other factors which cannot be easily denied. Television has overtaken movies as the prime source of audio-visual entertainment for most industrial nations. In fact, in the U.S., by the 1980s the "glass teat" had weaned approximately two-thirds of the average weekly movie going audience of the 1940s (90,000,000 admissions) away from the big screen and into the arms of "the tube." It is an astounding statistic, especially when one factors in the growth of the American population during those four decades from 130,000,000 to 230,000,000. Secondly and more importantly, the *noir* style and themes have informed a significant number of important television shows since the medium's inception in the late 1940s, particularly in the 1950s and 60s in what might be called TV's "classic period" of *noir* with its black-and-white programs.

Although the *noir* ethos infused television in all genres and formats (dramatic anthology, episodic, television movie) much as it did film, for the purposes of this piece the focus is on episodic TV—week-to-week shows with the same protagonists in various situations, in the detective-mystery genre during the classic period of the 1950s and 60s—for three reasons. First of all, in practical terms, a study which spanned the four decades of TV and included movies and dramatic anthologies as well as episodic TV would be far too lengthy of an article, requiring instead a comprehensive volume. And, secondly, episodic TV, according to studies, leaves the deepest imprint on the average viewer who often finds him or herself buying into the life of a given protagonist, like Richard Kimble, the "fugitive," and then following that character's adventures on a weekly basis. Or in television programming lingo, the viewer makes an emotional commitment to the character which in turn produces "product loyalty."

Finally, as to the detective-mystery genre, it has supplied *noir* its most fertile ground for development. As Alain Silver and Elizabeth Ward point out in *Film Noir: An Encyclopedic Reference*, the "contemporary urban setting" and "the concept of a complex protagonist with an existential awareness"[3] as well as a fatalistic streak are prerequisites for *noir*, qualities less commonly found or completely absent from genres like the Western, gangster film, science fiction, and the police drama (another staple of television) with, of course, notable exceptions like the classic *Blade Runner* (1982) and the *noir*ish sci-fi TV anthologies like *The Outer Limits* (1963-65) and *The Twilight Zone* (1959-64).

The key to *noir* in any medium is its style, influenced visually by German expressionism of the first part of the century and narratively by the labyrinthine mysteries and cynical tone of the detective genre in print (Hammett, Chandler, Cain, Goodis, Woolrich, etc.) and celluloid. What Janey Place and Lowell Peterson described in their discussion of visual motifs as a "mise-en-scene designed to unsettle, jar, and disorient the viewer in correlation with the disorientation felt by the *noir* heroes" has become inseparably bound in the mind of most viewers to the detective film as opposed to the more naturalistic, socially realistic mode of the police dramas which are more concerned with the everyday lives of cops and the mechanics of crime-solving (e.g., *The Untouchables, M-Squad, The Naked City, NYPD, Police Story, Hill Street Blues*, etc.). In addition, the visual features of police dramas are more naturalistic in setting and traditional in camera work, editing and lighting while *noir* favors chiaroscuro lighting, baroque camera angles, and languorous camera movements.

The *noir* style makes an early appearance on TV in 1952 with the series *China Smith* (1952-54). The series was produced by Bernard Tabakin (whose *World for Ransom* [1954] was a low-budget *film noir* which recycled the sets and protagonist of *China Smith*) and Buck Houghton (who had worked for Val Lewton in that producer's series of moody horror films and would later bring this style to the *noir*ish science fiction anthology *The Twilight Zone*). Several early episodes were directed by Robert Aldrich, who went on to such classic low-budget *film noir* features as *World for Ransom* and *Kiss Me Deadly*. The show featured Dan Duryea as world-weary, sarcastic Irish reporter adrift in the Far East. Within the limits of a two-day shooting schedule, the episodes managed to create some genuine *noir* moments— dark, labyrinthine streets; burning sampans dotting the harbor at night; shadowy patterns over the faces of villains.

China Smith also established several constants for TV *noir* "detectives." Firstly, he is an outsider, seeming to find comfort only in the bars and clubs where he invariable "hangs out." Secondly, he is quite sardonic in his hard-boiled repartee as well as first-person narration. Thirdly, he has a personal set of ethics which he will not violate. It is a code unique to him and as rigorous as those of classic *noir* detectives like Philip Marlowe and Sam Spade. For instance, in "Pagoda in the Jungle" Smith blows up a Buddhist shrine revered by the local inhabitants in order to foil gun runners, confirming what he has avowed about himself in an earlier episode ("Devil in the Godown"), "It's the devil I am."

Four Star Playhouse (1952-56), a dramatic anthology, created and eventually spun off an episodic series called *Dante* which originally featured Dick Powell in the title role as a dapper, cynical proprietor of a club called appropriately "Dante's Inferno." Several of the episodes from *Four Star Playhouse*—directed by Robert Aldrich, written by TV *noir* pioneer Blake Edwards, and starring *noir* icon Powell—express a *noir* sensibility with a lighter touch. In both "The Hard Way" and "The Squeeze" camera and lighting in the classic *noir* method create a feeling of mystery and anxiety.

In the opening of "The Hard Way" the camera tracks with Dante from the restaurant area of his club through an imaginary wall and into the low-key inner circle of this "inferno"—an illegal gambling casino. There he confronts with typical *noir* sarcasm a heavily perfumed, dimwitted gangster played by Jack Elam. Dante's insults return to haunt him, however, when the hood reappears and threatens Dante because he believes he has been cheated. In a long take typical of *noir*, Aldrich builds the tension of the scene by not only lengthening the shot beyond the traditional norm but also by having the nervous gangster move in and out and around the frame. At times he even blocks the camera. This unsettling technique emphasizes the menace of the character, particularly as Dante is confined to his seat for most of the shot while the hood prowls around him like an animal stalking his prey.

Mickey Spillane's Mike Hammer (1956-59) brought the protagonist of Spillane's series of detective novels to the small screen in diluted form. The hard-bitten Hammer of the novels differs significantly from such predecessors as Spade and Marlowe in his lack of a moral center. While the protagonists of Hammett and Chandler were definitely hard-bitten and cynical, they also expressed and demonstrated personal ethics and which permitted sporadic moments of compassion. Mike Hammer evidenced little of either. He was brutal, misogynistic, and self-serving. In bringing the character to the small screen, the creators of the series mitigated some of Hammer's brutality by transplanting the heart of the earlier detectives into this new Hammer incarnation. In fact, TV's Mike Hammer (played by Darren McGavin) even helps "old ladies." In "To Bury a Friend" he takes the case of one such senior citizen, searching out the murderer of her son. Although this Mike Hammer willingly descends at the behest of a gray-haired client into a "no man's land of filthy streets and rotten tenements," as his first-person narration so graciously describes his old neighborhood, his methods are not that distant from his literary antecedent. He's sarcastic as in his remark to the lazy police chief: "If I were you, Checkers, I'd shoot myself." And he's brutal, destroying the cherished clock collection of a suspect in order to extract the information he needs.

In "Dead Men Don't Dream" Hammer returns to his old community ("My old neighborhood was dying, and I was back for the wake") to wreak revenge on the murderer of his friend. As he says to Pat Chambers, Spillane's quintessentially frustrated representative of the law enforcement bureaucracy, "I don't have to worry about rules," and true to his word he proceeds to track down the killer, breaking the arm of a callow hood and "putting the make" on his dead friend's girl in the process.

In "Letter Edged in Blackmail" the series introduces a *femme fatale*, another iconic staple of *noir*. Played by Angie Dickinson, Lucille is a married woman who seduces Mike into helping her retrieve some jewels from a supposed blackmailer. But, reflecting the deep misogyny of much of the *noir* ethos, Lucille proves to be a "spider woman." She double crosses Hammer, shoots her partner in crime, and finally expires in Mike's arms, whispering seductively even in death, "I had it all figured out." Mike answers fatalistically and flatly, "The payoff is always grief."

The Man with a Camera (1958-59) was created by the producers involved in the *Dante* episodes at *Four Star Playhouse*, Don Sharpe and Warren Lewis, and is based on the exploits of crime photographer Weegee, who was also technical advisor on the show and the inspiration for the recent neo-*noir* film *The Public Eye* (1992). Rather than a detective with a gun, Mike Kovac, the protagonist of the show, is a shamus with a camera. As played by Charles Bronson, the character has an angry intensity. He seems always on the verge of erupting into violence when frustrated in his photographic/investigative quests.

Kovac spends his nights listening to police calls announcing fresh crime scenes and then racing off to get the first salable photo of the gruesome details. In between he hires himself out for investigations involving surveillance and photographic evidence. His is a lonely existence, or as he says at the end of "Black Light," after being scorned by the police for exposing corruption in their department: "All I do is take pictures. That's all I ever wanted to do."

Kovac's single-mindedness and anger pervade all the shows to varying degrees. However in an episode like "The Big Squeeze," it is most pronounced. In that story he tries to retrieve some negatives taken from a mobster by threatening the innocent girlfriend of a man the mobster murdered. He terrorizes her with statements like, "You'll see how far a man can be pushed and turned into an animal." Her defiance pushes him to the brink of a violent response. The viewer is totally convinced by Kovac's demeanor that not only could he beat her, but under slightly different circumstances he would.

The *noir* mood of the series is also notable, most emphatically showcased in an episode entitled "Close-up on Violence" (directed by William Castle). The episode begins in Kovac's womb-like darkroom where he listens to police calls as he develops prints. As he hears of a likely scene, he rushes off, camera in hand. "It's fun, money, and people. I don't know which I like best," he cynically informs the viewer in voice-over. As he reaches a conflagration he continues to narrate while shooting the faces of the people watching the burning building. Each close-up in the montage tells its own story. As Kovac points out, "A whole book is written on that face."

Suddenly a young hood grabs his camera and runs out of frame. When Kovac catches up with him his distress at the near loss of his only real companion is so extreme that he violently smashes the hood against a wall. As the gun mediates between the traditional detective figure and a hostile, alienating universe, so the camera, in its various sizes and formats, acts as Kovac's talisman. He is lost without it and so erupts when someone tries to deprive him of it.

The resolution of the episode further reinforces Kovac's obsession with his camera work. While helping the police locate a famous mobster, whose daughter (played by Angie Dickinson) Kovac had unknowingly photographed during the fire, he stumbles upon a hideout. A gang of local toughs are holding the mobster prisoner. In order to attract the police to the hideout, Kovac convinces the mobster to empty a suitcase full of money down on the street below. As the crowd looks up in shock, the mobster first sullenly then gleefully showers greenbacks down on them. Kovac positions himself on the ledge to snap that special photo which "tells a whole story." From his high angle POV, the camera focuses on the ecstatic bystanders under a rain of bills and then ends on a freeze frame of the smiling mobster dumping the cash. The freeze frame is immediately replaced by the same shot, now on a magazine cover. Kovac has gotten the prize he so desired.

Peter Gunn (1958-61), another creation of the prolific Blake Edwards, introduced a TV detective who epitomized 50s "cool" and foreshadowed James Bond in attitude and style. Like Bond, Gunn rarely let his feelings take him to either end of the love/hate spectrum. He was all business, a character who learned to deal with a hostile universe by "shutting down" emotionally. As an example, his scenes with his girlfriend Edie reveal a man who wanted sex and affection but only on his terms. Obviously because of censorship, Edwards could not show Gunn and Edie's actual intimate moments. So instead he utilized the time-honored cinematic signifiers of screen sex, the pan away from and/or the fade out on the amorous couple. However, beyond the sexual act, Gunn seems incapable of connecting with others emotionally. There are repeated scenes in the series of Edie—a submissive 1950s stereotype, not given to loud complaining—evincing her displeasure by a look of annoyance or a word of disappointment when Gunn leaves her for business and refuses to make a simple verbal commitment to her before he leaves. In "The Torch" they stand on the balcony where their contrasting clothing externalizes their conflict. He is in black, she in white, and both are contained by a tight two-shot which runs in one long take, as he tries to "sweet talk" her. He leaves her alone on the balcony at the end of the conversation, as she shakes her head in disgust and disappointment.

Gunn's detachment carries over to the violence and angst permeating the series. Most episodes open with a violent act, usually at night, which establishes the hostile universe in which Gunn must operate. In "The Comic" Gunn investigates the case of a possibly paranoid comedian, played by real-life comic Shelly Berman. In the first sequence of the episode the viewer sees the comic running in fear down a dark street, in flight from some yet unknown threat. As a drunk turns the same corner the comic has just maneuvered, he assaults the inebriated man with a brick, caving in his skull. The scene in which the comic tries to enlist Gunn's services and compassion is particularly revelatory. Gunn sits expressionless and motionless as the man paces around him, relating his fears that his wife is trying to kill him. The comic's anxiety, whether based in fact or not, is nonetheless real to him; however Gunn shows no sympathy, agreeing to investigate as a matter of business.

Even in the final sequence when he has discovered that the comic is a paranoid schizophrenic, Gunn refuses to give himself away. His only reaction is to call the police to insure that the comic is arrested before he does more damage to himself and others. In a tour de force of noir style, director Edwards has the comic give one final performance as the police surround him. The sequence is subjectified, allowing the TV viewer to feel the man's anxiety. The viewer hears the crowd whispering, unsure of whether the comic is going to perform or not, and sees their hostile and confused faces in slightly out-of-focus close-shots as they become impatient with him. When he finally begins his "routine," it is a harangue directed at the audience who, conditioned to the cruelty of humor, laugh uproariously. The final shot is a close-up of the comic, his head dipping as the camera irises in on this image of defeat and fatalistic acceptance.

In "Lynn's Blues" the mood of fatalistic acceptance is further extended through the title figure, a blues singer. Blues and jazz, both used extensively in this series, are traditional signifiers in noir.[4] Here they are used to signify the alienation and despair of the main character. Lynn has "sold herself" to a mobster named Kreuger and now regrets it. Kreuger's possessiveness ("I own you") includes killing any man who dares to court her. Lynn has turned to sad songs and the bottle for solace and even attempts suicide. "Nobody's going to cry for me. And I'm tired of crying for myself," she tearfully tells Gunn who breaks into her darkened, gas-filled hotel room and slaps her into consciousness beneath a single shaft of light from a nearby window. Although Gunn does manage to dispatch Kreuger in a violent shoot-out beginning in an elevator and ending under the streetlights, Lynn's alienation remains. In the final shot she sings into the moving camera, "Too well I know the meaning of the blues."

In 1959-61 Blake Edwards brought his radio detective series *Richard Diamond* to TV. Starring David Janssen the show was much lighter in tone than either *Gunn* or *Dante*. In the same year Raymond Chandler's tarnished knight-errant Philip Marlowe made an appearance for one season (1959-60) while Jack Webb, most famous for his groundbreaking cop show *Dragnet*, tried to adapt in the same year his moody film *Pete Kelly's Blues* (1955) to the small screen, also with limited commercial success.

But the show which made the greatest critical impact of that 1959-60 season was *Johnny Staccato*. Although many reviewers considered it a pale imitation of *Peter Gunn*—pointing out superficial similarities such as the title, the low-key photography, the jazz score, and nightclub hangout (Mother's in *Gunn*; Waldo's in *Staccato*)—others saw it more in the traditions of *noir* novelist David Goodis and director Orson Welles.

The series revolves around a self-avowed "mediocre" piano player "My talent was an octave lower than my ambition," Staccato's first-person narration tells the viewer in "The Naked Truth." Reminiscent of Goodis' protagonist in the novel *Down There (Shoot the Piano Player)*, Staccato is as edgy and volatile as his name and the bebop jazz he plays. John Cassavetes, who portrayed the main character as well as directed several of the best episodes, brings a street-wise, sardonic moodiness to the part, which is emotional light years away from Gunn's detached stoicism. While Gunn takes his beatings in the masochistic convention of *noir*, with typical aplomb, Staccato seems more vulnerable. The title sequence is symptomatic. Staccato runs down dark alleys to the syncopated jazz score by *film noir* regular Elmer Bernstein. In close-shot, his hand cradling a gun bursts through a plate of glass and he fires. The camera then cuts to a close-up of his face, not threatening or impassive but anxious, almost frightened.

Like the dialogue in Goodis' novels and *noir* in general, *Staccato*'s repartee is hard-boiled, filled with slang and sarcasm, spoken to the hip rhythms of the music. Or as Johnny says to a character in "The Collector's Item": "You play at your tempo. I'll play at mine." His tempo is a blend of street hip and jazz riffs. The pilot for the series, "The Naked Truth," opens on Staccato jamming with the house band at his favorite hangout. The fast tempo of the jazz piece continues as Staccato leaves the piano, answers a call, slides next to an attractive woman to "cop a feel," grabs his gun and exits. In this single sequence without dialogue, the filmmakers establish Staccato's character—hip, hyperactive, and slightly dangerous.

The pilot also seeks to establish Staccato in his milieu: the club, the urban streets of New York, the subway, and the seedy alleys. In describing a tabloid journalist's office, Staccato says, "From the outside it looked like the garbage dump it was." Like most of the TV *noir* of the classic period, *Staccato* uses real exteriors of the urban settings so vital to its literary and cinematic antecedents. Even though most of the shows were filmed in Hollywood, shots of the protagonists in New York, Chicago, LA, etc. were usually inserted to give them "authenticity" as well as further validate their *noir* credentials.

The violence of *Staccato*, like its predecessors in film and TV, is also heavily stylized in the *noir* fashion. The final shoot-out in "The Naked Truth" is typical. Set in an underground parking structure at night, the lighting is low-key. A killer pursues Staccato through the maze of the structure. The sequence climaxes in an orgy of violence as the killer fires at the delivery van Staccato has commandeered, forcing Staccato to crash into his assailant with the vehicle. Tired, alienated, and haunted by the death of the man, Staccato returns to his hangout, "Twenty-four hours I was still trying to get over the fact that I'd killed a man. That's why I need Waldo's." Like the protagonist of *Shoot the Piano Player*, Staccato retreats into his music for solace.

"Piece of Paradise" directed by Cassavetes tells the familiar *noir* story of a weak man, "Little Mack," driven to destruction by a *femme fatale* in the manner of *Double Indemnity*, *Criss Cross*, *Scarlet Street*, et al. The episode, like Cassavetes' other entries in the series, has the patina of a Welles film. It is filled with tight close-ups on anguished faces, low angles, deep shadows, and single key lights on the subjects. The final scene of the episode is typical. "Little Mack," a lame ex-jockey who became obsessed with a ruthless taxi dancer named Stella, confesses to her murder. The sequence staged in a stable consists largely of tight, low-angle close-ups of the three participants: Staccato, "Little Mack," and Gillin, the policeman who shared his obsession. "She drove me crazy. She got a kick out of it, " "Little Mack" tells Staccato as Gillin glowers in a corner. The fatalism of "Little Mack" is a quality he shares with so many *noir* characters and is exemplified in his final statement, "They had to destroy 'Old Poppa' [Mack's horse] after he fell. It's taken a little longer with me."

In "Evil" Cassavetes, the director, continues his extensive use of the close-up, a predilection he would carry over into his own feature films. The episode begins on a close-up of a storefront preacher, Brother Max, intoning his warning, "Evil comes through the thoughts you think." The camera pulls back across a crowd of frightened, mostly elderly congregation whom Brother Max exhorts to give him money in order to "fight evil." The preacher exits and the camera cuts to the interior of an expensive car. Brother Max enters and is caressed by the bejeweled and gloved hand of a woman. In a few shots the hypocrisy of this individual is established.

A more appropriate title for this episode might be "Anxiety." For the victims of Brother Max are not really haunted by demons, although they may claim to be, but rather by feelings of existential insignificance and absurdity. An elderly, lonely mark who has given large sums of money to Brother Max tells Staccato, "How can I justify this life? I haven't done anything important in my whole life." A drunken, wayward ex-acolyte of the preacher testifies to the congregation that what he experiences at night is a "kind of evil that won't let you sleep." These are individuals, like the protagonists of Camus' *The Stranger* and Sartre's *Nausea*, who are desperately trying to find some *one* or some *thing* on which to hang their existences.

Brother Thomas, the milquetoast-preacher from whom Brother Max snatched the storefront congregation, does stumble with Staccato's aid upon the only existential solution to this problem of guilt, loneliness, and alienation—action. In tight close-up, the bars of a stairway making him seem even more trapped, Brother Thomas has his own moment of existential epiphany, "I suppose one has to take some action." True to his word, he exposes Brother Max and thereby breaks the bond of dependence between the preacher and his blind followers.

The most self-conscious *noir* series and undoubtedly the most successful one, in the minds of public and critics alike, was *The Fugitive* (1963-67). Created by Roy Huggins, who would go on to produce and write other *noir*ish series in a lighter, more glamorous vein (*Run for Your Life, The Rockford Files*), *The Fugitive* reflected the creator's intellectual background (Huggins earned a doctorate from UCLA) as well as his secondary career as a detective novelist and referred back to literary and cultural sources (e.g., *Les Miserables, The Count of Monte Cristo,* American social themes, etc.). In his original pitch to the ABC network, Huggins succinctly summarized the themes of his new series: "...Kimble's life as a fugitive will relate to deep and responsive drives...not the least of which is that Kimble lives with alienation and anxiety. At the heart of the series is a preoccupation with guilt and salvation which has been called the American Theme."

The series also drew heavily for mood and theme from the works of *noir* writers and again most notably from David Goodis whose novel *Dark Passage* also features a fugitive unjustly accused of killing his wife and in search of the real murderer. In fact, Goodis sued the series unsuccessfully for plagiarism. But whether or not the litigation was resolved in Goodis' favor, the protagonist of *The Fugitive*, Dr. Richard Kimble, is a lineal descendant of the novelist's masochistic antiheroes. David Janssen as Kimble manages to convey the look and mannerisms of a frightened and hunted animal. His perpetually melancholy expression, his nervously darting eyes, his stooped posture, his occasional winces of pain—all telegraphed emotions far more effectively than pages of dialogue. In the series, afraid to give himself away, Kimble spoke rather sparingly. More often he reacted to what others said or did, reacted cautiously and with a minimum of words

The opening title sequence of the first season's episodes set the mood of alienation and fatalism which informed the entire four-year run of both the man and the show. Each opened on a two-shot of Kimble and Lt. Gerard, his nemesis throughout the series, on a train at night, a train headed for Death Row where he is to be executed for the murder of his wife. The camera moves into a close-up of Kimble—his face reflected in the glass of the train compartment window. The basso profundo voice of the narrator adds to the sense of doom as it describes the protagonist and his dilemma: "Richard Kimble ponders his fate as he looks at the world for the last time...and sees only darkness. But in that darkness fate moves its huge hand." A fortuitous, at least for Kimble, train crash "frees" Kimble to search for the one-armed man he saw run away from the crime scene the night of his wife's murder.

During his multi-season run, Richard Kimble is haunted and hunted by Gerard who, like the detective in *Les Miserables*, is obsessed with his prey's capture. "Nightmare at Northoak" opens with what the audience first assumes is a "real" (as opposed to "dream") sequence. Kimble is walking down a dark, deserted street, not unlike many others the viewer has seen Kimble traverse. Suddenly he hears footsteps and Lt. Gerard appears, as if out of nowhere. Kimble runs in silhouette down a cul-de-sac. He tries the door to a building. It won't open. He tries to climb a wall. He can't get a foothold. The sequence ends on his POV of Gerard holding a gun. The film then cuts on the sound of an explosion as Kimble awakes in a sweat. "This is Richard Kimble's nightmare," the narrator intones. Later in the same episode as Kimble is jailed by a local sheriff, the nightmare is repeated but the payoff is different. This time Gerard is actually there, staring at him sternly through the bars of the cell.

In "Home Is the Hunted" Kimble returns to the scene of the crime—Stafford, Indiana—to visit his ailing father. But as the narrator points out in lyrical prose typical of the literary pretensions of these framing narrations, "Always there is the hunter, the hunted, and the trap. Traps are of many kinds: of wind, of steel, of words. But this time the trap is a city." There is no succor for Kimble, even here in his own home. Although his sister and father receive him warmly, his brother is estranged from him; he blames Kimble for the collapse of his own life. When Kimble urges him to rebuild his life, he answers, "With your ghost hanging over me?"

Kimble then not only bears the guilt of his own bungled life but must face the fact that he has completely disrupted the lives of those around him. In "The Survivors" he visits the home of his dead wife's family in order to aid his father-in-law financially. Here, obviously, he is even less welcome. His mother-in-law has entombed herself in her dead daughter's room. There she listens over and over again to recordings of her daughter's voice.

In a particularly poignant scene, Kimble's mother-in-law plays a recording of her daughter complaining about her husband. As Kimble comes down the stairs, the camera focuses in on a close-up of his face, first registering shock at the voice, then anguish and pain as he comprehends what she is saying. When he finally does confront his mother-in-law, who is unaware that he is hiding there, she can only stare at him in hatred and say, with a violence in direct contrast to her elderly and enfeebled image, "I've planned out ways how an old lady can take you by the throat and strangle the life out of you." In the final scene of the episode, Kimble, looking for redemption and salvation, is again alone on a city street at night, the coda for many of the episodes of the series, while the narrator solemnly observes that "a man tries to arm himself against the lonely night, for he knows that at this time and place there is no homecoming for a fugitive."

The intellectual aspirations of the series are foregrounded in an episode similarly named to Samuel Beckett's absurdist play, *Endgame*. In "The End Game" Gerard tracks Kimble down through a photograph to an eight-block radius in a Chicago neighborhood. Kimble has found refuge in the home of two lifelong friends, Jake and Sam, who argue continually over every detail of life, including the guilt and innocence of their "guest." As the police conduct a block-by-block search, the three men, including Kimble, are immobilized much like the characters in Beckett's play. They can do nothing but argue and wait.

In chess, from which the term "end game" originates, and in most games the move which assures victory must be premeditated and shrewd. The viewers are at first not aware of the gambit Sam and Kimble have played. They see only Sam and Kimble's car flying over a cliff and bursting into flames to Gerard's solemn pronouncement, "So this how it ends." Only later is it revealed that they had staged the crash to cover Kimble's escape. "The end game he has won—but for how long," are the pessimistic words of the omniscient narrator who closes this chapter in Kimble's agony.

With "Escape into Black" the series' creators explore Kimble's psychological re-silience, his ability to withstand the stress that his heightened state of alienation and fear has produced. As a result of a gas explosion, Kimble is hospitalized with amnesia. But is the source of his illness physiological or, as Dr. Towne suggests when he says, "You don't want to remember who you are," psychological? The way back for Kimble is a painful one, a way along which his conscious mind seems to fight every step. Under the influence of pentothal, Kimble mumbles incoher-ently, his face twitching in pain, as pieces of his past slowly surface: his parents' names, the death of his wife, his profession. However, Kimble soon finds that he can only recover his painful past by reliving it in agonizing detail, much like the protagonist in Cornell Woorich's *The Black Curtain* or the detective in Alfred Hitchcock's *Vertigo* (1958). In a newspaper morgue he reads of his trial. As the film cuts from his face to the headlines, random voices from the trial echo on the sound track. The collage of voices reach a peak as they pronounce the verdict: "Guilty! Guilty! Guilty!"

The final breakthrough comes as a conflicted Kimble boards a train which will take him back to the waiting arms of Lt. Gerard. As he rides the train, the past is layered onto the present. Shots of him, with gray hair, being taken to Death Row by Gerard in the past are matched with shots in the present of Kimble, this time with dyed black hair, sitting in a similar position on a similar looking train. Over this are layered yet more shots: of his wife's body, of the one-armed man running from the scene. When the breakthrough occurs and he realizes his innocence, he jumps from the speeding train; again he repeats an action from the past as he re-lives the experience which freed him from the original death train. The narrator, as always, has the last word, "...he again believes in himself. He again has the will to run and for a fugitive, this instinct is survival." In other words, Kimble's attempt to escape into nothingness, the void, blackness has failed; so he must, like Camus' Sisyphus, keep rolling his rock up his own peculiar mountain.

The Fugitive marks the end of the classic period of TV *noir*. As the 60s ended and color came to dominate the medium, exercises in *noir* on the small screen be-came, as they did on the movie screen, rare. There were a few notable excep-tions, on TV at least. Darren McGavin played an anachronistic detective who found himself acting out black-and-white *noir* ethics in an age of hedonism, color-ful psychedelia, and flower power in Huggins' short-lived series *The Outsider* (1968-69). In *The Night Stalker* (1974-75) McGavin, who along with Janssen had become an icon of TV *noir*, hunted down supernatural killers in the context of the *noir* ethos replete with first-person narration, hard-boiled dialogue, low-key light-ing, and self-deprecating masochism. Finally, in 1972-73 and 1975-76 respectively, Robert Forster and Wayne Rogers foreshadowed the retro craze of the 80s by portraying a Chandleresque detectives in 1930s Los Angeles in the series *Banyon* and *City of Angels*.

Noir did not really come into its own again until the success of the movie *Body Heat* (1981) and Michael Mann's TV series *Miami Vice* (1984-89). As a result of these neo-*noir* milestones, TV *noir* has resurfaced with a vengeance, not only in the episodic format—*Mickey Spillane's Mike Hammer* (1984-87), Stephen J. Can-nell's *Wiseguy* (1987-90), detective novelist Robert Parker's *Spenser: For Hire* (1985-88), Cannell's *Silk Stalkings* (1991-present), *Philip Marlowe, Private Eye* (1983), *Gabriel's Fire* with James Earl Jones (1990-91), etc.—but also in dramatic anthologies like *Fallen Angels* (1993) which adapted stories by classic *noir* authors like Woolrich and Jim Thompson and set them in the classic period. And in the format made-for-TV or for-cable movies the list of neo-*noir* entries is staggeringly long. Even MTV, which has left its visual mark on all popular art forms including movies, has developed its own neo-*noir* series for Generation X—a fugitive couple on the run from a government-sponsored cybernetic program which has planted chips in the brains of its guinea pigs, chips which explode when they reach twenty-one (*Dead at 21*, 1994-present). Grunge, wall-to-wall music, beer, babes, and angst—the perfect combination for a generation, purportedly, without hope.

Notes

1. This term is of uncertain origin. It was used by Todd Erickson in his 1990 thesis *Evidence of Film noir in Contemporary American Cinema* and popularized by Alain Silver in his essay on "Neo-*noir*" for the third edition of *Film Noir: An Encyclopedic Reference*.

2. One of the notable exceptions is Jeremy Butler's "Miami Vice: The Legacy of *Film noir*" in the *Journal of Popular Film*, reprinted below. Evidence of the growing awareness of the concept is a recent article on the cinematographer of the series *Gabriel's Fire* and *Under Suspicion* entitled "Victor Goss defines *Film Noir* Television" in *International Pho-tographer*, 66/2 (February, 1995), pp. 20-23.

3. See page 323.

4. See Robert Porfirio's work on aural signifiers in his dissertation, *The Dark Age of Ameri-can Film: A Study of American Film Noir*, which is excerpted in his essay on *The Killers* above.

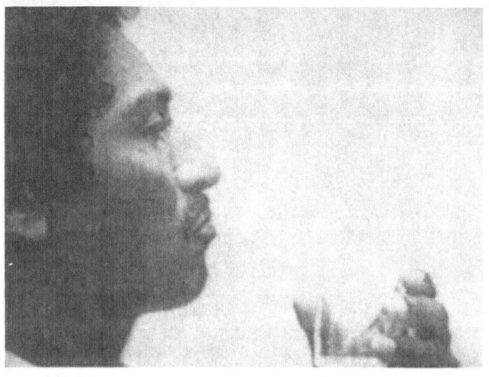

Above, **Figure** 1: a close-up of a man, profiled in a field of bleached white. Below,
Figure 2: the face of Ricardo Tubbs juts into the frame

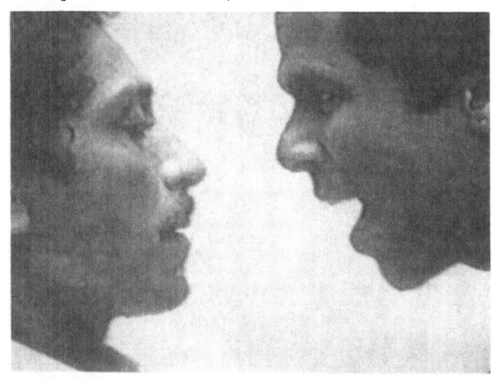

Miami Vice: The Legacy of *Film Noir*

Jeremy G. Butler

Presumably, broadcast television does not command our attention the way a film in a theater does. We gaze intensely at film but glance casually at television.[1] This widely held assumption about film and television is being challenged by *Miami Vice*, an NBC police drama that rewards the sustained gaze that is normally reserved for the cinema. Consider the following television fragment.

A television anchorman appears and reminds you that he'll return in an hour to give you the day's news. The screen is then filled with a close-up of a man, profiled in a field of bleached white (**Figure 1**); there is no music and very little ambient sound. A transparent drinking glass in his hand becomes visible as a clear fluid is poured into it from off screen. We are aware of the glass's presence mostly from the fluid's ambient sound, which is startlingly loud compared to the previous silence. The image disorients the viewer through absences: the lack of television's conventionally hyperactive imagery and the lack of television's invocatory soundtrack. This disorientation is soon replaced by mild shock as the glass is slapped from the man's hand by police detective Ricardo Tubbs, whose face juts into the frame (**Figure 2**). Another episode of *Miami Vice* has just begun.[2]

Critics have remarked on the fact that *Miami Vice* does not look or sound like conventional broadcast television. It seems too "cinematic" for the small screen. As Richard T. Jameson notes in *Film Comment*: "It's hard to forbear saying, every five minutes or so, 'I can't believe this was shot for *television!*'"[3] His remark indicates the well worn assumption that film is "art" and television is mere commerce. As John Ellis comments, "For broadcast TV, the culturally respectable is increasingly equated with the cinematic."[4] I take my starting point from Jameson and other critics who have correctly noted *Miami Vice*'s debt to cinematic traditions, but I hope to unload their prejudicial cinema-versus-television baggage. That approach can only generate more hierarchical boundaries and impede interdisciplinary studies in film and television. Granting the undeniable and mutual influence of these two media upon each other, my concern is to address their interrelationship as exemplified in *Miami Vice*. I choose this program not as a necessarily typical example of the film-television relationship but because it poses unique questions about genre and style.

Miami Vice has many antecedents, but most significant among them is the American cinematic genre known as *film noir*—the source of many of the program's thematic, narrative, and stylistic elements. *Film noir* complicates the film-television relationship, however, because it is a genre defined as much by style as by content. Indeed, some writers have gone so far as to insist that *film noir* is not actually a genre per se but rather a style or attitude. Paul Schrader, for example, has argued bluntly, "*film noir* is not a genre.... It is not defined, as are the Western and gangster genres, by conventions of setting and conflict, but rather by the more subtle qualities of tone and mood ."[5] Schrader's comments illustrate one major difference between *film noir* and his implicitly "normal" genres (the Western and the gangster film); *film noir*'s defining characteristics reside largely within style rather than within thematic and narrative structures. Moreover, content-heavy genres such as the Western, the gangster film, and the melodrama have made easy transitions to broadcast television, but because *film noir* depends so heavily on its *cinematic* visual style it is unclear how well the genre might adapt to broadcast television's constraints. In an effort to understand the "televisualization" of this stylized cinematic genre, I will consider *Miami Vice* in the context of more general questions of film and television analysis.

Components of *Film Noir*

Noir visual style is catalogued lucidly in J. A. Place and L. S. Peterson's "Some Visual Motifs of *Film Noir*."[6] They argue that *film noir* is fundamentally "anti-traditional" in its visual style—that it consistently violates the code of classical filmmaking that had evolved through the 1930s. These "violations" are summarized in the table below. To Place and Peterson's catalogue I would add only the use of black-and-white film stock, which is not anti-traditional for the time, but is still an essential part of *noir* visual style.

Classical Cinema	Film Noir
High key (low contrast) lighting	Low key (high contrast) lighting
Balanced, "three-point," lighting	Imbalanced lighting
Day-for-night	Night-for-night
Shallow focus	Deep focus
"Normal" focal length	Wide angle focal length
Symmetrical mise-en-scène	Dissymmetrical mise-en-scène
Eye-level camera	Extreme low and high angles
Open, unobstructed views.	Foreground obstructions

Place and Peterson stress that stylistic elements such as lighting, camera position, and *mise-en-scène* construct meaning as much as *noir* iconography.[7] Further, they argue that these stylistic elements are as responsible for the film's "meaning" as are conventional components of plot and theme. They note, "The characteristic *noir* moods of claustrophobia, paranoia, despair, and nihilism constitute a world view that is expressed not through the films' terse, elliptical dialogue, nor through their confusing, often insoluble plots, but ultimately through their remarkable style."[8] In effect, Place and Peterson (and many other writers on *film noir*) have created a metaphorical interpretation of cinematic style: imbalanced compositions equal an unstable world view.[9] The key to Place and Peterson's position is that *film noir* is anti-traditional; the significance of the genre is generated by its opposition to previous standards of visual style. Meaning is constructed from the contrast of *film noir* with classicism. This "meaning" includes the principal themes of the genre: the hostile instability of the universe (especially women), the impossibility of moral purity, and questions of identity that often involve a *Doppelgänger.*

Noir themes are defined in terms of their break with tradition. More specifically, many writers on *film noir* assume that "postwar disillusionment"—in contrast to wartime faith in America—is expressed in the genre.[10] Thus, *noir* thematics become significant, generate meaning, *in contrast to* a presumed traditional ideology.[11] *Noir* thematics are assumed to be the dark side of the American dream, a negative image of the 1940s status quo. This "dark" ideology expresses itself in recurrent *noir* narrative structures and character relationships. Indeed, most writers on the genre approach visual style in terms of how that style affects the representation of characters in the films. Place and Peterson, for example, contend, "...in the most notable examples of *film noir*, as the narratives drift headlong into confusion and irrelevance, each character's precarious relationship to the world, the people who inhabit it, and to himself and his own emotions, becomes a function of visual style."[12] Thus, style in *film noir* signifies character dynamics. It is not the presumably "neutral" style of the classical cinema.

Several generalizations can be made about the genre's conventional characters. Men are the ostensible heroes of most *films noir*. They are conventionally the protagonists, but there is seldom anything "heroic" about them. Most commonly they are men with an indiscretion in their past and unpleasantness in their future toward which the present rapidly carries them. The *noir* protagonist is alienated from a combustible, hostile world, driven by obsessions transcending morality and causality according to Alain Silver and Elizabeth Ward.[13] The obsessive *noir* protagonist is drawn into a destiny he cannot escape; he is impelled toward his fate by exterior forces beyond his power and interior forces beyond his control.

The women of *film noir* have been divided by Janey Place into two categories: the "rejuvenating redeemer" and the "deadly seductress," also known as the "spider woman."[14] The redemptive woman, according to Place, is strongly associated with the status quo, moral values, and stable identities. Her love provides an escape route for the alienated protagonist, but he is seldom able to join her world of safety.[15] The rejuvenating redeemer exists as more of an ideal than an attainable reality.

The spider woman is much more central to the genre. Rather than providing an escape or potential release for the protagonist—as does the redeemer—she usually contributes to his downfall. Indeed, she is the central disruptive force: disturbing narrative equilibrium, generating enigmas, and thus catalyzing the entire diegesis. As Mary Ann Doane notes, *film noir* "constitutes itself as a detour, a bending of the hermeneutic code from the questions connected with a crime to the difficulty posed by the woman as enigma (or crime)."[16] In many cases it is the woman who, as Annette Kuhn has observed, motivates the narrative—acting as "the 'trouble' that sets the plot in motion."[17] Consequently, the narrative can be closed off only when it solves the "problem" of the spider woman, when it neutralizes her (sexual) power.

Recently, feminists have been attracted to the spider woman because she provides one of the few instances in American cinema in which the woman is strong and sexually independent. She manipulates and uses men rather than performing as the victim or plaything. To understand the source of her power, we must return to the genre's visual style. The spider woman's diegetic power is directly expressed in her stylistic dominance. She commands the gaze of the camera and occupies a privileged position in the composition.[18] Laura Mulvey argues that this show of spectatorial dominance invokes severe castration anxiety in the male protagonist.[19] In so doing, it corrodes the very foundations of the narrative. Woman is unknowable, unattainable, and lethal. She is an enigma that goes beyond resolution, beyond understanding. Indeed, the desire/threat that she embodies threatens the very foundations of the classical cinematic apparatus. In her analysis of *Gilda* (1946), Doane argues that the spider woman generates a "crisis of vision":

> Since the epistemological cornerstone of the classical text is the dictum, "the image does not lie," *film noir* tends to flirt with the limits of this system, the guarantee of its readability oscillating between an image which often conceals a great deal and a voiceover which is not always entirely credible. Nevertheless, the message is quite clear—unrestrained female sexuality constitutes a danger. Not only to the male but to the system of signification itself. Woman is "the ruin of representation."[20]

According to Doane, the spider woman creates disturbances that are not merely on the level of narrative action but extend to visual style and the cinematic system of signification.

Miami Vice and Film Noir Thematics

Miami Vice shares at least three principal themes with *film noir*: moral ambiguity, confusion of identities, and fatalism (caused by a past that predetermines the present). These themes have recurred throughout the first season's episodes. For the sake of clarification, however, I will draw examples mainly from one particular episode, "Calderon's Demise." Originally broadcast early in the first season (October 26, 1984) and rerun as the second half of "The Return of Calderon," a two-hour special presentation, this episode brings the program's thematics into sharp relief.[21]

The shifting ambiguities of *Miami Vice*'s moral universe may well be its most salient characteristic. Unlike, say, *Dragnet*, the representatives of law and order in *Miami Vice* are quite similar to the sociopaths they stalk. There is no clear demarcation between forces of good and those of evil or at least that distinction is constantly changing. In "Calderon's Demise," the St. Andrews' police chief turns out to be corrupt, as does the kind father that Angelina believes Calderon to be. Such turnabouts are common in the program. In one episode, Crockett's friend turns out to be a cop on the take. In another, Crockett himself is suspected of taking a bribe. I would argue that these deceptions are more than just "plot twists." They underpin a fundamentally unstable universe, one in which black is white and white, black.

As Place points out in regard to *film noir*, identities, like values, are ever-changing and must constantly be reestablished. The main technique of vice police, of course, is to work undercover—in a complicated masquerade. They look, talk, and act much like the criminals they pursue. The identities of Crockett and Tubbs change time and again, depending on their assignments. In "Calderon's Demise," they are out of their regular jurisdiction, forced to rely on a corrupt Bahamian official. When they must cut off their ties with him they lose all official status and are, in effect, acting completely as vigilantes. They have no authority in St. Andrews. As Crockett comments, "We're so 'under' we may as well be on another planet." Identity switches are not limited to the police either. In the pilot episode, the viewer is misled into believing that a woman is murdering several persons. When the "woman" is apprehended, she turns out to be a man. On more than one occasion, the "criminal" who is apprehended turns out to be another police officer or an FBI undercover agent. Identities, allegiances, and even sexualities are constantly shifting in *Miami Vice*, resulting in a morally ambiguous universe.

This moral ambiguity also expresses itself in one of the program's main thematic oppositions: the conflict between performing police duties "by the book" and vigilante justice. In the latter, the policeman/woman's actions are motivated by an ambiguous mixture of public duty and personal vengeance. The supposedly neutral defender of society becomes an active participant in the breakdown of social order. *Miami Vice*'s police officers are conversant in the language of the underworld, skilled in its practices, and prepared to use both for their own ends. Most of the time, these ends coincide with the public good. Sometimes, however, they are not quite congruent. As Angelina points out to Tubbs at the end of "Calderon's Demise," it is no longer merely the police officer's job that governs Tubbs's actions, it is also a more base desire for revenge. This is further illustrated in "Rites of Passage," in which a policewoman from New York avenges the death of her sister. After cold-bloodedly shooting her sister's murderer, she calmly turns to Tubbs and asks him to read her her rights. The defender of social order has become its transgressor.

The form of detection that goes on in *Miami Vice* owes less to Sherlock Holmes-style ratiocination than it does to the *film noir* and, more generally, American hard-boiled fiction, in which the private eye is implicated in the crime that he is supposed to solve. The police work in *Miami Vice* is based on masquerade—bordering on entrapment—rather than well reasoned deduction. Indeed, the perpetrators of the crimes are often known from the beginning of the episode. When they are not and Crockett and Tubbs are forced to actually solve a mystery, they perform quite badly as deductive reasoners. More often than not, they solve it incorrectly as in "The Return of Calderon" and "Cool Running," in which they mistakenly believe they have captured the killer. Their ineptness as problem solvers emphasizes the fact that the true enigma in *Miami Vice* is not who killed whom or who set up the drug deal, but will the moral fabric of society remain intact? In this regard, each episode is a test of faith for the vice detectives.

Crockett and Tubbs are occasionally drawn out of the underworld by a redemptive woman. Crockett's dissolving marriage to Caroline (Belinda Montgomery) and his one episode romance with Brenda (Kim Greist), a career woman, involve redemptive women who could appear in a *film noir*: "She offers the possibility of integration for the alienated, lost man into the stable world of secure values, roles and identities."[22] In slightly different ways, Caroline and Brenda represent the morally stable world of the status quo. Each is outside Crockett and Tubbs's world. Each provides Crockett with an avenue of escape from the world of vice; they offer integration into the middle class. In each case, however, Crockett elects to return to the realm of vice after that realm threatens the redemptive woman. When Crockett attempts to spend time with his estranged wife and their child, for example, he lures Calderon's hit man to their home—a scene reminiscent of the car bombing of the policeman's wife in the Fritz Lang *film noir*, *The Big Heat*. Crockett's weary reimmersion in the underworld typifies the *noir* hero's attitude toward the "above-ground" world of the middle class: Not only does he not belong there, he also can destabilize that world simply by his presence. Consequently, he is fated to remain on the dark side of human existence.

Other elements also nurture the *noir*-like alienation of Crockett and Tubbs. As with many *noir* protagonists, each is haunted by events from the past—indiscretions, acts demanding revenge, humiliation—that intrude on the present. In "Calderon's Demise," Tubbs's obsessive desire to avenge his brother's murder poisons his romance with Angelina, a redemptive woman, when it soon becomes apparent that the man responsible for the killing is also Angelina's father. In a sense, the past determines the future. This is true of many *films noir*, particularly *The Locket* (1947) and the appropriately titled *Out of the Past* (1947). It is small wonder, therefore, that the *film noir* so heavily favored the flashback, a cinematic technique that became fashionable concurrent with the emergence of the *film noir* in the late 1940s. The flashback specifically suits *film noir*'s fatalism because its ending is predetermined. The viewer knows—to a certain extent—how the narrative will close.

The two flashbacks of "Calderon's Demise" serve different narrative functions. The first occurs while Crockett and Tubbs journey to St. Andrews. It includes shots from previous episodes involving Calderon, presented quickly and with no voice-over or, significantly, any sync sound. Instead, the entire sequence is accompanied by a rock music song (Russ Ballard's "Voices"). This flashback functions slightly differently from many cinematic flashbacks. The great majority of film flashbacks present diegetic material the viewer has not previously seen. Although this would be the case in "Calderon's Demise" for a viewer who has never watched the program before, *Miami Vice*'s regular viewers would have seen these shots previously. Thus, the reception of the flashback sequence would differ greatly between regular viewers and non-viewers of the program. For the former, this flashback functions as a quick review of past events. For the latter, it catalyzes an enigma: What do these events mean? For both viewers, however, the flashback connotes the influence of the past on the present. The second flashback (while Crockett and Tubbs return to Miami) serves an altogether different narrative function. It summarizes the episode, redundantly closing off the narrative that begins the first flashback—and could be traced back to the program's pilot. The enigma has been solved before the second flashback begins, so that it (the flashback) operates as a double closure. It emphasizes that the narrative that begins in the pilot and continues through two episodes is now finished.

The fact that Crockett and Tubbs's story continues the week following "Calderon's Demise" exemplifies a significant difference between cinema and television. A typical, classical film follows a conventional narrative progression: stasis, violence/disruption (the enigma posed), the process of solving the enigma, and resolution or closure. A television series, in contrast, must never have complete narrative closure.[23] Instead, each week's episode must work through a set pattern, one which forestalls complete closure . Ellis notes, "Its [broadcast television's] characteristic mode is not one of final closure or totalizing vision; rather it offers a continuous refiguration of events."[24] According to Ellis, television adopts the ever repeatable form of the dilemma—stable in its instability, as it were. Fresh incidents are continuously fed into the dilemma to maintain viewer interest, but the problem at its heart is never totally resolved. To do so would obviate the purpose of the series. In this context, I suggest that the core dilemma of *Miami Vice* is whether or not the police officers will surrender themselves to the world of vice. Each time they go undercover there is the implication that they might *stay* undercover. Each investigation threatens to move beyond neutral police work into personal vendetta. With the resolution of the dilemma in a particular episode, Crockett and Tubbs's decision to enforce the law is reaffirmed, but the knowledge that they will face the same temptations next week prevents complete closure. In some respects the program is little more than a contemporary morality play, in which temptable men are immersed in a world of temptations. Over the course of each episode they resist their more ignoble impulses and return to the socially approved fold, prepared to renew this internalized conflict next week.

Broadcast television's lack of closure undercuts a crucial element of *film noir*: its arch fatalism. Narrative closure is critical to *film noir* because it fulfills the doom that is prophesied implicitly at the film's start. *Noir* protagonists are paranoid with good reason; the world is generally pitted against them and their fate is invariably an unpleasant one. As is noted in James Damico's model of the typical *noir* narrative, the conclusion involves "the sometimes metaphoric, but usually literal destruction of the woman, the man to whom she is attached, and frequently the protagonist himself" (see, for example, *Out of the Past*).[25] By purging these morally contaminated characters, the *film noir* is able to achieve closure. Such a resolution—Crockett or Tubbs dying—would be aesthetically and economically impossible for *Miami Vice*. Aesthetically, broadcast television must have certain recurring figures with which to renew the series' dilemma. Economically, broadcast television depends on recognizable, bankable, "star" actors to nurture the ratings system. Consequently, the fatalism of *Miami Vice* will never be as cogent or as final as that of *film noir*.

Miami Vice also lacks one key *noir* character: the sexy, duplicitous woman. The sexually independent woman—disrupter of both narrative and visual style—has yet to appear in a central role in the program. Surprisingly, all of the women with whom Crockett and Tubbs have become involved have functioned as redeemers. Angelina, in "Calderon's Demise," may be the episode's central enigma and the evil Calderon's daughter, but she is not part of his world and does not lure Tubbs into danger. In a reversal of *noir* dynamics, it is the man who manipulates the woman, bringing her into the world of vice from which her father has insulated her. Similarly, none of Crockett's lovers have deceived him; instead, each has represented an escape from vice.

The significance of this lack of the "spider woman" becomes most apparent when one considers the voyeurism in *Miami Vice*. Practically every episode includes a scene of police surveillance of a suspect. Indeed, many episodes begin with pre-credit surveillance sequences. These scenes frequently include shots of women in revealing attire and the men usually make a casually sexist remark about their attractiveness. Unlike the voyeurs of *film noir*, however, Crockett and Tubbs are never enthralled with the woman as spectacle. They are never consumed by an obsession to possess those women as Johnny Farrell is with Gilda or Frank Chambers is with Cora Smith.[26] Thus, the image of a woman in *Miami Vice* does not have the same impact as it does in *film noir*. The woman is divested of her conventional power as spectacle and, consequently, she is no longer the narrative's central enigma, "the 'trouble' that sets the plot in motion."[27] Women continue to be displayed as specular objects, but they now attract the *glance* rather than the sustained *gaze*. As a result, they no longer exert an implicitly evil influence over men. As feminists have argued, this influence is the result of the woman's *masquerade*, of Gilda or Cora's manipulation of conventional feminine attractiveness to attain her own ends. The masquerade is thus the source of her power, giving her a sexual independence quite rare in classical cinema. In contrast, although women in *Miami Vice* are used for their masquerade (their conventional feminine attractiveness), they are denied the power and independence of *noir* characters such as Gilda or Cora.

In *Miami Vice* we may, therefore, observe a narrative text in which the act of looking holds a central fascination, but in which, strangely enough, a woman is not the object of the gaze. Instead, the gratifiers of Crockett and Tubbs's visual pleasure are *men* involved with narcotics, prostitution, or other criminal activities. Rather than the women of *film noir*, these men are the "trouble" that inaugurates the plot. (The exclusion of women from most of *Miami Vice* opens the program up to an analysis of a homoerotic subtext, especially since one episode, "Evan," specifically addresses homophobia in Crockett and another detective. Such an analysis, however, lies outside the purview of the present paper.) The substitution of men for women as objects of the masculine gaze severely alters the voyeuristic apparatus. Rather than the unknowable and castration-anxiety-provoking (according to Lacanians) woman, Crockett and Tubbs gaze at men who are very similar to themselves—mirror images, one might say. It is as if there is an imaginary unity between the vice detectives and the criminal element. This unity is inevitably broken when the object on display commits an act of violence, which forces the spectators to leave their positions as viewers and engage the object. Thus, their voyeuristic pleasure is disrupted by the aggressive action of the object under observation. Rather than an ostensibly passive woman on display for the active gaze of the male spectator, *Miami Vice* presents displays of active men that elicit the participation of the male spectator. To choose one example among many, in "Smuggler's Blues" Crockett and Tubbs use binoculars to observe a man making a narcotics payoff on a bridge. They then follow him to a boat, which violently explodes while Crockett watches on. Because of this murder, he and Tubbs must masquerade as drug dealers in Cartagena.

Just as conventional heterosexual voyeurism is disrupted, so is the conventional use of masquerade. Crockett and Tubbs's many undercover identities are just so many masquerades. In a sense, the masquerades of Crockett and Tubbs place them in a conventionally feminine position. They display themselves as narcotics dealers, as pimps, as derelicts for the benefit of the active gaze of the underworld figures they are attempting to lure into captivity—much as the spider woman lures her prey. Their masquerade is of legal necessity a passive one. If Crockett and Tubbs were to actively pursue criminals in this fashion, they would be guilty of entrapment. This passive masquerade cannot be maintained through an entire episode, however. Usually it is broken with an act of violence—for example, the car chase and subsequent dunking in "Calderon's Demise." The spectators of Crockett and Tubbs's masquerades respond violently when the truth is revealed. In turn, their violence triggers Crockett and Tubbs's retribution, making the detectives active forces in the repression of the violent figures. Crockett and Tubbs's final disavowal of the masquerade signals their shift from passivity to activity, allowing them to subjugate the forces of violence and restore the limited narrative equilibrium that television permits. Crockett and Tubbs must "unmask" themselves before the denouement in order to reestablish their position as law enforcers and prepare for subsequent masquerades in episodes to come. There is no conclusion, only a refiguration of events.

Cinematic Style and *Miami Vice*

> Impact on *Miami Vice* is first and foremost, a matter of style. (Richard T. Jameson)

> You load it up with pastels that kind of collide and vibrate by putting, say, a peach next to a mint green in a background, or, having Tubbs in a mint green shirt in a turquoise men's room with a violet tie. That's how you do it. (Michael Mann)

The style of *Miami Vice*, which is anti-traditional television, makes many points of contact with the anti-traditional style of *film noir*. In order to analyze the visual motifs of *Miami Vice*, as Place and Peterson do with *film noir*, I will consider the program's *mise-en-scène*, its "cinematographic" qualities, and its special effects—considering briefly its stylized sound.[28]

The *mise-en-scène* of *Miami Vice* is largely determined by its chosen setting of Miami in Dade County. Just as *film noir* is strongly associated with the image of squalid city streets, glistening from a recent rain, *Miami Vice* depends on the imagery of Miami: bleached white beaches, pastel mansions on the water, wide boulevards, crowded ghetto streets, ultramodern office complexes, and various bodies of water (the ocean, canals, rivers, concrete swimming pools). Indeed, the program's opening and closing credits serve as a catalogue of Miami iconography, constructing the city itself as a major figure in the narrative. This links *Miami Vice* to *film noir* in two ways. First, the paranoia of *film noir* is specifically associated with *urban* violence, the violence on a metropolis' mean streets and back alleys.

Noir cities are most commonly Eastern cities, but the genre does expand to include the Western decadence of Las Vegas and, most pertinently to *Miami Vice*, Los Angeles. The palm trees of Southern California in, say, *Kiss Me Deadly* (1955) are closely allied with those of *Miami Vice*. Secondly, *films noir* were among the first Hollywood films to reject the studio in favor of extensive location shooting, especially in post-World War II, semi-documentary *films noir* such as *The House on 92nd Street* (1945) and *The Naked City* (1948). To be sure, *Miami Vice* inherited this impulse toward location shooting, although it is far from unique in this respect. Several contemporary detective television programs use location shooting in a specific setting—for example, *Magnum, P.I.* and *The Streets of San Francisco*. The distinctiveness of *Miami Vice* lies in its choice of Miami and its stylization of that city.

Above, **Figure 3**.

Above, **Figure 4**.

Miami Vice's settings and costuming contribute to a marked visual scheme. Blindingly bright whites and translucent pastels dominate the daytime imagery (see **Figure 3**)—quite unlike most *films noir* (except, perhaps the sunlit *The Postman Always Rings Twice*). Most interiors are decorated in white with occasional patches of color, as can be seen in a variety of settings: Calderon's home (**Figure 4**), detective Switek's apartment (**Figure 5**), and the police department's interrogation room (**Figure 6**). Most of the color saturation is bleached out, leaving very light, pastel colors. In contrast, nighttime scenes are dominated by deep blacks. Scenes are shot night-for-night and employ unconven-

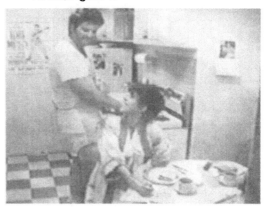

Above, **Figure 5**. Below, **Figure 6**.

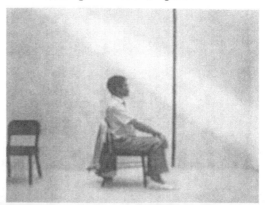

Above, **Figure 7**.

Above, **Figure 8**.

Above, **Figure 9**. Below, **Figure 10**.

tional *noir*-style lighting positions. Emily Benedek evocatively describes one such scene:

> ...following a long shot of Crockett and Tubbs in the Ferrari, the car rolls to a stop under an arching pink and blue neon sign that reads "Bernay's Cafe." Beneath the sign is a long, lit telephone booth. Everything else is blacked out. Sonny gets out of the car and steps to the phone. Edward Hopper in Miami.[29]

Rejecting standard "three-point" lighting, *Miami Vice* makes full use of lighting positions to create unusually dynamic, imbalanced compositions. In some scenes the blacks and whites contrast so strongly that one forgets one is watching a color film—as when a thug is propelled across black-and-white tiles by the force of a shotgun blast (**Figure 7**). As in *film noir*, blacks contrast starkly with whites in *Miami Vice*.

One final element of *mise-en-scène* is the positioning of figures/actors within the frame, or "blocking." Classical cinema and broadcast television conventionally position the actors for the most efficient transmission of narrative information. *Miami Vice*, in contrast, often positions the actors in such a way as to confuse the viewer, to deny him/her immediate narrative gratification. The opening shot of Mendez (Tito Goya) in "Calderon's Demise" is one such example (**Figure 1**). Positioned as he is, we have no sense of his location or narrative situation. Another shot later in the same episode is similarly unclear. When Crockett poses as a hired killer and goes to meet Calderon's man, the opening shot of the sequence is a long shot of both men in profile, silhouetted, with a large table occupying the foreground leading up to them and a roof cutting off the upper portion of the frame (**Figure 8**). Instead of performing the customary opening shot function of exposition, this shot obfuscates who the characters are and where they are located. The main visual pleasure of these two shots is their compositional arrangement; they perform inefficiently as narrative signifiers. They disconcert the viewer, *delaying* the progression of the narrative. As Roland Barthes has argued, this form of delay may well be a source of narrative pleasure. It allows the viewer the time to *look*, to grasp the image as image, rather than merely a signifier used to obtain a signified.

Above, **Figure 11**.

Miami Vice utilizes a broad variety of unconventional camera positions. Rather than rely on standard eye-level camera height, the program is peppered with extreme low-angle shots (for example, shooting through Crockett's arm while he is doing pushups [**Figure 9**]) and, less frequently, high-angle shots (**Figure 10**). Instead of a shallow depth of field, spatial relationships are constructed in deep focus—as when Tubbs approaches Angelina on the beach (**Figure 11**). Foreground objects often cramp the frame, obscuring our view of the scene. While Calderon dines in front of a captive Crockett, the foreground is filled with an unidentifiable object (**Figure 12**). Frames within the frame also constrict figure movement, confining characters in claustrophobic compositions, as in "The Maze" (**Figure 13**). In sum, set design, blocking, and camera position combine to create angular forms in strange, dissymetric, closed compositions—imagery that could function well in *film noir*, but which is quite uncommon in broadcast television.

Above, **Figure 12**. Below, **Figure 13**.

Variations on a Style

One of the most radically unconventional stylistic techniques in *Miami Vice* is its use of special effects—in particular, slow motion. The program uses the conventional slow motion in scenes of violence, but it twists those conventions slightly. Slow motion will frequently begin well before the violence does, creating a spooky foreshadowing of things to come. In "Calderon's Demise," for instance, Crockett and Tubbs are attacked while driving a car. The slow motion starts well before the gunfire, marking the impending violence. Additionally, slow motion sometimes continues after the violent act has concluded. When Calderon is machined gunned by Crockett, this death is (conventionally) presented in slow motion as he twists in agony. We cut away to two reaction shots (Crockett, and Angelina and Tubbs). Then, we cut back to Calderon—still in slow motion even though the violence is over—as he sits at the side of the swimming pool. Once he sits down, and *without cutting away*, the shot shifts into regular speed and he falls backward into the pool. The use of slow motion is echoed in some non-violent scenes that would not customarily incorporate slow motion. In "Return of Calderon," several shots of Crockett turning his head are done in slow motion, sometimes leading into the conventional freeze frame before a commercial break. In other episodes, shots of his car will be slowed into a hesitating slow motion—for no conventional reason. Slow motion in *Miami Vice* breaks the conventions of *film noir*, broadcast television, and classical cinema.

Perhaps the greatest seeming difference between *Miami Vice* and *film noir* lies not in any particular element in the imagery but instead in the soundtrack. *Miami Vice*'s audio style and its relationship with image are much closer to music videos than they are to *film noir*. In "Calderon's Demise," the two flashbacks are done without any dialogue whatsoever. In each, a rock song fills the soundtrack and suggests an interpretation of the images. As Crockett and Tubbs travel to the Bahamas, Russ Ballard sings "Voices." This song, with lyrics about looking to the future, accompanies images from past episodes. In "Smuggler's Blues," the entire narrative was suggested by a song written by Glenn Frey. In that instance and in others less literally, the song precedes the image. Images are constructed to "fill in," as it were, the soundtrack.

Several critics have remarked upon this as one of *Miami Vice*'s main innovations. In one respect, however, it is just the logical extension of television's heavy reliance on sound. Because the television viewer does not gaze at the screen with the intensity of the film viewer, television must use the soundtrack to invoke the viewer's attention. As Ellis maintains, "Sound carries the fiction or documentary; the image has a more illustrative function."[30] He contends that the visual poverty of television's images is compensated by the invocatory soundtrack—manipulating the viewer's attention. Thus, the "Smuggler's Blues" episode is the apotheosis of television: images redundantly restating the meaning of the sound. However, not all of the program's music video-style segments operate in this fashion. The images in the flashback in "Calderon's Demise," for example, do not so much illustrate the song as they operate in somewhat obscure counterpoint. The images are cut together quickly and enigmatically so that the viewer is forced to gaze intently at them at the same time he or she tries to make some connection between them and the song. Here and elsewhere in *Miami Vice*, the images are more allusive than illustrative. This is not only because the first "Calderon's Demise" flashback occurs toward the episode's beginning and thus is part of the construction of an enigma. Even the episode's concluding flashback—accompanied by Tina Turner's "What's Love Got to Do with It?"—points to no one specific meaning. Rather, sound and image interact with one another to create an elusive signification. Consequently, *Miami Vice* places demands on the viewer that are normally reserved to the cinema. We are invited to gaze—not glance—at the images and listen intently to the sounds.

Anti-traditional Television

All of the unconventional stylistic techniques articulated above work against the classical narrative model. They undermine the efficient presentation of narrative and by so doing they offer the viewer a pleasure that is not normally available on television: the pleasure of gazing, of considering the image as image. In this regard, one might apply Michel Mourlet's description of Fritz Lang' post-1948 work to *Miami Vice*:

> ...Lang's climactic period began in 1948 with a *mise-en-scène* which ceased being a prop for the script or a superficial decoration of space to become intense and inward, calling people and settings into question, predicated upon such fundamental problems as eyes, hand movements, the sudden illumination of abysses. Here the script supports the *mise-en-scène*, which becomes the end.[31]

Miami Vice's foregrounding of *mise-en-scène*, its anti-traditional slow motion shots, and even its stress on music that, ironically, heightens viewer awareness of the image, are elements that may be traced back to *film noir*—some more directly than others. It would be misleading, however, to assume that style is the only factor connecting *Miami Vice* to *film noir*. Crockett and Tubbs, alienated heroes in a hostile universe of shifting identities, are the Philip Marlowes of the 1980s. The lack of the spider woman and the ever repeatable nature of the televisual narrative form may somewhat eviscerate the fatalism of *film noir*, but the genre struggles on, attracting a new audience and developing new mechanisms to deal with the demands of the electronic medium.

Notes

1. "Gazing is the constitutive activity of cinema. Broadcast TV demands a rather different kind of looking: that of the glance," writes John Ellis. John Ellis, *Visible Fictions: Cinema: Television: Video* (Boston: Routledge & Kegan Paul, 1982), p. 50.

2. Executive producer: Michael Mann; producer: John Nicolella; created by Anthony Yerkovich; music: Jan Hammer; principal cast: James "Sonny" Crockett (Don Johnson), Ricardo "Rico" Tubbs (Philip Michael Thomas), Stan Switek (Michael Talbott), Larry Zito (John Diehl), Lieutenant Castillo (Edward James Olmos), Gina Calabrese (Saundra Santiago), Trudy (Olivia Brown).

3. Richard T. Jameson, "Men over Miami," *Film Comment*, April 1985, p. 66.

4. Ellis, p. 116.

5. Paul Schrader, "Notes on Film Noir," *Film Comment*, Spring 1972, p. 8.

6. J. A. Place and L. S. Peterson, "Some Visual Motifs of Film Noir," *Film Comment*, January-February 1974, pp. 30-35 [reproduced above, pp. 64-75].

7. Cf. Lawrence Alloway, *Violent America: The Movies 1946/1964* (New York: The Museum of Modern Art, 1971); Colin McArthur, *Underworld U.S.A.* (New York: Viking Press, 1972); and Edward Buscombe, "The Idea of Genre in the American Cinema," *Screen*, 11, No. 2, 33-45.

8. Place and Peterson, p. 30.

9. This is a legitimate link to make, as long as one recognizes that this signified (unstable world view) has been associated with this stylistic signifier (imbalanced compositions) through arbitrary or, at best, culturally determined, symbolic codes. Imbalanced composition need not necessarily signify disruption and instability.

10. Characteristically, Schrader writes, "For fifteen years the pressures against America's amelioristic cinema had been building up, and, given the freedom, audiences and artists were now eager to take a less optimistic view of things. The disillusionment many soldiers, small businessmen and housewife/factory employees felt in returning to a peacetime economy was directly mirrored in the sordidness of the urban crime film." Schrader, pp. 9-10.

11. This can be observed best when the *noir*/"normal" contrast is articulated within a single film as Pam Cook and Joyce Nelson have shown in *Mildred Pierce* (1945). See Pam Cook, "Duplicity in *Mildred Pierce*," in *Women in Film Noir*, ed. E. Ann Kaplan (London: British Film Institute, 1978), pp. 68-82; and Joyce Nelson, "*Mildred Pierce* Reconsidered," *Film Reader*, No. 2 (1977), pp. 65-70. See also Janey Place's comments on *The Big Heat* (1953) and *Night and the City* (1950): Janey Place, "Women in Film Noir," in Kaplan, pp. 35-67.

12. Place and Peterson, p. 32.

13. Alain Silver and Elizabeth Ward, eds., *Film Noir: An Encyclopedic Reference to the American Style* (Woodstock, NY: Overlook Press, 1979), pp. 4-5.

14. Place, pp. 42-54.

15. Place, p. 50.

16. Mary Ann Doane, "*Gilda:* Epistemology as Striptease," *Camera Obscura,* No. 11 (Fall 1983), p. 10.

17. Annette Kuhn, *Women's Pictures: Feminism and Cinema* (Boston: Routledge & Kegan Paul, 1982), p. 34.

18. See Place, p. 45.

19. Laura Mulvey, "Visual Pleasure and Narrative Cinema," *Screen,* 16, No. 3 (1975), 618.

20. Doane, p. 11, quoting Michele Montrelay.

21. A plot summary may help orient the reader who is unfamiliar with *Miami Vice.* Crockett and Tubbs travel to St. Andrews Island on the trail of Calderon (Miguel Pinero), the narcotics kingpin who in previous episodes killed Tubbs's brother and hired a professional killer to eliminate Crockett. Tubbs seduces Angelina (Phanie Napoli), a mysterious companion of Calderon's, who eventually is revealed to be his daughter. Crockett poses as the hired killer. After their cover is destroyed by the St. Andrews' police chief, Crockett and Tubbs are attacked in their car—winding up in the ocean, unharmed. At Angelina's invitation, they attend a masquerade festival, ostensibly to meet Calderon. Calderon's men capture Crockett, but not Tubbs. In the climax at Calderon's house, Tubbs apprehends Calderon, but a final gun battle erupts and Calderon is fatally shot by Crockett.

22. Place, p. 50.

23. Except for those very rare instances in which a program, is deliberately brought to a halt (for example, *The Fugitive*).

24. Ellis, p. 147.

25. James Damico, "Film Noir: A Modest Proposal," *Film Reader,* No. 3 (1978), p. 54.

26. Johnny (Glenn Ford) and Gilda (Rita Hayworth) are in *Gilda;* Frank (John Garfield) and Cora (Lana Turner) are in *The Postman Always Rings Twice.*

27. Kuhn, p. 34.

28. I here rely on David Bordwell and Kristin Thompson's articulation of these terms. See David Bordwell and Kristin Thompson, *Film Art: An Introduction* (Reading, MA: Addison-Wesley, 1979).

29. Emily Benedek, "Inside *Miami Vice,*" *Rolling Stone,* March 28, 1985, p. 56.

30. Ellis, p. 129.

31. Michel Mourlet, "Fritz Lang's Trajectory," in *Fritz Lang: The Image and the Look,* ed. Stephen Jenkins (London: British Film Institute, 1981), pp. 13-14.

Above, William Petersen as Will Graham in *Manhunter*.

Kill Me Again: Movement becomes Genre

Todd Erickson

Film noir was just a term, which French cinéaste Nino Frank reputedly invented it in 1946, when the movie houses of post-World War II Paris were deluged with a wave of hard-edged American crime pictures. After their first viewing of movies such as *Double Indemnity, Laura, Phantom Lady,* and *Murder, My Sweet,* other French critics picked up and fostered the use of the term in their writings, most notably Raymond Borde and Étienne Chaumeton in their groundbreaking study *Panorama du Film Noir Américain (1941-1953)* published in 1955. Remarkably, as Part One of this volume confirms, thirteen years passed before an English-language book—*Hollywood in the Forties* by Charles Higham and Joel Greenberg—used the term and formally recognized *film noir* as a distinct body of films. And, while there have been scores of English language articles and books dedicated to the subject since then, until recently, *film noir* was a term rarely encountered outside of film schools, cinema books, and motion picture retrospectives.

In 1995 thanks to the contemporary cinema's flourishing cycle of self-conscious *noir,* the term is rapidly being absorbed into everyday American life. The ubiquitous medium of modern television pays homage to *film noir* through period recreations such as Showtime Network's cable series *Fallen Angels,* and millions of viewers have been introduced to the stylistic decorum of the *noir* milieu through primetime programming like Fox Network's *X-Files.* Even journalists use fusion phrases such as "cable *noir,*" "TV *noir,*" "pop *noir,*" and "cyber *noir,*" to help them describe creations influenced by the somber mood and visual style of *film noir.*

The increased awareness of the term, *film noir,* can also be attributed to haphazard movie critics, who, seemingly anxious to show-off their cinematic IQs, assign the term to virtually any contemporary motion picture favoring dark, wet streets and/or a central character in jeopardy. In turn, the studios and mainstream independent distributors, none of which had ever promoted a theatrical release as a *"film noir"* prior to Orion Pictures' *The Hot Spot* in 1990,[1] have increasingly begun to rely on *noir*-descriptive quotes from critical reviews to market their pictures.

This evolution toward the acceptance and casual use of the term and its many variations has energized the long-standing argument over how *film noir* should be classified within the scope of cinema history and criticism. Is it a genre or a movement? A style? A mood? Was *film noir* time-bound, or does it still exist in the American cinema?

*   *   *

Fortunately, the passage of time, the accumulation of critical data, and most important, the contemporary cinema's new cycle of *noir*-influenced crime films, have given us a perspective on *film noir* not previously accessible. From this more favorable vantage point, we can understand *film noir* not only as a movement, but also as a genre, which developed within, and emerged from, the movement itself.

As a movement, the *film noir* incorporated a specific attitude; a cynical, existentially bitter attitude derived from the hard-boiled school of fiction, as well as the attendant socio-cultural influences of the day, which were visually expressed through lighting, design and camerawork assimilated from the German Expressionist cinema via the gangster and horror genres of the thirties.

Robert Porfirio cites *Citizen Kane* (1941) as the prototype of a visual style and narrative perspective from which the movement's tendencies were adopted.[2] The stylistic and narrative devices that Welles utilized in *Citizen Kane*, such as Gregg Toland's deep focus photography, extreme camera angles, optical effects, flashbacks, and voice-over narration became representative cinematic components of the overall *film noir* movement—a movement that darkened the mood, or tone, in virtually all of the cinematic product of Hollywood from that era.

Although *noir* found its best avenues of expression in the detective and the gangster genres, as a movement it cut across all generic lines. That's why social dramas (*It's a Wonderful Life*, 1946) and other genre films, such as the Western (*Pursued*, 1947) and Science Fiction (*The Day the Earth Stood Still*, 1951) were affected and transformed by the stylistic elements and thematic concerns of *noir*. Of course, these genre films were not *film noir*. To use a hybrid expression, they were "*noired*."

It was not until the *noir* genre had successfully emerged in the eighties (from its embryonic state in the sixties and seventies) that we could understand *film noir* on two distinct planes. First, as an overall cinematic movement which, to some extent, modified most of Hollywood's product during the forties and fifties, and secondly, as a (new) genre that emerged from the overall movement, utilizing the subject matter that was at the very core of its existence: the presence, or portent, of crime.

The detective and gangster genres were ripe for evolution within the context of the early forties American cinema, and the force of the *noir* movement made such an evolution possible. In theory, Robert Porfirio explained how this occurred:

> The *film noir* acted as something of a conduit, drawing from many of the major commercial genres of the thirties and transforming them (via its mood, style, etc.) into the more modern forms of the 1960s. To carry this metaphor a bit further, if the *film noir* served as a nexus or channel for the established genres to traverse, it was one whose function was short-lived, for as 'older' genres became 'newer' ones, the *film noir* itself died out, dissipating its energies among certain of the genres that displaced it.[3]

Because of the peculiar qualities that *film noir* brought to these existing genres, they were altered and re-codified so that they gradually built up their own specific generic expectations for the viewer. "The more a genre develops," observed Marc Vernet, "which is to say the more films it contains, the more the codes tend to play the role of a guarantee to the spectator."[4]

What made the *noir* films of the forties such as *Double Indemnity* (1944), *The Killers* (1946) and *Out of the Past* (1947) so revolutionary in their day was that they distorted the viewer's psychological reference points by establishing a new set of generic codes. This new set of generic codes incorporated iconography from the detective and gangster genres, the distinctive narrative voice (or attitude) of the hard-boiled writers, and the first-person sensibility of the expressionistic subjective camera, through which the underworld could be experienced vicariously by the viewer.

Using Raymond Chandler's character of Philip Marlowe as an example, J.P. Telotte explained how the narrative voice of the hard-boiled writers was significant in constructing the *noir* film:

> Thanks to Chandler's first-person narration, all that we see in the Marlowe novels is what the detective himself sees; his experiences—and his thoughts—are ours. This outer-directedness ultimately proves just as important as Marlowe's moral stance (style an equivalent of theme), since it equally defines our relationship to the world he inhabits. Through Marlowe we become different from, and in many ways stronger than, that world. We perceive its truth, understand its ways, and avoid its pitfalls as no one else in the novels can. What this singular experience produces, in effect, is a new vantage on the relation of the psyche and surface, as <u>how</u> we perceive becomes our one sure proof against <u>what</u> waits on those "mean streets."[5]

Fritz Lang, one of the great directors of the German Expressionist movement and later the *film noir*, explained the vicarious experience his films provided through the subjective camera:

> You show the protagonist so that the audience can put themselves under the skin of the man. First of all, I use my camera in such a

way as to show things, wherever possible, from the viewpoint of
the protagonist; in that way my audience identifies itself with the
character on the screen and thinks with him...in *The Big Heat* Glenn
Ford sits and plays with his child; the wife goes out to put the car in
the garage. Explosion. By not showing it, you first have the shock.
"What was that?" Ford runs out. He cannot even open the car. He
sees only catastrophe. Immediately (because they see it through his
eyes), the audience feels with him. [emphasis added][6]

By the mid-fifties, filmmakers as well as movie-goers had come to rely on these
new codes that were peculiar to a particular type of crime film, which endowed
the viewer with visual and psychological access—via the protagonist's first-person
perspective—to the nightmarish underworld of dead-end America. By the time
films such as *Kiss Me Deadly* (1955) and *Touch of Evil* (1958) were produced near
the end of the movement, it was evident a new genre had been created, based on
the stylistic and narrative conventions filmmakers had self-consciously absorbed
from the overall *noir* movement. "This process of evolutionary development
seems to be an almost natural feature in the history of any form—whether that of
a single genre or of Hollywood cinema as a whole," reasons Thomas Schatz. "As a
form is varied and refined, it is bound to become more stylized, more conscious
of its own rules of construction and expression."[7]

Even though American critics and filmgoers were unfamiliar with the term, at
that time, *film noir's* generic codes had become embedded in the filmmaker's cinematic vocabulary. However, this familiarity induced a new set of generic expectations which the genre was not ready—or capable—of fulfilling. These new
expectations could not be realized, in part, because they came at a time when
filming with black-and-white film in the Academy aperture was rapidly being
phased out.

American filmmakers were unable and unwilling to spontaneously translate the
cinematic vocabulary of the *film noir* to the widescreen, color format that was becoming the norm in American cinema's competition with television for the viewing audience. "Television, with its demand for full lighting and close-ups, gradually
undercut the German influence," stresses Paul Schrader in *Notes on Film Noir*,
"and color cinematography was, of course, the final blow to the '*noir*' look."[8]

In addition, the overall mood of the nation was in a vibrant upswing, drastically
reducing the scope of the *noir* canvas on which society's problems could be
painted. The House Un-American Activities Committee investigations were winding down, the Korean conflict had ended, industry and labor were setting records,
and reported crimes were at an all-time low in the nation, a sharp contrast from
the 1952 FBI report that Borde and Chaumeton cited, when crime had reached
record proportions.

In retrospect, the unique combination of elements fueling the *noir* movement,
and the *noir* genre it spawned, had dissipated (with the exception of the Cold

War) to such an extent that by the early 1960s the *noir* sensibility was barely decipherable in the American cinema.

*   *   *

Although the *noir* movement had exhausted its energies, as Porfirio suggests, by transforming several older genres into the new forms of the sixties, the *noir* sensibility never completely died. It remained dormant in the American cinema for nearly two decades, being kept alive through television series that paid homage to it, such as *The Fugitive, Dragnet, Lineup,* and *Peter Gunn.*[9] The seventies brought motion picture retrospectives, cable television, premium movie channels, and home video, all stimulating more demand for programming and greater interest in the original movement among film critics, historians, and filmmakers.

The American cinema's ongoing quest for greater realism was assisted by the Motion Picture Association of America's institution of a rating system in 1966, which permitted more explicit acts of sex and violence to be depicted on the screen. Occasionally, a *noir* film would surface, as evidenced by *Point Blank* (1967), *Hickey & Boggs* (1972), *The Friends of Eddie Coyle* (1973), *The Outfit* (1974), *Night Moves* (1975), and *Taxi Driver* (1976), giving validity to the idea that *noir* was capable of existing in the contemporary American cinema.

Below, "...in *The Big Heat* Glenn Ford sits and plays with his child; the wife goes out to put the car in the garage. Explosion."

More often than not, the *noir* attempts of the late sixties and seventies paral-
leled the wave of critical *noir* literature at the time, kindled by a nostalgic curiosity
which saw *Murder My Sweet* (1944) remade as *Farewell My Lovely* (1975), *They Live
By Night* (1949) as *Thieves Like Us* (1974), and *The Big Sleep* (1946) remade with
the same title in 1978. Among the remakes of this transitional/nostalgic period,
only *Farewell, My Lovely* was "more atmospherically faithful to the ethos" of the
original version.[10]

On the other hand, in spite of its faithfulness to the late thirties' Los Angeles
setting, *Chinatown* (1974) is the only "period *noir*" which manages to maintain an
air of timelessness in its presentation. Even its sequel, *The Two Jakes* (1990), and
other period attempts such as *The Public Eye* (1992) are wildly distracting in their
period perspectives, and ultimately fail to maintain the slightest notion of the true
noir spirit.

Summing up the wave of nostalgia that was sweeping through the American
cinema during that period, Richard T. Jameson contemplated the difference between the films of the original *noir* cycle and the remakes of the transitional period
in a 1974 article titled *Son of Noir*:

> If the *films noir* (or the *noir* descendants) of today are any sort of
> response, it must be of a markedly different kind. Of
> nostalgia-tripping, recreating the artifacts of the past for the sake of
> doing so...it is a decadent process, and if anything is illuminated
> thereby, it's the calculated self-interest of people who want to sell
> what the public is buying. That in itself is a cynical response to a
> cynical era hungry for optimism—an almost precise reversal of the
> climate in which *noir* was born.[11]

A few years later, Foster Hirsch echoed Jameson's observation, noting that "In the
sixties and seventies the genre was clearly a self-consciously resurrected form.
Thrillers made in the *noir* style became a nostalgic exercise, touched with that
note of condescension which often results when one generation reconstructs
artifacts of an earlier era's popular culture."[12]

However, near the close of the seventies, there were many socio-cultural factors present, ranging from post-Vietnam War disillusionment to the Feminist
movement, and an alarming wave of international terrorism, which mirrored many
of the factors present in post-World War II America. Added to that, the eighties
ushered in the era of the leveraged buyout on Wall Street, described by Bryan
Burrough as "a time when virtually everything—old standards, morals, sometimes
even the truth—was sacrificed in the almighty hunt for The Big Deal."[13] According to Fred Steeper, whose firm polled public opinion during the 1988 U.S. presi-
dential campaign, "The upcoming '90s have been prefaced by economic
uncertainty due to budget deficits, fear of the hazards of environmental pollution,
and sexual doubt fueled by the AIDS crisis. Such evolving dangers tend to make

people think that not everything should be tolerated. There's a sense that the moral fabric of society has been pulled asunder."[14]

When asked if he saw any parallels between the socio-cultural environment of post-World War II America and that of contemporary society, Lawrence Kasdan, the writer/director of *Body Heat* (1981), said he felt the women's liberation movement was "a comparable type of event" in America where "it created an atmosphere during the seventies where there was this same type of distrust of women that the guys returning from World War II had when they wondered where their women had been at night while they were away fighting the war."[15] Virginia Madsen, an actress who has portrayed a *femme fatale* in several theatrical features and pay-television movies including *Slam Dance* (1987), *The Hot Spot* (1990), *Gotham* (1988), and *Third Degree Burn* (1989) observed, "It's amazing, the leading men seem to be getting weaker, while the leading women are getting stronger, character wise. I think inevitably stories about women are fascinating to an audience—our society is fascinated by women. Men and women are both confused by females and why they do the things they do."[16]

Alan Waxenberg, publisher of a popular women's magazine, believes that a cycle that began in the early fifties with the infancy boom created a societal pressure that forced women to be nothing more than homemakers. "The sixties and seventies were years of experimentation, taking women away from the home. The materialism of the early eighties then set for a reactive re-emphasis on domesticity as a matter of choice."[17] Leslie Shelton, an advertising executive, added that "the pressure to achieve in a lot of areas within a relatively short period of time, which is new to women, has cre-

Right, Don Johnson and Virginia Madsen in *The Hot Spot*.

ated unsettling feelings, which are evidenced in guilt and insecurity."[18]

In addition to these various socio-cultural influences, there are three principal factors which have stimulated the resurgence of *noir* in the contemporary American cinema: (1) Technical advancements made with color film stock; (2) the pervasiveness of crime and the public's fascination with sensational crime stories; and, most importantly, (3) a definitive *noir* sensibility among contemporary filmmakers.

1. Technical advancements made with color film stock. The *noir* movement was heavily influenced by German Expressionism's quest to reveal the "deeper reality" (psychological motivations) of its characters through the intense interplay of light and shadow. Many of *noir*'s finest cinematographers came from the German Expressionist cinema, and the precedent of their black-and-white film sensibility dictated its use on the American screen. Black-and-white film was also a guarantee of realism for audiences of that period; it provided superior exposure latitude; and, the economics of filmmaking in the forties simply made color *film noir*, such as *Leave Her to Heaven* (1945), the striking exception.

Unlike the color film stock used in the sixties and seventies, modern high-speed color negative films provide filmmakers exceptional low-end latitude, and render true blacks. This means that the shadowy, high contrast images familiar to *film noir* can now be realized with color film.

By the mid-sixties, motion pictures filmed in color were standard in the industry, which meant that color film had gradually supplanted black-and-white film as a guarantee of realism to movie audiences. The rapid advancements made with color film stock contributed not only to an expanded ability to create realism on the screen, but also an increasing reliance on natural light, and ultimately, faster shot set-ups. Referring to the Kodak 5293 high speed film that was first available in 1982, Ric Waite, the cinematographer of *48 Hours*, said:

> It allowed us to shoot with minimum lighting in our night exteriors and almost nothing but natural lighting and maybe a few 60-watt bulbs, for the interiors. I started to light a scene one night and I decided to believe that if I could see it in the lens, then I would be able to see it in the rushes the next day. That was taking a real chance. We did in four nights a complicated chase scene that covered four to six blocks, and it was a scene we'd have needed at least twelve days to light and set up had it not been for this new stock.[19]

Five years later, Kodak introduced a superior color stock rated at 400 ASA, the 5295. "The '95 is very fine grained and holds the shadowy blacks extremely well," said Jack Green, the director of photography for *Bird* (1988), a dark, brooding bio-pic on the late jazz great, Charlie "Bird" Parker. Continuing, Green said that Clint Eastwood, the director, wanted a stylized look with *Bird*:

He told me to work with the idea that this was a black-and-white film which we just happened to be shooting with color stock.... Black is by far the hardest of all visual tones to keep. The blue sensitivity of the '95 is what helps keep the black dense.[20]

Yet again, in 1989, Kodak introduced an even faster film stock, the 5296 500 ASA (which Fuji Film Co. matched with its own 500 ASA film). Cinematographer Marc Reshovsky explained the benefits of the 5296 stock:

It has great sharpness of image and extreme low graininess.... The only thing you have to be careful of is not over lighting and bringing the fill up too much, because the stock's so sensitive. We filmed in this huge hangar, and there was a shadowy area on the set that I thought was too dark. But when I saw the dailies, it was brighter than it was to the eye at shoot time, which is pretty amazing.[21]

In photographing the remake of *D.O.A.* (1949), Yuri Neyman, the cinematographer for *DOA* (1988) shot the beginning and end of the remake in black-and-white, in a style he called "an homage to the naive, subjective camera of the forties." The rest of the film was shot in color because, as Neyman says, "we wanted to create a *film noir* in color. That suggested a very muted palette."[22] While the black-and-white sequences parenthesize the color portion of the *DOA* remake from a critical perspective, the juxtapositioning of the two film stocks illustrates that color cinematography can provide the exposure latitude necessary

Below, neo-*noir* lighting, a gang of bike-riding *yakuza* menace Andy Garcia in *Black Rain*.

to achieve the expressionistic lighting effects that *noir* depends on for heightened suspense and psychological insight.

Undoubtedly, the technical advancements made with color film during the past decade has greatly contributed to the distinct ambience of modern *noir*, as well as boosting the confidence of filmmakers desiring to project their *noir* sensibilities on the screen. The quality and range of modern high-speed color film stock means that virtually all lighting in contemporary filmmaking can now be effected for artistic purposes rather than for exposure.[23]

2. The pervasiveness of crime and the public's fascination with sensational crime stories. Crime stories abound in modern America, with newspaper headlines shouting *Cocaine Worth $20 Billion Seized in Biggest Bust Ever,*[24] *Crooked Cop Tapes Wrenching Tale,*[25] and *Contract Killings in Suburbia.*[26] Magazines have echoed the spread of crime with headlines such as *Victims of Crime,*[27] *The Cotton Club Murder: Cocaine and Hit Men in Hollywood—A 1980s Film Noir,*[28] and *Fear in the City: Darkness Descends on the City of Angels.*[29]

As for television, America's most popular news medium, there were at least nineteen network or nationally syndicated tabloid programs on the air in 1989,[30] two of which aired interviews with the infamous mass murderer Ted Bundy just hours before he was executed for his crimes by the Florida State Correctional System. In 1995, CNN News' ratings skyrocketed as millions of viewers tuned in daily during the court proceedings of Hall of Fame football hero/celebrity product endorser, O.J. Simpson, on trial for the double-murder slayings of his ex-wife and her friend. "Crime is the dark shadow spreading across TV," warns Howard Rosenberg, television critic for the *Los Angeles Times*. "The small screen is now the nation's rap sheet, offering tragedy as entertainment via tabloid programs and lurid dramas that mindlessly regurgitate or distort front-page stories."[31]

Echoing a 1989 survey of 690 city officials from across the United States, which indicated that two of the three worst problems facing American cities were drugs and crime,[32] Mike Shumacher, Chief Probation Officer for Orange County, California, admitted that "kids are more criminally sophisticated now. They seem to be more violence-prone and more drug-prone."[33]

Of course, it stands to reason that with crime's headline status and its social implications in daily American life, Hollywood would be anxious to cash in. Many former law enforcement officers, crime victims, and even criminals, have written books and sold the movie rights to their personal stories, spawning embittered legislative battles over the rights of criminals to profit from their crimes.

Referring to the allure of television crime shows in the book, *TV Genres*, Brooks Robard points out that "A little like voyeurs, the audience gets to ride in the back seat of the squad car and experience firsthand the seamy side of life. Implicit in such vicarious adventure is the audience's secret wish to explore its own darker impulses."[34] Much of *film noir*'s appeal is that it allows us to encounter characters and situations that we would never experience in our normal lives. We want to witness the nightmare, so to speak, but we want to do it from a safe perspective.

Motion pictures are not the only artistic medium reflecting and profiting from crime in modern America. Art, literature and music all demonstrate, in some way or another, crime's influence in their creative efforts. For example, the art world of the eighties experienced a revival of interest in expressionistic art. One of the most widely publicized, exhibited and collected artists of the decade, Robert Longo, "deals almost exclusively in social paranoia—Apocalyptic Pop."[35] The modern versions of the expressionistic movement are known as "neo-expressionism" and "agit-pop," both styles known for their ability to "restore our moral vision, and help us see the hell behind the headlines," according to Michael Kurcfeld in an article titled, *Dark Art for a Dark Age*.[36]

Hard-boiled fiction also witnessed a significant growth in its appeal to mainstream audiences. Besides the increased interest in the original hard-boiled writers such as Cain, Chandler and Woolrich, several of fifties pulp novelist Jim Thompson's works were reprinted, optioned for film development, and eventually made into films. Contemporary crime novelists, such as James Ellroy, Gerald Petievich, Joseph Wambaugh, and Walter Walker have brought an even greater realism to the sex, violence and underworld milieu typical of the hard-boiled tradition. And, some of these writers readily admit the influence of *film noir* in their work, as James Ellroy relates:

> There's a scene from the movie *Out of the Past* where Robert Mitchum has been sent down to Mexico to pick up Bad Girl Jane Greer, who shot Kirk Douglas and stole 40 grand from him. Mitchum has seen her in a bar, and you take one look at him as he sees this woman, and you know he's going to flush his f—-ing life down the toilet for this woman. In the chaste manner of '40s melodramas, they meet a couple of times for a drink, speak elliptically, and they end up on the beach one night and the waves are breaking, and they're holding each other and she says to him, You don't want me. You don't need me. I'm no good, I shot Kirk Douglas, I stole 40 grand from him, I'm bad, I'm evil, you don't want me, you don't need me; and Mitchum draws the woman to him and says, Baby, I don't care. And that's it, essentially, for me. I'm too ambitious and circumspect to flush my life down the toilet for a woman, and I'm happily married to a woman who's eminently good and strong and sane; but I love the romantic notion of it, and can also see through it in a hot f—-ing flash. One of the things I've tried to do with obsession in my books is feel the sensuality that's personally incomprehensible to me. I want the reader to be sucked into the vortex of that sensuality, into the perspective of demonic and obsessed heroes and psychotic killers.[37]

Even contemporary music, with its ability to convey lyrical messages rapidly, emits a restlessness used to underscore various moods in film. In the case of *To Live and*

Die in L.A. (1985) the title lyrics by the rock group, *Wang Chung*, emphasize the entrapment and existential repercussions of the city:

> In the heat of the day
> Every time you go away
> I have to piece my life together
> Every time you're away
> In the heat of the day
> In the dark of the night
> Every time I turn the light out
> I feel that God is not in Heaven
> In the dark of the night
> In the dark of the night
> I wonder why I live alone here
> I wonder why we spend these nights together
> Is this the room I'll live my life in forever?
> I wonder why in L.A.
> To live and die in L.A.
> I wonder why we waste our lives here
> When we could run away to paradise
> But I am held in some invisible vice
> And I can't get away
> To live and die in L.A...[38]

Below, a fence (Miichael Chong, right) is robbed by corrupt federal agents Vukovich (John Pankow, center) and Chance (William Petersen) in *To Live and Die in L.A.*

3. A definitive noir sensibility among contemporary filmmakers. Referring to the key distinction between *film noir* of the classic period and contemporary *noir* films, Alain Silver noted that "if there is a significant difference between then and now, it is in what motivates the creation of the films." [emphasis added][39] Undoubtedly, the primary motivating factor in the creation of *noir* films today is the peculiar attraction and high level of self-consciousness contemporary filmmakers have for the stylistic and narrative conventions of the classic *film noir*. Why the peculiar attraction? "*Noir* has a timeless appeal," explains Eugenio Zaretti, art director of *Slam Dance* (1987). "Because a *noir* hero has no exit, no options, and is constrained to do what destiny bids. People respond to *noir* because it is an element of daily life. We are all constrained, because of conditioning, to do things we'd prefer not to do."[40]

Modern filmmakers are clearly unabashed in their affinity for *noir*, and the function of self-consciousness in their work. Regarding his motivation for making *Johnny Handsome* (1989), Walter Hill said, "...This seemed to be a *film noir*. I could see this movie being made in 1948 with John Garfield."[41] When asked about his attraction to *film noir*, director John Flynn (*The Outfit*, 1974; *Rolling Thunder* 1977; *Best Seller*, 1987) said:

> Whenever anybody asks me that, I go back to Louie Calhern's line in *The Asphalt Jungle* when his wife—remember she is bedridden, and he stops before he went out to his retreat to meet Marilyn Monroe, and he was playing with her (his wife), and she said, "Why do you deal with all those terrible people?" And he said, "Crime is simply a left-handed form of human endeavor." It's just another way of looking at things. It's kind of fascinating. Hemingway said about war, not that he liked war, but that the pressures of war were so great that it stripped people of their veneers and you saw what was really in their hearts. I suppose that most crime stories happen in such desperate and dangerous circumstances, that the same rule would apply—you might have an aspect of someone's character revealed to you that you would not get in a more mainstream story.[42]

Bob Swaim, director of *Masquerade* (1988), spoke of the dichotomy between sex and love, and the role crime plays in his pictures:

> It's not that I think crime is an aphrodisiac, I just like putting ordinary people in extreme situations, and crime is a convenient circumstance. I am fascinated by the dark side of sex, and how love is its redeeming element.... What I tried to do with *Masquerade* was create a classic *film noir* without imitating the great films of the genre. I tried replacing the forties' style of long shadows with the wholesome look of a Bruce Weber ad for Ralph Lauren and hired adolescents to play grownups.... What I like about *film noir* is that

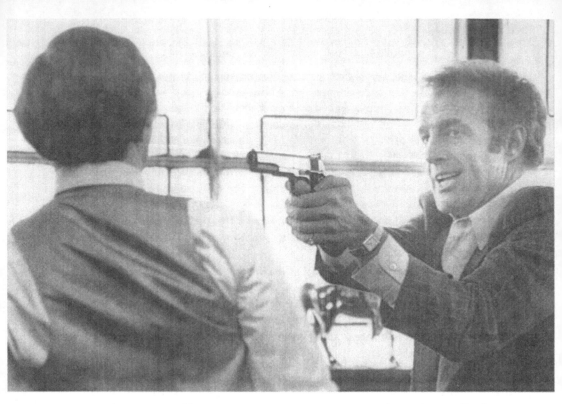

Above, Attaglia (Tom Signorelli, left) is menaced by Frank (James Caan) in *Thief.*

> it's desire rather than action that is the motivation. Love is the
> element you can never plan out. It changes everything.[43]

Michael Mann, director of *Thief* (1981) and *Manhunter* (1985), and creator of the
television series *Miami Vice*, explained his interest in the thematic concerns of *noir*:

> The darkness in working at night and the romance of wet, shiny
> streets is appealing to me for the same reason it was appealing in
> the forties and fifties. Most importantly, the questions about our
> society that cause the thematic ideas behind both pictures [*Thief*
> and *Manhunter*] are the same thematic ideas that were prevalent in
> the forties and fifties (more the forties, pre-McCarthyism) and
> channel one into the same cinematic tools and formal devices to tell
> these stories: man, man's condition, living a contradiction. These
> are modernist problems and have their roots in themes apropos to
> the forties and early fifties and to Weimar Germany in the 1920s.[44]

In an article for *Film Comment* magazine, Joel and Ethan Coen, the brothers who
produced and directed *Blood Simple*, acknowledged their sensibility, and affinity for
noir's antecedents:

> When people call *Blood Simple* a *film noir*, they're correct to the
> extent that we like the same kind of stories that the people who

made those movies liked. We tried to emulate the source that those movies came from rather than the movies themselves. *Blood Simple* utilizes movie conventions to tell the story. In that sense it's about other movies—but no more so than any other film that uses the medium in a way that's aware that there's a history of movies behind it. [45]

Because of their familiarity with the original *noir* films, filmmakers working from a contemporary *noir* point of view readily refer to titles from the *noir* index as influential reference points. Nestor Almendros, the cinematographer for Robert Benton's *Still of the Night* (1982), said that to achieve the look that they wanted for their film they sought inspiration from Edward Hopper's paintings and certain classic *films noir*:

> We looked at a lot of Fritz Lang movies—*Secret Beyond the Door*, *The Woman in the Window*, *Scarlet Street*. We also saw *The Criminal Life of Archibaldo de la Cruz*, by Luis Buñuel, another wonderful thriller. We watched all of these movies before we started working. So, *Still of the Night* is like a film that eats other films. [46]

Contemporary *film noir* is a new genre of film. As such, it must carry the distinction of another name; a name that is cognizant of its rich *noir* heritage, yet one that distinguishes its influences and motivations from those of a bygone era. The term for this new body of films should be "neo-noir," because these films still are *noir* films; yet a new type of *noir* film, one which effectively incorporates and projects the narrative and stylistic conventions of its progenitor onto a contemporary cinematic canvas. *Neo-noir* is, quite simply, a contemporary rendering of the *film noir* sensibility.

To illuminate the relationship between *film noir* and *neo-noir* more precisely, consider the following excerpt from John Belton's essay, *Cinemascope in Historical Methodology*, with my word substitutions in brackets:

> [Neo-noir], then, is not an old wine in a new bottle. It must be understood not as a product of the period in which it was invented, but as a product of the period in which it was finally innovated. The form it takes is determined by the forces that prompted its (re)creation in the [seventies and eighties]. The [neo-noir] could not have existed during the [classic *film noir* period]. Neither the technology nor the conditions under which it was ultimately developed were the same. As the protomaterialist Heraclitus once observed, "you cannot step twice into the same river, for other waters are continually flowing on." [47]

It would be impossible to recreate the *noir* film of the forties and fifties within the context of the contemporary American cinema because our perspective of that era is one that is shaped by the burden of experience and hindsight. The "period" remakes of the seventies as well as *Chinatown* illustrate this point, for even if they succeed in capturing the authentic narrative voice, or sensibility of the archetypal *film noir*, (which regrettably few manage to do), they are not, and never can be, the same.

A film could be shot today with black-and-white film stock in the Academy aperture and it could be designed to look like the urban milieu of the forties; the buildings, the automobiles, the clothing, etc.; yet, you could not recreate the awareness and sensitivity to that era's popular culture that a filmmaker living and experiencing life in that era did.

Even if Billy Wilder or Fritz Lang or Robert Siodmak were to attempt to make a *noir* film with a perfectly recreated period setting, their final product would not be the same as what they produced during the original cycle because they would not be able to divorce themselves from the reservoir of their own personal experiences and the modern sensibility with which they are necessarily burdened. Perhaps their modern *noir* vision would be even more compelling and disturbing than their contributions to the original cycle, but all the same, it would be different, it would be *neo-noir*. This applies not only to the director, but also the writer, the cinematographer—in short, anyone creatively involved with the film.

It is interesting to note that contemporary filmmakers believe that in working from the *noir* perspective, they are actually working with the conventions of a

Below, more cynical portrayals of contemporary officials: a corrupt lawyer (William Hurt, left) in *Body Heat* and a corrupt cop (Richard Gere) in *Internal Affairs*.

"genre." But the *noir* films of the contemporary American cinema are different from the *films noir* of the forties and fifties, for the *noir* movement was a phenomenal occurrence in cinematic history that will never be duplicated. *Film noir*, at its inception was an innocent, unconscious cinematic reaction to the popular culture of its time. The contemporary *film noir* is self-conscious, and well aware of its heritage. As Stephen Schiff wrote in reference to *film noir* in his article entitled *The Repeatable Experience*, "It's a matter of ontology. When a being is aware of itself, it becomes a different being."[48]

* * *

Since 1971, over 300 *noir*-influenced pictures have been released as theatrical features by the major studios or independents. Another 400-plus *noir* attempts were distributed directly into ancillary markets such as home video, pay cable, foreign, and in some instances, syndicated or network television.[49] The fact that such a large number of contemporary films have attempted to achieve the *noir* ambience clearly indicates the extent of self-consciousness at play in the modern cinema.

But, despite the breadth of *noir*-consciousness among filmmakers in the American cinema, relatively few pictures—perhaps one in five—actually succeed as authentic *noir*. Why so few? Because there's a virtual checklist of elements that have to coalesce on any given production for a film to achieve *noir*vana.

As with any film, it all starts with the script. Is the story "voiced" properly? Are the characters and dialogue believable? Does it have a plausible plot that enhances the suspension of disbelief? Are traditional *noir* stylistics such as the subjective camera, first-person sound effects, and extreme visual perspectives utilized properly? Is *noir* iconography appropriately utilized? Is the casting plausible? Does the music score appropriately highlight character nuances, emotions, plot points and overall mood shifts? If all of these elements come together in a single production, there's a good chance the picture will provide the of viewer with a vicarious experience of the nightmarish world of *noir*. While it is not feasible within the scope of this observation to discuss every contemporary *noir* attempt released, a brief overview can help provide an overall perspective of the breadth of the *noir* influence in the contemporary American cinema.

Which films of the contemporary cycle actually succeed as authentic *neo-noir*? The following chronologically listed titles, while not inclusive, provide a good reference point to begin with: *Who'll Stop the Rain?* (1978), *Thief* (1981), *Body Heat* (1981), *Breathless* (1983), *Blood Simple* (1984), *To Live and Die in L.A.* (1985), *Witness* (1985), *Manhunter* (1986), *Blue Velvet* (1987), *Best Seller* (1987), *House of Games* (1987), *Cop* (1988), *The Grifters* (1990), *Kill Me Again* (1990), *Internal Affairs* (1990), *Presumed Innocent* (1990), *Delusion* (1991), *Reservoir Dogs* (1992), *Red Rock West* (1992), *Pulp Fiction* (1994), *The Last Seduction* (1994), *The Usual Suspects* (1995), and *The Underneath* (1995).

The Underneath, a remake of Criss Cross (1949) is a product of the current trend to mine ideas from Hollywood's classic period. Remakes of films noir have steadily increased from the seventies to the present—with mixed success—critically, and at the box office. One of the more successful remakes (in terms of gross box office dollars) was No Way Out (1987), a political/espionage thriller loosely based on The Big Clock (1947). The Postman Always Rings Twice (1946) was remade under the same title with the Depression era setting of the Cain novel in 1981. Out of the Past (1947) was heavily diluted in 1984 as Against All Odds, The Blue Gardenia (1953) became The Morning After (1986), and D.O.A. (1949), The Narrow Margin (1951), Detour (1945), and Kiss of Death (1947) were modernized with the same titles in 1988, 1993, and 1995 respectively.

Unfortunately, noir remakes, such as those cited, rarely manage to achieve the soul-piercing anxiety that authentic noir successfully invokes in its audience. Nevertheless, it appears the trend of remaking the classic films noir from the forties and fifties will continue well into the cinematic future, as several more remakes are being readied for release, including Brute Force (1947) and Kiss Me Deadly (1955).

The high-tech revolution and sci-fi imaginations converged during the eighties to influence futuristic noir visions such as Blade Runner (1983), Terminator (1985), and RoboCop (1987). Often referred to as "tech noir," from the name of a nightclub in James Cameron's Terminator, these films are distinctively recognizable by their use of robotic characters and apocalyptic cityscapes. Comic book noir like Batman (1989), which Andrew Sarris said captured "both the dynamic expressionism of Fritz Lang's Metropolis and the morbid futurism of Ridley Scott's Blade Runner,"[50] falls on the fringe of the tech noir category, with exceptional technical achievements providing an atmosphere that overshadows its ineffectual story line and cardboard characters.

Buddy-cop films such as Lethal Weapon (1987), which spawned two sequels; Stakeout (1987); Colors (1988); Tango & Cash (1989); and Bad Boys (1995) have been popular during the last few years, as well as variations which paired a cop and a criminal in 48 Hours (1982), and a cop and a public defender in Shakedown (1988).

While all of these pictures attempt to maintain a noir look with their night-for-night photography, wet pavement, and mannered, low-key lighting, with the exception of Colors, the noir atmosphere is substantially undercut by an over-emphasis on the humorous aspects of the relationships. There is room for humor, albeit black humor, in a noir picture, as Blood Simple (1984), Cop (1988), and Pulp Fiction (1994) aptly demonstrate.

Pictures like 52 Pick-Up (1986), At Close Range (1986), Someone to Watch Over Me (1987), and Fatal Attraction (1987) are valid attempts, but fall short of tapping into the noir spirit because they fail to maintain the tense narrative/visual perspective that can be realized through identifying intimately with a particular character. For instance, in *Fatal Attraction*, the audience is forced to digest the unfolding events through the eyes of not only Dan Gallagher, but also his wife, Beth, and the antagonist, Alex Forrest. The result is that we "watch" the protagonist (Gallagher) struggle through his crisis rather than experiencing it vicariously along with him.

While there are several other films that effectively inhabit *neo-noir* terrain such as *Suspect* (1987), *True Believer* (1987), *Mortal Thoughts* (1991), and *Guilty as Sin* (1993), the majority of contemporary *noir* attempts fail to render the heightened level of co-experience authentic *noir* provides. As Alain Silver notes in reference to modern *noir* attempts, "Whether from a position of ignorance or knowledge, the interaction of the protagonist and viewer seems much more seldom to reveal the instability, the dark undercurrent that served as a thematic constant of the *noir* cycle."[51]

*   *   *

Since *neo-noir* has become firmly established in the American cinema, it is reasonable to assume that audiences will continue to be fascinated with the genre because the *noir* film communicates to us about our fears and desires more realistically than any other film formula. Alfred J. Appel wrote that the *noir* vision

Below, a new twist on "police brutality": hardbitten Detective Hopkins (James Woods, left) terrorizes Deputy Sheriff Haines (Charles Haid) in *Cop*.

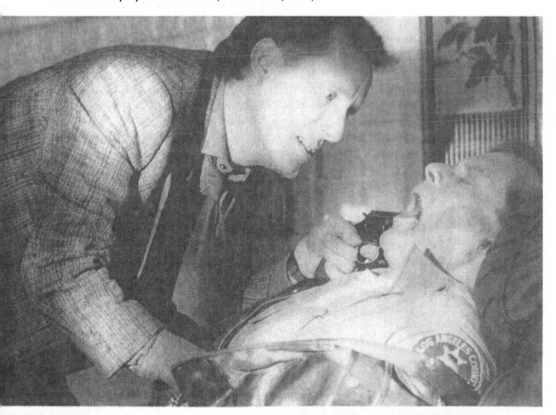

"touches an audience most intimately because it assures them that their suppressed impulses and fears are shared responses."[52] J.P. Telotte noted that we are always seeking patterns of order and continuity in both our individual and cultural experience, because they offer us a defense against the contradictions of the problem-free lives we want to lead. By confronting (in cinematic terms) the very issues we seek to avoid in real life, Telotte suggested, we engage in a psychoanalytic practice often referred to as a "talking cure." Continuing this line of reasoning, he said, "In trying to articulate our personal and cultural anxieties, the *film noir* similarly works out such a cure, offering a better sense of ourselves, or at least a clearer notion of who we are individually and socially."[53]

Film noir and its contemporary descendent, *neo-noir*, offer some of the most fascinating insights the cinema has provided on topics such as including ambition, corruption, redemption, greed, lust, and loyalty. The best of the *noir* films work on a poetic level; with their conscientious interplay of light and shadows, duplicitous imagery, deceptive plots, elliptical dialogue, and multiple forced perspectives, adding layers of connotative meaning to their film-texts. Most important, however, is the heightened level of co-experience with which the truly authentic *noir* grips its audience.

As we emerge from the darkness of the cinema (and the nightmarish darkness of the *noir* film) into the light of the theatre lobby, we breathe a sigh of relief, and contemplate our tense encounter with the flip side of the American Dream. By vicariously confronting the *noir* world on the screen, whether through the *film noir*, or its modern offshoot, *neo-noir*, we are able to validate the patterns of order and continuity we seek to establish in our lives. More precisely yet, "by means of the night...we see the light of day."[54]

Notes

1. Dennis Hopper, personal interview, 18 March 1993. Hopper wrote the copy and designed the one-sheets that were utilized in Orion's marketing campaign for *The Hot Spot*.

2. Robert G. Porfirio, *The Dark Age of American Film: A Study of the American Film Noir* (diss., Yale University, 1979), pp. 112-116.

3. Porfirio, p. 11.

4. Marc Vernet, "Genre" in *Film Reader* (Evanston: Northwestern University, February 1978), p. 16.

5. J.P. Telotte, *Voices in the Dark: The Narrative Patterns of Film Noir* (U. of Illinois Press, 1989), p. 22.

6. Peter Bogdanovich, *Fritz Lang in America* (New York: Praeger, 1967), pp. 86-87.

7. Thomas Schatz, *Hollywood Genres: Formulas. Filmmaking. and the Studio System* (Philadelphia: Temple University Press, 1981), 149.

8. Paul Schrader, "Notes on Film Noir," *Film Comment* (Spring, 1972), p. 12.

Above, a neo-*noir* perspective, looking up at a betraying *femme fatale* (JoAnne Whalley-Kilmer, left) and her menacing accomplice (Michael Madsen) in *Kill Me Again*.

9. Brian G. Rose, ed., *TV Genres* (Westport, CT: Greenwood Press, 1986), p. 34.

10. Alain Silver and Elizabeth Ward, eds., *Film Noir: An Encyclopedic Reference to the American Style* (Woodstock, NY: Overlook Press, 2nd Edition, 1987), p. 101.

11. Richard T. Jameson, "Son of Noir," *Film Comment* (November, 1974), pp. 31-32.

12. Foster Hirsch, *The Dark Side of the Screen: Film Noir* (San Diego: A.S. Barnes, 1981), pp. 202-203.

13. Bryan Burrough, "Top Deal Maker Leaves a Trail of Deception in Wall Street Rise," *The Wall Street Journal* (22 Jan., 1990), p. 1.

14. Ron Gales, "As the '80s Wane, a New View of the Good Life Emerges," *Adweek* (13 Feb., 1989), p. 34.

15. Lawrence Kasdan, personal interview, 10 November 1989.

16. Paula Parisi, "Virginia Madsen: This Versatile Femme Fatale Keeps Hollywood Guessing," *The Hollywood Reporter* (26 May, 1989), p. 18.

17. Gales, p. 38.

18. Ibid., p. 34.

19. Samir Hachem, "48 Hours," *Millimeter* (December, 1982), p. 191.

20. Ric Gentry, "Bird: DP Jack Green Creates a Black-and-White Style Film on Color Stock," *Film & Video* (September, 1988), p. 10.

21. Iain Blair, "Look at New Methods for Lighting Music Videos," *Film & Video* (January, 1990), p. 50.

22. Laurie Halpern Smith, "Yuri Neyman's Compelling Vision," *Movieline* (April, 1988), p. 27.

23. Stephen Gersor, "Expressionism in Film," *Crimmers: the Harvard Journal of Pictorial Fiction* (Winter, 1975), p. 49. For those apprehensive about color cinematography's compatibility with the modern *noir* vision, consider a remark by Wassily Kadinsky, leader of the "Blue Rider" German Expressionist group: "Color directly influences the soul; color is the keyboard, the eyes are the hammer, the soul is the piano with many strings. The artist is the hand that plays, to create vibrations in the soul."

24. Stephen Loeper, *Los Angeles Herald Examiner* (1 Oct., 1989), p. 1.

25. Ralph Blumenthal, *Los Angeles Herald Examiner* (18 Sept., 1989), p. 4.

26. Stephen Braun, *Los Angeles Times* (10 Feb., 1995), p. 1.

27. Ted Gest, *U.S. News & World Report* (31 July, 1989), p. 16-19.

28. Jeanie Kasindorf, *New York* (24 July, 1989), p. 24-33.

29. Harlan Ellison, *Los Angeles* (September, 1988), p. 103-107.

30. Howard Rosenberg, "It's a Crime What They Offer to TV," *Los Angeles Times* (27 Jan., 1989), p. F1.

31. Howard Rosenberg, *Los Angeles Times* (23 Sept., 1989), p. F1.

32. Paul Leavitt, "Drugs Top Cities' Fears," *USA Today* (13 Jan., 1989), p. 3.

33. *Los Angeles Times* (26 Feb., 1989), p. A56.

34. Rose, p. 12.

35. William Wilson, "Art from the Dark Side," *Los Angeles Times*, Calendar (1 Oct., 1989), p. 8.

36. Michael Kurcfeld, *L.A. Weekly* (16 Sept., 1988), p. 19.

37. Steve Erickson, "James Ellroy: Crime Fiction Beyond Noir," *L.A. Weekly* (21 July, 1989), p. 19-20.

38. Wang Chung, "To Live and Die in L.A.," (Geffen/Warner Bros. Records, M5G 24081), p. 1985.

39. Silver and Ward, p. 370.

40. Kristine McKenna, "L.A. Noir: 'Slam Dance'—The Look of a Lonely Paradise," *Los Angeles Times*, Calendar (27 Sept., 1987), p. 44.

41. Jeff Schwager, "Walter Hill: The Good, the Bad, and the Handsome," *Village View* (6 Oct., 1989), p. 7.

42. John Flynn, personal interview, 22 August, 1989.

43. Hal Rubenstein, "Crazy Love," *Vogue* (April, 1988), p. 82.

44. Michael Mann, written interview, 22 Nov., 1989.

45. Hal Hinson, "Bloodlines," *Film Comment* (February, 1986), p. 18.

46. John A. Gallagher, "Nestor Almendros: The Master Eye," *Millimeter* (February, 1983), p. 118-122.

47. John Belton, *Cinema Journal* 28:1 (Fall, 1988), p. 29-30.

48. Stephen Schiff, *Film Comment* (March/April, 1982), p. 35.

49. Sources include *Daily Variety*'s annual anniversary issues, American Film Market and Cannes Film Festival issues of *The Hollywood Reporter*, *Exhibitor Relations Company*, *NATO News*, *Boxoffice*, and *The Comprehensive Guide to Home Video* (1995 edition).

50. Andrew Sarris, *Video Review* (January, 1990), p. 54.

51. Silver and Ward, p. 372.

52. Alfred Appel, "Dark Cinema and Lolita," *Film Comment* (September, 1974), p. 26.

53. Telotte, p. 222.

54. Jon Tuska, *Dark Cinema: American Film Noir in Cultural Perspective* (Westport, CT: Greenwood Press, 1984), p. xvi.

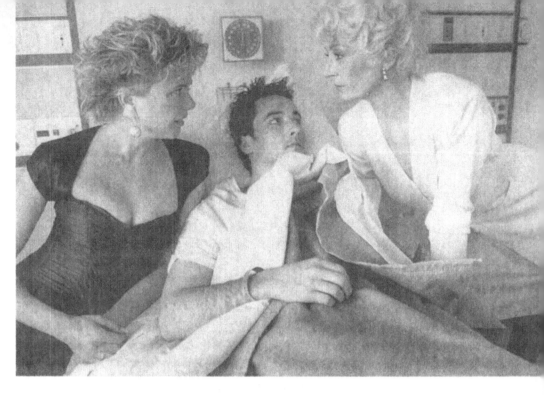

Above, Annette Bening (left) as Myra Langtry, John Cusack as Roy Dillon, and Anjelica Huston as Lilly Dillon in *The Grifters*. Below, Michael Madsen as "Mr. Blonde," Harvey Keitel as "Mr. White," and classic *noir* icon Lawrence Tierney as boss Joe Cabot in *Reservoir Dogs*.

Son of *Noir*:
Neo-*Film Noir* and the Neo-B Picture

Alain Silver

The "Classic" period of American *Film Noir* encompasses several hundred motion pictures from *The Maltese Falcon* (1941) to *Touch of Evil* (1958) produced by scores of different filmmakers between roughly 1940 and 1960. While that *noir* cycle of production never formally concluded, the attempts to sustain its viewpoint were few in the 1960s and 1970s. Particularly near its end, however, the decade of the 1980s brought a significant resurgence of interest in the themes and protagonists that typified classic *film noir*. The 1990s so far have added scores more to the titles of the preceding decade. If there is a most significant difference between then and now, it is in what motivates the creation of the films.

At the height of the movement individual *noir* films transcended personal and generic outlook to reflect cultural preoccupations. From the late 1970s to present, in a "Neo-*Noir*" period, many of the productions that recreate the *noir* mood, whether in remakes or new narratives, have been undertaken by filmmakers cognizant of a heritage and intent on placing their own interpretation on it. David Mamet put it most succinctly regarding *House of Games* (1987): "I am very well acquainted with the genre, both in print and on film, and I love it. I tried to be true."[1]

Guncrazy (1992) is not a remake, but a mixture of fugitive couple and "kid *noir*" concepts. The film does echo classic period titles, particularly the visual imagery of Joseph H. Lewis' 1950 original *Gun Crazy* in scenes of the couple locked in a parody of embrace while they shoot at cans and bottles. The ingenuous dialogue is more in the manner of Nicholas Ray's *They Live by Night* (1947). Because the characters themselves, Howard and Anita, are much more like Ray's Bowie and Keechie than those in Robert Altman's aimless, direct remake, *Thieves Like Us* (1974), they naively romanticize their sordid dilemma, epitomized when they break into a house and dress up for a candle-lit dinner.

Guncrazy, like its namesake and many recent productions, is also a low-budget picture. In the classic period, *film noir* may have been disproportionately involved with productions done on limited means. The original *Gun Crazy*

Above, Drew Barrymore as Anita and James Legros as Howard, juvenile fugitive couple in *Guncrazy*, recalling characters from both the original *Gun Crazy* and *They Live by Night*.

as well as *Kiss Me Deadly* (1955), *D.O.A.* (1950), *Detour* (1945) and scores of others were all made on limited budgets and shooting schedules, which seemed to mesh well with the spare, ill-lit locales that typified the *noir* under-world. In many ways, the resurgence of interest in the *noir* style by low-budget filmmakers represents a return to the roots of the cycle. The "B-film" or "pro-grammer," the less costly productions of the 40s and 50s from the major stu-dios, such as *Thieves' Highway* (Fox, 1949), *Scene of the Crime* (MGM, 1949), or *Black Angel* (Universal, 1946), whose second-tier actors, writers, and directors were featured on the bottom-half of double bills, has transformed itself into the limited release and made-for-video efforts of the 80s and 90s. The low-budget feature, made at a cost ranging from less than $500,000 to $3 or 4 mil-lion cannot be financed based on U.S. theatrical prospects alone but must follow the dictates of the foreign, video, and cable markets. Not only do those markets still prize the "action" picture or "thriller," whose spare narratives translate more easily for non-English speaking audiences, but the violence and compulsive sexual behavior that has always been part of film *noir* are more "saleable" than ever. Since many productions of the classic period were criticized at the time for their violence and unsavory themes, this is just another aspect of neo-*noir*'s return to its roots.

Like *Guncrazy*, many films like the three 1990 adaptations of Jim Thompson's novels, from *The Grifters* and *After Dark, My Sweet* at the high end to *The Kill-off* at the ultra-low end have worked within the range of limited budget and successfully evoked the *noir* tradition. In fact, in the worst of neo-*noir*, the failing is seldom because of monetary restrictions. *Hit List* and *Relentless* (both 1989) are two low-budget examples by the same director, William Lustig. What imbalances the former picture are the performances, with Rip Torn, Lance Henriksen, and Leo Rossi acting at one level and Jan-Michael Vincent and Charles Napier at another. While *Hit List* turns on the concept of the wrong address, the modus operandi in *Relentless*, where the killer chooses his victims by opening a page at random from the telephone directory, is even more arbitrary. Although Judd Nelson's portrayal of the psychopath brought the picture much opprobrium, his manic interpretation works within the context much as did Richard Basehart's performance in the classic *He Walked by Night* (1948). The ironies of the displaced cop (Leo Rossi) trying to prove himself and the old veteran (Robert Loggia) dying because of his carelessness are reinforced by the iconographic context of prior work, particularly Loggia's in *Jagged Edge*. In this sense, *Relentless* maximizes the impact of its limited means. While the flashbacks to the killer's abused childhood at the hands of his police officer-father may seem an "antique" device, it economically fulfills a necessary narrative function. Both films use actors with big-budget credits both to mask their limited means and to exploit the audience awareness of screen personas.

Sean Young's androgynous, "hysterical" performance in *Love Crimes* (1992) is part of this same low-budget tactic. In pop-critical jargon, director Lizzie Borden takes a cinematic ax and gives her audience forty whacks. The net effect, however, is a more direct statement about social patriarchy and prejudice against women in law enforcement than in similarly themed pictures with bigger budgets such as *Blue Steel* and *Impulse* (both 1990).

Not only is such economy the key in "neo-B," it helps generate a higher percentage of films that are rooted in the *noir* tradition without overwhelming it, like such self-conscious, high-budget efforts as *Shattered* (1991) or *Final Analysis* (1992). In copying *Fatal Attraction* (1987), *Body Chemistry* (1990) must circumvent the obstacles of short schedule and less celebrated actors; and it certainly had no budget to re-shoot endings after test screenings. Despite that, the result is both stark and affecting. Without the clutter of freight elevators or operatic arias, *Body Chemistry* focuses relentlessly on the central premise; and when its "hero" is gunned down it arrives literally and figuratively at a very different conclusion. *Mortal Passions* (1990) takes types from the hard-boiled mold of James L. Cain. Its plot turns fraternal loyalty into betrayal, literally buries bodies in the back yard, and has a would-be *femme fatale* fall in love with a prospective victim. In its final sequence it recalls more than anything Cain's ending to *Double Indemnity*, the novella.

Cain is not credited here, of course, nor even in *Kiss Me A Killer* (1991), which is an "unauthorized" Latino version of *The Postman Always Rings Twice*. The high-budget 1981 remake with Jack Nicholson and Jessica Lange in the John Garfield/Lana Turner roles restored the impulsive sexuality but little of the determinism of Cain's original or the 1947 adaptation. *Kiss Me A Killer* borrows sub-plots liberally from other classic films from Siegel's *Crime In the Streets* (1956) to Hitchcock's *I, Confess* (1953) but centers on the Mexican-American wife of a white bar owner and a guitar-playing drifter named Tony who helps transform the place into a salsa hot spot. Like Visconti's 1942 *Ossessione*, this unsanctioned adaptation of the novel emphasizes the loutish qualities of the husband to build empathy with the killers and captures Cain's obsessive and fateful mood better than its costlier counterparts.

The $1 million-budgeted *The Killing Time* (1987) and *Jezebel's Kiss* (1990) both feature youthful revenge seekers. Both use actors such as Beau Bridges, Malcolm MacDowell, Wayne Rogers, and Meredith Baxter-Birney to mask

Below, Tom Berenger (left) as the amnesiac real estate developer in *Shattered* with Corbin Bernson as his partner.

their fiscal origins. The key to both stories is revealed in flashback: they have returned to obtain reprisal for the death of a parent which they witnessed as children. As it happens both films are situated in small California coastal communities, and the deaths are tied to land swindles. For both films, the location and the limited cast allow production values to be maximized. *The Killing Time*'s protagonist murders and takes the place of the small town's new deputy sheriff and features a performance by Kiefer Sutherland that evokes Jim Thompson's Deputy Lou Ford. *Jezebel's Kiss* has a title character who rides into town on a Harley, and a lead performance that is best left undescribed.

More recent, modestly-budgeted pictures, which consider the issue of criminal "professionalism," *Diary of a Hitman* and *Reservoir Dogs* (both 1992), use stylized performances to create a *noir* ambience. Dekker, the title character of *Diary of a Hitman*, is a throwback and the film's narrative style follows suit. The story unfolds as a flashback, a message which Dekker is leaving on his "booking agent's" answering machine, and his voiceover narration is used heavily throughout. Forest Whitaker's portrayal of Dekker, who early on confesses to being troubled by his work and maintaining the illusion that "it's not personal," recalls Mark Stevens in *The Dark Corner* (1946) or *Cry Vengeance* (1954) in the best "B" manner.

Dekker's key comment is "I was a pro. A pro is a pro, right?" The answer from Mr. Pink in *Reservoir Dogs* is "a psychopath ain't a professional." From the perspective of the classic *noir* style and narrative, *Reservoir Dogs* is pointedly aware of a relationship to those conventions. The sociopathic "Mr. Blonde" might well be alluding to *Point Blank* when he confesses to being "a big Lee Marvin fan." The plot of *Reservoir Dogs* derives from the caper film. An organizer brings a group of otherwise unrelated criminals together for one job and keeps their true identities from each other with "colorful" names. The botched robbery itself is never seen, only its aftermath as the survivors come to the rendezvous point and argue over what happened and what to do now. Flashbacks within flashbacks economically create narrative layers that are both "traditionally" *noir* and endistance the modern viewer from identification with the criminal protagonists. Equally endistancing are slow motion optical effects and moments of grisly humor. While it shares the multiple points of view of writer/director Quentin Tarantino's later, more expensive, and much more celebrated *Pulp Fiction* (1994), *Reservoir Dogs* is a more tightly constructed and ultimately much darker film.

In *Genuine Risk* (1990), *Delusion* (1991), even *Femme Fatale* (1991), the titles are completely unambiguous and the budgets even lower. Equally remarkable is how well these pictures succeed in the *noir* tradition. *Femme Fatale* is the most complicated, recalling elements of *The Locket* (1947) and *Chicago Deadline* (1949), in which a man marries a woman who turn outs to be someone else or, more accurately, someone suffering from a multiple personality disorder. Like the reporter in *Chicago Deadline*, her husband pieces her other lives together through a succession of leads, while dodging some street hoodlums whom another of her personalities swindled. In the end the protagonists survive only because of a whim of these hoodlums.

The plot of *Delusion* owes even more to Al Robert's "mysterious force" in the classic *Detour* or to the chance events in Ida Lupino's *The Hitch-hiker* (1953). Embittered over his longtime employer's sale of the company, George O'Brien has embezzled a million dollars and is driving to Las Vegas with the cash in his trunk. He stops to help a young couple, Patti and Chevy, in a car that has swerved off the road, and they abduct him. O'Brien does not realize that the young tough has not been planning to kill him and does not know about the money, until Chevy kills someone else. Now O'Brien is a witness;

Below, neo-*noir femme fatales*: left, Katherine Barrese as the revenge-seeking, motorcycle-riding, and possibly amnesiac title character in *Jezebel's Kiss*. Right, Jennifer Rubin as the opportunistic Patti, who sings "These boots are made for walking" at the close of *Delusion*.

and they dump him in the desert. He survives; but by the time he tracks them down, Patti has found the money and is preparing to go off on her own.

Stylistically both of these films benefit from the isolated or seedy locales, which permit a spare and stark visualization in the manner of *Border Incident* (1949) or *On Dangerous Ground* (1952). As in *After Dark, My Sweet* or *Kill Me Again* (1990), the desert locations in *Delusion* permit an arrangement of figures in a landscape that create a sense of otherworldliness or mirage (the film's original title), of acting out a bad dream without having recourse to optical effects or mood lighting. At the victim's trailer site or in a rundown motel at the aptly named Death Valley Junction, the isolated environment underscores the narrative tension in the classic *noir* manner. The last shot literally drives off from O'Brien as he stands looking at the wounded Chevy lying in the dusty driveway, and it continues moving away down the road as the end credits roll, figuratively abandoning the protagonist to his fate.

Genuine Risk may be the most self-conscious neo-*noir* and neo-B of these three films, as locations, lighting style, and art direction constantly underscore the sordidness of the milieu. The script is outrageous and features lines like "A racetrack is like a woman...a man weathers so much banality in pursuit of the occasional orgasmic moment." What distinguishes *Genuine Risk* is the offhandedness of its violence, where people are beaten or die painfully, abruptly and without reason in stagings that capture the disturbing tone of videotapes of real events from surveillance cameras. It also has some wryness and novelty in its plot and casting, most notably Terence Stamp as a 60s British pop-star turned petty mobster. Although deceived by this mobster's wife, the "hero," a hapless petty criminal and compulsive gambler named Henry, survives. And while just about everyone else perishes, he goes back to the track for another play.

The plots of these pictures, all budgeted at under a million dollars, take only what they can afford from the classic tradition; but that is a considerable amount. All have enough money for a *femme fatale*, a hired killer or two, a confused and entrapped hero, an employer ripped-off, a shakedown. Two have flashbacks, two have gang bosses, and one a psychiatrist. The locations vary from Los Angeles to Las Vegas, from Death Valley to Big Bear Lake, but two have mansions, two cheap motels, and two isolated rural locales where killers take their proposed victims. Like its antecedent, neo-*noir* and neo-B in particular makes few if any extravagant demands in terms of production value.

From television to comic books, *film noir* has exerted and continues to exert its narrative and stylistic influence. It has been a while since *Dragnet, Naked City, Johnny Staccato, The Fugitive, Run for Your Life,* and *Harry-O* were on network; but movies-of-the-week and cable originals frequently explore the *noir* terrain on a limited budget. While both were given after-market theatrical releases, such recent and extremely self-conscious neo-*noir* projects as John Dahl's *Red Rock West* (1992) and *The Last Seduction* (1994) originated as made-for-cable movies. After the short-lived, animated cop series *Fish Police*, can it be long before an angst-ridden Bart Simpson puts on a fedora and skateboards down his own mean streets?

The resurgence of interest in the themes and styles of *film noir* in recent tears has benefited filmmakers at all budget levels. If *film noir* is no longer *the* American style, certainly no other movement has emerged to replace it. Unless and until filmmakers discover another mirror to hold up to American society, none ever will.

Notes

1. Mamet quoted in Todd Erickson, *Evidence of Film Noir in Contemporary Cinema*, p. 168.

Young guns: left, a childlike pose by Anita (Drew Barrymore) holding her .357 magnum in *Guncrazy*. Below, Chevy (Kyle Secor, right) prepares to execute Larry (Jerry Orbach) in *Delusion*.

Notes on Contributors

Linda Brookover is a researcher and writer who has worked extensively in the fields of multi-cultural edutcation and community outreach. She has recently written on Native American subjects for *oneWorld*, an on-line magazine, and previously edited several resource guides and corporate newsletters. She is currently creating electonic learning aids for Edutainment for Kids. She also works as a focus group moderator and educator.

Jeremy G. Butler is an associate professor in the Telecommunication and Film Department at the University of Alabama. He edited *Star Texts: Image and Performance in Film and Television*, and has published articles in *Cinema Journal, Journal of Film and Video, Jump Cut*, and other periodicals. His most recent book is *Television: Critical Methods and Applications*.

James Damico wrote critical articles for *The Journal of Popular Film, Cinema Journal*, and wrote about *film noir* comedies of the Forties for *Movietone News*. He also contributed to the two-volume anthology *Cinema: A Critical Dictionary* and to *Movies as Artifacts*.

Raymond Durgnat is currently Visiting Professor at the University of East London, Docklands, and sometime Head of History of Art at the St. Martin's School of Art. He has previously taught at Dartmouth College, the University of California at Los Angeles, Berkeley, and San Diego, Columbia College New York, and the Royal College of Art and has lectured on aesthetics in Italy, India, Finland, and New Zealand. His articles have appeared in *The London Times, The Independent, Film Comment, Cinema* (U.K.), and *Positif.* His books touching on *film noir* include *The Crazy Mirror, Eros in the Cinema, Jean Renoir, Buñuel, A Mirror for England, Sexual Alienation in the Cinema*, and (with Scott Simmon) *King Vidor, American*.

Glenn Erickson is the co-author of *The Making of 1941* (1980), on the production of which he also served as Coordinator of miniatures and other effects. He has also written program articles for FILMEX. He works primarily as a film and videotape editor whose credits include several independent features and is currently a staff editor at MGM/UA.

Todd R. Erickson is an entertainment marketing executive with Hill and Knowlton, the international public relations firm. He previously served as creative services director at Rogers & Cowan, Inc., wrote and produced training films for the U.S. Air Force, and worked in various production capacities with Tisch/Avnet Productions and WGN Television. While in the Masters program at Brigham Young University, he taught undergraduate film classes and managed the university's film society in order to screen as many *films noir* as possible. He co-authored *Introduction to Motion Picture Art & Analysis* (1985) for BYU Press and is currently adapting his thesis on neo-*noir* for publication.

Joel Greenberg, in addition to oft-cited *Hollywood in the Forties*, also wrote for *Sight and Sound* and conducted oral histories of Lewis Milestone and other notable figures for the American Film Institute. He was co-editor of *Film Journal* (Australia) and contributed numerous articles including the first in-depth study in English of the work of George Cukor. He is currently Senior Policy Officer with the Australian Office of Film and Literature Classification and Secretary of its Board of Review.

Charles Higham co-wrote *Hollywood in the Forties* while serving as editor of the Australian literary magazine *The Bulletin*. While Regents Professor of Literature and Film at the University of California, Santa Cruz, he completed *The Films of Orson Welles*. While spending eleven years as Hollywood feature writer for the *New York Times*, he wrote biographies of Katharine Hepburn, Errol Flynn, the Duchess Windsor, and several other contemporary personages as well as a literary biography of Sir Arthur Conan Doyle and five volumes of verse. His biography of Howard Hughes is the basis for a forthcoming television miniseries. His articles and interviews have appeared in numerous periodicals. His latest book is *Rose: The Life and Times of Rose Fitzgerald Kennedy*.

Karen Hollinger co-edited, with Virginia Wright Waxman, a monograph on *Letter from An Unknown Woman* for the Rutgers Films in Print series and has published articles on film and literature in *Film Criticism, Literature/Film Quarterly, The Quarterly Review of Film and Video, The Journal of Film and Video*, and *Studies in Short Fiction*. She is currently developing aspects of her dissertation on the role of the narrator in *film noir* and women's film, including a book-length study of representations of female friendship in contemporary film. She teaches film and literature at Amstrong State College in Savannah, Georgia.

Paul Kerr has written on film and television for *Screen*, also serving on its editorial board, and a range of other specialized journals. He also produced two anthologies, *The Hollywood Film Industry* and *MTM: Quality Television*. He has lectured at the University of London and worked at the British Film Institute until becoming series producer for Channel Four's *Media Show*. He is currently series editor of *Moving Pictures*, a weekly program on BBC2 and has just produced the documentary, *The Projection Racket*, concerning the role of organized crime in the projectionist union in the 1930s for BBC2/A&E.

Richard Lippe is a lecturer in Film at Atkinson College, York University. He serves on the editorial board of *CineAction* and had contributed articles to that magazine and *Movie*. He is currently completing a book-length study of George Cukor and the melodrama.

Lowell Peterson worked as an assistant cameraperson and camera operator on numerous feature and television productions in the Hollywood film industry and is now a cinematographer whose credits include *Knots Landing*, *Hotel Malibu*, and *Lois and Clark*. He has contributed articles to *Film Comment* and *International Photographer*. His recent work on the neo-*noir*ish series, *Second Chances*, was nominated for Best Photography by the American Society of Cinematographers.

Janey Place wrote *The Western Films of John Ford* (1974) and *The Non-Western Films of John Ford* (1979). She was a contributor and assistant editor to *Cinema* (U.S.) and taught film at the University of California, Santa Cruz. Her other work on *film noir* is the title essay in the anthology *Women and Film Noir*; a reconstruction through frame enlargements of the visual style of *Thieves' Highway* housed in the Museum of Modern Art; and as a commentator on the PBS series on American Cinema. She has worked as a communications executive for Hughes Aircraft, Wells Fargo Bank and is currently Exec Vice-President and Director of Strategic Technology for Nationsbank.

Robert Porfirio began his extensive work on *film noir* while in the Master's program at U.C.L.A. which culminated in his 1979 dissertation for Yale University *The Dark Age of American Film: A Study of American Film Noir (1940-1960)*. His articles include contributions to *Continuum*, *Dialog*, *Literature/Film Quarterly*, and *Sight and Sound*. As co-editor of *Film Noir: An Encyclopedic Reference to the American Style* (1979), he wrote over sixty entries on individual films. He was formerly assistant professor of American Studies at California State University, Fullerton and is presently a real estate broker in Southern California. When pressed he occasionally lectures on *film noir*.

Paul Schrader wrote *Transcendental Style in Film: Ozu, Bresson, Dreyer* (1972), was the editor of *Cinema* (U.S.), and published reviews and articles in the *Los Angeles Free Press*, *Film Quarterly*, and *Film Comment*. Since beginning a career as a screenwriter (*Taxi Driver*, *The Yakuza*, *Rolling Thunder*, *Raging Bull*) and going on to direct numerous feature films such as *Blue Collar*, *Hard Core*, *American Gigolo*, *Cat People*, *Mishima*, *Light Sleeper*, and the *film noir* parody *Witch Hunt*, he has been actively involved in such film industry issues as artists rights and film preservation. His comments on *film noir* anchored that segment of the PBS series on American

Cinema and many of his critical writings were reprinted in *Schrader on Schrader* (1990).

Alain Silver wrote *The Samurai Film* (2nd Edition, 1983). Two other genre studies and two auteur studies—based on his Master's thesis on Robert Aldrich and his dissertation on David Lean—were co-written with James Ursini [see his entry below]. With Elizabeth Ward, he co-wrote *Raymond Chandler's Los Angeles* (1987) and co-edited *Film Noir: An Encyclopedic Reference* (3rd Edition, 1993). Shorter pieces have appeared in *Film Comment, Movie, Literature/Film Quarterly, Wide Angle, Photon,* the *DGA Magazine* and the *Los Angeles Times.* He has produced feature films (*Night Visitor, Cyborg^2*), documentaries, and music videos and has lectured on film production at U.C.L.A. and the Directors Guild of America.

Robert E. Smith, a self-described "unrepentant auteurist," lectures on film history and criticism at the University of Connecticut and the Graduate Liberal Studies Program at Wesleyan University. He has previously administered retrospectives of American film with a particular emphasis on 35mm original or restored prints and has also written on the work of DeMille and Borzage and subversive melodramas of the 30s such *The Devil Is A Woman, Desire,* and *Back Street.*

James Ursini is the co-author, with Alain Silver, of *What Ever Happened to Robert Aldrich?* (1995); *More Things Than Are Dreamt Of* (1994); *The Vampire Film* (2nd Edition, 1993); and *David Lean and His Films* (2nd Edition, 1992). He was co-editor on the 3rd Edition of *Film Noir: An Encyclopedic Reference* and has also written *Preston Sturges: An American Dreamer* (1972) and contributed articles to *Mediascene, Cinema* (U.S.), *Photon, Cinefantastique, Midnight Marquee,* and the *DGA Magazine.* He has produced Oral Histories and been a researcher for the American Film Institute and has also been associate producer and producer on feature films and documentaries for various school districts and public broadcasting. He has lectured on filmmaking at UCLA and other colleges and continues to work as an educator in Los Angeles.

Elizabeth Ward is co-editor of *Film Noir: An Encyclopedic Reference to the American Style* (3rd Edition, 1993) and co-wrote and co-photographed *Raymond Chandler's Los Angeles* (1987). She also co-authored with Alain Silver, *The Film Director's Team* (2nd Edition, 1992) and *Robert Aldrich: a guide to references and resources* (1979). Other of her articles and interviews related to *film noir* have appeared in *Movie* and the *Los Angeles Times.* She has worked extensively as a production manager, assistant director, and stage manager in motion picture and television production for Paramount Pictures and independent producers and as an editor and researcher. She currently works as a primary school educator.

television production for Paramount Pictures and independent producers and as an editor and researcher. She currently works as a primary school educator.

Tony Williams is the co-author of *Italian Western: Opera of Violence* (1975), co-editor of *Vietnam War Films* (1994), and author of *Jack London: the Movies* (1992) and the forthcoming *Hearths of Darkness: the Family in the American Horror Film*. His essays have appeared in the anthologies *Making Television* (1990); *From Hanoi to Hollywood* and *Inventing Vietnam* (both 1991); *Fires Were Started: British Cinema and Thatcherism* and *Crisis Cinema* (both 1993); and *Re-viewing British Cinema, 1900-1992* (1994). He has also written articles for *CineAction, Film History, Jump Cut, Movie, Viet Nam Generation*, and *Wide Angle*. He is Associate Professor of Cinema Studies in the English department of Southern Illinois University at Carbondale.

CPSIA information can be obtained at www.ICGtesting.com
Printed in the USA
LVOW11s2136221115

463751LV00001B/39/P